THIRD EDITION

OUTCOMES

INTERMEDIATE

Hugh Dellar

Andrew Walkley

NATIONAL
GEOGRAPHIC
LEARNING

Australia · Brazil · Canada · Mexico · Singapore · United Kingdom · United States

Contents 3

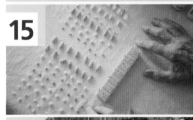

GRAMMAR	VOCABULARY	READING	LISTENING
• Present perfect simple and present perfect continuous • Comparing now and the past	• Describing homes • A place to live	• An article about housing in South Korea and the UK	• Two people talk about their friends' new apartment • Four conversations about places to live
• Quantifiers • Future in the past	• Cultural events • Idioms • Describing events	• An article about nights out around the world	• Two friends arrange to go out • Three conversations about what people did last night
• *Managed to, be able to* and *be forced to* • Passives	• Identifying animals • Challenges and achievements • Natural resources	• An article about a mountain climber	• Three conversations about animals • A lecture about natural resources
• Talking about memories • Expressing regret using *wish*	• Talking about character • Friendships	• An article about becoming a grandparent	• Two friends discuss what other people are like • Five people talk about a shared friend
• Third conditionals • *Should have*	• Phrasal verbs • Extreme adjectives	• An article about one refugee's remarkable journey	• Two conversations about bad journeys • Four conversations about travel problems
• Articles • Infinitive with *to* or *-ing* form	• Computer problems • Apps and gadgets	• An article about jobs in the gaming industry	• Four phone calls reporting IT issues • A podcast about apps
• Adverbs • Reported speech	• Symptoms and treatments • Word class and suffixes • Accidents and injuries	• A blog post about parental health warnings	• Two patient-doctor conversations in a hospital • A conversation about an accident
• Reporting verbs • Defining relative clauses	• News stories • Important figures	• An article about celebrity news	• Five short conversations about news stories • Three conversations about historic figures

VOCABULARY REFERENCE page 193   **INFORMATION FILES page 194**   **AUDIO SCRIPTS page 200**

Contents 5

1

First class

IN THIS UNIT, YOU:

- get to know people you've just met
- share and discuss language-learning tips
- compare studying needs and wants, and find a study partner

SPEAKING

1 Work in pairs. Look at the photo. Discuss the questions.

1 What do you think the class is learning?

2 Do you know anyone who can use sign language?

3 Why do you think people might decide to take a course like this?

4 Would you like to take a course like this? Why? / Why not?

2 Work with a new partner. Discuss the questions.

1 Why are you learning English?

2 What English classes have you done before? Where?

3 Do you know anyone in this class?

4 Are you still friends with people from previous classes? Tell your partner about them.

Learning sign language at the Charles W. Howard Santa Claus School, Michigan, US.

Nice to meet you

IN THIS LESSON, YOU:
- get to know people you've just met
- talk about yourself and people you know
- practise listening to conversations in which people meet for the first time
- practise asking follow-up questions

Students learn English at Midwestern Career College, Chicago, US.

VOCABULARY All about me

1 Decide which two of these words could replace the words in italics in sentences 1–6 to talk about the same topic.

Architecture	engaged	Engineering	a flight attendant
hiking	a laboratory	a nursery	an only child
separated	a translator	a twin	working out

1 I'm *the youngest of five kids*.
2 I'm *a software engineer*.
3 I work in *a university*.
4 I did a degree in *Law*.
5 I'm really into *travelling*.
6 I'm *single*.

2 [P] [▶] **Listen to the words from Exercise 1 and practise saying them on their own and in a phrase. Which words / phrases do you find hard to say? Practise saying them again.**

3 Work in groups. How many true things can you say about yourself or people you know using the language from Exercise 1?

LISTENING

4 [▶] Listen to two conversations in which people meet for the first time. Answer the questions for each conversation.

1 Where do they meet?
2 Why are they there?

5 [▶] Work in pairs. Answer the questions. Listen again and check your answers.

Conversation 1

1 How is Harry feeling? Why?
2 Is Olivia a new student?
3 When did Harry start studying Spanish?
4 What does he think his strengths and weaknesses are?
5 According to Olivia, where is Spanish an official language?

Conversation 2

6 How did Noah feel about the talk he attended?

7 Where is Noah from? Where is he living now?

8 When did Noah move to his current home?

9 Has Giuliana visited the city Noah is living in?

10 What does Noah do for a living?

6 **Who was the last new person you met? Tell a partner as much as you can about them.**

GRAMMAR

Auxiliary verbs

There are three auxiliary verbs: *be*, *do* and *have*. They're used with different forms of a main verb to make questions, negatives and other structures.

How's it going? (present continuous)

Did you enjoy it? (past simple)

I don't know. (present simple)

I haven't tried that. (present perfect simple)

I've learned quite a lot of vocabulary. (present perfect simple)

I'm employed on a temporary contract. (present simple passive)

7 **Work in pairs. Read the questions from the conversations in Exercise 5 and answer questions 1–4.**

a **Do** you know it?

b **Did** you enjoy it?

c **Have** you studied here before?

d Where **are** you based?

e What **are** you doing there? **Are** you working?

f How long **have** you **been** learning Spanish?

1 Which auxiliary goes with the infinitive form of the verb?

2 Which auxiliary goes with the *-ing* form of the verb?

3 Which two auxiliaries go with a past participle (often an *-ed* form) of the verb?

4 Which two auxiliaries can be used together?

8 **Complete the questions with the correct form of *be*, *do* or *have*.**

1 Where _____ you live?

2 Who _____ you live with?

3 How long have you _____ living there?

4 Where _____ you born?

5 How long _____ it usually take you to get to work / school?

6 What _____ you do last weekend? Anything interesting?

7 Why _____ you studying at this school?

8 _____ you ever been to an English-speaking country?

9 _____ anyone else in your family speak English?

10 _____ anyone you know ever lived abroad? Where?

9 **Work in pairs. Ask and answer the questions in Exercise 8.**

G See Grammar reference 1A.

DEVELOPING CONVERSATIONS

Asking follow-up questions

After someone answers a question we've asked, we often ask a follow-up question. This helps us find out more details and keeps the conversation going.

A: *So* **have you studied here before?**

B: *Yeah, last term.*

A: *Oh really? OK.* **And did you enjoy it?**

B: *Yeah, it was amazing.*

10 **Match the questions (1–6) with the follow-up question pairs (a–f).**

1 What are you studying?

2 Have you studied here before?

3 What do you do when you're not studying?

4 Have you got any brothers or sisters?

5 What did you do at the weekend?

6 What do you do?

a Which class were you in? / Where did you learn your English?

b What year are you in? / What does that involve?

c Older or younger? / Where do they live?

d Where do you work? / Do you enjoy it?

e How often do you do that? / Did you get anything nice?

f How long have you been doing that? / What kind of music are you into?

11 **Write one more follow-up question you might ask after someone answers questions 1–6 in Exercise 10.**

CONVERSATION PRACTICE

12 **Choose six questions from this lesson that you think are good to ask people when you first meet them. Then think of two more questions you could ask.**

13 **M** **Imagine you're at a party for language students from different countries.**

- Using your questions, start conversations with other students and get to know them. You can answer in ways that are true for you or choose a person from File 3 on page 195 and pretend to be them.

- Try to find two things you have in common and two things that are different.

What did you do last weekend? Anything interesting?

Yes, actually. I saw a horror film at the cinema with my brother and sister-in-law.

Me, too! Well, I went to the cinema, but I watched a drama.

1B

Learning languages

IN THIS LESSON, YOU:
- share and discuss language-learning tips
- talk about your language-learning experiences
- read a blog post about amazing language learners
- write a comment in response to a blog post

VOCABULARY Learning languages

1 Work in pairs. How many of these languages do you recognize?

2 Complete the sentences with these words.

accent	accuracy	express	fluently
get by	mastering	picked it up	struggled

1 I'm a bit embarrassed to speak sometimes because I know I have a strong _____ .

2 I grew up bilingual, so I speak Ukrainian and English _____ .

3 I really _____ with French when I was at school, and in the end, I just gave up.

4 I hate it when I can't _____ myself properly.

5 I never took any classes. I just _____ from talking to people.

6 I'm not interested in _____ the language. I just want to be able to read it for my job.

7 I know the basics – enough to _____ when I'm travelling there.

8 _____ is very important to me. It's not enough to just make myself understood.

3 Work in pairs. Discuss the questions.

1 Why might people struggle with a language?

2 Apart from talking to people, how else can you pick language up?

3 What else do you think you can master – apart from a language?

4 What kinds of things can you say / do if you can get by in a language?

4 Work in groups. Discuss the questions.

1 What languages have you studied? How well do you speak each one?

2 What languages do you know at least a few words in? What can you say?

3 How did you learn? Do you use these languages now?

READING

5 Read the blog post about language learning on page 11. Find out:

1 which three world records are mentioned.

2 what happened to one of the record holders.

3 what a hyperpolyglot is.

4 what hyperpolyglots and athletes might have in common.

6 Complete the blog post with these sentences. There are two sentences you don't need.

a This would explain their excellent memories and ability to process speech sounds.

b Knowing such people exist gives me hope and pushes me to learn more myself.

c Obviously, none of it was true.

d Accept mistakes and uncertainty.

e Anyone that could do this was a hero to me – someone I wanted to be like.

f Practice makes perfect.

g However, the damage was done and his name was taken out of the record books.

7 Work in pairs. Read the comments at the end of the blog post. Say which ones you agree with and which you disagree with. Explain why.

8 Write your own comment in response to the blog post. Then share your comments in groups. Which do you agree with? Which do you like best?

SPEAKING

9 Work in pairs. Look at the advice on language learning in the last paragraph of the blog post. What do you think is the best tip? Why? Which pieces of advice do you already follow?

10 With your partner, write three more pieces of language-learning advice that you think other students might find useful.

11 Ⓜ Work in groups. Share your tips. Ask each other to give reasons why these tips are useful, and suggest ways of rephrasing or improving each other's tips. Then decide on the two best pieces of advice.

What the best can teach the rest

Like many of you, I'm sure, I loved *The Guinness Book of Records* when I was a kid. Every Christmas, my parents used to give me the latest edition and I remember how much I enjoyed finding out about things like the tallest dog in the world (1.12 metres, in case you're wondering) and the most tennis balls held in one hand (27, believe it or not).

However, growing up bilingual (I spoke Arabic at home and Dutch in the world outside), one record impressed me more than any other: it was for most languages spoken by one person, and it was held by a man called Ziad Youssef Fazah, who claimed he could speak fifty-nine languages. As I was struggling to learn my third, fourth and fifth languages – English, German and French – at school, the idea that someone might master twelve times more than this seemed incredible! [1]_____

Hyperglot Richard Simcott speaks over 12 languages.

I recently found out, though, that not everything was as it seemed. In 1997, the year I finished high school, Ziad Fazah appeared on a TV show in Chile and was asked questions in Arabic, Greek, Hindi, Farsi, Chinese, Russian and Finnish – and only managed to answer the first question. He later said he that the test had been a surprise, that he hadn't had time to prepare and so got nervous – and on top of that, he was tired after a long flight. [2]_____

By now, though, Ziad had got me interested and I found myself wanting to learn more about these abilities. I mean, being able to speak, say, ten languages fairly fluently and get by in several more is incredible, right? [3]_____

People who are fluent in six or more languages are known as hyperpolyglots – and there are only a tiny number in the world. While some make a lot of money from their talents, and others like Richard Simcott and Timothy Doner have become quite well-known, many other hyperpolyglots are quiet, shy people who study for fun and don't always use their languages to communicate.

Researchers believe that hyperpolyglots – like many top athletes – may have genetic advantages. [4]_____ However, making the most of whatever natural gifts you're born with requires years of hard work, and while most hyperpolyglots say it's important to find your own approach, there are certain pieces of advice that can help any language learner.

For instance, understand that the road is long and getting good takes time. Forget the idea of achieving 100% accuracy or having a native-like accent. It's not going to happen. Most people are happy if they can express themselves when talking about a range of subjects. [5]_____ And, finally, read and listen to the language as much as you can.

What do you think? I'd love to see your thoughts on hyperpolyglots and language learning in the comments.

COMMENTS

BobbyG: I know it's wrong of me to say this, but I kind of hate hyperpolyglots! I mean, I'm struggling to learn *one* new language.
♡ LIKE   ↳ REPLY

unconvinced: I get that you can make good money if you speak lots of different languages, but I think you need to be rich to become a hyperpolyglot in the first place! Who has that much time to study?
♡ LIKE   ↳ REPLY

daveD: I think you have to start learning languages when you're really young. If you don't, you'll never become fluent.
♡ LIKE   ↳ REPLY

Emoling47: When people say they're bad at languages, they usually just mean that they don't want to spend the time required to learn.
♡ LIKE   ↳ REPLY

r_sewell: You have to learn vocabulary in context. I never learn single words. I always learn words in groups.
♡ LIKE   ↳ REPLY

Study buddies

IN THIS LESSON, YOU:
- compare study goals and needs and find a study partner
- discuss the role of traditional culture in education
- practise listening to people talk about language learning
- make plans and reject suggestions

LISTENING

1 Work in pairs. Discuss the questions.

1 Look at the photo. What do you know about the Maori people and their culture?

2 What did you learn at school about traditional culture in your country?

3 Which parts of traditional culture are most / least interesting for you? Why?

4 Do you think schools should teach a country's traditional languages? Why? / Why not?

2 ▶ Listen to four short extracts. Answer the questions.

1 Which speaker doesn't talk about studying a language?

2 Which languages are the other speakers studying?

3 FS ▶ Linking words like *and* and *but* are often unstressed in fast speech. Listen to eight phrases. Which contain *and* and which contain *but*?

4 ▶ Listen again and write the phrases you hear.

5 ▶ Listen to the four extracts again. Choose the correct option (a–c) to answer the questions (1–4).

1 Why is the man in Extract 1 taking language classes?

a He's married to someone who speaks the language.

b He has a job in advertising that requires it.

c He wants to connect better with a colleague.

2 Why don't the speakers in Extract 2 arrange a time to meet?

a She doesn't want to practise the language.

b She's busy on the days he suggests.

c She's working on Friday and Saturday.

3 Why are people surprised that the man in Extract 3 speaks German?

a Because no-one in his family comes from Germany.

b Because he's Brazilian.

c Because he's never been to Germany.

4 Which sentence summarizes the woman in Extract 4's feelings?

a Translating improves her French accent.

b It's useful to translate from one language to another.

c Translating texts helps you remember them better.

6 Work in pairs. Discuss the questions.

1 Do you know any families which speak more than one language? Why?

2 Where and when do you use English outside the classroom?

3 Have you ever practised English with your classmates outside of class?

4 Have you ever translated for people outside of class? If yes, when?

Maori boys perform a haka, Roturua, New Zealand.

GRAMMAR

Present simple and present continuous

We can use the present simple and the present continuous to talk about both the present and the future.

Present simple

a I **speak** German at home.

b The flight **doesn't leave** till eleven.

c Where **does** she **work**?

Present continuous

d I**'m working** all day tomorrow.

e I**'m not making** much progress.

f **Are** you **coming** to class on Friday?

7 Work in pairs. Look at the examples in the Grammar box. Answer the questions.

1 Which two examples are about habits / regular, repeated activities?

2 Which example is about a future timetable?

3 Which example is about a temporary, unfinished activity?

4 Which two examples are about things in the future that are already decided and planned / arranged with other people?

5 What is the connection between the verbs in the box?

agree	believe	belong	disagree	forget
like	need	own	seem	want

8 Complete the conversations with the present simple or present continuous form of the words in brackets.

1 A: How _____ ? Are you still enjoying it? (your course, go)

   B: Yeah, I am, but _____ it a lot harder than before. (I, find)

2 A: Are you busy this weekend? _____ something? (you, want, do)

   B: Yeah, maybe. _____ Saturday mornings, but I'm free in the afternoon. (I, work)

3 A: What's your sister doing these days? _____ ? (she, still study)

   B: Yeah. She graduated last year, but now _____ a Master's. (she, do)

4 A: _____ a coat? _____ outside? (I, need / it, still rain)

   B: Yeah, _____ worse, actually. (it, get)

5 A: _____ any plans for tonight? (you, have)

   B: Yeah. _____ an old friend of mine for dinner, actually. (I, meet)

6 A: Some of us _____ after class tomorrow. _____ come with us? (go out / you, want)

   B: I'd love to, but I can't, I'm afraid. _____ late tomorrow. _____ until ten. (I, work / I, not finish)

9 Write reasons to explain why you can't or don't want to do the things (1–5). Use the present simple or present continuous.

1 A: Could you help me move this table to the back of the classroom?

   B: Sorry, but I can't. _____ .

2 A: We're meeting after class today to practise. Would you like to join us?

   B: I'd love to, but I can't, I'm afraid. _____ .

3 A: Can I borrow your dictionary for a few minutes?

   B: No, sorry. _____ .

4 A: Can you turn the TV off? I can't study with all that noise.

   B: No! _____ .

5 A: Would you like to go out with me on Friday?

   B: Oh, it's nice of you to ask, but I can't. Sorry. _____ .

10 Work in pairs. Take turns to read out the questions in Exercise 9. Say your responses and then continue each conversation for as long as you can.

G See Grammar reference 1C. ⟫⟫

SPEAKING TASK

11 You're going to ask other students questions to find the best study partner for you. Read these questions (1–6) and think about how you'd answer them. Then add two more questions of your own (7–8).

1 Why are you learning English?

2 What are your strengths and weaknesses in English?

3 How much time do you spend studying outside of class?

4 Do you use English when:
   - playing games?
   - watching TV?
   - listening to music?
   - using social media?

5 Do you ever use translation to help you study?

6 What are you doing over the next few days to practise your English?

7 _____ ?

8 _____ ?

12 Choose a study partner to work with. Think about:

- what you have in common.
- how you can help each other in areas where you'd like to improve.

13 Work with the study partner you chose in Exercise 12. Suggest ways of helping each other with your studies.

▣ MY OUTCOMES ▣

Work in pairs. Discuss the questions.

1 What was fun to learn in the unit?

2 What can you do better now and why?

3 What did you find challenging in this unit?

4 What can you do at home to revise what you have learned?

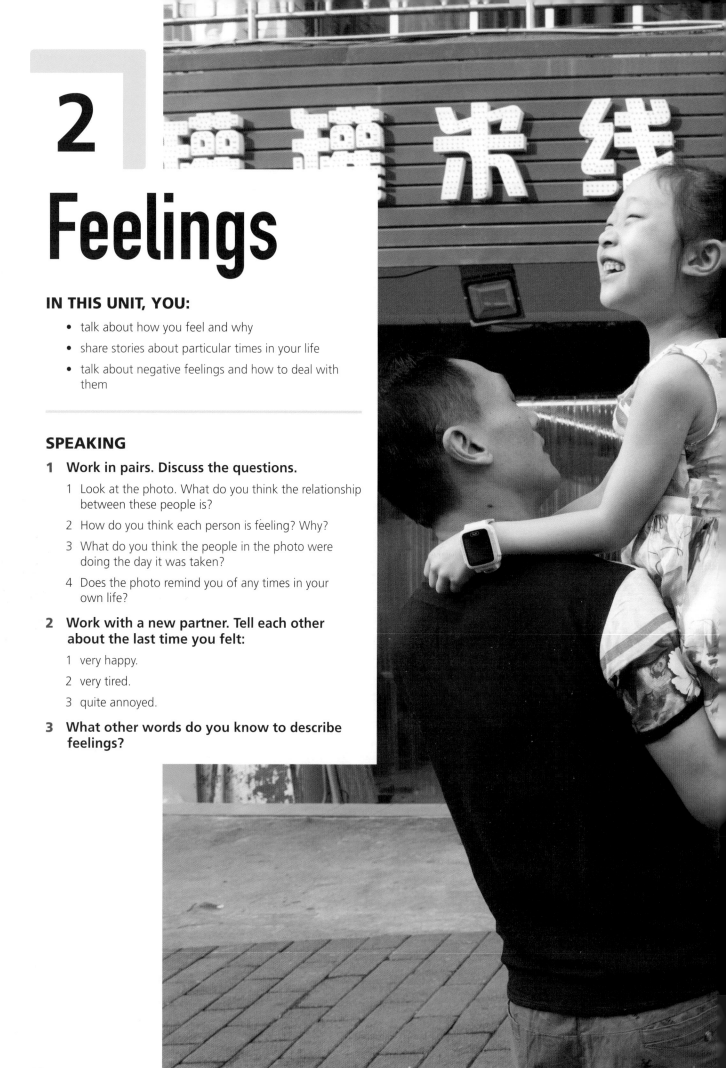

2 Feelings

IN THIS UNIT, YOU:

- talk about how you feel and why
- share stories about particular times in your life
- talk about negative feelings and how to deal with them

SPEAKING

1 Work in pairs. Discuss the questions.

1 Look at the photo. What do you think the relationship between these people is?

2 How do you think each person is feeling? Why?

3 What do you think the people in the photo were doing the day it was taken?

4 Does the photo remind you of any times in your own life?

2 Work with a new partner. Tell each other about the last time you felt:

1 very happy.

2 very tired.

3 quite annoyed.

3 What other words do you know to describe feelings?

Family members walk along Huangjueping Street in Chonqing, China.

Are you OK?

IN THIS LESSON, YOU:
- talk about how you feel and why
- practise listening to two conversations about how people are feeling
- comment on how you think people are feeling
- respond to good and bad news

VOCABULARY Feelings

1 Match the words in bold in the sentences to these basic meanings: happy, tired, annoyed, bad, sad, angry, worried.

1 We left at six in the morning and didn't get back till midnight. I was **exhausted**.

2 You must be **delighted** with the results. They're great.

3 He says he's not **bothered** by what his boss said, but I can see it's upset him.

4 I'm finding work very difficult at the moment. I feel stressed and **tense** all the time.

5 His granddad's ill at the moment, so he's upset about that. He was **in tears** when I saw him.

6 I'm so sorry. I feel really **guilty** about leaving you with all the work to do.

7 Ask her now. She looks like she's **in a good mood**. She might say yes.

8 It was good to see her enjoying herself because I know she's been a bit **down** recently.

9 I was **pleasantly surprised** by the film. I really didn't expect it to be so good.

10 I'm **fed up** with this weather. It's so hot you can't do anything. I just want it to stop.

2 **P** ▶ **Listen to the words from Exercise 1 and practise saying them on their own and in a phrase. Which words / phrases do you find hard to say? Practise saying them again.**

3 Work in pairs. Answer the questions.

1 Can you find five prepositions connected to the adjectives in bold in Exercise 1?

2 Which words from Exercise 1 can you use to describe the people in the photos?

3 Why might you feel exhausted?

4 How do you know if someone is delighted with something?

5 When might you feel tense?

6 What things might you feel guilty about?

7 What things might put you in a good mood?

8 What's the opposite of being pleasantly surprised?

9 Can you think of three things you might be fed up with? Explain why.

LISTENING

4 ▶ **Listen to two conversations between friends. How do these people feel? Why?**

1 Karim

2 Belinda

3 Alisha

5 ▶ **Listen again. Are the statements true (T) or false (F)? How do you know?**

1 Clara hasn't seen Karim for a while.

2 Ryan feels bad because he hasn't contacted Karim recently.

3 Karim is quite a quiet person.

4 Alisha is in the middle of her exams.

5 Belinda accepts Alisha's offer to help.

6 Alisha orders cake for Belinda, but not for herself.

6 Work in pairs. Discuss the questions.

1 What would you do or say if a friend was upset? Would it depend on the reason?

2 How do you cheer yourself up if you're a bit down?

3 Are you good at sorting out problems?

4 Who do you talk to if you have a problem?

GRAMMAR

Linking verbs

Look, seem, feel, sound, taste and *smell* are all linking verbs. They are used to introduce a description of the subject of a sentence or a clause. Linking verbs can be followed by different patterns.

*That chocolate cake **looks** nice.*

*He **seemed** down.*

*She **looks like** she's in a good mood.*

*He **sounded as if** he might cry.*

*That **sounds like** a nightmare.*

*It **smells like** a hospital in here.*

7 Work in pairs. Look at the examples in the Grammar box. Answer the questions.

1 What is the pattern when an adjective comes after a linking verb?

2 What two patterns are possible when a clause comes after a linking verb?

3 What is the pattern when a noun comes after a linking verb?

8 Complete these sentences with the correct form of the verbs in brackets. You may also need to add other words.

1 Are you OK? You _____ a bit tense. (look)

2 Are you alright? You _____ you've had a bit of a shock. (look)

3 Is Bruna OK? She _____ disappointed when I spoke to her. (sound)

4 Is Bukayo alright? He _____ a bit down yesterday. (seem)

5 Are you OK? You _____ you've got a cold. (sound)

6 Is your friend OK there? He _____ a bit confused. (look)

7 Have you seen Ana recently? She _____ so well, so relaxed when I last saw her! (look)

8 Hi. You _____ you're in a good mood today. (look)

9 Match the items in Exercise 8 (1–8) with the responses (a–h).

a Yeah, I am. I've just been offered a new job and I'm delighted about it.

b Yeah, I know. She's so much better after that holiday.

c Yeah, I feel terrible. I think I may have the flu.

d I am. I'm really stressed about work and I'm exhausted.

e Oh, yeah. You're right. I'll just go and see what's going on.

f Yeah. Well, on my way here I was almost hit by a car.

g He's just split up with his partner and he's quite upset about it.

h Yeah. I think she expected to get a better mark as she'd studied so much.

10 Write your own responses to the items in Exercise 8. Then work in pairs. Take turns to read out the items and give your responses.

G See Grammar reference 2A.

DEVELOPING CONVERSATIONS

Response expressions

We use lots of short expressions to respond to news and we often then ask questions as well.

A: *Apparently, she's quite ill and he's just very worried about her.*

B: ***Oh no!*** *That sounds like a nightmare. What's wrong with her? Is it very serious?*

A: *I think I'm going to need to find a new place to live.*

B: ***What a pain!*** *What's the problem with your current place?*

11 Complete the conversations with these words.

Congratulations	Oh no	pain
relief	what a shame	Wow

1 A: I'm going to Canada to study English.

  B: _____ ! That's great! How long are you going for?

2 A: I'm afraid I can't meet you tonight.

  B: Oh, _____ ! Are you sure?

3 A: Hey, I've got some big news – I'm pregnant!

  B: Really? _____ ! When's the baby due?

4 A: My brother's not very well.

  B: _____ . I'm really sorry. I hope it's not serious.

5 A: I lost my wallet somewhere last night.

  B: Oh no! That's a _____ ! Did it have much in it?

6 A: I've found my wallet!

  B: Phew, that's a _____ ! Where was it?

CONVERSATION PRACTICE

12 Think of a piece of good or bad news. Then work in pairs and have conversations similar to the ones you heard in Exercise 4. Take turns to be Student A and Student B. Use this guide to help you.

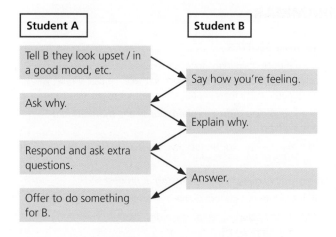

2B

Don't take it personally

IN THIS LESSON, YOU:
- share stories about particular times in your life
- discuss rejection and fear of rejection, and how to deal with them
- read an article about how one man overcame his biggest fear
- work out the function of different parts of an article

READING

1 **You're going to read an article about how one man overcame his fear of rejection. First, work in groups and discuss the questions.**

1 In what kind of situations might you be rejected? How would you feel in each situation?

2 What problems could a fear of rejection cause? How could you overcome this fear?

2 **Read the article on page 19. Find out:**

1 what rejection therapy is.

2 why Jia Jiang decided he needed it.

3 what the title of the article means.

3 **M** **Work in pairs. Don't use a dictionary. Discuss what you think the words and phrases in bold mean, or decide how to translate them into your first language.**

4 **Which paragraph (A–H) mentions these things?**

1 where the fear of rejection often comes from

2 what Jia Jiang learned from being rejected

3 two opportunities that Jia Jiang missed

4 how Jia Jiang became successful

5 the damage that fear of rejection can do

6 some general lessons we can all learn from

7 the main goal of rejection therapy

8 an example of Jia Jiang using someone else's idea

5 **Work in groups. Discuss the questions.**

1 Are you good at asking for help? Are you good at offering to help others? Give examples.

2 What might the benefits of saying yes to requests be?

3 What could you say to persuade a stranger to:

lend you money?	give you a 'burger refill'?
let you plant a flower in their garden?	let you read the weather forecast on TV?

GRAMMAR

Telling stories

We use three main forms to tell stories: past simple, past continuous and past perfect simple. To make the past simple, we usually add -ed to the verb, but some past forms are irregular.

*The young man **didn't explain**, but simply **thanked** him and **walked** away.*

To make the past continuous, we use *was / were* + *-ing* form of the verb.

*The security guard **was** just **sitting** at his desk.*

To make the past perfect simple, we use *had* + past participle.

*After he'**d had** a couple of rejections, though, something amazing happened.*

6 **Look at the examples in the Grammar box and answer the questions.**

1 Which form is often used at the beginning of stories to describe a situation?

2 Which form shows the order of events?

3 Which form shows an action that happened before something else in the past?

4 Which form shows an action was still in progress when another action happened?

7 **Choose the correct options to complete the story.**

I ¹*sat / was sitting* on the bus the other day on my way to work when a woman with two small kids ²*got / was getting* on. They ³*had looked / looked* exhausted. She ⁴*told / was telling* the driver where she wanted to go, but in Spanish. Then the driver tried to tell her where to get off, but she didn't understand. By now, her kids ⁵*cried / were crying* and she seemed very stressed. The driver then ⁶*asked / had asked* if anyone on the bus spoke Spanish. I ⁷*was standing / stood* up because I ⁸*had lived / was living* in Mexico when I was younger and I'm quite fluent. The driver explained where she needed to get off and I then ⁹*had translated / translated* what he ¹⁰*had said / said*. She ¹¹*was getting / got* off at the right stop – and I felt great because I ¹²*had helped / was helping* someone in need.

8 **Work in pairs. Add extra details to the story in Exercise 7. Use at least one more example of the past perfect simple and the past continuous.**

9 **Complete the sentences with your own ideas.**

1 When I saw her, I suddenly realized …

2 I didn't recognize him at first because …

3 He wasn't looking where he was going and …

4 This guy approached me in the street and...

5 I had wanted to … but in the end, I actually...

6 I found out later that …

G **See Grammar reference 2B.**

SPEAKING

10 **You're going to tell a story. Choose one of these ideas. Spend a few minutes thinking about what happened and how to tell your story.**

- a time you asked someone for a favour
- a time you helped someone in need
- a time a stranger helped you
- a time you were rejected

11 **Work in groups. Share your stories. Which was the funniest and which was the most interesting?**

How to win even when you lose

A The security guard was just sitting at his desk when a young man approached him and asked if he could borrow $100. 'No,' he immediately replied, before asking why. The young man didn't explain, but simply thanked him and walked away. The following day, Jia Jiang, the thirty-year-old who had made the request, ordered a burger in a fast-food chain and then tried to get a 'refill' – another burger for free. Again, he was sent away empty-handed.

Jia Jaing giving his TED Talk.

B By now, you might be wondering who Jia Jiang is and what on earth he was doing. In fact, these were the first two days of Jiang's 100-day rejection therapy challenge, a **concept** first created by Canadian entrepreneur Jason Comely. In short, rejection therapy challenges people to go up to strangers and ask for unusual favours. Comely claimed that after a month of hearing 'No!' every day, you develop a **thicker skin** and become **tougher**.

C Many of us experience the fear of being rejected at one time or another in our lives. We worry about not **fitting in**; we're scared of being on our own; we decide not to apply for that promotion at work after **convincing** ourselves that we wouldn't get it anyway. This fear of rejection means we might struggle to speak our minds or end up staying in unhealthy relationships longer than we should.

D Overcoming these fears can be hard as they often have their **roots** in childhood. This was certainly true for Jiang, whose earliest experience of being rejected came while he was at school. The negative feelings this caused stayed with him for many years, affecting his confidence and career.

E To deal with this, he decided to do something scary – actively look for rejection. Feeling that the 30 days suggested by Comely weren't enough, he set himself a 100-day challenge. Using ideas he **came up with** himself as well as suggestions from his online followers, he made a list of simple but strange requests to make: Could he, for example, plant a flower in a stranger's garden or read the weather forecast on TV?

F The first few rejections were hard for Jiang. After he'd had a couple, though, something amazing happened: people actually started agreeing to do what he asked of them, and as time went by, he got better and better at persuading people too. He realized that many people were far nicer than he'd expected – and that every potential rejection was also a potential opportunity. For instance, he learned that if he asked *why* people were rejecting him, he could often turn a 'no' into a 'yes'. By giving them the chance to share what made them uncomfortable about his requests, he could then try to earn their confidence.

G Before long, Jiang's video diaries of his daily **encounters** started going viral and he was offered a TED talk and a book deal. He now has a new career helping others to overcome their fears of rejection.

H Perhaps what Jia Jiang's story most clearly shows us is that if you don't ask, you don't get. However, it also reminds us that we're all connected. We can all benefit from asking for help more often – and in fact by doing this, we also give others the opportunity to say yes.

2C

You live and learn

LISTENING

1 Work in pairs. Read the quotes and answer the questions.

Anger is like fire. It burns it all clean.
—Maya Angelou

Relax. No-one else knows what they're doing either.
—Ricky Gervais

Every man is guilty of all the good he did not do.
—Voltaire

Depression, suffering and anger are all part of being human.
—Janet Fitch

I think, therefore I am … confused.
—Benjamin Hoff

1 What do you think the quotes mean? How might you translate them into your first language?

2 How far do you agree / disagree with each quote? Why?

3 Can you think of an example from real life that connects to each quote?

4 Which is your favourite quote? Why?

2 Work in groups. Look at the people in the photos. What kind of difficult situations might each person get into?

3 ▶ Listen to four people talking about difficult situations. Match each speaker (1–4) with one of the photos. There are two photos you don't need.

4 FS ▶ In fast speech, past simple and past perfect forms often sound very similar. Listen to eight phrases and decide whether you hear the past simple or the past perfect. Then listen again and check your ideas with a partner.

5 ▶ Listen again. Match the speakers (1–4) with the sentences (a–f). There are two items you don't need.

a They got into an argument.

b They were badly prepared.

c They deal with pressure well.

d They calm people down.

e They changed their approach.

f They made someone laugh.

6 Work in pairs. Discuss the questions.

1 How well does each speaker deal with their problems?

2 Have you ever given a talk in public? When? Where? How was it?

3 What was the last interview you had? How did you prepare for it? Did it help?

4 Is your town / city good for cyclists? Why? / Why not?

5 Have you ever got into an argument in the street? What happened?

6 How often do you go to the dentist? How do you feel about going?

VOCABULARY Adjectives with -ed and -ing

V See Vocabulary reference 2C. »»

7 Complete the pairs of sentences with either the -ed or -ing adjective form of the verbs in the box.

amaze	confuse	disappoint	embarrass
fascinate	shock	thrill	

1 a Can you just explain it one more time? I'm still a bit _____ .

 b The instructions for how to put this together are really _____ . I'm totally lost.

2 a It's _____ to think she was only 23 when she wrote that book.

 b I have to say, I was _____ by the size of their house.

3 a The violence in the film was pretty _____ .

 b I was really _____ to see so many homeless people on the streets there.

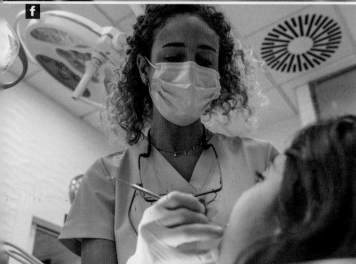

4 a I knew I was wrong, but I was too _____ to say so.

 b I couldn't remember his name. It was so _____ !

5 a Obviously, I'm a bit _____ that I didn't get the job. I thought I might.

 b I loved her last film, but to be honest, I found this one quite _____ .

6 a It was a _____ game. I couldn't take my eyes off it.

 b Brilliant! I'm _____ to hear you did so well in your exams.

7 a I've always been _____ by technology.

 b It's a _____ place. I'd love to go back one day.

8 Complete the sentences to make them true for you.

1 I've always found … fascinating.

2 I still remember how amazed I was when I found out …

3 One thing I found really disappointing was …

4 I still get quite confused about …

5 One of the most shocking things I've ever seen was …

6 One of the most embarrassing things that's happened to me was ….

7 One of the most thrilling experiences of my life was when …

9 Work in groups. Compare and explain your sentences. Who do you have the most in common with?

SPEAKING TASK

10 Think of times when you feel, or have felt, at least three of the feelings in the box. Make notes about the situations and the causes.

anxious	disappointed	down	embarrassed
fed up	guilty	scared	stressed

11 M Work in groups. Follow the instructions:

1 Take turns to share one of your experiences.

2 Work together to think of advice you can give each other to help deal with these feelings.

3 Decide which advice is the most helpful for you.

■ MY OUTCOMES ■

Work in pairs. Discuss the questions.

1 What classroom activities did you enjoy doing?

2 Can you talk about feelings and experiences better? If so, in what way?

3 What did you find challenging about the reading or listening texts?

4 What are the three most important things to revise from this unit?

Keeping in touch

SPEAKING

1 Work in pairs. Discuss the questions.

1 Are you good at keeping in touch with people?

2 What's good / bad about these ways of keeping in touch?
- emails
- social media
- phone
- messaging apps
- video calls
- letters

3 Think of someone you know who you haven't been in touch with for a while.
- Why haven't you been in touch?
- What was their situation last time you were in touch?

WRITING

2 Read an email from Luca to Jun, a friend he made while studying English in the UK. Put the paragraphs in the correct order. Then work in pairs and explain your order.

To: Jun@email.ml

From: Luca83@email.ml

Hi there Jun,

a **Apart from** getting married, looking for a flat and working six nights a week, I'm also working out a lot at the gym. To be honest, I'm exhausted, but **also** really happy, if you know what I mean!

b When I last wrote, I told you I'd met a woman called Jean, right? Well, guess what? We're getting married! I proposed when we were having a meal to celebrate our first six months together. I know it seems quick, but she's really wonderful. It now looks as if I'm going stay in Scotland for a long time!

c Anyway, what about you? What are you up to these days? When you wrote last, you said you were thinking of going to see Reo in Japan. Did you go? How was it? How's Reo? I often think of you both and the great times we had at school here.

d Write to me soon and tell me your news.

e How are you? Sorry I haven't written recently, but I've been busy. So many things are happening in my life at the moment it's difficult to find time for anything else!

f **As well as** getting married, we're looking for a place to live. It's expensive here, so it's good that I **also** started a new job two months ago. I'm working in an Italian restaurant. The basic wages aren't great, but I get a lot of tips. The owner's grandparents were Italian, but he doesn't speak the language, so it's good for my English **too**. I've picked up a lot of things. And, of course, I speak English with Jean and her family.

All the best,
Luca

3 Use words from the email to complete the phrases for catching up with news.

1 How are you? Sorry I haven't _____ recently, but I've _____ very busy.

2 When I _____ wrote, I told you …

3 _____ what? We're getting married!

4 _____ , what about you? What are _____ these days?

5 I often think _____ you both and the great _____ we had.

6 Write to me _____ and tell me your _____ .

4 Work in groups. Discuss the questions.

1 Do you think Luca and Jean have decided to get married too quickly? Why? / Why not?

2 What might be good / bad about studying abroad?

3 Do you have any friends from other countries? How did you meet? How do you keep in touch?

4 Apart from emails, what other ways can you think of to practise writing in English? Which do you think is the best way?

USEFUL LANGUAGE

As well as, apart from, too and also

We use *as well as* and *apart from* to join ideas and different parts of sentences. These phrases can start a sentence and are followed by an *-ing* form. At the end of the clause starting with *as well as / apart from*, we add a comma.

As well as getting married, we're looking for a place to live.

Apart from getting married, looking for a flat and working six nights a week, I'm also working out a lot at the gym.

Too and *also* add ideas, but you need another word such as *and*, *but* or *so* to join the two parts of a sentence. *Too* goes at the end of a sentence / clause. *Also* usually goes in the middle.

I am exhausted, but I'm also really happy.

He doesn't speak Italian well, so it's good for my English too.

5 Join the pairs of sentences. Use the words in brackets and make any other necessary changes.

1 I started a new job last week. I'm moving house. (also)

2 I'm studying a lot. I'm training hard for a marathon. (as well as)

3 My brother is living with me at the moment. I'm busy looking after him. (too)

4 I helped to organize my mum's 50th birthday party. I've been busy at work. (apart from)

6 Use *as well as* / *apart from* or *too* / *also* to write three sentences about your life recently. Then read your sentences to a partner.

Referring back

When we write to catch up with news, we often refer back to the situation the last time we wrote to / spoke to / saw the person we're writing to. We use the past perfect simple or the past continuous to show if the action happened before we spoke, or around the same time.

When I last wrote, I told you I'd met a woman called Jean. (= We met before I wrote.)

When you wrote last, you said you were thinking of going to see Reo in Japan. (= You were thinking around the same time as you wrote.)

7 Complete the sentences with the correct form of an auxiliary verb. You may need to use negative forms.

1 The last time we spoke, you said you _____ feeling a bit down.
2 The last time I saw you, you _____ doing your exams.
3 The last time I saw you, I _____ have a job.
4 The last time you wrote, you said you _____ planning to move.
5 The last time we spoke, I still _____ graduated.
6 The last time I wrote, I _____ still going out with Karina.

8 Match the sentences in Exercise 7 (1–6) with the follow-up comments / questions (a–f).

a How are you now? I hope you're better.
b Did you find anywhere nice? What's your new address?
c How did you do? Did you pass them all?
d Well, guess what? I'm now the manager of a local café.
e Well, I finished last July and now I'm doing a Master's.
f Well, unfortunately we've split up.

9 Complete the sentences with your own ideas. Then add a follow-up question or comment.

1 The last time you wrote, you said …
2 The last time I saw you, I think I …
3 The last time I spoke to her, …

PRACTICE

10 You're going to write an email to someone you haven't been in touch with for a while. You want to catch up with their news. Think about:

- why you haven't been in touch.
- the situation you were both in when you last spoke and / or what you talked about.
- your situation now, things you're doing and events that have happened to you recently.
- questions you want to ask your friend.

11 Write your email. Use the model email and language from this lesson to help you. Write 180–220 words.

12 Work in pairs. Swap emails. Can your partner's email be improved? Discuss these questions.

1 Have they included phrases from Exercise 3?
2 Have they used *as well as*, *apart from*, *too* and *also* correctly?
3 Have they referred back to a past situation / conversation?

Preparing food in an Italian restaurant, London, UK.

THE BEST LEVONI SALUMI
CREAMY BUFFALO MOZZARELLA
PECORINO CHEESE WITH SWEET

BY THE LOVE, PASSION &
VERVE FOR FOOD, FAMILY &
LIFE ITSELF THAT JUST ABOUT
ALL ITALIAN PEOPLE HAVE &
THAT'S WHAT I'M PASSIONATE
ABOUT - GOOD FOOD FOR
EVERYONE. BIG LOVE

VIDEO Out and about

1 Work in pairs. Discuss the questions.

1 Where and when do you use English outside the classroom?

2 What's been your best moment using English outside the classroom? Why was it so good?

Understanding accents

Some accents use a /t/ sound instead of a /θ/ sound, so *thin* /θɪn/ may sound more like *tin* /tɪn/.

2 ▶ **Watch four people answer the same questions. How much can you remember about what they said? Then work in pairs. Did anyone have similar experiences to you?**

3 ▶ **Watch again. Match one or two sentences with each speaker. There are two extra sentences.**

a They use English when they go out after class.

b They use English in their job.

c They had an interview which was partly in English.

d They're studying Engineering in English.

e Someone admired their English.

f They read novels in English.

g They feel their English has become a bit easier to use.

h They occasionally use English to help tourists.

4 Discuss the questions with your partner.

1 Have you ever done an interview or public speaking in English?

2 What jobs should require English? Why?

3 What English magazines or newspapers do you know? Do you ever read them? Why? / Why not?

4 Why might tourists come to where you live? Do you ever talk to them?

VIDEO Developing conversations

5 ▶ **You're going to watch two people sharing their personal news. Watch and take notes.**

6 ▶ **Work in pairs. Compare what you understood. Watch again if you need to.**

7 FS ▶ **Watch again. Complete the sentences with three to five words in each gap.**

1 Well, you know how long _____ sell my flat?

2 I can see how relieved _____ . That just must be a weight off your shoulders.

3 At last I can just say 'yes!' _____ I have to find somewhere to live!

4 I'm going to need _____ some properties.

5 Not so great. _____ good news.

6 I've completely _____ . Don't feel sorry for me.

7 So now I need _____ – I need to collect my car and pay a fine.

8 So _____ on the way home, I can pick up my car.

CONVERSATION PRACTICE

8 Work in pairs. You're going to practise a conversation.

1 Choose a Conversation practice from either Lesson 1A or Lesson 2A.

2 Look at the language in that lesson.

3 Check the meaning of anything you've forgotten with your partner.

4 Have the conversation. Try to improve on the last time you did it.

Grammar and Vocabulary

GRAMMAR

1 **Complete the text with one word in each gap. Contractions count as one word.**

[1]_____ I ever told you how my parents met? Well, they met in the middle of nowhere in Peru. My dad [2]_____ walking on his own to Machu Picchu. He was very fit at the time, but he found he was getting slower and slower, and then he stopped and was really sick.

Apparently, it [3]_____ caused by being up in the mountains. Eventually, he got to a village to ask for help, which was difficult as he [4]_____ speak much Spanish. Fortunately, there was another group who [5]_____ just visited Machu Picchu and [6]_____ on their way back to the nearest city, Cuzco. My mum was in that group. She had done Spanish at university, so she translated for him. She told me that [7]_____ she first saw him, she was shocked because he looked [8]_____ if he hadn't eaten for days! Anyway, my dad recovered and they fell in love. And that's why they [9]_____ going back to Machu Picchu this year to celebrate their wedding anniversary. My dad still [10]_____ been there!

2 **Write the words in the correct order to make two questions.**

1 Where / What / does / are / that / you / based / involve
2 Have / Are / you / you / working / been / here before / at the moment
3 Where / When / does / was / she / she / live / born
4 Did / Has / you / she / go out / seen / it / last night
5 What / How / kind of music / often / do / are / you / you / into / do that
6 How many / How long / have / brothers and sisters / do / you / you / been / have / doing that

3 **Choose the correct option to complete the sentences.**

1 What do you do when *you're not / you don't* working?
2 Are you OK? You *look / look like* a bit confused.
3 I can't speak to you now. *I do / I'm doing* something.
4 *We have / We're having* a barbecue on Friday.
5 We couldn't get back into the house because I *left / had left* my key inside.
6 Is he OK? He *sounds / sounds like* he's getting a cold.
7 It was stupid. I *was trying / had tried* to carry too many things and in the end I dropped everything.
8 I asked them to turn their music down because I *was studying / studied*.
9 He said he can't come on Friday because he *has / is having* too much work.
10 We *met / were meeting* some clients when we *heard / was hearing* the news.

4 ▶ **Listen and write the six sentences you hear.**

VOCABULARY

5 **Match the two parts of the collocations.**

1	express	a	in a laboratory / from home
2	have	b	a slight accent / a lot in common
3	pick it up	c	with English grammar / to understand him
4	work out	d	myself clearly / his feelings
5	work	e	as you go along / from talking to people
6	do	f	three times a week / to music
7	struggle	g	the language / the basics first
8	master	h	a Master's / a degree in Engineering

6 **Decide if these words are connected to personal information, language or feelings.**

accent	accuracy	not bothered	down
fed up	get by	mood	only child
single	separated	twin	

7 **Complete the sentences with the correct form of the words in bold.**

1 I didn't expect much, so I was _____ surprised. **pleasant**
2 I struggled with German at school. I always got _____ by the grammar. **confuse**
3 We were quite _____ with the results. **disappoint**
4 Did you see the news yesterday? It was quite _____ , wasn't it? **shock**
5 I think her work is really _____ . **fascinate**
6 He can speak six languages _____ . **fluent**
7 After I asked where her dad worked, there was an _____ silence. **embarrass**
8 My flight was overnight and I didn't sleep at all, so I'm _____ . **exhaust**

8 **Complete the extract from an email with one word in each gap. The first letters are given.**

Hey, guess what? I saw Gabriel the other day. It was lovely to see him and he was in a really good [1]m_____ . I felt [2]g_____ that I hadn't been in touch for so long as he's had quite a [3]to_____ time since we last met. Do you remember that he was [4]e_____ to Kasia? Well, they split up, but then he got married six months later to someone he met online. That didn't last and they're now [5]s_____ . He said he started feeling quite [6]do_____ about everything after that, and his job was making him [7]an_____ as well. He didn't [8]f_____ in there and was working such long hours that in the end, he decided to quit. He then went through quite a confusing time where he didn't know what to do before he then [9]c_____ up with the idea of using his language skills to be a [10]tr_____ and that's what he's doing now.

3
Time off

IN THIS UNIT, YOU:

- roleplay a conversation recommending places to visit
- talk about public holidays and your plans for the next one
- research and plan a one-week holiday

SPEAKING

1 Work in groups. Discuss the questions.

1 Look at the photo. Would you like to go to a place like this for a holiday? Why? / Why not?

2 What's the best place to get a view where you live? What can you see from there?

3 What's the highest building or place you have been up? How was it? When did you go there?

City view from Cerro Santa Lucia,
Santiago, Chile.

Can you recommend anywhere?

IN THIS LESSON, YOU:
- roleplay a conversation recommending places to visit
- describe places of interest in a city / area you know
- find out about places of interest in Kraków
- practise giving and responding to suggestions

VOCABULARY Places of interest

1 Complete the sentences with these words. Check you understand the words in bold.

architect	district	gallery	religious
restored	rides	royal	ruins
stalls	theme park	tower	

1 There's an incredible castle on the edge of the town. You can get great views walking along the walls and from the top of the _____ .

2 There's a fantastic street market in the east of the city with _____ selling everything from antique furniture to apples.

3 There's a 17th century _____ **palace** down by the river. It's recently opened again after it was _____ .

4 There's a great _____ an hour out of the city along the coast. They've got some really exciting _____ there.

5 The main nightlife is in the **historic** _____ near the port. There are lots of bars and restaurants there and it's always very lively.

6 There are **ancient** _____ all over this part of the country. They discovered some near here recently when they were building a new supermarket.

7 There's a variety of old _____ buildings representing the people of different religions that have lived in the city.

8 They built a new modern art _____ recently. It's an amazing building. It was designed by a famous Brazilian _____ .

2 **P** ▶ Listen to the words from Exercise 1 said on their own and then in a phrase. Practise saying them. Which words / phrases do you find hard to say? Practise saying them again.

3 Work in pairs. Think of another word or phrase connected to the words in Exercise 1.

gallery – put on an exhibition

district – financial district

4 Complete the phrases with prepositions from Exercise 1.

1 It's about 10 miles / 60 kilometres / an hour _____ of town.

2 You can walk _____ the walls / the river / the beach.

3 It's _____ the east of the city / the old town / the financial district.

4 It's _____ by the river / the beach / the port.

5 It's _____ the edge of the town / the city / a lake.

6 You find them all _____ this part of the country / this area / the city.

5 **M** Work in pairs. Choose a city / area you both know. Create an itinerary or list of places and things for tourists to do.

LISTENING

6 Work in pairs. Look at the places to visit in Kraków, Poland's top tourist destination. If you were in Kraków for a day, which places you would go to? Why?

7 ▶ Listen to a conversation between a tourist and a hotel receptionist in Kraków. Which places in the text are mentioned? What does the tourist decide to do? Work in pairs and compare your ideas.

8 ▶ Complete the sentences with one word in each gap. Then listen again and check your answers.

1 Hello there. I _____ if you can help me.

2 I'm _____ of going sightseeing today.

3 Can you _____ anywhere good to go?

4 It depends on _____ you like.

5 I'm not really a big _____ of looking around old religious buildings, to be honest.

6 Well, in that case, you _____ try Kazimierz.

7 How _____ a guided tour of Nowa Huta?

8 I can call and _____ a _____ for you.

DEVELOPING CONVERSATIONS

Giving and responding to suggestions

There are number of semi-fixed phrases you can use to get suggestions for things to do.

To ask for suggestions: ***I'm thinking of … Can you recommend anywhere?***

To suggest something: ***Well, you could try … / In that case, how about (going to) … ?***

To disagree with a suggestion: ***I'm not really a big fan of / I'm not really into …***

To agree with a suggestion: ***Oh, that sounds interesting / great / better.***

We can also ask other practical questions such as *How much? / Where? /* etc.

9 Put the two conversations in the correct order.

Conversation 1

a Well, you could try Oxford Street. There are lots of big department stores there.

b Oh, OK. Well, in that case, how about Portobello Road? It's a big street market. You can find lots of bargains there.

c To be honest, I'm not really a big fan of department stores.

d Oh, that sounds great. I love that kind of thing. Is it easy to get to?

e I'm thinking of doing some shopping today. Can you recommend anywhere? *1*

f Yes, very. I'll show you on the map.

Conversation 2

g   Right. I'm not really into museums, to be honest.

h   Well, you could try the local museum. That's quite close to here. They've got lots of interesting things in there.

i   No, it's quite cheap. It should only be about $10.

j   I'm thinking of doing some sightseeing today. Can you recommend anywhere?

k   Oh, that sounds better. Are they expensive to get into?

l   That's OK. In that case, how about going to the Roman ruins down by the lake? There are also some nice cafés and you can swim there.

10 ▶ **Listen and check your answers. Then work in pairs and practise reading the conversations.**

CONVERSATION PRACTICE

11   Work in pairs. Roleplay a conversation between a tourist and a hotel receptionist. Use your ideas from Exercise 5. Take turns to be Student A and Student B.

Student A: You're a tourist. You're thinking of going sightseeing. Ask for recommendations. Reject some before deciding on one.

Student B: You're a hotel receptionist. Suggest some different places to the tourist when they ask you for recommendations. Explain why they're good.

KRAKÓW
PLACES TO VISIT

Rynek Główny

A huge medieval square in the centre of the old town where there is a market with some great stalls.

Rynek Underground

The popular hi-tech museum, below the square, allows you to experience the full history of the city of Kraków.

St Mary's Church

The city's most important church, originally built in the thirteenth century, contains some wonderful pieces of art.

Wawel Royal Castle

See the beautiful rooms of the royal palace and get great views of the Vistula River and Kraków from the castle walls.

MOCAK

Kraków's modern art gallery, designed by the Italian architect Claudio Nardi, holds exhibitions of the latest international art.

Oskar Schindler Factory

During World War II, the factory was the site of a movement that saved over 1,000 Jewish people from being killed by the Nazis. It was restored and is now a museum with exhibitions on the war and life in Kraków at the time.

Nowa Huta

Take a tour round the model industrial and housing district built in the 1950s and visit the Nowa Huta museum to experience life in communist times.

Kazimierz

The historic Jewish district, with its narrow streets and squares, is now a lively area with small shops and excellent nightlife.

Pasaż 13

Go to this small shopping centre in central Kraków for the best shops and fashion boutiques.

Ulica Józefa

For those who prefer vintage styles, go to Józefa and the nearby streets to explore some great second-hand stores.

The medieval square of Rynek Główny, Krakow, Poland.

A day off

IN THIS LESSON, YOU:
- talk about public holidays and your plans for the next one
- explain the significance of different public holidays
- read and share information about different public holidays in the world
- tell people about plans you have for different days / times

VOCABULARY Public holidays

1 **Work in pairs. Don't use a dictionary. Discuss what you think the words in bold mean, or decide how to translate them into your first language.**

1 It's named after our first president and celebrates the day the country **became independent**.

2 It celebrates the royal family and the birth of our king. There's usually a big loud **fireworks display** at night.

3 It's in memory of those who died fighting for our **freedom** during the war of independence. An **official ceremony** takes place in the main square.

4 It's in memory of **a tragic event** in our history when many people died in a huge flood.

5 It celebrates winning an **important battle** when we had to **defend** the country.

6 Families **get together** and share a big meal where we roast a whole lamb over a fire.

7 It celebrates **the role** of women in our society, and on that day we usually **take our mothers out** for lunch.

8 On the day, we usually visit the **cemetery** and take flowers and **remember our ancestors**.

9 **It's held** in October and is a celebration of nature and the start of spring. Family and friends often have **a day out at the seaside**.

2 **Work in groups. How many of the words in Exercise 1 can you use to describe public holidays or festivals that you know of?**

READING

3 **Work in pairs. Read the article introduction on page 31 and discuss the questions.**

1 Why might people not like a public holiday?

2 Do people get enough holiday or too much? Why?

4 **Work in pairs. Read about two public holidays and find out when and why they're held.**

Student A: Read the paragraphs on page 31.

Student B: Read the paragraphs in File 4 on page 196.

5 **Work in pairs. Decide which would be the best public holiday for you to experience together.**

6 **Work with your partner to decide which holiday(s) each sentence refers to.**

1 The writer is thinking of celebrating all night.

2 The writer might take part in one of the events this year.

3 The festival celebrates an unusual natural event.

4 People can see the main events on TV.

5 The writer is not going to have the day off this year.

6 Not many people take part in the events on the day.

7 The writer might not be in the country this year.

8 The writer mentions problems related to this public holiday.

7 **Discuss the questions about holidays in your country.**

1 Are there any big sporting / cultural events on particular holidays? Do you like them? Why? / Why not?

2 Do any holidays have a history that people don't think about much? How do you feel about that?

3 Do some parts of the country get special holidays? Why?

4 Do any events attract a lot of tourists? Why?

5 Do you get problems on any public holiday?

GRAMMAR

Future plans

We can talk about future plans using a variety of forms:

present continuous	*I'm working* all weekend.
be going to + verb	Our team *is going to compete* there.
be thinking of + -ing	*I'm thinking of taking* an extra day off.
will probably + verb	*I'll probably go* out with my friends as usual.
might + verb	I *might take* the boat to Sicily.

8 **Look at the examples in the Grammar box. Answer the questions.**

1 Which sentences show plans that are already arranged?

2 Which sentences show plans which are less certain?

3 What are the negative forms of each structure?

9 **Complete the conversation with one word in each gap. Contractions count as one word.**

A: Do you have any ¹_____ for the weekend?

B: Well, I'm going ²_____ have an exam next week so I ³_____ spending most of the weekend revising, but I'm ⁴_____ a friend on Sunday morning to go to the MOCAK gallery. We ⁵_____ go for lunch too. It depends how much work I do on Saturday. Why? What about you?

A: Well, I'm ⁶_____ of maybe going to the cinema on Saturday night and thought you might like to go.

B: Maybe. I'll probably be tired and ⁷_____ want to work late. What are you ⁸_____ of seeing?

A: I haven't decided. Let's have a look now.

10 **Work in pairs. Ask each other about your plans:**

- in the summer
- for the weekend
- after this course
- after the class
- for your birthday
- other times

G See Grammar reference 3B.

SPEAKING

11 **Work in pairs. Answer the questions.**

1 Which public holiday do you like most / least? Why?

2 What are your plans for the next public holiday(s)?

Public Holiday
HISTORY

Everyone loves a public holiday – that occasional extra day, where you don't need to get up early or you can have a day out with family. Some countries get a bit more of that holiday feeling than others – although calculating who actually gets the most is a bit difficult because of regional variations, and because there may be unofficial extra days that people take to bridge the weekend to the official public holiday. Still, Liechtenstein, Cambodia and Egypt all have 20 or more, while the unlucky Dutch have just eight. And the Dutch sometimes get even fewer if the 'holiday' falls on a weekend because they aren't replaced by a day off on the following working day as in some countries. Still, at least workers in the Netherlands have the right to 20 days of paid holiday a year, unlike in the US, so I suppose it's not all hard work and no play for them.

While many public holidays have a link to a country's culture and history, quite often these links can be forgotten as people focus on getting together and celebrating. We're all for people having a good time, but we think there's still room for education too. Read more here to find out about public holidays around the world and our contributors' plans for this year.

Bon om touk

We have three days of public holiday during the autumn, at the end of October or beginning of November. The festival which is held then celebrates the water and moon because at this time of year the Tonle Sap river changes direction after the heavy rains of the monsoon season and the full moon is also at its biggest and brightest. It's a great festival. There are lots of traditions connected with it, such as lighting beautiful lanterns and playing a game where you try and make people laugh, but the main thing is boat racing. Races are held all over Cambodia, but the biggest ones take place in the capital, Phnom Penh, in front of the royal palace. I'm actually training hard now to be part of our team from Kampong Cham Province which is going to compete there. It's going to be difficult to get into the team, so it might not happen. Even if I don't compete, I'll still probably travel to the capital with my family. As well as supporting the team we're looking forward to seeing the great firework displays and enjoying all the other celebrations in the city.

Samnang, Cambodia

August bank holiday

The last Monday of August is always a public holiday in the UK. The name, *bank holiday*, goes back to a nineteenth-century law introduced by the politician and banker Sir John Lubbock. Before this law, bank workers couldn't take holidays like other people because the banks would lose money. So there's no other reason for the August bank holiday, apart from giving people a day off and creating a long weekend. I'm happy to have a day off, but personally would prefer it at another time of year – and maybe linking it with some historic event. A lot of people are away on holiday at this time of year anyway, but others may have a day out at the seaside or in the countryside. Unfortunately, the weather here is pretty unpredictable and my childhood memories of the day are either sitting inside avoiding the rain or sitting in a traffic jam on our way to the beach arguing with my brothers! The last couple of years I went to the Notting Hill Carnival, which is a Caribbean carnival, held every year in London and is apparently Europe's largest street festival. Unfortunately, this year I'm working all weekend, including the bank holiday, and I'm not even going to get extra pay!

Sadie, UK

My kind of holiday

IN THIS LESSON, YOU:
- research and plan a one-week holiday
- discuss what's important for you when going on holiday
- practise identifying the main ideas in a podcast on travel
- have conversations about your experiences of different places

A rainy photo opportunity, Machu Picchu, Peru.

VOCABULARY Choosing a holiday

1 **Match the descriptions (1–9) to the holiday words and phrases (a–i).**

1 There's an ancient temple there as well as some other **historic sites**.

2 I'm not bothered about trying the **local cuisine**.

3 I just want to **get away from** it all and not be **disturbed** by anyone.

4 I might spend a couple of weeks **volunteering** in a community project abroad.

5 I want to go **diving** and maybe even try **water-skiing**.

6 I'm looking for some **luxury accommodation**.

7 I don't want it to **pour down** or drop below about 30 and I don't like it if it's too **humid** either!

8 There were some woods nearby and we could also get great views from the **cliffs** above the sea.

9 There's so much to do on a **cruise**. They put on shows every night and there are all sorts of other activities to keep people entertained.

a a high-quality place to stay

b entertainment

c **guaranteed** good weather

d history and culture

e meeting local people

f beautiful **surroundings**

g good food

h peace and quiet

i activities and adventure

2 **Work in pairs. Individually rank the things in Exercise 1 (a–i) from 1 (= most important) to 9 (= least important). Then explain your choices to your partner and give examples.**

LISTENING

3 ▶ **Listen to the beginning of a podcast. Answer these questions.**

1 Who is the presenter?

2 Who is being interviewed?

3 What do you think the answer to the question at the end might be?

4 FS ▶ **The same word can sound different within different groups of words. Listen to the seven extracts. Which word do you hear in all of them?**

5 ▶ **Listen to the rest of the podcast. Decide which of the things in Exercise 1 Lois is interested in.**

6 ▶ Work in pairs. Are these statements true (T) or false (F)? Then listen again and check your answers.

1 Holly isn't interested in visiting Glasgow.

2 Lois's main reason for travel is to visit famous cemeteries.

3 Lois didn't really want to go to Père Lachaise.

4 Holly and Lois agree that guided tours are better than going on your own.

5 Lois doesn't like taking selfie photos.

6 Dark tourism can involve visiting sites of recent wars or crimes.

7 Lois sees cemeteries as providing a more positive view of history.

8 Holly and Lois have both been to the Merry Cemetery.

9 Lois sees WWOOFing as a cheap way to travel abroad.

7 Work in pairs. Choose three sets of questions to discuss.

1 What do you think of Lois's choices for holidays and travel? Does she sound like someone you would go travelling with? Why? / Why not?

2 Have you ever been to a place where a famous person lived / was buried? Who? Where?

3 How well do you know your city, region, country? Would you like to travel around them more?

4 What cheap ways of travelling can you think of? Have you done any of them? Where?

GRAMMAR

Present perfect simple

We often use the present perfect simple to start conversations about experiences. We're not interested in the specific time – only if you've had the experience or not. We form the present perfect simple with *have / has* + (*not / never*) + past participle.

I interview people I've met on my journeys.

I've never been there.

Have you visited anywhere interesting recently?

When we respond to a question in the present perfect simple, we can use a wide range of different forms.

A: *Have you been on holiday recently?*

B: *Yes, I have. / Yeah, a few weeks ago I went to Glasgow. / Not since I last saw you, but I'm going to Peru in the summer. / No, what about you?*

8 Work in pairs. Look at the examples in the Grammar box. Answer these questions.

1 Why might A ask that question?

2 What different verb forms are used in B's example answers?

3 Which of the answers do you think help develop the conversation and which one doesn't? Why?

9 Write present perfect questions and statements using these words (1–8).

1 you / be / anywhere good recently?

Have you been anywhere good recently?

2 they / do / that before ?

3 I / never even / hear / of that city

4 We / not / travel / very widely

5 you / ever / try / moqueca?

6 It's the first time / he / travel / abroad .

7 What's the best place you / ever / stay ?

8 She / write / a lot of books about travel .

10 Complete these answers to the question *Have you (ever) been to …?* with *Yes (I have)* or *No (never / I haven't)*.

1 _____ . What's it like?

2 _____ , but it's supposed to be amazing.

3 _____ . Several times. Why?

4 _____ , but I might actually go at the weekend.

5 _____ . I've never really wanted to.

6 _____ . I'd love to, though.

7 _____ . It's great. You should go.

8 _____ . I spent a week there on a business trip.

9 _____ . I'm going there this summer, though.

10 _____ . Have you? I've heard it's quite nice.

11 _____ . My brother has, though. He enjoyed it.

12 _____ . Once. Have you?

11 Write five questions starting with *Have you (ever) been to … ?* Ask about places you know and want to compare experiences of, or places you're thinking of going to and want opinions of.

12 Talk to other students. Ask your questions and answer other students' questions using the answers in Exercise 10. Give as many details as you can.

G | See Grammar reference 3C. »»

SPEAKING TASK

13 M Work in groups. You're going to decide where to go and what to do for a week's holiday together. Follow the instructions:

1 Discuss what you look for in a holiday and agree the kind of holiday you'd like to do.

2 Decide who will look at the holiday options in File 2 on page 194 and File 5 on page 196.

3 Read the holiday options and think about which you'd prefer to do and why. Which options do you think would be good for your group?

4 Discuss the options. Make suggestions based on what you read and what you know about the people in your group.

5 Agree on which holiday you'll take, where and when you'll go, and what activities you'll do.

■ MY OUTCOMES ■

Work in pairs. Discuss the questions.

1 What interesting information about the lesson topic have you learned?

2 What useful language have you learned?

3 What did you find challenging about the speaking tasks?

4 Which texts in the unit do you want to read or listen to again, and why?

4 Interests

IN THIS UNIT, YOU:

- have conversations about free-time activities
- talk about aspects of music and why you like / don't like them
- do a survey into people's use of local facilities and how to improve them

SPEAKING

1 Work in pairs. Discuss the questions.

1 Look at the photo. Have you ever done anything similar to this? When? Where?

2 Do you do anything to keep fit? What?

3 Are you more of a morning or an evening person?

4 What do you usually do early in the morning and late in the evening?

A woman wild swims in an icy lake in Slovakia.

Making the most of your time

VOCABULARY Free-time activities

1 Complete the sentences with the words in the box.

baking	basic steps	a bike ride	chess
a club	an early night	jogging	the NBA Finals
a quick workout	a rehearsal	sailing	sewing
stayed in			

1 I hung out with my brother and played _____ .

2 I just _____ and watched a few episodes of *House of the Dragon*.

3 I was tired so I just had _____ . I read in bed for a while, but I was asleep by 10 p.m.

4 I sat at home and did some _____ . I'm making a jacket for a friend.

5 I went to the gym for _____ . I usually do weights and use the rowing machine.

6 I went to my beginner's dance class. We're just trying to master some _____ at the moment.

7 I went to _____ with some friends. We danced all night.

8 I went for _____ in the country with my girlfriend. We did about 30km.

9 I went _____ . I didn't go far – just round the park a couple of times.

10 A friend of mine has got a boat and he took us _____ down the river.

11 I invited some friends round for drinks and to watch _____ .

12 I did some _____ for my sister's birthday party. I made her a lovely cake.

13 I play in a band and we had _____ last night.

2 Work in pairs. Think of three ways to complete each sentence.

1 I went … *-ing*

2 I went for a …

3 I stayed in and …

4 I invited some friends round …

3 Work in groups. Try to find examples of activities from Exercises 1 and 2 that:

1 you've all done recently.

2 you all only do occasionally.

3 none of you really like doing.

4 none of you have ever done.

LISTENING

4 ▶ Listen to three conversations. Which activities from Exercise 1 do the speakers talk about?

5 ▶ Work in pairs. Are the sentences true (T) or false (F)? Listen again and check your answers.

1 Brenda is a professional actor.

2 She has a major part in a play called *101 Break-ups*.

3 She's rehearsing more than she normally does.

4 Domi had poor weather when she went sailing at the weekend.

5 She got into sailing during childhood.

6 She's been out a lot recently with work colleagues.

7 Finn was out late playing chess with friends.

8 He and his friends meet up every two months or so to play.

9 Finn plays well and he's improving quickly in all aspects of the game.

Outdoor tango lessons, London, UK.

GRAMMAR

Habit and frequency

We use the present simple to ask about the frequency of activities.

How often **do** you **rehearse**?

Do you **go** sailing a lot / much?

Do you ever **play** chess?

We use a variety of time phrases in our replies. We may give a general frequency followed by more details. We may also say how our habits have changed.

We always meet **once a week**, but as we get nearer a performance, we have rehearsals **three or four times a week**.

A fair bit. Maybe **once every couple of months**.

Not as much as I used to in Brittany. At home, I went **all the time**.

I play online **sometimes**, but **not as much as I'd like to**.

6 Work in pairs. Look at the examples in the Grammar box. Answer the questions.

1 Which question do we use if we aren't sure whether the person we're talking to does this activity?

2 When do we use *every* and when do we use *a / an* with periods of time like *hour*, *day*, *week* etc.?

3 Which two forms can we use to talk about habits in the past?

4 Can you think of another way to end a sentence starting *Not as much as I … ?*

7 Complete the frequency phrases in the conversations with the words in the box.

all	hardly	like	much
nearly	quite	to	whenever

1 A: Do you go swimming a lot?
B: Yeah, _____ **every day**, unless I'm really busy.

2 A: Do you eat out a lot?
B: **Not as much as we used** _____ . Before we had kids, we went out all the time.

3 A: So, do you read much?
B: Yeah, _____ **the time**. I read at least a book a week.

4 A: Do you go to the cinema much?
B: Yeah, _____ **a lot**. I probably go once every two weeks.

5 A: How often do you play video games?
B: **Not very** _____ . I don't really have the time.

6 A: So how often do you go to the gym?
B: _____ **ever** now, to be honest. Today was the first time in ages! I used to go a lot more often.

7 A: Do you ever read books in English?
B: Yeah, _____ **I get the chance**. It's hard to find time, though. Work's so busy.

8 A: Do you ever go to see your favourite team play?
B: Yeah, but **not as much as I'd** _____ **to**. I only went four times last season.

8 Work in groups. Ask and answer questions about your habits. Use the frequency phrases in Exercise 7.

G See Grammar reference 4A. ≫≫

DEVELOPING CONVERSATIONS

Are you any good?

We usually use a short phrase to answer the question *Are you any good?* We then explain the phrase in more detail.

A: I play cards sometimes too. **Are you any good?**

B: Yeah, I'm OK. I mean, I'm not a professional or anything, but I enjoy it.

9 Choose the correct option to complete the sentences.

1 a *No, I'm useless. / I'm OK.* I can't even boil an egg!

b *Yeah, quite good. / Not really.* I do good soups and I bake quite a lot as well.

2 a *I'm OK. / No, not really.* I used to be OK when I was at school, but I lost interest.

b *No, I'm useless. / Yeah, quite good.* I usually hit the ball out of the court or into the net.

3 a *Yeah, quite good. / Not really.* Most people seem to trust me.

b *I'm OK. / No, I'm useless.* I usually end up telling everybody everything!

4 a *Yeah, quite good. / No, I'm useless.* I mean, I can hardly throw or catch a ball.

b *Not bad. / Not really.* I play a bit of table tennis and I'm OK at basketball.

10 Match the questions (a–d) with the answer pairs in Exercise 9 (1–4).

a Are you any good at sport?

b Are you any good at cooking?

c Are you any good at tennis?

d Are you any good at keeping secrets?

11 Write four more *Are you any good at … ?* questions. Then work in groups. Ask and answer the questions in Exercise 10 and your own questions.

CONVERSATION PRACTICE

12 Think of a free-time activity that you do quite a lot. Think about how often you do it, where you do it and if you're any good at it. Then have conversations with other students in the class. Use the guide below to help you.

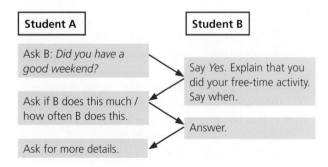

The soundtrack of our lives

IN THIS LESSON, YOU:
- talk about aspects of music and why you like / don't like them
- discuss and compare tastes in music, books, etc.
- practise understanding the main message of forum posts
- practise guessing meanings of new unknown words

SPEAKING

1 Work in pairs. Adapt the conversation below by replacing the phrases in purple with your own ideas. Have one conversation about music and another about films, TV or books.

A: Do you **listen to music** much?

B: **Not that much**. What about you?

A: **Yeah, all the time**.

B: What kind of **music** are you into?

A: All sorts really, but mainly **pop music and R&B**.

B: Oh right. Anyone in particular?

A: I don't know … **Billie Eilish, The Weeknd**, stuff like that.

B: Oh OK. **I quite like The Weeknd**. So, have you **heard** anything good recently?

A: Well, I love *Last Last* **by Burna Boy**.

B: Never heard of **him**.

A: Oh, **he's fantastic**. So if you do **listen to** anything, what kind of thing do you like?

B: **Rock**, mainly, I guess. **Wet Leg** – that kind of thing.

2 Change partners. Have a conversation to find out each other's tastes in music / TV / films / books. How similar are your tastes?

VOCABULARY Musical tastes

3 Work in pairs. Don't use a dictionary. Discuss what you think the phrases in bold mean, or decide how to translate them into your first language.

1 I don't listen to **the charts**. I'm not interested if a song is a hit or not.

2 The best songs have **a good chorus** that everyone can sing along to.

3 A good tune is less important to me than songs with interesting **lyrics** that mean something.

4 I saw my dad dance once, but he had absolutely **no sense of rhythm**. It was quite embarrassing.

5 I never listen to a whole album. I just **pick the tracks** I like and add them to a playlist.

6 **New versions** of old songs are never as good as the original.

7 I can't study or work with any music **on in the background**. I need complete quiet.

8 I often find myself **whistling a tune** that I don't know the lyrics of and don't even like that much!

9 If I see live music, I prefer to go to **a small venue** where you're close to the performer.

10 If I don't like **the first verse** of a song, I stop listening to it. I don't even wait for the chorus.

11 I like to work out to music. Something that's full of energy, with **a strong beat**.

12 I usually listen to music on my phone with my **headphones** on.

4 **P ▶** Listen to words from Exercise 3 said on their own and then in a phrase. Practise saying them. Which words / phrases do you find hard to say? Practise saying them again.

5 Work in pairs. Discuss if the statements in Exercise 3 are true for you or not. Give examples.

READING

6 You're going to read an online forum where people post music playlists. Look at the headings. What do you think the writer will talk about in each post?

a Best playlists from the streaming services

b The album is dead; long live the playlist!

c My best year so far

d In memory of a very special person

e Music to teach people a lesson

f No more heartache

g Family favourites

h Secret loves

7 Read the online forum on page 39 and match each post (1–6) with a heading in Exercise 6 (a–h). There are two headings you don't need.

8 Work in pairs. Discuss the questions about the posts.

1 Which post do you like best? Why?

2 Which person do have most in common with? Why?

3 Is there anything you found strange / surprising / funny / silly / true about the posts?

SPEAKING

9 Choose two playlist titles. For each one, make a list of three songs you want to include.

- My current favourites
- Family memories
- Childhood dreams / nightmares
- Music to fall asleep / wake up to
- Music for a romantic evening
- Karaoke classics

10 Work in groups and compare your playlists. Say as much as you can about the songs you have chosen. Ask questions to find out why people have chosen their songs.

11 **M** Work in pairs. Create a playlist of six songs that represents aspects of your English class and the people in it. Take turns to present and explain your lists.

1

While complete albums are still produced and sold with a title and 'cover', few people buy the CD or record. Most don't even sit and listen to the whole thing from start to finish, unless it's left on in the background by accident. It's the playlist which is king now. Streaming services provide playlists by genre (Hot Latin or Rap Français), mood (Relax or Sad Songs) or a combination of the two (Feel-good Indie Rock), but the best aspect of the playlist is that we can pick our own tunes and make it personal. Tell us about your playlists and share the links here!

2

Music is sometimes about being in 'a gang' with people who agree what music is cool and what's not. It can be embarrassing to admit you like certain things, but here is a list of my guilty pleasures. My friends don't see Maluma as pure enough reggaeton now he's been so successful in the charts, but I really like *Corazón*. *I'm A Believer* was in Shrek, which I probably watched a hundred times with my sister when I was growing up. It was probably the first English I learned! Then, my parents are big fans of Romeo Santos and they played *Héroe Favorito* a lot. Sometimes when you hear a song enough, you can't help liking it. **Marcos, Colombia**

Corazón – **Maluma ft. Nego do Borel**

I'm A Believer – **Smash Mouth**

Héroe Favorito – **Romeo Santos**

Tú Sin Mí – **Dread Mar I**

Aserejé – **Las Ketchup**

3

After I graduated in 2017, I had a fantastic trip to the UK, thanks to my gran, who encouraged me to go and partly paid for it. She was always very young at heart and loved rock music, especially The Beatles and The Clash, so these songs really remind me of her. *Kojo no Tsuki* is a traditional song, but she used to play this rock version and it always brings a tear to my eye when I hear it. **Emi, Japan**

London Calling – **The Clash**

Let It Be – **The Beatles**

Cum on Feel the Noize – **Slade**

Kojo No Tsuki – **Scorpions**

Kimi No Mado Kara – **The Dylan II**

4

Last year I broke up with my boyfriend. I'd shut myself in my room for a week when a friend shared a playlist with me. It had sad and angry songs and more positive music to cheer me up. It matched all the mixed emotions I was experiencing. Obviously, the list includes Adele – I think that woman has been very unlucky in love – but my favourite is Taylor Swift. *Shake it Off* has a great chorus, which basically says forget all about anyone who doesn't love you or tells lies. Just move on. **Jo, Australia**

Shake it Off – **Taylor Swift**

Someone Like You – **Adele**

All I Could Do Was Cry – **Etta James**

Fighter – **Christina Aguilera**

Shout Out to My Ex – **Little Mix**

5

I find it so annoying when people play music on public transport without headphones. I think it should be banned. And then, if anyone broke the law, the punishment would be to listen to this playlist on repeat for 24 hours. I know some will be shocked that I've included *Imagine*. Yes, the lyrics are all very positive, but the music? It has a really boring rhythm and sounds miserable. *Baby Shark* is obviously the worst though, and has the added punishment that you can't ever get it out of your head after hearing it. **Tyrone, UK**

Baby Shark – **Pinkfong**

Macarena – **Los del Río**

Imagine – **John Lennon**

My Heart Will Go On – **Céline Dion**

I Like to Move It – **Alvin and the Chipmunks**

6

Back in 2018, I spent a term in Amsterdam. There were loads of other international students there and we became quite close. We all worked hard and partied hard too. *Blinding Lights* was our absolute favourite song. From the first beats everyone used to jump up and dance – and we used to really shout out the chorus together. Now, if it comes on the radio, it immediately takes me back to that time. **Greta, Germany**

Blinding Lights – **The Weeknd**

Zoutelande – **BLØF**

One Kiss – **Calvin Harris and Dua Lipa**

Blah Blah Blah – **Armin van Buuren**

For You – **Liam Payne and Rita Ora**

Hidden talent

IN THIS LESSON, YOU:
- do a survey into people's use of local facilities and how to improve them
- practise taking notes on a conversation about a hidden talent
- discuss competitions and events
- talk about you how long you did / have done activities

LISTENING

1 **Look at the photo and discuss the questions.**

1 What do you know about different martial arts? Do you know anyone who does a martial art? Are they any good?

2 What abilities / qualities do you need to do martial arts? (strength, balance, patience, etc.)

3 What other ways could you develop these skills?

2 **FS** ▶ **Content words are often stressed and easy to hear. However, to understand a message, we also need to hear the unstressed words before them, which might be said more quickly.**

Listen to eight unstressed phrases and write down what the next word(s) could be.

3 ▶ **Listen to Ian talking to his Japanese colleague, Rika. Make notes on Rika's hidden talent. Then compare your notes with a partner.**

4 ▶ **Listen again. Add one more piece of information to your notes. Then compare answers in groups.**

5 **Work in groups. Discuss the questions.**

1 Do you understand why Rika doesn't talk about her talent at work?

2 Do you know anyone who has an unusual hobby or 'hidden' talent? What is it?

3 Is learning a martial art the best way to deal with bullying? Why? / Why not? What else could be done?

4 Do you know anyone who's been out of action because of an injury? What happened? How are they recovering?

VOCABULARY Competition

6 **Complete the sentences with the word pairs in the box.**

advantage / home	cheat / excuse
confidence / a win	performance / quarter-finals
round / tournament	season / champions
took part / proud	

1 She lost **in the first** _____ , but her game was against the best player **in the** _____ .

2 They did badly **last** _____ , but this year they could become the _____ . They haven't lost any games.

3 The other team **had an** _____ because they were **playing at** _____ in front of their own crowd, so it wasn't surprising they won.

4 My sister _____ **in a national chess tournament** and she came ninth. We were so _____ **of her**.

5 I lost because I'm too honest and didn't _____ like some other people. **That's my** _____ , anyway.

6 I was quite pleased with **my** _____ , because I **got to the** _____ of the competition.

7 He was beaten really badly and he **lost** _____ after that. He just **needs** _____ to get it back.

7 **Work in groups. Discuss the questions.**

1 Do you know anyone who has ever taken part in a competition or tournament? Explain who, what and how they did.

2 Do you follow any teams or sportspeople? How well are they doing in their sport at the moment?

3 What competitive sports and activities do / did you do at school? How do / did you normally do?

4 Do you know anyone who cheats at games? How? Have you heard of any examples of cheating in professional sport? What happened?

GRAMMAR

Present perfect continuous and past simple for duration

We can use both the present perfect continuous and the past simple to ask *How long … (for)?* and talk about the duration of an activity or situation.

I: So **how long have you been doing** judo, then? (present perfect continuous)

R: **Ever since** I was a kid.

R: I had a back injury that stopped me from training.

I: Really? **How long did you stop** for?

R: Well, **I didn't do anything for** a couple of months. (past simple)

8 **Work in pairs. Look at the examples in the Grammar box. Answer the questions.**

1 Does Rika still do judo?

2 Is Rika still injured?

3 What's the difference between *for* and *since*?

4 Why can't we say *How long have I been knowing you now?*

9 **Respond to the comments by writing a *How long … ?* question. Use the verb in brackets.**

1 He gets quite nervous when he's on the motorway. (drive)

2 I can't meet you tonight – I have my kickboxing class. (do)

3 I used to be quite good at basketball before I gave up. (play)

4 He only started playing again after the injury two months ago. (be injured)

5 I should have warmed up more. I think I've pulled a muscle! (warm up)

6 My parents are having a party for their wedding anniversary on Saturday. (be married)

7 Her Arabic is pretty good already. (learn)

8 At last! You're here. I was beginning to worry. (wait)

10 **Work in pairs. Have conversations starting with the comments and questions from Exercise 9. Continue each conversation for as long as you can.**

A: He gets quite nervous when he's on the motorway.

B: How long has he been driving?

A: Only a year or so.

B: Right. Well, it can take a while to feel confident.

11 **Work in groups to answer the questions below. Find out two more details, such as how long, when, where, how often, why or how.**

1 Who is the sportiest person?

2 Who has run the longest distance?

3 Who has given up a hobby or sport recently?

4 Who plays a musical instrument well?

5 Who has got to this level of English the quickest?

6 Who has been on the longest journey?

7 Who has experienced the longest wait for a plane or train?

8 Who has lived in their home for the shortest time?

9 Who has seen the longest film?

10 Who had the shortest journey to get here?

G   See Grammar reference 4C.

SPEAKING TASK

12 **M** **Work in pairs. You're going to give suggestions for how to improve local facilities around where you're studying now. Follow the instructions:**

1 Write six to ten questions to find out what facilities people know about, if they use them, and what they think of them.

2 Conduct your survey by asking other people in the class your questions.

3 Collect your results and decide what the most important findings are.

4 Decide two or three things you would do to improve the situation.

5 Report and explain your suggestions to the rest of the class.

▨ MY OUTCOMES ▨

Work in pairs. Discuss the questions.

1 What conversations or discussions did you enjoy?

2 How confidently can you talk about your interests now? How could you improve further?

3 What pronunciation problems did you have with the language in this unit?

4 What speaking or writing activities would you like to try again, and why?

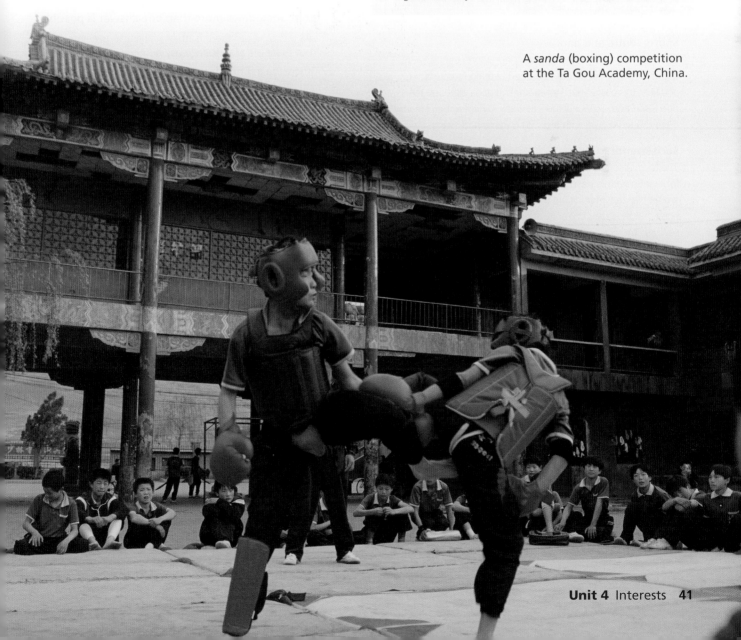

A *sanda* (boxing) competition at the Ta Gou Academy, China.

Unit 4 Interests   **41**

Writing a report

IN THIS LESSON, YOU:
- practise writing a report about a local issue
- discuss facilities for young people and the community
- notice features of a report and use of formal language
- highlight one aspect of a situation to comment on

SPEAKING

1 Work in pairs. Discuss the questions.

1 Look at the photos. What age groups do you think the activities / places are good for?

2 What other activities / places are good for the following age groups?

3–6	7–11	12–15	16–18

3 What facilities are there for young people where you live? Do you think there are enough? Why? / Why not?

Availability of activities for young people

Introduction

The town has a population of approximately 9,000, including approximately 2,000 young people under the age of 20. At present, there are a limited number of things for young people to do in the town. As a result, the main free-time activity is simply hanging out in the street.

Sports centre and park

Currently, the town has a small outdoor sports centre, with a football pitch, basketball court and two tennis courts. In addition, there is an outdoor swimming pool, although this is only open from July until the first week in September. Nearby, there is a small park with a climbing frame and swings.

Social centre

The town also has a social centre that runs dance classes for teenagers two days a week. For younger children, there are art classes. In addition, there are yoga classes open to all ages, but these are currently attended by mainly adults and seniors. The centre has a small cinema screen and auditorium. However, this is rarely used.

Recommendations

As far as classes are concerned, the council could provide a wider range for all age groups. For example, they could offer drama classes or run music groups. More could be done with the cinema, such as showing films on Friday evenings or Saturday mornings.

In terms of sports facilities, the council could organize more team sports and provide coaches for training sessions. Finally, the council should consider building a cover over or heating the swimming pool so it could be used in the winter.

WRITING

2 Read the report on facilities for young people in a town. Then work in pairs and discuss the questions.

1 Do you think the area is better or worse for young people than where you live? Why?

2 Can you think of any other services or facilities that could be provided for the young people in the town?

3 Which five of the features (1–7) are typical of reports? Find examples of each in the report.

1 Clear sections with headings

2 An explanation of why the report is being written

3 Contractions (e.g. *it's, they're, they've*)

4 A summary of facts about the current situation

5 A conclusion and suggestions for change at the end

6 Writing from a personal point of view (e.g. *I, you, we*)

7 More formal language (e.g. *would like* not *want*)

4 Complete the sentences with a word from the report. Sometimes more than one answer is possible.

1 **At** _____ , there is no availability in evening classes, but there is a plan to increase numbers in the future.

2 There are **a limited** _____ **of** sports facilities at the university.

3 The canteen **is** _____ **closed** for repairs and will not re-open for a number of weeks.

4 There is one metro line that crosses the town from east to west. **In** _____ , there are a large number of buses that go into the centre.

5 It appears that the station ticket offices **are** _____ **used** and could be closed without affecting services.

6 **As far as** train services **are** _____ , a number of improvements could be made.

7 **More could be** _____ with the existing facilities, for example by opening them in the evenings.

8 The council **could** _____ more support for talented sports people to compete.

9 The council **should** _____ **providing** electric bicycles for the public to use.

5 Work in pairs. Can you think of simpler / less formal ways to say the phrases in purple in Exercise 4?

USEFUL LANGUAGE

As far as / In terms of

We often highlight particular things in a report using *as far as … is / are concerned* or *in terms of … .*

As far as classes **are concerned**, the council could provide a wider range for all age groups.

In terms of the sports facilities, the council could provide more organized teams.

6 Match the first parts of the sentences (1–6) with the second parts (a–f).

1 As far as public transport in the area is concerned,

2 In terms of the canteen,

3 As far as the hotel facilities are concerned,

4 In terms of security,

5 As far as French classes are concerned,

6 In terms of the park,

a the number of students should be reduced.

b the owners should consider building a swimming pool.

c more could be done to stop robberies.

d most people are satisfied with the quality of food.

e there's a good range of play equipment for younger kids.

f many people complain that the trains do not run late enough.

7 Think of the area where you live. Complete the sentences with your own ideas, explaining how people feel or how things could be different.

1 As far as public transport is concerned, …

2 As far as schools are concerned, …

3 In terms of sports facilities, …

4 In terms of activities for young people, …

8 Work in pairs. Discuss your sentences from Exercise 7. Do you agree with your partner's ideas?

PRACTICE

9 You're going to write a short report about a local issue and make recommendations. Work in pairs. Do the following.

1 Choose one of the following topics for your report.

- Facilities for young people in the place where you live
- Public transport where you live
- Work / Study conditions at your workplace / school / university
- Sports facilities where you live

2 Discuss the questions.

- Why might you write the report?
- What is the current situation? What aspects are good / bad?
- What could be done to improve things?
- What should the council / school / company consider doing?
- How are you going to organize the report? What headings will you use?

10 Write your report about the topic you discussed in Exercise 9. Write 150–200 words.

11 Work with a new partner. Read your partner's report. Discuss:

1 Do you agree with their recommendations? Why? / Why not?

2 What mark would you give the report out of five? Think about the elements in Exercise 3. What improvements could the writer make?

VIDEO Out and about

1 Work in pairs. Discuss the questions.

1 Are you any good at cooking?

2 Are you any good at sports?

3 Are you any good at keeping secrets?

Understanding accents

Some accents use an /eə/ sound instead of an /ɜː/ sound, so *shirt* /ʃɜːt/ may sound more like *shared* /ʃeəd/.

2 ▣ Watch five people answer the same questions. How much can you remember about what they said? Then work in pairs. Did anyone have similar experiences to you?

3 ▣ Watch again. Match one or two sentences with each speaker. There are two extra sentences.

a They make a variety of dishes, especially with spices.

b They don't like sweets and cakes.

c They work out on a bike to keep fit.

d They're quite good at tennis.

e They aren't as good as they used to be at sport.

f They love to chat to everyone and share other people's news.

g They don't like situations where they need to keep secrets.

h Their friends always trust them with secrets.

i They may tell a secret in some situations.

4 Tell your partner about people with these characteristics. Give examples.

1 They love to gossip.

2 They are happy to experiment and try different things.

3 They can always / never be trusted.

VIDEO Developing conversations

5 ▣ You're going to watch two people talking about visiting Rome. Watch and take notes.

6 ▣ Work in pairs. Compare what you understood. Watch again if you need to.

7 FS ▣ Watch again. Complete the sentences with three to five words in each gap.

1 OK, _____ recommendations for me?

2 Very historic. _____ as well it's beautiful.

3 What time _____ go there?

4 In that case, _____ go in the morning.

5 There's a lot to see. In the main square _____ Trevi fountain.

6 Generally _____ there is so much history there.

7 That sounds too expensive for me. _____ to travel there?

8 In that case you could try the train. _____ recall it wasn't too long.

CONVERSATION PRACTICE

8 Work in pairs. You're going to practise a conversation.

1 Choose a Conversation practice from either Lesson 3A or Lesson 4A.

2 Look at the language in that lesson.

3 Check the meaning of anything you've forgotten with your partner.

4 Have the conversation. Try to improve on the last time you did it.

Grammar and Vocabulary

GRAMMAR

1 Complete the text with one word in each gap.

I'm really into surfing and I've been doing it [1]_____ about seven years now. I don't go as much [2]_____ I'd like to, because I don't actually live that close to the sea, but [3]_____ two or three weeks I drive to a beach for the weekend. I've also [4]_____ to several places abroad to spend a couple of weeks surfing every day. In March, I'm [5]_____ to Taghazout in Morocco. I've never been there, but it's supposed to be one of the best places in the world for surfing, with some big waves, so I'm really [6]_____ forward to testing myself. A friend of mine is thinking [7]_____ coming with me. We've known each other [8]_____ we were kids, but he only started surfing a few months [9]_____ , so he feels he's not quite ready. I've told him he could go sightseeing, or just lie on the beach and relax as it's warm and sunny [10]_____ every day at that time of year.

2 Read the first sentence in each pair. Complete the second sentence so that it has a similar meaning. Use between two to five words, including the word in bold.

1 Before I started work, I read a lot more.
  I don't read as _____ .   **USED**

2 I go to the gym as much as I can.
  I go to the gym _____ .   **CHANCE**

3 I joined the club ten years ago now.
  I _____ of the club for ten years now.   **MEMBER**

4 We might go to see a show while we're there.
  We're _____ to see a show while we're there.   **OF**

5 I've never been there, but it's supposed to be great.
  I haven't been there, but I _____ great.   **HAVE**

6 When did you start working here?
  How _____ here now?   **WORKING**

3 Choose the correct option to complete the sentences.

1 A: Have you ever been to Europe?
  B: Yeah, I *spent / have spent* some time in Spain a few years ago.

2 A: What's the forecast for tomorrow?
  B: They said it's *going to rain / raining* all day.

3 A: *Do you have / Are you having* any plans for the weekend?
  B: Yeah. *We're going to / We will* visit some friends who live in Milan.

4 A: *Do you go / Are you going* to the cinema much?
  B: Hardly *never / ever*. I usually watch films online.

5 A: I *played / was playing* basketball a lot, but I gave up after I injured my knee.
  B: How long *have you played / did you play* for?

6 A: *Do you ever eat out? / Have you ever eaten out?*
  B: Quite often – maybe once *a / every* couple of months.

4 ▶ Listen and write the six sentences you hear.

5 Write a sentence before and after the sentences from Exercise 4 to create short dialogues.

VOCABULARY

6 Match the two parts of the collocations.

1	have	a	a play / a tournament
2	get to	b	an early night / an excuse
3	go for	c	me sailing / us out
4	pick	d	a tune / to yourself
5	pour	e	an ancient site / the old palace
6	restore	f	the quarter-final / the end
7	take	g	some tracks / the teams
8	take part in	h	with rain / down
9	whistle	i	a bike ride / a jog

7 Decide if these words are connected to places of interest, music or sport.

beat	cemetery	champions	charts
cheat	gallery	headphones	rhythm
round	ruins	season	stall
tower	verse	workout	

8 Complete the sentences with the correct form of the words in bold.

1 National Day celebrates our country's _____.
  independent

2 There are a number of _____ sites to visit in the city.   **history**

3 It is believed that the stone circle had a _____ purpose.   **religion**

4 The room was OK, but the hotel was in very nice _____ .   **surround**

5 It was a bit embarrassing because I'm _____ at dancing.   **use**

6 We were invited to watch a _____ before the musical opened.   **rehearse**

7 I lost the match, but I was pleased with my _____ .   **perform**

8 Since I had my injury I've lost quite a lot of _____ .   **confident**

9 Complete the text with one word in each gap. The first letters are given.

Bastille Day, on 14th July, is a [1]p_____ holiday in France. The holiday is on the date that the people of Paris first won a [2]b_____ against the king's army during the revolution, and it celebrates France's [3]f_____ . On the day, there are some serious [4]o_____ ceremonies to give thanks to the current army and to remember people's [5]an_____ who fought to [6]d_____ the country. But families also get [7]t_____ for the day – they go to street parties with music and dancing and watch firework [8]d_____ .

5

Working life

IN THIS UNIT, YOU:

- talk about jobs and what they involve
- make and discuss work-related predictions
- discuss rules and freedoms at work

SPEAKING

1   **Work in pairs. Look at the photo. Discuss how the seaweed might be used or what products might it be used in.**

2   **Work in groups. Which of these jobs are needed to bring the seaweed products you thought of to market? Which other jobs might be involved?**

accountant	builder	designer
engineer	marketing manager	model
lawyer	security guard	truck driver

3   **Work in groups. Discuss the questions.**

1   Are the jobs in Exercise 2 good or bad jobs to have in your country at the moment? Why?

2   Do any of your friends or family do any of these jobs?

3   Who do they work for? Do they enjoy it?

A seaweed grower collects her crop on the coast of Zanzibar, Tanzania.

5A

You must enjoy it

IN THIS LESSON, YOU:
- talk about jobs and what they involve
- practise listening to conversations about what people do
- practise asking for more details about people's jobs
- comment on other people's experiences and feelings

VOCABULARY Describing jobs

1 **Work in pairs. Check you understand the words in bold. Then think of at least one job that each item could describe.**

1 It's very **varied**. You get to do lots of different things.

2 It's very well-paid. He gets £90,000 as well as a **bonus** at the end of the year.

3 You have to do a lot of **paperwork**, which isn't much fun.

4 It's quite **insecure**. You could lose your job at any time.

5 It's easy. You don't have much **responsibility**. You do the job, go home and forget about it.

6 It's a bit **dull.** I basically just sit at a desk all day.

7 It's a very stressful job. You're always **under pressure**.

8 It's very physically **demanding**. You have to be strong and fit to do that kind of work.

9 It's a very competitive **field**. There are hundreds of **applicants** for every job.

10 I'm **head** of the department. I **manage** a small team of six people.

2 **P ▶ Listen to the words from Exercise 1 and practise saying them on their own and in a phrase. Which words / phrases do you find hard to say? Practise saying them again.**

3 **Work in pairs. Answer the questions.**

1 Why might someone get a bonus?

2 What kinds of things might paperwork involve?

3 What important responsibilities might a job have?

4 What might make a job a bit dull?

5 Why might you feel under pressure at work?

6 What else can you manage at work apart from a team?

LISTENING

4 **▶ Listen to three conversations about what people do. Answer these questions for each conversation.**

1 What does the second speaker do?

2 What's good / bad about their job?

5 **▶ Listen again. Decide in which conversation (1–3) someone:**

1 isn't worried about losing their job.

2 says their job can get a bit boring sometimes.

3 sounds happy about their salary.

4 talks about their family.

5 comments on how they work in stressful situations.

6 mentions the people they manage.

6 **Work in pairs. Discuss the questions.**

1 Which of the three jobs do you think is best? Why?

2 Are you good at dealing with stress? Do you work well under pressure?

3 What are the most secure jobs in your country at the moment?

4 Do you like the idea of travelling for work? How much travel would be too much?

DEVELOPING CONVERSATIONS

Doing what?

When people reply to the question *What do you do?* by talking about their place of work, we often try to find out exactly what work they do by asking *Doing what?* The other person will usually reply with a more specific description of what their job involves.

I: *So what do you do, Amanda?*

A: *I work for a mobile phone company.*

I: *Oh yeah. **Doing what?***

A: *I work in the design department. I'm involved in designing what you see on the screen.*

7 **Match the jobs (1–5) with the specific job descriptions (a–e).**

1 I work for a big fashion company.

2 I'm in the accounts department of a big law firm.

3 I work for the police department.

4 I work in the education department of a big college in town.

5 I work in a fast-food place.

a **I'm involved in** community work and events, and also **do some work with** prisoners.

b **I mostly** find models for our shows, **but I also do a bit of** design **work**.

c **I take** all the orders and get them ready for delivery.

d **I'm responsible for** helping new teachers feel at home.

e **I deal with** all the pay and finances.

8 **Have five conversations starting with *What do you do?* Follow the pattern in the Developing conversations box and use some of the phrases in bold in Exercise 7.**

GRAMMAR

Must / can't comments and replies

We often use *must* and *can't* + verb to comment on other people's experiences and feelings. When people respond to these comments, they often use the present simple.

A: *I was 25 when I joined, so eight years. Time goes so fast!*

I: *You **must enjoy** it.*

A: ***Yeah, I do, generally.** It's quite varied.*

A: *Sometimes I do 50 hours a week.*

I: *Really? That **can't be** easy.*

A: ***It's actually OK.** I mean, it is a bit stressful sometimes, but I work better under pressure.*

9 **Look at examples in the Grammar box. Are these statements true (T) or false (F)?**

1 We use *must* + verb when we think something is the case.

2 We use *can't* + verb when we think something is not the case.

3 When responding to comments, we usually repeat the verbs and adjectives used in the comments.

10 **Write comments for these sentences (1–8) using *must* and *can't*.**

1 I'm the marketing manager for the whole of Latin America.

Wow! That must be really demanding.

2 I travel a lot round Europe and the Middle East.

3 I care for people who are very ill.

4 She's a tax lawyer for a top accountancy firm.

5 I really see my students develop and improve.

6 Basically, I just sit in front of a screen all day.

7 It's very insecure. I never know if I'm going to have work from one month to the next.

8 They said they're going to give us all a bonus.

11 **Work in pairs. Practise having three-part conversations starting with the sentences in Exercise 10.**

A: *I'm the marketing manager for the whole of Latin America.*

B: *Wow! That must be interesting.*

A: *It is. I really love it.*

G See Grammar reference 5A.

CONVERSATION PRACTICE

12 **Either think about the job you do at the moment or choose a job you'd like to do. Make a list of what's good / bad about the job.**

13 **M** **Work in small groups. Find out about the jobs your partners have chosen by having similar conversations to the ones you heard in Exercise 4. Comment on what others say using *must* or *can't* at least once.**

The future starts now

IN THIS LESSON, YOU:
- make and discuss work-related predictions
- read about jobs that weren't common 20 years ago
- summarize short paragraphs using key vocabulary
- practise using phrases with *be* and *get*

READING

1 Work in groups. Read the introduction to the magazine article on page 51. Then discuss these questions.

1 How do you feel about the Luddites? Why?

2 What kind of jobs do you think are most likely to be replaced by automation and AI?

3 Can you think of jobs that have more or less disappeared in recent years? Why do you think this has happened?

4 Think of two jobs that no-one had heard of 20 years ago. Do you think they're good jobs? Why?

2 You're going to read about these four jobs. Work in pairs. What do you think each job involves?

a Content moderator   c Data scientist

b Sustainability manager   d Online dating ghostwriter

3 Match the groups of words (1–4) to the jobs in Exercise 2 (a–d). Check your ideas with a partner and explain what the connection to each job might be.

1 a bow and arrow / clients / a match

2 the dark side / marked as inappropriate / quit their jobs

3 the climate emergency / green policies / new recycling systems

4 collecting and analysing / working with numbers / decision-making processes

4 **M** Read about the four jobs on page 51 and check your ideas. In pairs, summarize the connections.

5 Work in pairs. Discuss which of the four jobs you think each sentence describes. Explain why.

1 They must be very good at seeing patterns, those people.

2 I'm guessing you just need to know the rules very well and then follow them.

3 You'd need to get to know your clients very well to do that kind of thing.

4 It can't be easy, trying to get everyone in the company to change their habits.

5 It must be nice knowing you've helped to bring people together.

6 It must be frustrating if governments aren't acting as quickly as your company is.

7 I'm guessing the most important part of the job is knowing what to do with all that information.

8 It can't be good for you, all that. It must really affect your mental health.

6 Discuss the questions with your partner.

1 Which of the four jobs do you think is the best / worst?

2 Which do you think is the most varied?

3 Which has the most responsibility?

4 Do you think your job now – or the job you want to do – is safe from automation and AI?

VOCABULARY Phrases with *be* and *get*

V See Vocabulary reference 5B.

7 Work in pairs. Discuss the difference in meaning between the phrases in bold.

1 How did you **get interested** in computer science?

2 He**'s** really **interested in** fashion and design.

8 Choose the correct option to complete the sentences.

1 How *did you get / are you* into that field of work?

2 I think I need to start looking for something else. *I'm just / I just get* sick of my job.

3 I'm still *getting / being* used to everything, but *it's / it gets* easier than it was, anyway.

4 It's not easy for anyone at the moment – and it's *being / getting* tougher all the time.

5 *I'm still / I still get* in touch with some people who work there, so I can ask them if you like.

6 The boss wants to talk to me. I think *I'm / I get* in trouble.

7 She *got / was* in trouble at work because of something she posted on social media.

8 It took me a while to *get / be* used to working from home, but now I really love it.

9 If things don't *be / get* better at work, maybe you should *be / get* in touch with a lawyer.

10 *Getting / Being* good at any job takes time.

11 Working nights was hard to begin with, but *I'm totally / I got totally* used to it now.

12 *He's / He gets* really into his job, which is great, but it also means we don't see each other much.

9 Work in pairs. Compare your answers and explain your decisions.

10 Choose two topics to talk about. Plan what you want to say. Work in small groups and share your ideas.

1 something that was hard to begin with, but that you're totally used to now

2 a time you got in trouble

3 someone from your past who you'd like to get in touch with again

4 something that you're really sick of

5 something that you're really into

6 how you got into something you now love doing / are really interested in

SPEAKING

11 Work in pairs. Make three work-related predictions for the next 10 years and three for the next 50–100 years.

English is going to be more important than ever.

12 Work with another pair. Compare your lists. Discuss how likely each prediction is and explain why.

THE FUTURE OF WORK

Your dream job may not even exist yet

In the early 19th century, a group of English textile workers formed a secret organization and started planning attacks on the new machines that were appearing in factories up and down the country. The group became known as the Luddites. Their attacks were driven by a fear that they would be replaced by machines that produced cloth faster and more cheaply than they could.

Of course, their actions didn't stop the development of technology, and today we still hear many of the same fears – and with good reason, as more and more jobs are replaced by automation and AI (Artificial Intelligence). In fact, Oxford Economics recently predicted that up to 20 million manufacturing jobs around the world could soon be lost to robots.

However, as some jobs slowly disappear, new ones are created. Many children starting school today will end up doing jobs that don't even exist yet. These jobs are often – but not always – driven by technology. Here we look at four jobs that no-one had heard of twenty years ago.

Content moderator

The Internet influences all areas of our lives and helps us do many wonderful things. However, like any other great invention, it has its dark side and that's where content moderators come in. Hired to go through things that are uploaded by users onto sites like Facebook or YouTube, they check whether content breaks the rules of the site and often remove items people have marked as inappropriate. Perhaps unsurprisingly, many people in this field get depressed by some of the darker content and some quit their jobs after a while as they simply can't get used to seeing so many awful things day after day.

Sustainability manager

Sustainability means using methods that cause little or no damage to the environment. As the climate emergency becomes an ever bigger issue, more and more companies are turning to sustainability managers to think of green policies and to then put them into practice. This can involve anything from working out how to waste less energy to introducing new recycling systems. All companies can benefit from lower gas and electricity bills, and it's sometimes possible to get money from the government to help develop a more sustainable approach as well.

Data scientist

Every time we use our phones or computers, we produce digital data – and the amount we produce is increasing year on year. Data science is about collecting and analysing this data and making decisions based on the findings. If you're used to working with numbers, you love technology and you have good communication skills, it's a great area to get into because many leading companies and organizations now use data scientists in their decision-making processes.

Online dating ghostwriter

In ancient Rome, Cupid was the god of love. He was usually shown as a child with wings and he went around shooting people with a bow and arrow. If you got hit by one of his arrows, you suddenly found you were interested in someone you'd maybe not noticed before. Well, online dating ghostwriters are the Cupids of the modern world. They help people create interesting profiles for dating apps – and they sometimes even help with online conversations when clients find a match.

Play by the rules

IN THIS LESSON, YOU:
- discuss rules and freedoms at work
- consider what might be good / bad about different rules
- practise listening to three conversations about rules at work
- talk about work rules and laws

LISTENING

1 Work in pairs. Look at the cartoons. Which do you like most / least? Why?

2 M Read the workplace rules (a–j). Then work in groups and discuss the questions.

a Employees have to wear dark colours to work.

b We have to take our breaks at set times.

c We have to agree time off with our boss. We can't just take holidays when we want.

d We have to work 9 to 5. We can't work overtime, even if we wanted to.

e We have to wear a hard hat at all times.

f We can't access social media on company computers.

g We can't turn our cameras off during online meetings.

h We can't talk to each other while we're working.

i We have to wash our hands at least twice an hour.

j We can work from home one day a week.

- Why do you think companies have these rules?
- Do you think they're sensible? Are they fair?

3 ▶ Listen to three conversations about rules at work. Match each conversation (1–3) with a rule in Exercise 2 (a–j).

4 FS ▶ In fast speech, the word *have* is often unstressed and links to words that come before and after it. Listen to eight phrases and write what you hear.

5 ▶ Listen to the conversations again. Complete the sentences with no more than two words.

1 Davina's company say that if everyone can see each other, there'll be a ¹_____ in online meetings.

Being able to see facial expressions might help reduce ²_____ .

Davina is glad she can work ³_____ .

2 Ulrika doesn't usually wear ⁴_____ .

The law firm has a strict ⁵_____ . For example, tattoos are completely ⁶_____ .

A colleague of hers was ⁷_____ because of the shoes she was wearing.

3 Adam wants to watch his son perform in a ⁸_____ .

One of Adam's colleagues is ⁹_____ this week.

The company has to complete an important ¹⁰_____ by Saturday.

4 The rules say you should book time off a month ¹¹_____ .

6 Work in pairs. Who do you agree with more in each conversation – the company or the workers? Why?

'It's OK to take your work home with you. It's not OK to bring your home to work with you.'

'Obviously, we need to readjust to in-office meetings.'

Office rules
NO:
- Yawning
- Eye Blinking
- Day Dreaming
- Texting
- Doodling
- Smiling

'I'm not a rule breaker, but the no eye blinking is going to be a tough one.'

VOCABULARY Work rules and laws

7 Complete the sentences with these words.

adequate	banned	court	entitled
guarantees	guilty	obey	obliged
overtime	prohibit	requirement	won

1 The company _____ **the use of** social media during work hours, which was quite an unpopular decision.

2 It's **a legal** _____ to pay the minimum wage. Companies that don't _____ **the rules** are punished.

3 Companies aren't **legally** _____ **to** pay their employees extra for **working** _____ .

4 In Belgium, you**'re** _____ **to** take up to a year off. You don't even have to take it in one go.

5 The workers **took the company to** _____ because they had been exposed to dangerous chemicals – and they _____ **their case**.

6 There's no specific law in the US that _____ **employees** will get a toilet break. Luckily, though, most companies don't _____ **people from** using the bathroom.

7 They were **found** _____ **of** breaking health and safety laws after failing to **provide** _____ **training** for staff.

8 Work in pairs. Discuss the questions.

1 What employment laws do you know? Think about: safety at work, equal rights, number of hours worked in a week, the workplace environment, sick pay, etc.

2 Do you think these laws are good? Why? / Why not?

3 Do you know any other things that companies are legally obliged to do / provide?

4 Do you know how much time off new parents are entitled to?

5 Have you heard of any companies being taken to court? Who by? Why? Who won the case?

6 What kind of things might companies be found guilty of? Have you heard of any examples?

GRAMMAR

Talking about rules

When we talk about rules we generally use *have to*, *can / can't*, *be (not) allowed to*, *be (not) supposed to*. We often use these forms instead of *must / mustn't* because *must / mustn't* can sound too direct and rude.

We**'re allowed to work** from home.

You**'re not allowed to turn** your video off during online meetings.

Guys **can't have** beards.

You **have to wear** blue, black or grey.

You**'re supposed to arrange** time off with me a month in advance.

9 Look at the examples in the Grammar box. Complete the sentences (1–4) with the structures in bold.

1 We often use _____ instead of *must*.

2 We often use _____ or _____ instead of *mustn't*.

3 We often use _____ instead of *can*.

4 We often use _____ when a rule has just been broken or is often not followed.

10 Replace the words in italics with the correct form of *be allowed to*, *be supposed to* or *have to*.

1 One other rule we have is that you *mustn't use your personal mobile* on any part of the company property.

2 Is there a dress code? *Can I wear* jewellery?

3 *I shouldn't really help* you. It's basically against the rules, but I'll make an exception.

4 Our contract says we *must be* in the office a minimum of 35 hours a week. They're very strict about it.

5 *Must you work* overtime if the company asks you to?

6 Most people *can't work* from home, but they let me because my mum is ill.

7 We sometimes *must work* late or at the weekend, but we *can take* time off the following week if we do.

8 I'm sorry, but only senior staff *can use* these toilets. You *must go* to the ones downstairs.

11 Complete the sentences with your own ideas. Then work in pairs and compare your ideas.

1 I'm always surprised people are allowed to _____ .

2 I don't really understand why we we're not allowed to _____ .

3 I'm not happy about it, but I have to _____ .

4 My boss / teacher / parents told me that I can't _____ .

5 I'm not supposed to _____ at work / school / home, but I sometimes do.

6 I'm supposed to _____ at work / school / home, but I usually don't.

G See Grammar reference 5C. »»

SPEAKING TASK

12 M Work in pairs. Decide if you're going to talk about rules where you work, where you study or at home. Follow the instructions:

1 Work on your own and think of the following:
- two rules you don't like – and why
- two rules you like – and why
- two rules which are often broken and whether that's a problem
- two questions for your partner about rules where they work / study / at home

2 Compare your ideas with your partner. Then make a list of five useful rules for a workplace, a school or a home.

■ MY OUTCOMES ■

Work in pairs. Discuss the questions.

1 Which listening activity did you like best?

2 What can you do better after Unit 5?

3 What did you find most challenging in this unit?

4 Which phrases and expressions from this unit do you intend to remember and use?

6
Buying and selling

IN THIS UNIT, YOU:

- roleplay a conversation in a phone shop
- discuss how the way we shop is changing
- practise buying / selling things and trying to get a good price

SPEAKING

1 Work in pairs. Discuss the questions.

1 Look at the photo. Do you have a place like this where you live? Do you ever go there?

2 What do you think is good / bad about shopping in a place like this?

3 What kinds of things do you most / least like shopping for?

4 What was the last thing you bought?

2 Work with a new partner. Discuss the questions.

1 Do you know anyone who works – or has ever worked – in a shop? Doing what?

2 Do you know anyone who runs their own shop? What kind?

3 Do you have a favourite shop? If so, what makes it so special?

4 Which shops do you go to most often? Why?

The spectacular dome of the Galeries Lafayette, built in 1912. Paris, France.

Get a good deal

IN THIS LESSON, YOU:
- roleplay a conversation in a phone shop
- discuss tech devices
- practise listening to a conversation in a phone shop
- practise different ways of comparing things

VOCABULARY Choosing new technology

1 Complete the sentences with these words.

battery life	comparison	deal	features	make
price range	storage	stylish	switch	upgrade

1 No wonder it's slow. You're using the old version of the software. **You need to** _____ **to the latest** one.

2 You need to **go onto one of those price** _____ **sites and see** what's best for you.

3 Wow! **You've got an electric car. What** _____ **is it?**

4 It's almost full. **You either need to delete some of these videos or else buy more** _____ .

5 **The design's great – it's very** _____ , and it's easy to use and good value for money.

6 **The** _____ **on this phone is amazing**. I only need to charge it once every few days.

7 **It's a bit out of my** _____ , **I'm afraid.** Have you got anything cheaper?

8 If you're interested, **I could show you some of the new** _____ **they've added**.

9 Whichever company you're with at the moment, **I'm sure that we can offer you a better** _____ .

10 I've been with them for a while, but **the service isn't great so it might be time to** _____ .

2 🅿 ▶ **Listen to the words from Exercise 1 and practise saying them on their own and in a phrase. Which words / phrases do you find hard to say? Practise saying them again.**

3 Look at the chunks in purple in Exercise 1. Work in pairs and think of three ways each chunk could be changed.

I should upgrade to the latest version.

I really want to upgrade to the ePhone5.

I'd like to upgrade to business class.

4 Work with a new partner. Discuss the questions.

1 How often do you upgrade your technology?

2 Do you ever use price comparison sites? What for?

3 What's the most stylish piece of technology you own?

4 What are your favourite features on the tech devices you own?

5 Which phone company are with? Why? What kind of deal do you have?

6 Have you ever switched phone companies? Why?

LISTENING

5 ▶ **Listen to a conversation in a mobile phone shop. Complete the table with the correct information. Then work in pairs and compare your answers.**

	S620	N570
Monthly payments	£50	1 _____
Screen	fairly small	2 _____
Battery life (hours)	15–16 hours	3 _____
Camera (megapixels)	4 _____	48
Storage for photos	5 _____	holds at least 10,000
Speaker	fairly small	6 _____

6 What deal is suggested at the end of the conversation? Would you accept this? Why? / Why not?

GRAMMAR

Comparisons

When we want to compare two things, we use a number of different patterns with adjectives or nouns. We can also use words like *much* and *a bit* to show how big the difference is.

*The camera is **much more powerful**.*

*It's **a bit easier** to use.*

*The battery in the other phone is**n't as good as this one**.*

*It**'s about twice as big as** the speaker on the S620.*

*The screen folds out so it**'s about twice the size of** your current phone's.*

7 Work in pairs. Look at the examples in the Grammar box. Answer these questions.

1 Why does the comparative adjective in the first example use *more*, but the comparative adjective in the second doesn't?

2 Do you know any other words that show how big / small a difference is?

3 Which sentence is a negative comparison? Which structure is used?

4 How are the structures in bold in the last two examples different from each other? Why are they different?

8 ▶ The words in italics in the sentences about the two phones in Exercise 5 are factually incorrect. In pairs, try to correct them. Then listen again and check your answers.

1 With the N570 you get a *slightly* better user experience.
2 The N570 *isn't as easy* to use *as* the S620.
3 The battery in the N570 lasts a *tiny bit* longer than the other one.
4 The camera on the N570 is *almost* twice as powerful.
5 The N570 has *three times* the amount of storage.
6 The speaker on the N570 is quite a lot *smaller*.

9 Choose the best option to make the sentence below true for you. Then write four more sentences to explain your choice using the patterns in the Grammar box. Work in pairs and share your ideas.

Now that so many people have got smartphones, our quality of life is *way better / quite a lot better / slightly better / a bit worse / much worse* than it was in the past.

G See Grammar reference 6A. 〉〉〉

DEVELOPING CONVERSATIONS

Avoiding repetition

To talk about the differences between things, we often use *one / ones* to avoid repeating nouns. To join contrasting parts of a sentence together, we often use *whereas / while*.

*The camera is much better too. This one is 48 megapixels, **whereas** the **one** on the S620 is just 20.*

10 Match the first parts of the sentences (1–6) with the second parts (a–f).

1 This phone comes with unlimited data,
2 These ones only have 64 gigabytes of memory,
3 This one is only €79.99,
4 These tablets are on special offer,
5 These ones all use a touch ID system,
6 You can store up to 2,000 songs on this watch,

a whereas those ones have 128.
b whereas those ones aren't.
c whereas that one doesn't.
d while that one only holds around 500.
e while those just use a password, which isn't as secure.
f while that one is €149.99.

11 Work in groups. Compare the features of any phones or other tech devices you have. Find at least three ways in which each one is different from the others. Use *one / ones* and *whereas / while*.

CONVERSATION PRACTICE

12 Work in pairs. Roleplay a conversation in a mobile phone shop.

Student A: You're a customer. Read File 6 on page 196.

Student B: You're a salesperson. Read File 8 on page 196.

Shopping around

IN THIS LESSON, YOU:
- discuss how the way we shop is changing
- describe clothes and accessories
- read about clothes shopping habits
- do a quiz about your shopping habits

VOCABULARY Clothes and accessories

1 **Work in pairs. Tell each other as much as you can about the clothes and accessories you're wearing at the moment. Think about:**

1 why you chose them.

2 where you got them.

3 how long you've had them.

2 **With your partner, check you understand the words in bold. Then decide which is the odd one out in each group. Explain your decisions.**

1 necklace / **bracelet** / chain / **outfit** / ring

2 top / shirt / jacket / **leggings** / jumper

3 scarf / gloves / **bikini** / wool hat / thick socks

4 jeans / trousers / earrings / **tracksuit bottoms** / skirt

5 **slippers** / trainers / **sandals** / boots / **high heels**

6 **messy** / fashionable / smart / cool / nice

7 **colourful** / stripy / **tight** / bright / **plain**

3 **Work in pairs. How many words from Exercise 2 can you use to describe what you see in the photos? Which of the things would you wear / not wear? Why?**

I (don't) think that top / shirt would suit me.

That coat would go well with a jumper I have at home.

Those trainers would / wouldn't really look good on me.

READING

4 **Work in groups. Read the introduction to a quiz about clothes shopping habits. Then discuss the questions (1–4).**

Over recent years, the way we shop for clothes has changed a lot. While many of us still like to buy our clothes in-store, where we can look at, touch and try on items, more and more people are shopping online instead.

Because of these changes, traditional clothes shops have needed to rethink the way they attract customers. People are encouraged to shop locally, many businesses offer a click-and-collect option, and lots of shops now understand how important sustainability is for shoppers. For example, while demand for cheap fashionable clothing is still high, there's also a growing trend for buying second-hand or even renting clothes. This is not only better for the environment, but it also helps people save money during hard times.

So, what kind of shopper are you?

Take our quiz to find out.

1 Have you noticed any of these changes where you live?

2 Have you seen any other changes in the way people shop?

3 What advantages and disadvantages of shopping online can you think of?

4 Can you think of any other ways that traditional shops can attract customers?

5 **Read the quiz on page 59. Complete the quiz items (1–12) with the questions (a–l).**

a Do you ever buy designer brands?

b When you include trainers, boots and sandals, how many pairs of shoes do you own?

c If you go shopping and come back without having bought anything, how do you feel?

d Do you have any clothes you haven't worn much?

e What's the most important thing when you buy clothes?

f How often do you look at blogs / social media pages / magazines about fashion?

g How do you usually find new clothes that you want to buy?

h Do you prefer shopping online or shopping in-store?

i Do you ever buy second-hand clothes?

j Do you believe in retail therapy?

k Do you have any clothes you only wear at home?

l How do you choose which shops or sites to buy from?

6 **Do the quiz. Choose the answers that are most true for you. Then work in pairs. Compare answers and explain your choices.**

7 **With your partner, look at File 9 on page 197. Calculate your scores and read the descriptions. Is the description of you accurate? Why? / Why not?**

SPEAKING

8 **Work in groups. Discuss the questions.**

1 How much pressure do you think there is on people to have expensive products and designer brands? Where does the pressure come from? Do you worry about it at all? Why? / Why not?

2 Do you ever check where / how the things you buy were produced?

3 Do you buy much online? Is online shopping having an effect on shops in your country? How?

4 Can you think of any shops that have had bad publicity because of the way they make / get their products or how they run their business? What happened?

Shop till you Drop?

1 _____

a Neither. I find shopping boring and stressful and avoid it if I can.

b Going out is OK if you're with friends or you have nothing else to do.

c I like both. I shop all the time. I just love it.

2 _____

a They're cheap.

b They'll last a long time.

c They look good on me.

3 _____

a A bit annoyed, but I like to shop around for the best bargains and sometimes that takes time.

b I don't mind. Sometimes it's nice just to do some window-shopping.

c It never happens! What's the point of looking if you don't buy anything?

4 _____

a Five pairs or fewer.

b Six to 19 pairs.

c I've lost count. It must be at least 20.

5 _____

a Yes, they have holes in, but they're OK to wear around the house.

b Yes. They're not fashionable, but they're comfortable.

c No. You never know who will call by! I always look my best.

6 _____

a Not really, but I have one outfit I only wear on special occasions.

b Yes. They don't fit me at the moment, but they will one day!

c Yes. One item still has the price tag on.

7 _____

a I always shop locally and support independent shops.

b I try to buy socially responsible brands.

c I always just go for the famous international brands.

8 _____

a Never. They're far too expensive. You're just paying for the label.

b Sometimes – especially if they're in the sales.

c All the time. Designer labels are just better.

9 _____

a Not at all. Buying things doesn't make you happy.

b Shopping isn't the first thing I think of to cheer myself up, but it does work sometimes.

c Absolutely. If I'm feeling down, shopping always cheers me up.

10 _____

a Only if they fit OK and they're really cheap!

b Of course! You can find some great-value second-hand clothes.

c No. I can't stand the idea of wearing something that someone else wore before me!

11 _____

a Never. They're a complete waste of time.

b Sometimes. If a post comes up on social media or if I'm killing time somewhere, I might have a look.

c Pretty regularly, actually. I like to keep up with what's going on.

12 _____

a I just go straight to the sale section and see what's on offer.

b I search for something similar to an item I already own.

c I have a look at what's 'new in' and see if there's anything I like.

That's my final offer

IN THIS LESSON, YOU:
- practise buying / selling things and trying to get a good price
- explore ways to get lower prices
- describe souvenirs and presents
- practise listening to four people describe different souvenirs

VOCABULARY Buying and selling

1 Work in pairs. Look at the photos and discuss these questions.

1 Where do you think each of the souvenirs is from?

2 How would you put the souvenirs in order – from the best to the worst?

3 Which might make good gifts for different people you know? Why?

4 How much would you be happy to pay for each of these things? Why?

5 When you buy souvenirs, do you usually pay the asking price? If not, what do you do?

2 Complete the conversations with these pairs of words.

antique / discount	brand / profit	genuine / deal
handmade / fixed	on sale / sold out	silk / bargain

1 A: It's _____ leather, that. Here. Feel it.

B: Yeah. It is nice, but it's damaged. Look. Maybe you could do me a _____ on it?

2 A: It's _____ , that mask is. It's over two hundred years old.

B: Yeah. It's lovely. Would you give me a _____ if I pay in cash?

3 A: It's _____ , that carpet. It's not the cheap factory-made type.

B: Yeah, it's nice. Is that price there _____ or could you go down a bit?

4 A: How much are you asking for this _____ scarf?

B: 300 – and it's a _____ at a price like that.

5 A: I thought these would be cheaper. I heard they were _____ at the moment.

B: Yeah. I'm afraid all the cheaper ones have already _____ . This is all we have left.

6 A: 250 is a good price. I mean, look at the _____ . That's a quality product.

B: Listen. I'll give you a hundred. Take it or leave it.

A: A hundred? That's an insult. I wouldn't make a _____ if I let you have it that cheap.

3 Work in pairs. Discuss the questions.

1 Can you think of three other things often described as 'antique'?

2 Can you think of five famous fashion brands?

3 Why might you get / ask for a discount?

4 What else can be handmade?

5 When do things usually go on sale?

6 What's the opposite of making a profit?

4 Work with a new partner. Think of three more ways a buyer might try to get a price down and three things a seller might say to keep a price up.

LISTENING

5 ▶ Listen to four speakers talking about gifts and souvenirs. Match the speakers (1–4) with the descriptions (a–f). There are two you don't need.

This person …

a threw a gift away.

b wasn't pleased with a gift.

c was given a useful souvenir.

d   mentions a souvenir that broke.

e   collects models of famous buildings.

f   prefers food or drink as souvenirs.

6   **FS** ▶ **In fast speech, you often hear a /z/ sound when a word that ends with the letter _s_ joins a word that starts with a vowel sound. Listen and write the eight phrases you hear.**

7   **M** ▶ **Work in pairs. Discuss which speakers had these souvenirs and where each one was from. What can you remember about how they described them? Listen again and check your ideas.**

a   an apron   d   a paperweight

b   a panettone   e   a model

c   a drink   f   a tie

8   **Work in groups. Discuss the questions.**

1   What are typical souvenirs from your country?

2   Do you agree that the best souvenirs are things you can consume? Why? / Why not?

3   Is Speaker 2 ungrateful for not wanting gifts? Why? / Why not?

4   What's the most useful souvenir you've ever bought or been given?

5   Have you ever got upset about breaking something? What was it? What happened?

GRAMMAR

Noun phrases

We often add information before and after a noun to help describe it. This longer group of words is called a noun phrase. Look at how longer noun phrases can be added to.

They bought me a **silk tie**_._

They bought me a very **unusual** _silk_ **tie**_._

They bought me a very unusual **red** _silk_ **tie**_._

They bought me a very unusual **bright** _red silk_ **tie**_._

They bought me a very unusual bright red silk **tie with pictures** _on it._

They bought me a very unusual bright red silk tie with pictures **of scary masks** _on it._

9   **Work in pairs. Look at the examples in the Grammar box. Are these statements true (T) or false (F)?**

1   The compound noun _silk tie_ describes a kind of silk, not a kind of tie.

2   Both nouns in the compound noun _silk tie_ can be made plural (i.e. _silks ties_).

3   The general rule for the order of adjectives is opinion first, then facts such as size or colour.

4   We can add information after a noun using phrases that start with prepositions (e.g. _with_, _of_, _from_, _in_, etc.)

10   **Put the words in brackets into the correct order before the noun in the sentences (1–6). Add a preposition after the noun where necessary.**

1   My most precious possession is my _____ (gold / grandmother's / old) ring.

2   My favourite piece of clothing is a _____ (wool / lovely) hat _____ Bolivia that my dad bought me.

3   People there often cook in these _____ (stone / wonderful) ovens _____ big metal doors.

4   I recently bought this _____ (leather / nice / brown) coat _____ the winter.

5   We were lucky enough to find this _____ (washing / German / amazing) machine _____ sale.

6   My brother went to Tanzania and brought me back this _____ (handmade / wooden / amazing) mask _____ a woman. It's on my wall at home.

11   **Complete the sentences with noun phrases. Then work in groups and share your ideas.**

1   When I was on holiday in … I bought …

2   My most precious possession is …

3   When I was younger, I used to have a … that I loved.

4   The strangest souvenir I think I've ever seen was a …

5   My favourite piece of clothing is …

G   See Grammar reference 6C.   »

SPEAKING TASK

12   **Work in pairs. You're going to roleplay a conversation in a souvenir shop.**

1   **Student A:** You're a tourist thinking of buying one of the things in the photos in this lesson. Decide how much you want to pay and think of what you can say to get a good price. Use some of these phrases:

   How much do you want for / is that / are those … over there?

   Is that the best price you can do?

   Can't you go a bit lower?

   I'll give you … Take it or leave it.

   Student B: You're the seller. Decide how much you want for each of the things in the photos. Think about what you are going to say to make sure you get the price you want. Use some of these phrases:

   It's a bargain at that price.

   Look at the quality / brand.

   I can't go any lower than that, I'm afraid.

   If I let you have it for that price, I'll make a loss.

2   Work in pairs. Roleplay the conversation. Try to find a price you can agree on.

3   Swap roles and have another conversation.

■ MY OUTCOMES ■

Work in pairs. Discuss the questions.

1   What pairwork or groupwork activities did you find enjoyable?

2   What useful language have you learned?

3   How challenging did you find the reading and listening texts?

4   What homework do you plan to do to revise language from this unit?

WRITING 3
Writing a review

IN THIS LESSON, YOU:
- write a review of a product, place or service
- discuss what might be good / bad about different products and places
- read three different reviews
- look at different ways of recommending

SPEAKING

1 **Work in pairs. Discuss the questions.**

1 Which of these things (a–f) have you spent money on, or in? Would you recommend them?

2 What good / bad things might people write in reviews of these things?

a a pack of six plain white T-shirts

b a pet hairbrush

c special powder that makes your teeth whiter

d a small Bluetooth speaker

e a large furniture store

f a famous hotel

WRITING

2 **Read three reviews and match each one to an item (a–f) in Exercise 1.**

3 **Decide which review in Exercise 2 (1–3) is five-star, which is three-star and which is one-star. Then work with a partner and explain your choices.**

4 **Work in pairs. Look at the advice for writing a review. Find examples of these things in the three reviews.**

1 Explain benefits and features.

2 Tell a story to make the review more personal.

3 Use strong descriptive adjectives.

4 Where there are problems, suggest what the company could do to make things better for you.

5 Make it clear if you're recommending the product / service or not.

---

1 This place really has nothing to recommend it. It's hard to find the words to explain quite how terrible our experience here was. We booked a three-day break as it was my husband's birthday, but in the end, we left after just one night. It was that bad! As you enter, you see that the carpet in the reception area is dirty – and you then have to spend half an hour trying to find someone who can check you in and give you your room key.

The room itself was even worse. The bed sheets had clearly been there for some time – days perhaps, or maybe even weeks. No-one had cleaned the bathroom and the whole place smelled really bad. To make matters worse, the window didn't open at all.

I've written to the manager three times now asking for a full refund as soon as possible, but so far, I haven't heard anything back. Avoid this place unless, of course, you want to know what it's like to stay somewhere with furniture from the 1970s!

2 As I have three beautiful Persians, I was delighted to discover this – and I've been delighted with how well it works, too. Compared to other items I've used, it's very efficient and does a great job without causing any pain or problems. My three always seem very relaxed and happy as I'm using it. You could even say that they enjoy it, which is very unusual!

It's easy to clean and wash after use – you just press the button on the back and that's it. It's so simple that even my four-year-old can use it. It fits nicely into your hand, it's well-made and it looks like it will last. Oh, and top of all that, it's excellent value for money too.

Put simply, this has made a huge difference to the way I care for my beauties. I can't recommend it enough.

3 As far as the delivery is concerned, I ordered them on a Monday and they arrived on Tuesday, so I've got no complaints there. When I got them, I thought the material felt OK. It was good quality and felt nice against my skin. They all seemed to fit OK as well, though maybe they were a little bit on the large side to begin with.

They go well with a range of different things. I've worn them, on their own, under a coat and under jumpers and they've generally looked quite good.

However, the real problem came when I first washed them, as they came out much smaller than they went in. I can still wear them, but I'm not sure I'd buy this brand again. They're not the cheapest on offer, and for the price I paid, I'd expect something that lasts a little bit longer.

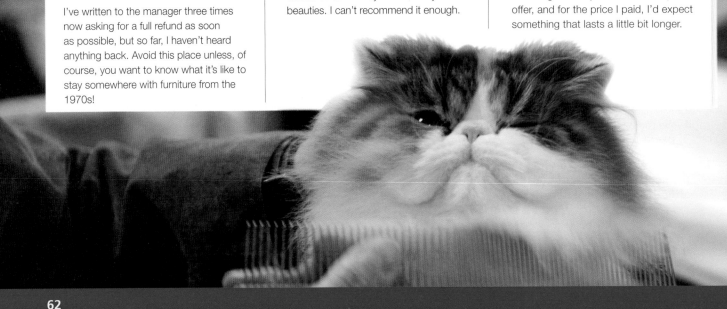

USEFUL LANGUAGE

Recommending

When writing reviews, we often recommend certain products and services – or recommend that people avoid them and save their money. The word *recommend* is used with lots of different patterns and expressions.

*I can't **recommend** it enough.*

*Highly **recommended**.*

*This place has nothing to **recommend** it.*

*I'm not sure I'd **recommend** them.*

5 **Complete the sentences by putting the words in brackets in the correct order.**

1 If you decide to visit, _____ (recommend / can / I) the seafood. It's delicious.

2 The food wasn't great and the service was terrible. _____ . (it / recommend / wouldn't / I)

3 It's a great product, but I _____ (shop around / you / recommend / that) to find the best price.

4 They get very busy in the evenings, so _____ . (advance / recommend / I / booking / in)

5 I expected better from this because _____ . (recommended / came / highly / it).

6 To be honest, the place _____ (it / recommend / little / has / to) and I wouldn't visit again.

7 I _____ (anyone / would / for / it / recommend) wanting to try something a bit different.

8 A friend of mine _____ (place / me / this / recommended / to) and I'm glad she did.

6 **Write true sentences about four of these things, using different patterns with *recommend*. Then work in pairs and compare your ideas.**

- a video game you've played
- a book you've read
- a place you've worked
- an app you use
- a place you sometimes eat in
- a place you've been to on holiday
- something you've bought recently
- a shop you go to a lot

As

As is sometimes used to mean *while*. We also use *as* to mean *because*. *As* is used in common expressions like *as far as*, too.

a *I've written to the manager three times now asking for a full refund **as soon as possible**.*

b ***As** you enter, you see that the carpet in the reception area is dirty.*

c ***As** I have three beautiful Persians, I was delighted to discover this.*

d *My three always seem very relaxed and happy **as** I'm using it.*

e ***As far as** the delivery is concerned, I've got no complaints.*

f *The real problem came when I first washed them, **as** they came out much smaller.*

7 **Look at the examples in the Useful language box. Decide in which two sentences:**

1 *as* means *while*.

2 *as* means *because*.

3 *as* is used as part of an expression. What's the whole expression in each case?

8 **Work in pairs. Complete the sentences from reviews by adding activities or reasons. How many sentences can you add both to?**

1 I only ended up with this as _____ .

   … it was a present from a friend.

   … I was bored and so started looking at things online.

2 I'm glad we booked a table in advance, as _____ .

3 I asked if they could deliver free of charge, as _____ .

4 This has already become the most-used app on my phone, as _____ .

5 I'm giving this a one-star review because it broke as _____ .

6 The customer service was terrible, particularly as _____ .

7 I usually listen, as _____ .

9 **Complete the sentences (1–6) with these expressions.**

as a result	as a matter of fact
as far as I know	as far as the design is concerned
as long as	it's just as well

1 They last for years _____ you take care of them.

2 It's certainly not cheap. _____ , I'd recommend saving your money and buying something different.

3 Mine got damaged in the post, I think, and _____ , the top doesn't fit on properly anymore.

4 It didn't come with any instructions, so _____ it was easy to put together and use.

5 It's not the cheapest one on the market, but _____ , I'd say it looks better than anything else out there.

6 I haven't tried using it in other countries, but _____ , it should work all over the world.

PRACTICE

10 **M** **Work in pairs. Think of a product you've both bought, a place you've both been to or a service you've both used.**

1 Decide how many stars out of five you'd give it.

2 Make a list of what you liked / didn't like about it and why.

11 **Write your review about the product / place / service you discussed in Exercise 10. Write 150–200 words.**

12 **Give your review to your partner. Read your partner's review. Discuss:**

1 what you wrote similarly / differently.

2 if you both followed the five points mentioned in Exercise 4.

3 how much of the Useful language you managed to use.

VIDEO Out and about

1 Work in pairs. Discuss the questions.

1 How keen on shopping are you?

2 What's the most important thing when you buy clothes?

Understanding accents

Some accents use an /ɒ/ instead of an /ɔː/ sound, so *court* /kɔːt/ may sound like *cot* /kɒt/.

2 🎥 **Watch four people answer the same questions. How much can you remember about what they said? Then work in pairs. Did anyone have similar experiences to you?**

3 🎥 **Watch again. Match two sentences with each speaker. There is one extra sentence.**

a They don't go out shopping as much as they used to.

b They're not into buying clothes as much as another kind of shopping.

c They love shopping.

d They like to take their time to choose what to buy.

e They tend to go at a particular time of year.

f They keep in mind health and the environment when shopping.

g They only really buy online when it's something they've bought before.

h They like to wear bright clothes.

i Price isn't really a factor in their choices.

4 Discuss the questions with your partner.

1 Do you have a favourite time of year to do shopping?

2 What are the best bargains you've found when shopping?

3 What things might you describe as 'a necessary evil'?

4 How sustainable is your lifestyle?

VIDEO Developing conversations

5 🎥 **You're going to watch two people talking about their jobs. Watch and take notes.**

6 🎥 **Work in pairs. Compare what you understood. Watch again if you need to.**

7 FS 🎥 **Watch again. Complete the sentences with three to five words in each gap.**

1 Not that cool! _____ – science centre exhibits.

2 It is mainly for children, _____ big children.

3 Anytime you build something, _____ and you can play with it.

4 I met someone, _____ company.

5 It is very fancy, actually, _____ .

6 _____ I prefer it cos it's quiet on the weekends.

7 You should come some time if you want – I _____ guest pass.

8 Oh really. _____ kick me out?

CONVERSATION PRACTICE

8 Work in pairs. You're going to practise a conversation.

1 Choose a Conversation practice from either Lesson 5A or Lesson 6A.

2 Look at the language in that lesson.

3 Check the meaning of anything you've forgotten with your partner.

4 Have the conversation. Try to improve on the last time you did it.

Grammar and Vocabulary

GRAMMAR

1 Complete the conversation with one word in each gap.

A: What do you do?

B: I'm an electrician for a construction company.

A: Oh, OK. I thought most electricians were self-employed.

B: Yeah, they are. I used to be too, but with this job, the work is a bit [1]_____ secure. Also, I don't [2]_____ to work weekends very often and I'm [3]_____ to work flexible hours. The money isn't [4]_____ good as it was when I was self-employed, but I don't mind that. And I've met lots of good people there as well.

A: So it [5]_____ be quite a big company, then?

B: Yeah, it [6]_____ . It's huge. They're involved in lots of projects here and abroad, so I get to travel a bit, too.

A: That sounds great.

B: Yeah, it is. And I [7]_____ use a company car as well.

A: So do you do any private work at all now?

B: Well, we're not really [8]_____ to, but I do occasionally – for people I know, usually.

2 Read the first sentence in each pair. Complete the second sentence so that it has a similar meaning. Use between two and five words, including the word in bold.

1 The company dress code doesn't allow jeans.

We _____ at work.   **CAN'T**

2 When we go to the toilet, we mustn't leave our desks for more than five minutes.

We _____ a toilet break of more than five minutes. **ALLOWED**

3 I shouldn't really leave before six, but I could maybe go at five.

I'm _____ until six, but I could maybe go at five. **STAY**

4 This design's nicer, but the battery life is shorter than on the other one.

This design's nicer, but the battery doesn't _____ on the other one.   **LAST**

5 Paris has around 11 million people, compared with about 22 million in Mexico City.

Mexico City is twice _____ Paris.   **SIZE**

3 Put the words in brackets in the correct order to complete the sentences.

1 He bought me a _____. (nice / really / scarf / wool)

2 They sell a lot of _____ (Big Ben / cheap / of / plastic / models).

3 She was wearing a _____ ('Peace' / blue / with / T-shirt / dirty / written) on it.

4 I like it, but I've seen _____ (that / ones / much / cheaper / similar / are) than this one.

5 His favourite piece of clothing is _____ (a / shirt / name / Argentina / classic / with / Messi's) on it.

4 ▶ Listen and write the six sentences you hear.

VOCABULARY

5 Match the two parts of the collocations.

1	obey	a	sides / to another company
2	win	b	a small team / your time better
3	upgrade	c	my phone / to the latest version
4	guarantee	d	a lot of comments / used to it
5	manage	e	school exams / social media at work
6	switch	f	the rules / orders
7	get	g	a legal case / a competition
8	prohibit	h	workers' rights / you'll love it

6 Decide if these words and phrases are connected to buying and selling, new technology, or clothes.

bargain	battery life	deal	discount
messy	new features	outfit	plain
profit	storage	tight	

7 Complete the sentence with the correct form of the word in bold.

1 There's a legal _____ to give workers two weeks' holiday pay.   **require**

2 We usually interview around 20 _____ for each job.   **apply**

3 Have a look one of those price _____ sites to see what the best price is.   **compare**

4 It's never boring, because the work is always _____. **vary**

5 It looks amazing. It's a very _____ design.   **style**

6 My main _____ is to make sure everyone gets paid on time.   **responsible**

7 We got this beautiful, _____ painting on holiday. It really brightens up the room.   **colour**

8 It's cold out there. If you're going to play football, wear _____ under your shorts.   **leg**

9 Being a teacher is a very _____ job.   **demand**

8 Complete the text with one word in each gap. The first letters are given.

I recently got in [1]t _____ with a friend from school and he told me a crazy story. He's recently got [2]i _____ buying and selling second-hand stuff, and he's always looking for [3]a _____ rugs, tables – that kind of thing. He recently found a painting that he thought was by a famous artist. He was sure it was [4]g _____ and as it was only £50 it seemed like a real [5]b _____. He thought he could make a [6]p _____ by selling it to a collector. When he tried to sell it, though, he got in [7]t _____ with the police, as it had actually been stolen! They took him to the police station, told him he was [8]e _____ to one phone call and then kept him there for the night. Luckily, though, he didn't end up in [9]c _____ . I have to say, my life feels [10]d _____ and boring in comparison!

7
Eating

IN THIS UNIT, YOU:

- create and explain a menu in your language to someone in English

- talk about personal and cultural habits in diet and eating

- make plans for a food business and present it to the class

SPEAKING

1 Work in pairs. Discuss the questions.

1 Look at the photo. Why do you think they are making the dish?

2 Would you like to eat it? Why? / Why not?

3 Are there any dishes like this where you live? What are they called? How are they similar / different to the paella in the photo?

2 Work with a new partner. Discuss the questions.

1 Are you any good at cooking? If you are, how did you learn?

2 What's the best dish you can cook?

3 What kind of thing do you usually eat in the morning / for lunch / in the evening?

4 Are you a fussy eater or will you try anything? Do you know other people like this?

5 Do you prefer to eat out at a restaurant or to eat at home? Why?

Preparing a giant dish of paella, Altea, Spain.

I'll go for that

IN THIS LESSON, YOU:
- create and explain a menu in your language to someone in English
- talk about food you like / dislike
- practise listening to someone explaining a Peruvian menu in English
- explain foods and dishes when you don't know the name in English

VOCABULARY Talking about food

1 Work in pairs. Discuss what you think the words in bold mean. Then match the sentences (1–9) with the responses (a–i).

1 It's a mix of potatoes and beans, so it really **fills you up**.

2 It smells bad. Do you think it's **off**?

3 I don't like the meat. It's really dry and **tough** too.

4 I liked that cheese, but they gave me such a small **portion**.

5 It's delicious, but I'm not sure I can finish it all. Go on, have a **bite**.

6 How hot is the curry here?

7 I have an allergy. Does it contain nuts?

8 Did you put anything on the salad?

9 How is it cooked?

a Just some olive oil and **vinegar**.

b I know, you really have to **chew** it a lot and there's not much fat on it.

c No. It's supposed to be like that. It has a slightly **sour** taste too. Not everyone likes it.

d Yeah. It did have a strong **flavour**, but it was really **thinly-sliced**!

e It's **deep-fried**, so the outside is hard and the cheese on the inside is soft.

f I'm not sure – let me check the **ingredients**.

g I'd say it's very mild, but then I'm used to **spicy** food.

h Mmm, yes, that's very **rich**. You couldn't eat a lot of it.

i OK. I'll have something a bit lighter. I'm not that hungry.

2 🅿 ▶ Listen to the words from Exercise 1 and practise saying them on their own and in a phrase. Which words / phrases do you find hard to say? Practise saying them again.

3 Work in pairs. Discuss the questions.

1 Why might meat be tough?

2 How else can you tell food or drink is off?

3 Why might someone ask you for a bite of your food? How could you reply?

4 What foods are deep-fried? What's good / bad about cooking like that?

5 What happens if you eat a lot of rich food?

6 What ingredients does a burger typically contain?

7 How can you improve the flavour of something?

8 Which eight words below also have a -y adjective, like salt – salty and spice – spicy?

boil	chew	crisp	fat
juice	oil	roast	slice
smell	taste	tough	vinegar

LISTENING

4 Work in pairs. Look at the menu from a Peruvian restaurant. Answer the questions.

1 Do you know what kind of dishes they might be or what might be in them?

2 Do any of the words sound similar to food or dishes in your first language?

STARTERS
Papa Rellena

Anticuchos

Ceviche

Sopa de Carne

Tallarín con Mariscos

MAINS
Bistec Apanado

Arroz con Mariscos

Arroz con Pato

Lomo Saltado

Seco de Cabrito

DESSERTS
Arroz con Leche

Crema Volteada

Helado de Lúcuma

Mazamorra Morada

5 ▶ Listen to a conversation between Aurora, a Peruvian woman, and Claes, a colleague who's visiting Peru. Tick (✓) the dishes they each decide to order and note the ingredients of the dishes.

6 ▶ Work in pairs. Which dishes on the menu do these sentences refer to? Then listen again and check your answers.

1 The man can't eat them.

2 It's crispy.

3 It's nice and juicy.

4 They contain the same kind of meat.

5 It's the national dish of Peru.

6 It's a bit like a dish from another country.

7 It's similar to lamb.

8 Order it if you aren't full.

7 Work in pairs. Discuss the questions.

1 Would you order any of the dishes mentioned? If yes, which one(s)? If not, why not?

2 Do you like steak? How do you usually like it cooked?

3 Do any of the dishes sound similar to any dishes from your country?

4 Do you think your country has a national dish? What would it be?

5 Do the speakers mention any ingredients you often / never use in your own cooking?

DEVELOPING CONVERSATIONS

Describing dishes

To help us describe different foods or dishes, we often use these phrases.

It's a kind of *vegetable / side dish / spice.*

It's a bit like *lamb,* **but with** *a stronger flavour /* **but not as** *fatty.*

It's made from *fruit and purple corn / a special kind of bean.*

It's cooked with *tomatoes, onions and spices.*

8 Work in pairs. Each think of four foods or dishes you've eaten in the last week. Take turns to describe your foods/dishes to each other. Can your partner guess what you're describing?

9 Think of three different drinks, dishes, fruit or vegetables from your country. Write a description of them.

CONVERSATION PRACTICE

10 Work in groups. Agree a menu of six to eight of the most typical dishes from your country. Write it in your first language.

11 M **Work with a new partner. Roleplay a conversation like the one you heard in Exercise 5.**

Student A: You're visiting the country on holiday or for work. You don't speak the local language. Student B will explain the menu and make suggestions. Reject at least one suggestion and explain why. Then decide on two or three dishes to order.

Student B: Explain the menu for Student A and make suggestions of what to order.

Eat with your eyes

IN THIS LESSON, YOU:
- talk about personal and cultural habits in diet and eating
- discuss aspects of the food industry
- practise reading an article on colour and food
- practise different ways of making generalizations

VOCABULARY Diet and the food industry

1 Complete the sentences with these words.

associated with	consume	diet
manufacturing	prepared	preserve
process	source	substance
weight		

1 Food production and _____ are the most important industries here.

2 In general, people here have a balanced _____ with lots of fruit and veg. There aren't many people with _____ problems.

3 Generally speaking, people _____ a lot of meat here. Most people have it every day.

4 I buy a lot of frozen food and other _____ meals that I can put in the oven or microwave.

5 I worry about the manufacturing _____ of lots of food products – companies add too many things to flavour and _____ food.

6 I always check the list of ingredients on a packet. If I don't recognize a _____, I don't buy it.

7 I try not to consume too much sugar because it's _____ heart disease.

8 I check the _____ of the vegetables and meat I buy to know where it comes from.

2 Work in pairs. Discuss if the statements in Exercise 1 are true for you and where you live.

READING

3 Work in pairs. You're going to read an article about the use of colour in food and the food industry. Discuss why you think the following are mentioned.

- grape juice
- people died
- the colour of the plate
- blue steak
- taste sour
- kill bacteria

4 Read the article on page 71 and check your ideas. Find three things you didn't know before.

5 Work in pairs. Complete the article (1–7) with these sentences (a–h). There is one extra sentence.

a And another found adding red food colouring can make people think food tastes sweeter.

b Red tends to make us more active and increase our appetite.

c These days, there's a huge variety of colours available, but they're mainly produced from natural sources.

d Each different colour naturally contains different chemicals that feed different kinds of healthy bacteria.

e Some of these colourings were actually poisonous and there were incidents where people died.

f Studies have shown these substances that are unhealthy.

g For example, the colour blue is often associated with food that has gone off.

h Of course, that doesn't mean such products are healthy.

6 Work in pairs. Discuss the questions.

1 What was the most surprising thing in the article? Why? Does the article make you want to change your behaviour in any way? Why? / Why not?

2 Have you heard of any stories in the news about food? Were they scary or positive?

GRAMMAR

Generalizations and *tend to*

We can show that something is generally true by using an adverb like *usually* or *hardly (ever)*, an adverbial phrase like *generally speaking,* or the structure *tend to* + verb.

*In restaurants, people **(don't) usually** order individual dishes for themselves.*

***Generally speaking**, people eat a lot of meat.*

*Red **tends to** make us more active.*

*People **tend not to** stay long in yellow rooms.*

*I **don't tend to** cook meat at home.*

7 Look at the examples in the Grammar box. Answer these questions.

1 Where does an adverb like *normally* go in a sentence?

2 Where does an adverbial phrase like *on the whole* or *in general* go?

3 How is the negative of *tend to* formed?

8 Rewrite the sentences using the words in brackets.

1 On the whole, we eat food with our hands. (tend)

2 I hardly ever have a dessert if I go out for dinner. (tend)

3 I tend not to have breakfast during the week. (normally)

4 As a rule, our family doesn't eat out. (hardly ever)

5 People don't usually leave tips here – unless it was an unusually good meal. (speaking)

6 I don't usually have time to have a big lunch, so I normally just have a sandwich. (whole / tend)

9 Write five generalizations about your country. These could be about food, eating, shopping, work, education or behaviour.

G See Grammar reference 7B.

SPEAKING

10 M Work in groups. Find out the following.

1 Who's had the most colours in their food today / this week.

2 The most / least popular colour of food.

3 What people know about the health benefits of different-coloured foods.

Eat your greens ... and reds and yellows

Colour has always been important when it comes to food. The Roman food lover Apicius observed that 'we eat first with our eyes' and ancient Egyptians used to colour sweets using grape juice to make them more attractive. As food manufacturing grew in the 19th century, all kinds of substances were used to colour and disguise cheap products. [1]_____ Eventually, laws had to be introduced to protect the public and the producers of more expensive, natural products. In some parts of the US, manufacturers were banned for many years from using yellow dye to make margarine look more like butter. However, these laws have not stopped food businesses from using colour to their advantage. [2]_____ Furthermore, the food industry has a greater understanding of how colour can affect our mood.

For example, red and yellow are popular with fast-food chains partly because of their effect on behaviour. [3]_____ Bright yellow may also encourage us to eat more by creating a happy mood. At the same time, it seems people tend not to stay long in yellow rooms, leaving space for new customers.

We may also find ourselves eating more or less depending on the colour of the plate we use. Studies suggest that when the colour of the plate contrasts strongly with the food (white pasta on a blue plate) we tend to serve ourselves less. When the food matches the colour of the plate more closely people may eat more – although that might not be the case for all colours. [4]_____ One experiment reported to show how colouring a steak blue made people feel sick, even though the food was perfectly fresh. People started eating the meal under a low light, which meant they could not see that the food had been dyed. When the lights were turned up and they saw their off-coloured food, several of them immediately left the table saying they felt ill.

In contrast, green tends to represent health and naturalness. One fast-food brand changed the decoration in its restaurants from red to green to suggest its menu was healthier and better for the environment, and supermarkets often use green packaging for vegetarian meals. [5]_____ They can still contain too much salt, fat or sugar.

Yellow food colouring may fool few people into thinking that margarine is butter, but some studies do suggest that adding colour can affect how we experience flavours. It seems that people associate yellow with a sour taste and expect white food to be salty. [6]_____

If adding colour allows manufacturers to reduce salt or sugar content, then that might be a good thing. However, some research suggests artificial food colourings can be associated with hyperactivity, while other studies have found that eating highly-processed foods may cause weight and other health problems. It seems that additives used to preserve, flavour and colour food can kill bacteria in our bodies that control weight and keep us well.

And what's the suggested solution to this problem? Well funnily enough, it's more colour in your diet – colours that come directly from fresh fruit and veg. [7]_____ And it seems the more varied the bacteria in your gut, the healthier you'll be.

Ingredients for success

IN THIS LESSON, YOU:
- make plans for a food business and present it to the class
- practise listening to a podcast about starting a food business
- share examples of food businesses and what makes them successful / unsuccessful
- discuss plans and actions and raise possible issues

SPEAKING

1 **Work in pairs. What's good and bad about food places in these descriptions? Would you go to them? Why? / Why not?**

1 You can't book a table.

2 There are always tables available.

3 It's on top of a cliff with views over the sea.

4 It has a lively atmosphere and music in the background.

5 It serves really big portions.

6 It has a menu with nine courses.

7 All the products they use are organic or from local sources.

8 It does an international buffet where you serve yourself.

9 The place provides work for unemployed people.

10 It's unusual.

LISTENING

2 ▶ **Listen to the introduction to a podcast. Answer these questions.**

1 Who is the show for?

2 What is the episode going to be about?

3 Who do you know that might be interested in it? Why?

3 **FS** ▶ **Adverbs (*really*, *probably*, *very*, etc.) may be emphasized or reduced in fast speech. Listen to eight extracts and write the adverbs you hear.**

4 ▶ **Listen to the podcast on starting a food business and take notes. Then work in pairs. Do you think the information would encourage someone to start a food business, or not?**

5 ▶ **Listen again. Complete the notes with one to three words or a number in each gap.**

1 On average, up to _____ of restaurants in the US fail in the first year of business.

2 Food businesses generally do _____ than other kinds of businesses.

3 By 2029, it's estimated that food services will be worth around _____ .

4 A lot of restaurants fail because they didn't budget for _____ .

5 You can start small by hiring space in kitchens set up in _____ .

6 When starting a restaurant, it's better to be near _____ .

7 Having a clear concept means thinking about the kind of food, price and _____ .

8 As well as a good chef, you need people who are _____ .

9 Antonia's new project, called _____ , will open in _____ .

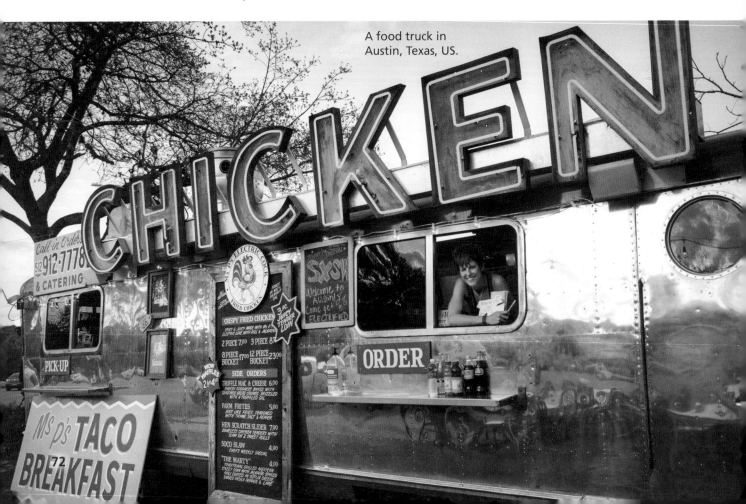

A food truck in Austin, Texas, US.

72

6 Work in pairs. Think of an example for each food or drink place (1–6). Then answer the questions for each place.

1 a place which has been around for a long time
2 a place which has opened recently
3 a place which closed down
4 a place which is popular with young people or students
5 a mobile place or delivery service
6 a chain of places

- What is / was it like?
- Why is it successful or why did it fail?
- How does it fit in with the advice in the podcast?

GRAMMAR

First conditionals

We use first conditionals to talk about plans, make predictions and give advice for likely situations now or in the future. We use *What (will you do) if … ?* questions to raise possible issues.

a *If* everything *goes* to plan, we*'re going to launch* in around four months.

b And *if* they*'re* successful online, we *might help* them set up their own physical businesses.

c *If* you *don't sell* tasty food, you *will fail*.

d *If* you *don't have* much money, *start* small.

e *If* you *take care* of the food, I*'ll deal* with all the business side of things.

f What *will* you *do if* you *don't get* as many customers as you hoped? What *if* your chef *is* sick?

7 Look at the examples in the Grammar box. Match the purposes (1–6) with the examples (a–f). Which verb form shows the purpose in each example?

1 give advice
2 make an offer or promise
3 give a definite prediction
4 ask about situations that might affect your plan
5 explain a definite plan
6 explain a possible plan

8 Complete each conversation with the correct form of these verbs.

| give | hire | let | need | open | refuse |

A: I hear you're thinking of getting into the food business.

B: Yeah, if I can get a loan from the bank, I'm ¹_____ a restaurant.

A: Really? That's brave. What if they ²_____ the loan?

B: I ³_____ space in a commercial kitchen and do online deliveries. I have some savings.

A: Oh, OK. Well, if you ⁴_____ help with your website, ⁵_____ me know and I ⁶_____ you a hand.

B: Wow, that's a very generous offer. Thank you!

| be | call | eat | go for | pick you up | rain | stay |

C: If the weather stays nice till Friday, we ⁷_____ a picnic on the beach. Do you want to come?

D: Sure, if it ⁸_____ too early. I have to do some work in the morning.

C: We're thinking of meeting there around two, so if you come, I ⁹_____ from your house about 1.30 pm.

D: OK – that sounds good. What if it ¹⁰_____ ?

C: We ¹¹_____ in one of the restaurants near there.

D: OK. If that happens, I ¹²_____ here. I can't afford to eat out at the moment.

C: Alright. Well, see what you think on Saturday. Just ¹³_____ me in the morning if you decide not to come.

9 Write down five plans, promises or predictions you have for the next year using different first conditional patterns.

10 Work in pairs. Share and discuss your ideas from Exercise 9. Your partner should suggest at least one possible issue using a *What (will you do) if … ?* question.

G See Grammar Reference 7C.

SPEAKING TASK

11 Work in groups. You're going to give a presentation for a new food business. Follow the instructions.

1 Choose one of these options to suit your group.
- a drink or fast-food place with potential to become a chain
- a food delivery company in your city
- a restaurant in the area of your school
- a mobile food or drinks van

2 Discuss what skills, knowledge and other resources people in the group could contribute to the business.

3 Decide what concept your business will have and what it will look like (e.g. type of food and customer, pricing, etc.).

4 Decide how you're going to get it started, who will do what and if you will employ people.

12 In your group, present your ideas to the class.
- Other groups should ask questions to find out more.
- As a class, decide which business you think has the best chance of success.

■ MY OUTCOMES ■

Work in pairs. Discuss the questions.

1 What speaking activities did you find enjoyable?
2 What grammar have you learned?
3 What problems did you have when doing written activities?
4 What can you do at home to revise language from this unit?

8 Education

Schoolboys in Germany, 1905.

IN THIS UNIT, YOU:

- have conversations about courses you've done / you're doing
- share information and discuss what's effective in education
- have a debate about educational issues

SPEAKING

1 Work in groups. Discuss the questions.

1 Are there any similarities between this classroom and classrooms you've studied in?

2 How has education changed over recent years?

3 Do you think these changes have been for the better or for the worse? Why?

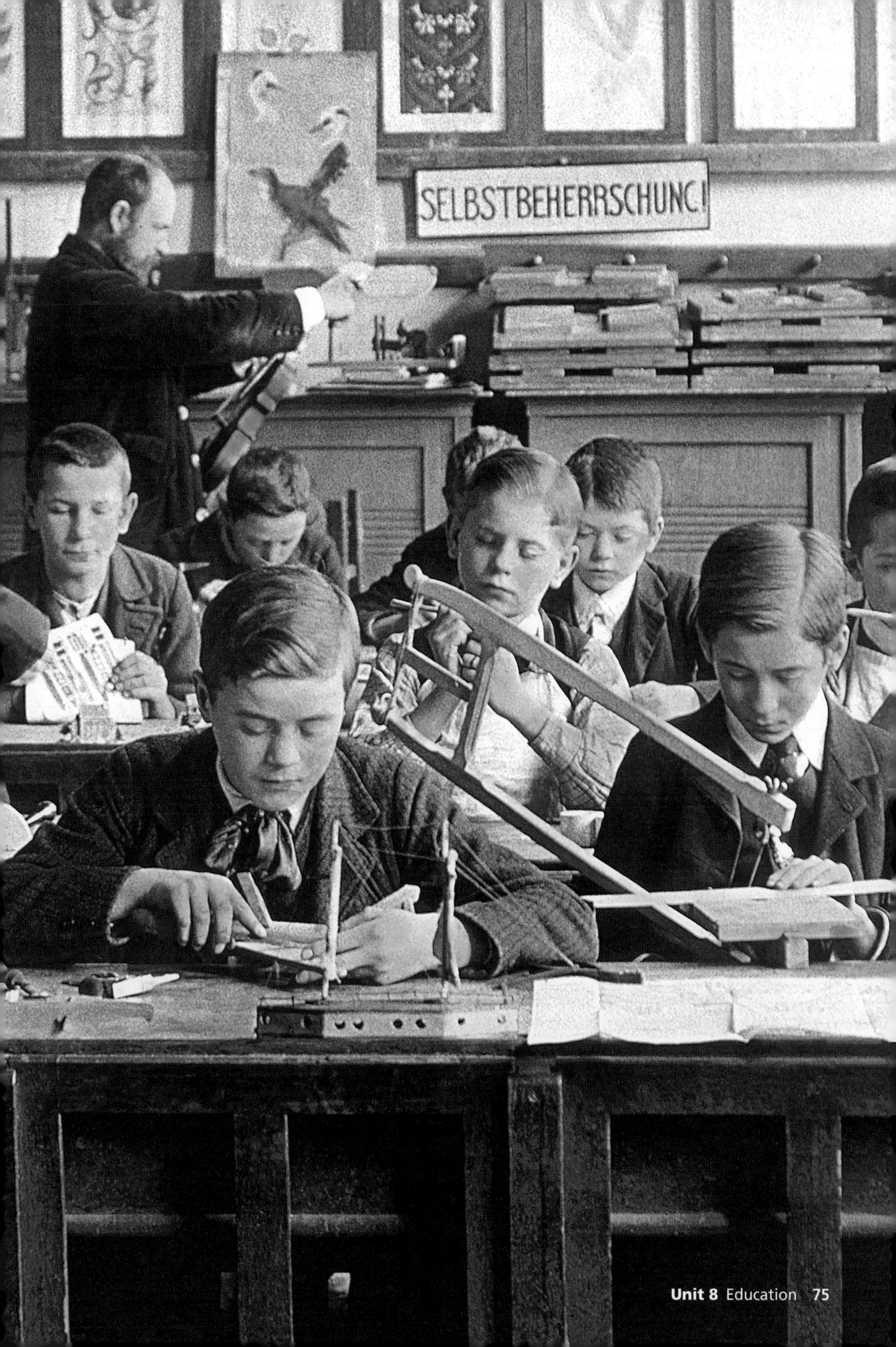
SELBSTBEHERRSCHUNG!

How's your course going?

IN THIS LESSON, YOU:
- have conversations about courses you've done / you're doing
- practise taking notes while listening to a conversation about a course
- ask about and explain future plans related to a course
- practise using different phrases to show empathy and understanding

VOCABULARY Describing courses

1 **Match the questions (1–8) with the answers (a–h). Check you understand the words in bold.**

1 Why are you doing the course?

2 How's it going?

3 How was it taught?

4 Did you enjoy it?

5 What were the **tutors** like? Were they helpful?

6 Did you have much **coursework** outside class?

7 Did you find it useful?

8 How is it assessed? Is there an exam?

a Yes there is, but 60% of **the overall mark** is based on your coursework.

b Well, I'd done the basic training and I wanted to **progress** to an advanced level.

c I'm struggling a bit, to be honest. I failed my last **module**, so I can't afford to fail another.

d Yes and no. I mean, I guess having some knowledge and skills in Excel is **good for my CV**, but I never use it at work, so it wasn't that **relevant.**

e Yes, they were really **encouraging** and gave us a lot of **feedback** on how we could improve.

f It was all done through **lectures**, so unfortunately it wasn't very practical.

g Not that much. I was interested in the subject, but the course wasn't really what I expected and I lost **motivation.**

h Yeah, it was quite demanding. We had regular **assignments** and the **seminars** involved a lot of reading before them too.

2 **Work in pairs. Answer the questions.**

1 If course tutors are encouraging, what do they say to you? Think of two more adjectives to describe a tutor.

2 What percentage / grade might mean you fail a module? What could happen if you do?

3 How do you usually get feedback? What might be good / bad feedback? Why?

4 What things could be good for a CV? Why?

5 What can be good / bad about lectures?

6 Why might you struggle on a course? What's the opposite of *struggling on a course*?

7 What things might help you maintain or increase your motivation on a course?

8 What kind of things might you do for an assignment / coursework?

LISTENING

3 **FS ▶ People often say time phrases quickly. Listen and write the six time phrases you hear.**

4 **▶ M Listen to two colleagues, Daniel and Paulina, talk about a counselling course Paulina is doing. Take notes about these things:**

1 who the counselling is for

2 how the students learn

3 the tutors and students

4 the length of the course

5 assessment and qualification

5 **▶ Work in pairs. Based on your notes, complete the sentences with one or two words or a number in each gap. Then listen again and check your answers.**

1 It's a course for speech therapists where you learn some _____ in counselling.

2 There are some lectures _____ .

3 They have _____ who are very knowledgeable.

4 Everyone is very supportive apart from two people who are quite _____ .

5 The classes take place _____ a week.

6 To pass the course you need to complete an assignment and have _____ attendance.

7 There is quite a bit to read for _____ , but you don't have to look at all of it.

6 **Discuss the questions with your partner.**

1 Do you agree that encouragement from teachers and classmates is always better than criticism? Why? / Why not?

2 Do you think you would be good at counselling? Why? / Why not?

3 Do you know anyone who has studied something that they don't use anymore?

4 Do you agree with the idea of stopping studying at a certain age / point in life? Why? / Why not? Do you know anyone who's continued studying into old age?

Students study at The Blatnavik School of Government, University of Oxford, UK.

GRAMMAR

Future time clauses

When we want to specify the time at which a future action will happen, we often use a clause starting with a time expression such as *when, after, once,* etc.

*I'm going back **after** I've had this coffee.*

*So what are you going to do **when** it ends?*

*I might do another course **once** I've finished this one.*

***As soon as** I find a proper job, I'll probably stop studying.*

***When** you're ready, give me a call.*

7 **Look at the examples in the Grammar box. Answer these questions.**

1 Do you know any other time words that can join two parts of a sentence?

2 What tenses follow the time expressions?

3 Do the time clauses refer to now or to the future?

4 Can we start a sentence with a time clause?

8 **Complete the sentences with a pronoun and the correct form of the verb in brackets.**

1 How much revision *will you have to* do before *you take* your final exams? (have to / take)

2 After _____ this course, _____ to her old job? (finish / go back)

3 Is he going to look for a job as soon as _____ or _____ some time off? (graduate / take)

4 Before _____ , send me your CV and _____ it if you like. (apply / look through)

5 I bet you'll be bored when _____ and _____ any more studying to do. (leave / not have)

6 Once you _____ this qualification, _____ more? (have / get paid)

7 You must be quite stressed, studying so hard. I bet _____ relieved once _____ all over. (be / be)

8 _____ and see me once _____ . (come back / qualify)

9 **Work in pairs and take turns to say the sentences in Exercise 8. Respond and try to continue the conversation.**

> **G** See Grammar reference 8A.

DEVELOPING CONVERSATIONS

Showing you understand

When someone makes a statement about how they feel or how they find a situation, you can show you believe them or sympathize with them by saying *I'm sure, It sounds it, I can imagine* or *I bet*.

P: *They can be a bit more critical than the others, which is a bit annoying.*

D: **I can imagine.**

10 **Complete the sentences about courses with your own ideas.**

1 _____ , so I'm struggling.

2 _____ , which was annoying.

3 _____ , so I'm really pleased.

4 _____ , which was fascinating.

5 _____ , so it's quite demanding.

6 _____ , which is really helpful.

11 **Work in pairs. Take turns to read your sentences and show you understand by responding with *I bet,* etc.**

A: *We have to do a huge amount of reading at home every week, so I'm struggling.*

B: *I bet. It must be hard.*

CONVERSATION PRACTICE

12 **Work in pairs. You're going to have conversations about courses you've done / you're doing. Follow the instructions:**

1 Choose a course from the box that you have done, or choose a role from File 10 on page 197.

- a degree course
- an evening course
- training in first aid
- IT training
- an online course
- a postgraduate course
- professional development training
- training in using something

2 Think about how you might answer the questions in Exercises 1 and 8.

3 One of you start the conversation by saying: *I'm doing … at the moment / I did … ago.*

4 Continue the conversations for as long as you can. Make sure you've both talked about your courses.

Making a difference

IN THIS LESSON, YOU:
- share information and discuss what's effective in education
- talk about different groups' concerns about education
- practise reading and responding to an article about educational research
- learn different ways nouns are formed from verbs and practise using them

READING

1 Work in pairs. What do you think the following people worry or complain about when discussing schools and the education system?

businesspeople	parents	politicians
students	teachers	

2 Compare your ideas in groups. Then discuss the questions.

- What do you think is the biggest education issue in your country at the moment?
- What solutions have been suggested?
- Do you agree with them?

3 Read the first part of the article on page 79 about John Hattie, author of *Visible Learning*™, and his research into achievement in schools. Find out:

1 if any of the worries or issues you thought of were investigated.

2 why these figures are mentioned.
- 30
- 270
- 96,000
- 300 million

3 what Hattie believes is the most important influence.

4 Read the article again and mark it in the following way:

✓ – Anything which you think is true in your country

X – Anything which you think would be different in your country

! – Anything which you find surprising or interesting

? – Anything which you aren't sure about

5 Work in pairs. Compare your ideas from Exercise 4. Can your partner explain anything you weren't sure about?

VOCABULARY Forming nouns

V See Vocabulary reference 8B.

6 Complete the phrases (1–12) with nouns from the article based on the verbs in bold.

1	**improve** standards	need further _____
2	**impact** badly on kids	have a positive _____
3	**specialize** in science	a _____ in Maths
4	not be **assessed**	for the final _____
5	standards **differ** widely	make a huge _____
6	**debate** the issue	cause much _____
7	**affect** behaviour	have a positive _____
8	**expect** great things	have low _____
9	**fail** an exam	a complete _____
10	**know** a bit of French	have little _____
11	when you **compare** them	in _____ to theirs
12	**analyse** the results	do a simple _____

7 **P** ▶ Listen to the nouns from Exercise 6 and practise saying them on their own and in a phrase. Which words / phrases do you find hard to say? Practise saying them again.

8 Work in pairs. Take turns to give examples about you or education where you are. Use the verbs and nouns in Exercise 6.

A: *I think more homework would improve standards at school.*

B: *My essay writing needs further improvement.*

SPEAKING

9 Work in groups of three. Read the influences on student learning (a–i) that Hattie's analysis looked at. Discuss any that you aren't sure about and what they might mean. Which influences do you think will be the most positive for learning and which the least positive?

a Teachers' subject knowledge

b Vocabulary programmes

c Independent charter schools

d Reducing class sizes

e Summer holidays

f Self-reported grades

g Spaced practice v. mass practice

h Doing homework

i Deliberate practice

10 **M** In the same group, read about three of the influences in Exercise 9.

Student A: Read the information in File 1 on page 194.

Student B: Read the information in File 7 on page 196.

Student C: Read the information in File 14 on page 199.

Work together to rank the influences from 1 (= the most effective for improving learning) to 9 (= the least effective). What effect-size score do you think each might have?

11 Work in pairs. Discuss the questions.

1 What do you think of the research results? Did you find anything surprising or obvious? Why? What explanations could you give for the results?

2 How many of these influences were present in schools you have been to? Does that make you think the results are true or not true?

3 Do you think the results would be the same in all countries in the world? Why? / Why not?

4 Would you like to read more about the research? Why? / Why not?

What works in education

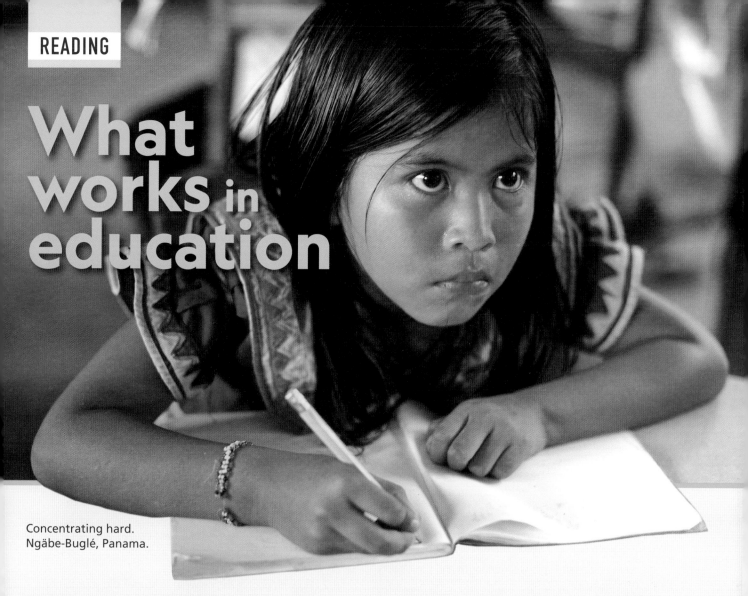

Concentrating hard.
Ngäbe-Buglé, Panama.

Few things cause more worry and debate than education. Wherever you go in the world, you will rarely find a place where everyone is happy with the education system they have. Parents worry about their kids' grades; businesses complain that students don't have the right skills; politicians look at other countries' education systems and see only failure in their own. All want to see higher achievement, but the debate is how to do it. Should it be smaller classes or more homework, wearing school uniform or better pay for teachers?

Not only are there a huge number of things that people say will make education better, but people also disagree about whether each factor actually improves learning or not. So who's right? This is the question that the New Zealand academic John Hattie has been trying to answer. Over 30 years of work, he has analysed 96,000 studies into student achievement carried out with around 300 million students, mainly from Western countries. It's an amazing piece of work and the analysis has produced some surprising results.

Hattie discovered that nearly every factor (or 'influence', as he prefers to calls them) improves students' achievement when compared with doing nothing, but that the strength of each influence differs widely. He therefore realized that rather than asking what policies and actions are positive, he needed to compare the size of the improvements. These measurements are represented in a league table that currently covers around 270 possible influences, showing which ones help most and which ones are less effective.

Hattie's conclusion from this research is that what makes the biggest difference in education is having passionate teachers who communicate well with students and other teachers. These teachers do not have to be specialists in their field with MAs or PhDs, but they need to think about their impact on students. Through listening and talking to students, these teachers understand what level their students are at, show them how to exceed their expectations and share this knowledge with colleagues. This openness about what is expected and what needs to be learned is one of the reasons he calls his work *Visible Learning*.™

Hattie's work is not without its critics. Some people think that in giving an average effect-size for different studies, he may fail to show that some influences are stronger in certain situations, for example younger students or the most talented pupils. However, Hattie argues that these are not big problems and do not change his basic conclusions: that the non-teaching solutions which are often talked about most – wearing uniforms, reducing class sizes or investing in IT – have a relatively small impact compared to good teacher–student relationships. Hattie suggests that these influences continue to get more attention because they are the things that parents and politicians can see, whereas we do not see teachers and students at work. Through his research, Hattie also wants to acknowledge and support the expert teaching that already takes place in classrooms all over the world.

Pay attention!

IN THIS LESSON, YOU:
- have a debate about educational issues
- talk about what makes a good school / university
- listen to people discuss educational situations and issues
- explain the reactions or consequences that might come from different situations

SPEAKING

1 Work in pairs. Discuss the questions.

1 Do people have much choice about what secondary school / university they can go to in your country? Do you think it's a good thing?

2 Is it easy for older people to study at university where you live? Where else can older people get further education and training where you are?

3 Why do some schools and universities have a better reputation than others? Do you think this is fair?

VOCABULARY Schools and universities

2 Work in pairs. Complete the sentences with the phrases in the box. Then decide if each sentence refers to a school or a university.

academic reputation	alternative approaches
bilingual school	entry requirements
Master's programme	research facilities
scientific discoveries	sporting success
strict discipline	

1 It's a _____ , so some subjects like PE and science are taught in English.

2 It's very traditional. Pupils wear uniforms and there's very _____ .

3 It has a big _____ that attracts a lot of international graduates who want to study more.

4 It has a very good _____ . They really push pupils to achieve high grades and get into the top universities.

5 It's difficult to get into, because the _____ are very high, especially for subjects like Law.

6 They do a lot of research and a larger number of _____ have been made there.

7 Lectures are very crowded, and the library and other _____ are a bit limited.

8 They have some _____ to teaching and learning, which the headteacher introduced.

9 They're very proud of their _____ and you don't have to pay fees if you're a good athlete.

3 Work in groups. Discuss the questions.

1 Would you like to attend or send kids to the different places in Exercise 2? Why? / Why not?

2 Have you heard of any places like those described in Exercise 2? What else do you know about them?

3 What places have you studied at? What were they like?

LISTENING

4 ▶ Match the sentences (a–f) with the four extracts you hear. There are two sentences you don't need.

a Someone explains why they want free university education.

b Someone talks about the difficulties of working in a school.

c Someone complains about an exam they're doing.

d Someone talks about their choice of degree.

e Someone explains why they are changing career.

f Someone suggests changing schools.

5 ▶ Work in pairs and answer the questions. Then listen again and check your answers.

1 Why do the speakers start talking about teaching?

2 Why is the woman surprised that the man doesn't want to study medicine?

3 What does the speaker say are the benefits of having a degree?

4 What does Angela like / not like about her school?

6 Work in pairs. Choose three sets of questions to discuss.

1 Would you like to be a teacher? Why? / Why not? Do you think teachers should be allowed to go on strike? Why? / Why not?

2 How do people decide what to study? Did your family help you make any decisions about what you've done in life? How? How much should parents push their kids?

3 Have you ever done a debate (e.g. at school / university)? What about? What skills can you learn from doing them? Do you think education should be free? Why? / Why not?

4 Do you agree changing a child's school might do more harm than good? Why? / Why not? What else could parents do if their child is unhappy, struggling or bored at school?

Studying science at the Colégio Santo Agostinho, Belo Horizonte, Brazil.

GRAMMAR

Second conditionals

We use second conditionals to talk about the consequences of imagined situations that are not currently true or that we don't believe will happen.

a I **wouldn't be** able to teach 30 kids, especially **if** they **were causing** trouble.

b I'm sure **you'd be** OK.

c **Would** you **study** it **if** you **could get** the grades?

d No, my mum's a doctor and **I don't think I'd enjoy** it.

e Maybe she**'d do** better **if** she **was** somewhere else.

f No, she**'d have to make** new friends.

7 **Look at the examples in the Grammar box. Answer the questions.**

1 Are the *if* clause and the result clause always together in the same sentence?

2 Does the past form in the *if* clause refer to something that has happened or that we expect to happen?

3 Why do speakers use *might* instead of *would*?

4 Are all of these sentences correct?

   a *I would never do that.*

   b *I wouldn't do that.*

   c *I don't think I'd do that.*

5 For these two comments, which speaker is probably doing better in their studies, a or b?

   a *I'm going to study medicine if I can get the grades.*

   b *I would study medicine if I could get the grades.*

8 **Choose the correct options to complete the conversations.**

1 A: If I *could / can* go back to university, I'd study Art.

   B: Really? I think *I'd / I'll* do something more practical, like Engineering.

2 A: I could never be a teacher.

   B: Me neither. *I get / I'd get* very frustrated if students *didn't / don't* understand me straight away.

3 A: Imagine what would happen if all the kids just *refused / refuse* to go to lessons.

   B: Yeah – that *was / would be* wild!

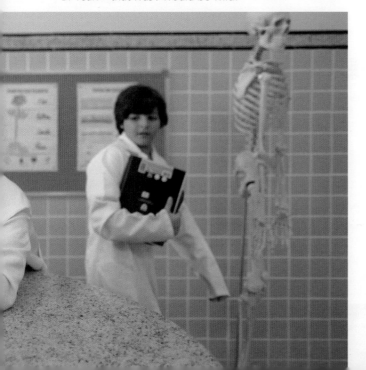

4 A: If I *am / was* in charge of education, I *would / will* just get rid of all exams.

   B: That's ridiculous. If they *did / would do* that, how would companies decide who to employ?

   A: The teacher *can / could* write a report.

   B: I don't think *they'd / they wouldn't* want to do that. They have enough work already!

9 **Complete the sentences with your own ideas.**

1 As a student, what would you do if …

2 As a teacher, what would you do if …?

3 What would you study if … ?

4 What would you do if you were a parent and your child … ?

5 If I was in charge of education, I … .

6 Imagine what would happen if … .

10 **Say your questions and statements to other students in the class and get their responses.**

G See Grammar reference 8C. ⟫

SPEAKING TASK

11 **M** **As a class, choose two proposals (a–e) to debate. Then divide the class into two groups – one group arguing for both proposals and the other group arguing against them. In your group, follow the instructions (1–5).**

> a We should ban exams in schools.
>
> b We should provide a healthy free school meal to every child every day.
>
> c We should get a yearly amount of money to pay for education throughout our lives.
>
> d No-one should be able to get a degree if they haven't got an Intermediate level of English.
>
> e Teachers should be paid according to the exam results of their students.

1 Look at the arguments in File 11 on page 197.

2 Discuss why the opposing arguments might be wrong and / or what you might do instead.

3 Think of examples or research information to support each argument.

4 Add one or two more arguments if you can.

5 Write a short speech for each proposal together.

12 **Have the debates. Follow the instructions:**

1 The speaker *for* the proposal presents their argument.

2 The speaker *against* the proposal presents their argument.

3 Anybody can ask questions to the speakers.

4 Take a vote on each proposal and the best arguments.

5 Repeat steps 1–4 for the second proposal.

■ MY OUTCOMES ■

Work in pairs. Discuss the questions.

1 What speaking activities did you find enjoyable?

2 What grammar have you learned?

3 What problems did you have when doing written work?

4 What can you do at home to revise language from this unit?

Making requests

IN THIS LESSON, YOU:
- make requests in different styles of writing
- discuss different kinds of requests and responses to them
- learn ways to make requests more polite / formal
- practise making writing more or less formal

SPEAKING

1 Work in pairs. Discuss the questions.

1 When was the last time you did a friend a favour? What was it?

2 When was the last time you asked a friend to do you a favour? What was it? How did you ask? What did they say?

3 Have you ever requested something at one of these places? Why? How? What was the reply?
- a place where you were studying
- a restaurant
- a hotel

4 Have you ever sent out a request on a group chat or social media? What for? What was the response?

WRITING

2 Work in pairs. Read the messages (1–5) that ask for a favour or make a request. Answer the questions.

1 Would you give a positive answer if you were the recipient of the message?

2 What reason might you give if you refused? What might you suggest instead?

3 Work in pairs. Match the replies (a–e) with the messages (1–5).

a I would, but I'm away all this week. Any chance you could do it?

b Here you go! Loved it too!

c Of course! No probs. Just let me know the details when you have everything sorted.

d That is not something I would expect, so I think I would prefer to cancel and look elsewhere.

e I'll be happy to do it if you don't need it back immediately.

4 Look at the messages again. Answer these questions.

1 What phrases are used to introduce the requests?

2 Do the writers give any explanations for their requests? Why? / Why not?

3 What words / phrases are used to show thanks?

1

To: Osman123@shotmail.ml

Subject: Restaurant booking

Dear Ms Osman,

We have received your booking for 16 people via bookatable. com. We would very much like to accommodate you, but we cannot confirm the booking without a deposit of £200. Could you possibly call us today on 0842 111 639 so we can take your card details over the phone? And could you please inform us of any dietary requirements in advance?

We look forward to hearing from you.

Yours faithfully,
Sandra Schafernaker

2

Do you want to sort out the cake for Kwame's birthday then? We can get everyone to pay something towards it.

3

 Camden

Hey there! What a night! Just want to say a big thank you to everyone for coming out to celebrate. I had a fantastic time. I was too busy enjoying myself to really take any photos, so if anyone has any nice ones, could you share them on here? Cheers.

4

To: Margot122@shotmail.ml

Subject: Favour

Hi Margot,

Long time, no see. How are you? I've been very busy finishing my final dissertation for my Master's. It's 20,000 words, so I haven't been out much! I've attached it here. As your English is so good, could you possibly do me a big favour and have a look through to check it's OK? I'd be really grateful – I'll even buy you lunch sometime. If it's really too much at the moment, don't worry. I could maybe ask my English teacher to help. Anyway, let me know.

All best,
Olaf

5

To: Mario@shotmail.ml

Subject: Flights

Mario,

I'm just looking at flights to Milan for Dana's wedding. They're all seem to be very expensive, except one on the 12th to Malpensa which doesn't get in till 12:00 at night. I was wondering if you could possibly pick me up though, as I'll probably miss the last train – especially if there are any delays. Either way, could you let me know as soon as you get this message as I need to make a decision?

Cheers!
Andre

Transporting a cake
in Hanoi, Vietnam.

USEFUL LANGUAGE

Polite questions

In English, we often use question phrases like *Do you think you could …* or *I was wondering if you could …* when making a request. We do this to be more polite (as English doesn't have polite verb form) and show we understand we're asking a big favour and aren't necessarily expecting a positive answer. If it's a very big favour, you might add other words like *possibly*, *at all*, *please*, etc.

I was wondering if you could possibly *pick me up?*

Could you possibly do me a big favour and *have a look through to check it's OK?*

5 **Complete the requests by putting the words in the correct order.**

1 you / think / you / do / could   … pick me up?

2 me / you / a / could / and / do / favour   … buy it for me?

3 to / would / it / possible / be   … give him a call?

4 could / there / is / any / you / chance   … translate this for me?

5 if / I / wondering / you / was / could   … re-do it.

6 **Complete the requests with these words.**

at all	do you think	huge
please	possibly	there's any chance

1 I was wondering if _____ you could print out this document for me?

2 Would it be _____ possible to provide an answer by tomorrow?

3 Is there any chance we could _____ stay at your home?

4 _____ could you share this information with anyone who may be interested?

5 _____ you could do me a _____ favour and lend me your car?

7 **Write five requests / favours using different polite question phrases.**

Synonyms

In email 1, Sandra asks Ms Osman to inform her of any dietary requirements. *Inform* is a synonym for *tell*. We can use synonyms to make something sound more or less formal, though often there's no difference in formality.

8 **Match the verbs in italics (1–8) with their synonyms (a–h). Which verbs are more formal?**

1 *request* a refund   a pick up

2 *collect* Maria from the airport   b send on

3 the flight *arrives* at five   c get in

4 *inform* me when it is ready   d fill in

5 *enquire* about prices   e ask for

6 *complete* the form   f say sorry

7 *forward* the email to him   g ask

8 *apologize* for the error   h tell

9 **Work in pairs. Tell each other about the last time you:**

1 requested something by email.

2 informed someone of something by email.

3 made an enquiry about something by email.

4 completed a form.

5 sent on an email, photo or link.

6 apologized for something.

PRACTICE

10 **Work in pairs. You're going to write two requests. Imagine you're organizing a wedding, birthday or other kind of celebration. Think of one or two examples for each kind of requests:**

1 a request to the venue manager / service provider

2 a big favour of a friend

3 an easy / general request to friends

11 **With your partner, write your requests. You should write one email and one text message. Use language from the lesson and write around 60 words for each request.**

12 **Swap your requests with another pair. Then, with your partner, write an appropriate reply to each one.**

VIDEO Out and about

1 Work in pairs. Discuss the questions.

1 What makes a good teacher?

2 What makes a good student?

Understanding accents

Some accents use a /r/ sound instead of a /l/ sound, so *play* /pleɪ/ may sound more like pray /preɪ/.

2 📹 **Watch five people answer the same questions. How much can you remember about what they said? Then work in pairs. Did anyone have the same ideas as you?**

3 📹 **Watch again. Match one or two sentences with each speaker. There is one extra sentence.**

A good teacher:

a understands the level of students and what they could achieve.

b gives emotional support to the students.

c provides interesting material for students to discuss.

d uses a variety of tasks in their classes.

e obviously enjoys what they're doing.

A good student:

f understands the approach their school is taking.

g doesn't expect the teacher to motivate them.

h develops an interest in what they're learning and wants to find out more.

i makes the most of the opportunity to practise.

4 Discuss the questions with your partner.

1 Have you experienced different approaches to teaching English? How were they different?

2 Have you ever had a teacher that inspired you?

3 Which lessons in this course have been most relevant for you so far? Why?

4 What things are you curious about?

VIDEO Developing conversations

5 📹 **You're going to watch two people talking about what to cook for a dinner party. Watch and take notes.**

6 📹 **Work in pairs. Compare what you understood. Watch again if you need to.**

7 FS 📹 **Watch again. Complete the sentences with three to five words in each gap.**

1 I'm going to have friends for dinner tonight and I don't know _____ .

2 I know that you're a really good cook, so do you have _____ ?

3 I don't know _____ , to be honest.

4 You just need that pasta that _____ and some stock from fish as well.

5 It sounds quite complicated; I'm not _____ .

6 You need to boil them – _____ .

7 It makes _____ , trust me.

8 You just have to prepare the guacamole on the side, so avocado, tomato, a bit of chilli if _____ a bit spicy.

CONVERSATION PRACTICE

8 Work in pairs. You're going to practise a conversation.

1 Choose a Conversation practice from either Lesson 7A or Lesson 8A.

2 Look at the language in that lesson.

3 Check the meaning of anything you've forgotten with your partner.

4 Have the conversation. Try to improve on the last time you did it.

Grammar and Vocabulary

GRAMMAR

1 Complete the text with one word in each gap.

Generally [1]_____ , when I was growing up, we had a traditional Sunday lunch. As a [2]_____ , my dad made roast chicken, although on very special occasions we had beef. It was served with roast potatoes, some boiled vegetables and a sauce called 'gravy'. I loved it, but now I live on my own and I [3]_____ ever have a Sunday lunch unless I visit my parents. Basically, cooking a roast dinner takes a long time and I [4]_____ to go out till late on Saturday, so I'm usually too tired to cook a big meal the next day. Maybe if I [5]_____ cooking for more than one person, I [6]_____ make an effort, but my flat's really small and I don't have space to invite anyone. I guess I'll have to wait until I [7]_____ my own family or a bigger place! But when that time comes, it [8]_____ still be hard to make a Sunday lunch which is as good as my dad's.

2 Choose all the correct options to complete the sentences.

1 If you feel ill, *take / you'll take / you'd take* the day off.

2 Hopefully, I'll get a job after *I graduate / I'll graduate / I've graduated*.

3 If I don't find anything soon, *I might look / I'll look / I look* for a job abroad somewhere.

4 I *almost never / tend not / don't tend* to eat out. It's just too expensive.

5 I'll let you know *as soon as / when / if* I hear anything.

6 I'll call you *when / once / if* I'm ready.

7 What if he *finds out / found out / will find out*?

3 Read the first sentence in each pair. Complete the second sentence so that it has a similar meaning. Use between two and five words, including the word in bold.

1 My main meal of the day tends to be lunch.

_____ , lunch is my main meal of the day.   **WHOLE**

2 First, I'm going to speak to this customer. Then I'll deal with your problem.

I'll deal with your problem _____ this customer.   **ONCE**

3 He will never pass his final exams because he hardly ever goes to class.

If he _____ so many classes, he might actually pass his final exams.   **NOT**

4 As a rule, I only have a coffee for breakfast.

I _____ anything for breakfast.   **TEND**

5 My plan is to retire at the age of 60.

I'm going to _____ 60.   **UNTIL**

4 ▶ Listen and write the six sentences you hear.

5 Write a sentence before and after the sentences from Exercise 4 to create short dialogues.

VOCABULARY

6 Match the two parts of the collocations.

1	cause / have	a	the main ingredients
2	attend / set up	b	an alternative approach
3	introduce / adopt	c	an advanced level
4	check / list	d	a big debate
5	progress to / reach	e	my motivation
6	lose / increase	f	red meat
7	give / receive	g	a bilingual school
8	consume / preserve	h	good feedback

7 Decide if these nouns are connected to food or education.

assessment	assignment	bite	diet
discipline	flavour	lecture	module
portion	reputation	substance	vinegar

8 Complete the sentences with the correct form of the words in bold.

1 The university has lowered its _____ requirements to attract more students.   **enter**

2 I have to say, the course didn't really meet my _____ .   **expect**

3 The school has faced a lot of criticism over its pupils' poor _____ in exams.   **perform**

4 The school is actually doing well in _____ to others nearby.   **compare**

5 The new head teacher has made an interesting _____ .   **discover**

6 Unfortunately, the new approach was a complete _____ .   **fail**

7 I've been training every day and I'm beginning to see a lot of _____ .   **improve**

8 I found the meat a bit tough and _____ .   **chew**

9 Complete the email extract with one word in each gap. The first letters are given.

I studied graphic design at university and as part of our [1]c_____ we had to create design ideas for a food business. It was very [2]re_____ for me because my parents had a restaurant, so I already had some [3]kn_____ and experience, and I got a really good mark when the project was [4]a_____ . Actually, doing that project had a big [5]i_____ on me because I realized I actually really loved the food industry, and after I graduated I decided to set up my own food company. To begin with, my parents weren't very [6]en_____ , because they knew how tough the business is. But when they saw how passionate I was, they gave me a lot of support, and now they can see I'm having some [7]su_____ . I have a van selling kimchi burgers. The chilli in the kimchi means it is quite [8]sp_____ and it also has a slightly sour [9]t_____ . We sell to office workers at the weekend and go to festivals during the summer.

9 Houses

IN THIS UNIT, YOU:

- roleplay a conversation about a friend's new home
- talk about social and economic changes
- roleplay a conversation between a student and a host

SPEAKING

1 Work in pairs. Discuss the questions.

1 Look at the photo. What do you think would be good / bad about living in a place like this? Think about:

- the house.
- where it is.
- the local facilities.
- the people who live there.
- the way of life.

2 Would you like to live there? Why? / Why not?

2 Work with a new partner. Discuss the questions.

1 Which of these things are common in homes in your country?

back garden	garage	gas central heating
open fire	roof garden	spare room
swimming pool	wood floors	

2 Which things make the biggest difference to the price of a home in your country?

3 What other things have a big effect on prices? Why?

The Aurora Borealis (Northern Lights) shine over a Sami village, Finland.

Home sweet home

IN THIS LESSON, YOU:
- roleplay a conversation about a friend's new apartment
- describe different houses and flats
- practise listening to a conversation about some friends' new home
- explain how big different places are

VOCABULARY Describing homes

1 Match the sentences (1–10) with (a–j) to make descriptions.

1 It's lovely and **bright** in the summer. g
2 I'm on the sixth floor and I've got a **balcony**. d
3 It's very **central**. c
4 We're building an **extension** at the back of the house. i
5 It's very **spacious**. a
6 I live in a **newly built** apartment block. e
7 It was in a terrible **state** when we moved in. h
8 My partner has a little **studio** in the back garden. b
9 We're planning to **convert** the spare bedroom into an office. j
10 We've got a **basement**, which is really useful. f

a It's the biggest place I've ever lived in by a long way!
b He paints and writes out there.
c I can walk into town in ten minutes.
d You get a great view of the city from there.
e It's great – everything is in perfect condition.
f We keep loads of stuff down there.
g It faces south, so we get a lot of sunlight.
h We had to do quite a lot of work on it.
i It'll mean we get a much bigger kitchen.
j That'll make it easier for me to work from home.

2 **P** ▶ Listen to the words from Exercise 1 and practise saying them on their own and in a phrase. Which words / phrases do you find hard to say? Practise saying them again.

3 Work in pairs. Which of the words in bold in Exercise 1 describe where you live? Explain why.

LISTENING

4 ▶ **Listen to Andy and Gitte talking about their friends' new apartment. Answer the questions.**

1 Why did Jon and Sara move?
2 What's nice about their new place?
3 What are the problems with the new place?

5 ▶ **Listen again. Complete the sentences with two words in each gap.**

1 Did I tell you I _____ to see Jon and Sara the other day?
2 I haven't seen them _____ .
3 They said _____ 'hello' to you.
4 The last time I heard from them they were still renting that place near _____ .
5 That must be nice for them now the kids are _____ .
6 They wanted _____ for the kids.
7 It's on the _____ of an old block.
8 It's not in a _____ .
9 There's a little balcony where you can sit _____ in the summer.
10 I must go round and see them _____ .

DEVELOPING CONVERSATIONS

6 **Work in groups. Discuss the questions.**

1 How many times have you moved in your life? Why?
2 Have you ever done any work on your place? What?
3 Have you ever shared a room? How was it?

DEVELOPING CONVERSATIONS

Explaining how big a place is

We often explain the size of places by comparing them with things both speakers know, including the room we're in. We may also point, gesture and use these forms:

*The front room is huge. It's **about twice the size of / three times the size of** this room.*

*It's got a great kitchen. It's **a similar size** to yours – **maybe a bit bigger**.*

*Her garden's nice. It's **about the size of** mine. / It's **about the same size as** mine.*

*Their bathroom is enormous. It's **about from that wall over there to here**, I guess.*

7 **Complete the sentences with one word in each gap.**

1 His bedroom's tiny. It's about half ___the___ size of this room.
2 The kitchen is huge. It's three ___times___ the size of mine.
3 It's much bigger than my old place. It's maybe double the ___size___ .
4 The bathroom's OK. It's about the ___same___ size as yours – maybe a little bit bigger.
5 They've got a huge garden. It's at least ___twice___ the size of yours.
6 They've got a small basement. It's a ___similar___ size to this room – maybe a bit smaller.
7 It's not that big. It's maybe about ___from___ here to where that desk is.
8 They've got a lovely front room. It's ___about___ twice as wide as this room and maybe a little bit longer.

8 **Think of two rooms you know. How large are they compared to the room you're in now? Then work in groups. Share your ideas using the patterns in the Developing conversations box.**

CONVERSATION PRACTICE

9 Ⓜ **Work in pairs. You're going to roleplay a conversation like the one in Exercise 4. Together, invent a person and details about their new home. Think about the following.**

• the location: where they live, who with, when they moved there, and why
• the best / worst things about where they live
• the size of the place – and of the individual rooms
• the local area and facilities

10 **Work with a new partner and roleplay the conversation. Start by asking *Did I tell you I went round to see … the other day?* When you've finished, exchange roles and repeat.**

Starting out

IN THIS LESSON, YOU:
- talk about social and economic changes
- identify key facts in an article about housing in South Korea and the UK
- discuss possible solutions to housing problems
- discuss changes and why you think they happened

SPEAKING

1 Work in pairs. Discuss the questions.

1 At what age would you normally expect to do the following things? Does your partner agree?
- leave home
- start a serious long-term relationship
- buy your first place
- start earning a good salary
- start a family

2 Do you think the average age to do these things has changed in your country? Since when? In what way?

READING

2 Read the article about housing in South Korea and the UK on page 91. Then work in pairs. In what ways are the situations in South Korea and the UK similar to your country now or in the past? In what ways are they different?

3 With your partner, decide if these sentences are about South Korea (SK), the UK (UK) or both (B). Then read again and check your answers.

1 Many young people don't have the money to buy a home even if they're working.

2 Property prices have risen quickly in the last twelve months.

3 There aren't enough places for people to live.

4 The current situation may well change soon because of economic reasons.

5 House prices and high rents are having an impact on the number of children people have.

6 A lot of people from other countries buy property there as an investment.

7 Times are so hard that some young people are choosing not to have relationships.

8 People sometimes try to stop big building projects near where they live.

4 Work in groups. What do you think of the solutions to the problems talked about in the article? What might be the results?

- Make it more difficult for people from other countries to buy housing.
- Let people on lower incomes live in empty homes for free or at a discount.
- Take houses that are empty for more than six months and give them to people in need.
- Let house prices crash.
- Provide government financial help for young people to buy a home.

GRAMMAR

Present perfect simple and present perfect continuous

The present perfect simple and the present perfect continuous can both be used to talk about changes or trends from some time in the past to now.

a *Birth rates in the country **have been falling** steadily over the last decade.*

b *Over the last year, average prices **have increased** sharply.*

c *Investors from abroad **have bought** huge amounts of property.*

5 Work in pairs. Look at the examples in the Grammar box and answer the questions.

1 Which two phrases describe a period of time when the change took place?

2 Can both the present perfect simple and continuous be used with these phrases?

3 Why is the continuous used in example a?

4 Which of the two forms is used to show finished events before now?

6 Write sentences about changes using the ideas in 1–7 and a word or phrase from the box.

a lot	dramatically	fall	go down
go up	gradually	rise	slightly

1 Population / up from 57 to 60 million / 10 years

The population has been rising gradually over the last 10 years.

The population has risen from 57 to 60 million over the last 10 years.

2 The crime rate / 250,000 to 170,000 / 20 years

3 Unemployment / 8% to 15% / two years

4 House prices / down 27% / year

5 The birth rate / down from 2.4 to 1.9 / 10 years

6 The average wage / up €2 / three years

7 Petrol prices / up one dollar a litre / two months

G See Grammar reference 9B.

SPEAKING

7 Think of four social or economic changes that have taken place in your country in the last 20 years.

8 Think about what caused each of the changes you thought of in Exercise 7.

9 M Work in groups. Discuss the changes you thought of and what you think caused them. Decide what has been the most significant change. Try to agree on two possible causes.

Rooftop patios on apartment buildings in Jeju-do Province, South Korea.

Waiting for the
bubble to burst

Priced out of the market

It would be easy to mistake Lee Pyeong-su's modest apartment in Seoul for a storage room. Indeed, it was originally built to house a water tank and was only converted into a living space a few years ago. Despite the fact that it's just 23 square metres in size and freezing cold in winter, Lee is happy there – for now. 'I didn't want to spend 20 or 30 per cent of my pay cheque on housing every month, so I decided to save on housing and enjoy life,' he explains, adding that he can now afford to go snowboarding and camping more often.

Faced with high rents and rising property prices, Lee Pyeong-su is one of a growing number of South Koreans who have given up on the idea of buying their own homes. This trend is having serious consequences. Birth rates in the country have been falling steadily over the last decade and are now among the lowest in the world, as most people still believe that you need to be married before having children … and you need a home before marriage.

These pressures have led many to join what's known as the *sampo* generation. Literally, this translates as 'the three giving-up generation' and describes young people who have decided not to date, get married or have kids. Lee isn't giving up hope yet, though, and still wants to save money for a future relationship.

A worldwide problem

Of course, South Koreans aren't alone in experiencing these problems. From Lisbon to Tokyo and Vancouver to Santiago de Chile, young people in work are finding that high housing costs are limiting their opportunities to find a place of their own and settle down.

This is also true in the UK, where a shortage of housing keeps prices high. Over the last year, average prices have increased sharply and are now more than nine times the average income. The problem is particularly bad in London, where investors from abroad have bought huge amounts of property. This has

led 39-year-old Rioch Fitzpatrick, who works in the TV industry, to choose what's known as a 'microflat' – an apartment that's even smaller than Lee Pyeong-su's. At £900 a month, it's still far from cheap, but at least it's affordable and Rioch likes the area. However, there are still problems. For example, every time he wants to get to the fridge, he has to move his bike!

Hope in a crash

With the housing market the way it is, it's not surprising that many young British people expect to live at home until well into their 20s, and nearly 10% of adults aged between 30 and 34 still live with their parents. Rising prices are also affecting people's decisions about when – and whether – to start a family. As in South Korea, birth rates in Britain have been falling steadily.

So what chance is there for young people to get onto the housing ladder? Well, some experts believe their best hope is for the property market to crash. The high price of real estate is not good for standards of living or the economy in general and in many places – including South Korea – there are already signs of prices dropping.

Cultural barriers to change

However, there are also cultural attitudes that prevent change. One obvious solution to the UK's problems would be to build more apartments that are cheap to rent. However, while over 60% of South Koreans live in apartments, less than 15% of British people do. Persuading people to accept apartment living isn't easy. There's an old saying that 'an Englishman's home is his castle', and for most people – men and women – the long-term dream remains a house with a garden.

In fact, when there are plans to build new apartment blocks, local residents often protest about the increase in people, noise and traffic they would bring. Without a change of attitudes, the UK is less likely to see falling housing prices.

Room to rent

VOCABULARY A place to live

1 **Work in groups. Tell each other the best things about each of the following. Are there any things you'd like to change?**

- your room
- the place you live in
- the people you live with and / or your neighbours
- the area you live in

2 **Complete the sentences with these words and phrases.**

connected	cosy	in advance	landlord
laundry	neighbourhood	notice	outskirts
room	turns		

1 It's not very central. It's on the _____ of town.

2 There are five people living here and we all take _____ to cook.

3 It's very well _____ . It's easy to get public transport into the centre from there.

4 There's plenty of _____ for any guests who want to stay over.

5 It's a very quiet _____ . It's mostly just families and retired people round there.

6 You have to give six weeks' _____ if you want to move out.

7 You have to pay three months' rent _____ before you move in.

8 The _____ is great. He's always quick to sort out any problems.

9 It's not very big, but it's nice and _____ – especially in the winter.

10 There's no washing machine, but there's a place round the corner where you can do your _____ .

3 **Work in pairs. Discuss the questions.**

1 Which three things from Exercise 2 are important for you when looking for a place to live? What else is important?

2 Which two things might make you not want to live somewhere? Why?

LISTENING

4 ▶ **Listen to four short conversations about places to live. Match each conversation (1–4) to one of the descriptions below. There are two extra descriptions.**

a It's very spacious.

b It's cheap for a reason!

c There are lots of green spaces round there.

d It's more expensive than it used to be.

e It's a studio flat.

f It's not very central.

5 FS ▶ **When we make comparisons, *than* often sounds like /ðən/ in fast speech. Listen and write down the second part of six comparisons.**

6 FS ▶ **Listen and complete the comparisons from Exercise 5.**

7 ▶ **Listen to the four conversations again. Choose the correct option (a–c) to answer the questions (1–4).**

Conversation 1

1 Why is there a problem at the start of the conversation?

a because Paula is too early

b because Karina gets confused

c because lots of people want to rent the room

Conversation 2

2 What do the two speakers agree on?

a More and more people want to live in Northgate.

b Crime used to be a big problem there.

c It's better to buy than to rent.

Conversation 3

3 How has Woodlands changed?

a There are a lot more cars on the road now.

b The rents have gone up.

c The public transport there is better now.

Conversation 4

4 What's the caller worried about?

a the noise

b the internet connection

c the best time to visit

GRAMMAR

Comparing now and the past

We often make comparisons between situations and things as they are now and as they were in the past.

a *There are **fewer people** around **than before**.*

b *There's **much less crime** now **than there used to be**.*

c *It's **more popular than it used to be**.*

d *The highways are **much better than they were**.*

e *It was so **much cheaper in the past**.*

f *It's **not as cheap as it used to be**.*

8 **Work in pairs. Look at the examples in the Grammar box. Answer these questions.**

1 Which examples use nouns in the comparisons? Which use adjectives?

2 When do we use *fewer* to compare and when do we use *less*?

3 What time words and phrases are used to refer to the past?

9 Write comparisons with the past using these words.

1 They've cleaned up the area a lot. There / much / pollution / used to.

2 You have to pay to enter the city centre now, so there / far / cars on the road / before.

3 It / not / bad / it / past, but I still wouldn't want to live there myself.

4 They've extended the train line, so easy / get around / it / a few years ago.

5 There are lots of new places to eat and drink. It / a lot / lively / when / first moved here.

10 Work in groups. Discuss what's got better and worse about where you live in your lifetime. Talk about:

1 Traffic and public transport.

2 Green spaces for people to relax.

3 Places to eat and hang out.

4 Housing and accomodation.

G See Grammar reference 9C. ⟫

SPEAKING TASK

11 **M** Imagine you're going to study in Berlin for three months and are looking for a place to stay. Rank the homestay adverts (A–F) from 1 (= best) to 6 (= worst). Then work in pairs and explain your order.

A Close to U-Bahn underground station. 8km from the city centre – near airport, Lake Tegel and woods. Huge and beautifully-decorated house. This very friendly family offers two meals a day (€290 a week) or self-catering accommodation (€210 a week).

B This happy household consists of a young couple, two-year-old boy and baby. Breakfast and evening meal included. Lovely, spacious room in a flat in smart area near Tiergarten Park and embassies. (€350 a week)

C Bright apartment in fashionable area of Friedrichshain. Self-catering rooms for two single students sharing with a friendly lady owner. Relaxed atmosphere. Within walking distance of lively nightlife. (€200 a week)

D Beautiful country house in village 35km from Berlin. Very green! Young, friendly homeowner. High-speed wi-fi. 15 minutes' walk to train station. (€170 a week with breakfast)

E Cosy room with access to own kitchen facilities. Large old house owned by a retired couple offering quiet, comfortable accommodation. Very central. (€220 a week)

F Good-sized room in lovely apartment. A 45-minute bus ride from the centre. A very pleasant family of four (children aged 16 and 20). Beautifully-decorated apartment. Half-board (two meals a day: very good cuisine). Two dogs. Non-smoking women only. (€215 a week)

12 With your partner, roleplay a phone call between a student and the host you ranked the highest in Exercise 11. When you've finished, exchange roles and repeat.

Student A: You're the student. Ask questions about:

- the house.
- the area.
- rules.
- any special requests.

Student B: You're a homestay host. Answer A's questions. Ask some questions of your own to find more about them.

13 Work with a new partner. Tell each other which place you were interested in and if the phone call made you more or less keen on it. Explain why.

▪ MY OUTCOMES ▪

Work in pairs. Discuss the questions.

1 Which discussions did you enjoy most in this unit?

2 What useful language have you learned to talk about the topics in this unit?

3 What was most challenging about the language you used?

4 What can you do online or in daily life to revise or practise language from this unit?

City views and apartments in Friedrichshain district, Berlin, Germany.

10
Going out

IN THIS UNIT, YOU:

- invite people to a cultural event
- describe nights out
- research and plan a class outing

SPEAKING

1 Work in pairs. Discuss the questions.

1 Look at the photo. Do you like the art shown? Why? / Why not?

2 What point do you think the artist is trying to make with this piece?

3 How often do you go to art exhibitions / the cinema / the theatre?

4 What kind of art / films / theatre do you like?

5 Are there any exhibitions / films / plays on at the moment that you'd like to see?

2 Work with a new partner. Can you think of an example of each of these different kinds of people? Do you have any favourites?

a comedian	a director	a DJ
a painter	a sculptor	a singer-songwriter

Neon map of the United States, Smithsonian Art Museum, Washington DC, US.

What's on?

IN THIS LESSON, YOU:
- invite people to a cultural event
- describe and discuss cultural events
- practise listening to two friends arranging to go out
- practise explaining where places are

An outdoor performance by
theatre company Beiavass
at the Easter Festival,
Kautokeino, Norway.

VOCABULARY Cultural events

1 **Work in pairs. Decide whether the groups of words are linked to exhibitions, concerts, films or plays. Then explain how they're linked.**

1 a **portrait** / a video piece / a **landscape** / a **sculpture**

2 an **animated** comedy / a thriller / a **biography** / a documentary

3 a drama / a **tragedy** / a historical play / a **solo show**

4 a **soundtrack** / **special effects** / photography / the **plot**

5 a new **production** / acting / **lighting** / **scenery**

6 on tour / an audience / play live / a **gig**

2 **Work in pairs. Give examples of as many of the things in bold from Exercise 1 as you can.**

A: *The most famous portrait I can think of is the* Mona Lisa.

B: *I had the same idea! I guess some of Frida Kahlo's self-portraits are very famous too.*

3 **Match each question (1–6) with two possible answers (a–l).**

1 What's on in town at the moment?

2 What kind of exhibition is it?

3 What's it about?

4 When's it on?

5 Who's in it?

6 What was it like?

a The first showing's at 1:15 and then there's another at 6:45.

b Scarlett Johansson and Bradley Cooper.

c It's a drama about small-town life in 1950s Ireland.

d Not much, really. There's a musical on at the theatre that might be OK.

e It's a collection of historical objects from Central America.

f Well, the gallery's open between 10 a.m. and 8 p.m. and it's on till the end of the month.

g It was great. The scenery and the lighting were amazing.

h Nobody I've heard of.

i It's an animated movie that tells the story of life on a farm.

j There's the new film by that French director Audrey Diwan.

k It's a series of sculptures by a Romanian artist called Constantin Brâncuși.

l It was brilliant. The special effects were amazing.

4 **Work in pairs. Think of one more possible answer for each of the questions (1–6) in Exercise 3.**

LISTENING

5 ▶ **Listen to the first part of a conversation between two friends, Lyla and Zahra. Answer the questions.**

1 What does Lyla want to go and see?
2 What kind of thing is it?
3 Where's it on?

6 ▶ **Listen to the rest of the conversation. Answer the questions.**

1 Where's the gallery? Mark it on the map.
2 What time do Lyla and Zahra arrange to meet?

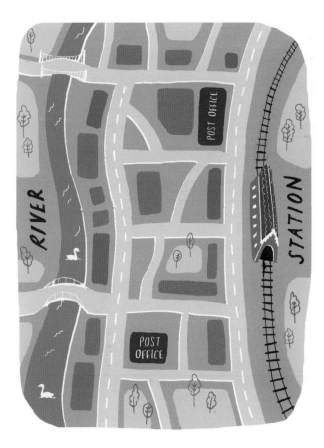

DEVELOPING CONVERSATIONS

Explaining where places are

When explaining where places are, we often start by mentioning places we think the listener will know and then giving directions from there.

You know Oxford Road, yeah? That's the main street that goes past the railway station. Well, if you have your back to the station, you turn right down Oxford Road.

7 Complete the sentences (1–5) and (6–10) with these words.

at	front	halfway	next	off

1 You know Main Street? Well, the restaurant's about _____ down there.
2 The bus stop is right in _____ of the main entrance to the station.
3 You know the post office? Well, Broad Street is the _____ turning down from there, on the other side of the road.

4 You know the cinema? Well, there's a car park _____ the back.
5 You know the main square? Well, Hope Close is one of the streets _____ there.

back	coming	facing	out	towards

6 If you have your _____ to the station, turn left.
7 If you're _____ the station, the shop will be on your right.
8 If you're _____ down the road away from the station, Beach Road's the second turning on the left.
9 If you're going up the road _____ the station and away from the river, Bond Terrace is the second on the right.
10 When you come _____ of the building, you'll see the cinema right opposite.

8 Work in pairs. Take turns to draw maps to illustrate each description in Exercise 7. As you draw, explain what your map shows. How good are your partner's drawings?

9 M **Think of three places near where you live or study to describe using language from Exercise 7. Then work in groups and explain where your places are. Can the rest of your group guess the places you mean?**

CONVERSATION PRACTICE

10 Work in pairs. Think of an exhibition, concert, play or film that you'd like to invite other students to tomorrow. It can be a real event or you can invent details. Decide what it is, why you think it'll be good, and where and when it's on.

11 Work with a new partner. Have conversations similar to the one in Exercises 5 and 6. Take turns to be Student A and Student B. Use the guide to help you.

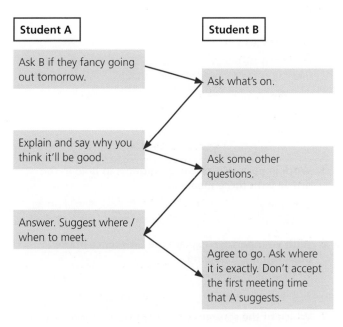

Big night out

IN THIS LESSON, YOU:
- describe nights out
- find out about nights out around the world
- practise finding specific information in an article
- practise using idioms

READING

1 Work in groups. Discuss the questions.

1 Do you go out at night much – or did you in the past? If yes, where do / did you usually go?

2 Which day of the week is the main night out where you live?

3 What do people you know normally do on a night out?

4 What's a normal time to go out and get back home after a night out?

5 How expensive is going out where you live?

2 Read the article about typical nights out around the world on page 99. Which night out sounds most like where you live?

3 Read the article again. Who says that:

1 they go to places because of the music played there?

2 they often go out into the countryside at night?

3 they're often so tired that their night out finishes early?

4 they love the view they get at the end of the day?

5 they got really into something after they moved?

6 they make a big effort with what they wear?

7 they really enjoy food prepared and eaten outside?

8 they prefer to spend time alone?

9 they can have a good meal that doesn't cost that much?

10 they sometimes stay out the whole night?

4 Work in pairs. Discuss the questions.

1 Which night out sounds the best to you? Why?

2 Which sounds the worst? Why?

GRAMMAR

Quantifiers

Quantifiers are words that go before nouns. They show the quantity of the noun we're talking about.

Very *few* locals go there.

There's *no* chance of that happening.

There *are lots of* good places to go.

5 Work in pairs. Match the quantifiers in bold in the article with these meanings.

1 not any	3 some	5 almost all
2 almost no	4 a lot of	6 all

6 With your partner, explain the difference in use between the following:

1 *a few* and *a little*	3 *much* and *many*
2 *a few* and *few*	4 *no* and *not*

7 Which of the sentences (1–6) are true for where you live? Rewrite the other sentences using different quantifiers to make them true.

1 Friday is the night that most people go out.

2 There's very little entertainment at night round here.

3 There are a lot of good clubs near here.

4 Not many people are interested in the cinema here.

5 There are a few good restaurants here.

6 There are no buses at night, so most people drive.

G See Grammar reference 10B.

VOCABULARY Idioms

V See Vocabulary reference 10B.

8 Complete the idioms with these nouns.

eye	eyes	feet	hand
lesson	middle	side	trouble

1 I asked my friend to **keep an** _____ **on** my bag, but when I came back, it had gone.

2 I won't be going there again. It was dreadful. I've **learned my** _____ now.

3 I don't feel like going out. To be honest, all I really want to do tonight is just **put my** _____ **up** and relax.

4 Going to a gig without booking is just **asking for** _____ .

5 He was just the most amazing looking person. I **couldn't take my** _____ **off** him all night!

6 We stayed **in the** _____ **of nowhere**, so there really wasn't much to do at night.

7 There was a huge crowd trying to get into the venue and it was starting to **get out of** _____ , so we left.

8 It was amazing – a bit **on the expensive** _____ , but well worth it.

9 P ▶ Listen to the idioms from Exercise 9 and practise saying them on their own and in a longer phrase. Which ones do you find hard to say? Practise saying them again.

10 Think of nights out (or in) you've had – or might have – that you can describe using at least three of the idioms in Exercise 9. Share your ideas with a partner.

My cousin was in town and he's from a little village, so when we went out we had to keep an eye on him.

SPEAKING

11 Choose one of the topics below. Think of what you want to say about it. Then work in groups and tell each other your stories. Decide which is the best night out.

1 a night out you'll always remember

2 a night out in a different town / city / country

3 a night when something unexpected happened

4 your idea of a perfect night out / in

HAVE YOUR SAY: nights around the world

The Blue Lagoon, Reykjanes Peninsula, Iceland.

As we come to the end of another working week, many of us start thinking about meeting friends and going out. We asked our readers to share with us what a typical night out where they live involves – here are five of our favourite responses.

HERDIS – AKUREYRI, ICELAND ▲

A Friday night out here in the summer is quite special, as the sun never sets, so there's basically no 'night-time'! I usually start with a light meal – sushi or something like that – and then, around midnight, I'll go and play eighteen holes of golf. I'm normally back home around 3 a.m. On Saturday, I sleep in till the afternoon and have an early dinner – maybe some grilled fish and some *skyr* (a sort of Icelandic yoghurt). I usually go for a swim in one of the natural hot springs around midnight. What I do next depends on my mood, but I enjoy my own company most, so I tend to go for a walk out in the middle of nowhere and just enjoy our amazing landscape instead.

AMINATA – ABIDJAN, CÔTE D'IVOIRE

Abidjan is widely considered to be one of the most modern West African cities, and me and my friends here love to dress up and hang out together. There's so **much** energy and colour here and there's also a lot of amazing street food. I personally love *garba*, which is *attiéké* – a bit like couscous, but made from cassava – with fried tuna and onions, tomatoes and peppers. At the weekend, I often meet friends and eat in an area called Yopougon and then we go on to a club. There aren't usually any problems in the clubs here, though there a couple of places we tend to avoid. Anyway, we have a couple of favourite places that we usually go to for the DJs and the atmosphere. Oh, and there are always **a few** restaurants open all night, in case you get hungry later.

MAYA – MONTEVIDEO, URUGUAY

On Thursday nights I occasionally go and see a comedy show, but at the weekend I mainly go clubbing as I love dancing. Because of the way I am and the way I want to live, I like to dress in a certain way, which sometimes attracts people's attention. But I'm not going to change – as Oscar Wilde said, you can never be overdressed or overeducated! My only rule is **no** high heels. I can't dance like I want to in them, and if you're out all night, your feet hurt too much by the time you get home!

LINDA – BUSAN, SOUTH KOREA

During the summer months, a Friday or Saturday night out will normally mean a trip to see the Lotte Giants baseball team. Before I came here, I had **little** interest in any sport, but one trip to a game here was enough to convert me to baseball. I go to **every** game now. The atmosphere is incredible. From start to finish, **most** people are cheering and singing the team song, even when the team is getting beaten badly. There's dancing, food, drink, good company – everything you need for a good night out. It usually finishes around nine, but by then I'm exhausted and head home rather than going on to somewhere else.

YOUNIS – MUSCAT, OMAN ▼

Many students like me go to the beach at the end of the day because we often get these amazing golden sunsets. After that, I'll sometimes go to Mutrah Souq, which is one of the biggest and oldest markets in the Middle East. It's open till ten at night and you can eat well without spending a fortune. If I'm meeting friends, we usually share a few dishes and have some coffee. Local people often go to each other's homes for dinner, and stay up talking and enjoying their guests' company into the early hours.

Muscat, Oman.

A change of plan

IN THIS LESSON, YOU:
- research and plan a class outing
- describe different kinds of events
- practise listening to friends talking about nights out
- practise talking about past plans that changed

VOCABULARY Describing events

1 Match the sentences (1–8) with the follow-up comments (a–h).

1 It was a great exhibition, but the paintings were quite **odd**.
2 It's not a terrible film, but it was a bit of a **disappointment**.
3 It was really **moving**.
4 It was completely **sold out**.
5 It **attracts** a much older crowd.
6 I saw them play live last year.
7 It was **boiling hot** in there.
8 The first band were great, but the main band were **rubbish**.

a Honestly, we were all sweating so much.
b I can't really describe them or say why I like them.
c I mean, it wasn't as great as everyone's been saying.
d It was absolutely **packed** in there.
e I was in tears by the end.
f They were so bad we actually left **halfway through.**
g We were the youngest people there – by about 20 years!
h They were **promoting** their latest album.

2 Work in groups. Think of examples of the following.

1 two artists / musicians / films that you think are quite odd
2 two films / TV shows / news events that you found really moving
3 two films / exhibitions / events / places that you agree were a bit of a disappointment
4 two places that might get absolutely packed
5 two other things you could leave halfway through, apart from a concert
6 two other things you could promote, apart from an album

LISTENING

3 ▶ Listen to three conversations about what people did last night. Answer the questions about each conversation.

1 What kind of event was it?
2 Did the speaker change their plans? If so, why?
3 Did they have a good night? Why? / Why not?
4 Did their experiences match what other people had said about the event?

4 **FS** ▶ In fast speech, the words *is* and *was* can sound very similar. Listen to nine extracts. Which contain *is* and which contain *was*?

5 ▶ Work in pairs. Are these statements true (T) or false (F)? How do you know? Then listen again and check your ideas.

Conversation 1

1 The film wasn't as good as the woman thought it'd be.
2 She thought the main story was great.
3 The man never watches Hollywood films.

Conversation 2

4 Hans picked his friend up at seven.
5 There was a massive queue outside the club.
6 It was so busy the speaker didn't have fun.

Conversation 3

7 Clara had bought an extra ticket for the woman.
8 Plenty of people have written good things about the play.
9 The man doesn't like the sound of the play.

6 Work in pairs. Discuss the questions.

1 Who do you think had the best night? Why?
2 Can you think of any recent films that have been heavily promoted?
3 Do you ever go to concerts? If yes, what was the last one you went to? Was it any good?
4 Can you think of anything that's had great reviews recently?

People dance at a club in Berlin, Germany.

GRAMMAR

Future in the past

We can talk about plans, promises or predictions made in the past using *was / were going to* + verb or *would / wouldn't* + verb.

a *Hans **was going to pick** me **up** at seven.*

b *I **was going to stay** in.*

c *It was brilliant – much better than I thought it **was going to be**.*

d *I didn't think it**'d be** anything special.*

e *I said I**'d go** with her.*

7 **Work in pairs. Look at the examples in the Grammar box. Answer the questions.**

1 Which example(s) describe plans, promises or predictions?

2 In examples a and b, did the plans actually happen? Why? / Why not?

3 What were the original thoughts / promises that examples c, d and e describe?

8 **Make sentences using these ideas (1–6). Link the ideas using *but* and *so*.**

1 I / go out / feel exhausted / just stay in and go to bed early

   I was going to go out, but I felt exhausted, so I just stayed in and went to bed early.

2 They / have a barbecue / start raining / have to cook indoors instead

3 We / go to the beach for the day / miss the train / end up going to the park instead

4 I / stay in and study / a friend call me / go out / meet him

5 She promised / give me a lift / she forget / have to get a taxi instead

6 I think / be too expensive / a friend give me a ticket / I get in free

9 **Work in pairs. Think of as many different endings for each sentence as you can.**

1 We were going to stay with friends, but …

2 I was going to go out last night, but in the end …

3 She said she'd call me, but …

4 I was going to buy a new one, but in the end …

5 I didn't think we'd get there in time, but …

10 **Work in groups. Discuss the questions. Use the future in the past to explain your ideas.**

1 Can you think of a time you had a last-minute change of plan? What happened? Did it turn out well / badly?

2 Have you ever been very disappointed or pleasantly surprised by a film / party / etc. you went to? Why?

3 Can you think of any predictions that have failed to come true?

G   See Grammar reference 10C.

SPEAKING TASK

11 **Work in pairs. You're going to plan a class outing.**

1 Carry out a survey. Talk to as many other students as you can and find out:

   • what kind of activities they like doing.

   • what kind of places they most like going to in their free time.

   • what time of day they usually go out.

   • whether they like to have definite, fixed plans or whether they're a bit more flexible.

2 Decide what the best activities for the class would be, where to go and when, and how fixed the plan should be.

12 **M** **Work with another pair. Compare your plans. How similar are your ideas? Can you agree on an ideal outing for the whole class?**

MY OUTCOMES

Work in pairs. Discuss the questions.

1 What was interesting about the topic of the texts in this unit?

2 What useful language have you learned in this unit?

3 Was any part of this unit particularly challenging? If so, in what way?

4 How will you practise the language and situations from this unit?

Writing a formal email

IN THIS LESSON, YOU:
- write a formal email requesting changes to a plan
- discuss ways of organizing different kinds of events
- practise reading an email that asks for changes to a plan
- identify useful phrases in a formal email
- practise describing contrasting statements and ideas

SPEAKING

1 Work in groups. Discuss the questions.

1 What things need doing when you organize the following?
   - a study / work meeting
   - a conference
   - a wedding
   - a party
   - a group trip

2 Which event above do you think would be the most difficult to organize? Why?

3 Have you ever been involved in organizing any of these events? How easy was it?

4 Did you have to make any changes or compromises?

WRITING

2 A group of students are going on a trip to Valencia, Spain. One of them has written to the organizers to ask for a change to the programme. Read the email. Then work in pairs and answer the questions.

1 How does Simon try to persuade Ms Roberts to agree to the changes?

2 If you were Ms Roberts, would you agree to the change? Why? / Why not?

3 The email should have paragraphs to organize and make the information easier to read. With your partner, decide where you would start each new paragraph.

To: roberts14@ex-spain-ge.es
From: simonholden@exploremail.com

Dear Ms Roberts,

I am writing on ¹**behalf** of the students who are going on the trip to Valencia in October. Firstly, can we say ²**thank you** for all your hard work organizing the trip. On the ³**whole**, it looks great and we are all very much looking forward to it. However, we were ⁴**wondering** if we could possibly suggest one change. The Sunday after we arrive, there is a motorcycle Grand Prix in Cheste and ten of us would like to go. Currently, we are ⁵**scheduled** to go to an exhibition at the Modern Art Institute that day and are free after lunch. Although we are sure the exhibition would be fascinating, it seems a shame to miss such a big event while we are there and Cheste is supposed to have a very special atmosphere. The four who are not interested in the motorcycling said they would not mind missing the exhibition either. ⁶**Alternatively**, we could go to the exhibition on Wednesday afternoon, which is currently free for shopping. We can take public transport to the Grand Prix as it is only 30km from Valencia. Obviously, we would pay for any extra cost. We are sorry if this causes any ⁷**inconvenience**, but we are all very keen to go. We really hope this change is possible and thank you again for all your work putting together the programme – we very much ⁸**appreciate** it.

Best wishes,

Simon Holden

City views from El Miguelete Tower, Valencia, Spain.

4 The features (1–5) are common in more formal writing. Find an example of each feature in the email.

1 Address people using their title and surname.
2 Use full forms, not contractions (e.g. *did not* rather than *didn't*).
3 Use polite question phrases.
4 Use more formal words (e.g. *request* rather than *ask for*).
5 Use formal ways to sign off.

5 Look at the words in bold in the email. Identify the whole phrase you could use for a similar email.

I am writing on behalf of ...

6 Work in pairs. Complete the email with the phrases from Exercise 5. Don't look back at Simon's email.

Dear Mr Wong,

I am writing ¹ _____ the students who are going on the trip to Whistler this weekend.

Firstly, we would like to ² _____ the work that has gone into organizing this trip. ³ _____ , it looks excellent and we are all looking forward to it.

However, we ⁴ _____ maybe suggest one small change. We ⁵ _____ leave Vancouver at ten and arrive around midday. Although we understand that no-one wants to get up too early at the weekend, we would really like to leave an hour or two earlier so we can do some skiing and snowboarding on arrival.
⁶ _____ return home later in the day.

We are sorry if this ⁷ _____ , but we are all very keen to make the most of the snow. We really hope this small change will possible and thank you again for all the work you have put into organizing this trip. We really ⁸ _____ .

Best regards,
Bruna Couto

USEFUL LANGUAGE

However, although and *but*

However, although and *but* can all be used to introduce contrasting statements or ideas. While they have a similar meaning, they use different grammar.

Although *we are sure the exhibition is fascinating, it seems a shame to miss such a big event.*

On the whole, it looks great and we are all really looking forward to it. **However**, *we were wondering if we could possibly suggest one change.*

We are sorry if this causes any inconvenience, **but** *we are all really keen to go.*

7 Complete the rules with *however, although* or *but.*

1 _____ and _____ connect two parts of the same sentence. _____ usually starts the sentence, but it can also come in the middle.
2 _____ connects a second sentence to an idea in a previous sentence. It usually starts the second sentence and is followed by a comma, but it can come in the middle or at the end of the second sentence, with a comma usually used before it.

8 Complete the sentences with *however, although* or *but.*

1 _____ it would be nice to visit the museum, we don't have enough time.
2 It's a very full programme. _____ , there is space for one more visit on Monday afternoon.
3 We would really like to go to the exhibition, _____ we were wondering if we could go on Tuesday instead of Sunday.
4 Thanks again for your help. _____ we realize these last-minute changes are inconvenient, we are sure they will improve the programme.
5 On the whole, everything seems to be very clear. I do have couple of queries, _____ .

9 Rewrite each pair of sentences as one sentence. Use the word in brackets and the correct punctuation.

1 Giving all the participants a souvenir is a nice idea. It might be a bit too expensive. (but)
2 I personally like rock music. Some of those attending might prefer something different. (although)
3 The menu for the dinner looks great. I think there should be a better option for vegetarians. (however)

PRACTICE

10 **M** Work in pairs. Plan and write a programme for one of these events.

- a week-long programme for a group of students visiting where you live
- an activity programme for a company team-building day

11 Swap your programme from Exercise 10 with another pair. With your partner, discuss what you would like to change in the programme if you were going, and why and how you would do this.

12 Write a formal email to the organizers requesting your changes. Use as much of the language from this lesson as you can. Write 150–200 words.

13 Exchange your email with a different partner. Can you see any ways your partner's email could be improved? Discuss these questions.

1 Have they used the features described in Exercise 4?
2 Have they organized their email into paragraphs correctly?
3 Have they used phrases from Simon's email?
4 Have they used words to introduce contrasting statements / ideas?

VIDEO Out and about

1 Work in pairs. Discuss the questions.

1 Which room do you spend most time in at home? Why?

2 Do you have any rules in your house?

Understanding accents

Some accents add a /k/ sound after a /ŋ/ sound, so *thing* /θɪŋ/ may sound more like *think* /θɪŋk/.

2 ▣ **Watch four people answer the same questions. How much can you remember about what they said? Then work in pairs. How many different rooms did they mention? What did they say?**

3 ▣ **Watch again. Match two sentences with each speaker.**

a They spend a lot of time alone in their room / house.

b People shouldn't come into their room without warning.

c People shouldn't wear shoes in the house.

d People should keep things very tidy.

e They don't have any brothers or sisters.

f They play a musical instrument.

g They like working with their hands and making things.

h Their favourite room has a lot of light.

4 Discuss the questions with your partner.

1 Do you like spending a lot of time on your own?

2 Do you know any families where one member spends a lot of time away from home? Why? Do they feel positively about it, like Nurgül?

3 Have you ever made anything? Do you know anyone who does woodwork, sewing, etc.? What do they make?

4 Do you know anyone who is a bit of a control freak? Give examples of what they do.

VIDEO Developing conversations

5 ▣ **You're going to watch two people arranging to go out. Watch and take notes.**

6 ▣ **Work in pairs. Compare what you understood. Watch again if you need to.**

7 FS ▣ **Watch again. Complete the sentences with three to five words in each gap.**

1 Are you free this weekend _____ ?

2 Do _____ *Avatar*?

3 OK, so _____ the station you've got supermarket on the left and High Street on the right.

4 So it's a bit hidden in that archway. _____ haven't seen it before.

5 _____ tickets and then …?

6 Don't you still owe me from that _____ ?

7 OK, _____ the tickets are only about 11 quid each.

8 I think the film starts about quarter past eight, so eight _____ !

CONVERSATION PRACTICE

8 Work in pairs. You're going to practise a conversation.

1 Choose a Conversation practice from either Lesson 9A or Lesson 10A.

2 Look at the language in that lesson.

3 Check the meaning of anything you've forgotten with your partner.

4 Have the conversation. Try to improve on the last time you did it.

Grammar and Vocabulary

GRAMMAR

1 Complete the text with one word in each gap.

1 In general, the crime rate [1] _____ fallen quite dramatically [2] _____ recent years. There are [3] _____ robberies than there [4] _____ five years ago and there is [5] _____ violent crime. There were [6] _____ any murders last year. This may well have something to do with the fact that there are [7] _____ police officers on the street than there [8] _____ to be.

However, online crime has [9] _____ increasing steadily over the [10] _____ few years. [11] _____ bank account is completely safe anymore and [12] _____ bank is working hard to improve online security.

2 Choose the correct option to complete the sentences.

1 House prices have *increased / been increasing* 50% in the last six months.

2 I have *little / few* interest in politics.

3 *All the / Every* people I work with really love the new boss we've got.

4 It was much better than I thought it *will / would* be.

5 The cost of energy isn't *as / more* low as it used to be.

6 We *are / were* going to go and see a movie, but we didn't in the end.

7 It's not a bad area, but it's not as *well / good* as it used to be.

8 Unemployment *has / has been* fallen steadily over recent years.

9 Would you like a *few / little* more cake?

10 I'm a bit fitter than I *would be / was* this time last year.

3 Read the first sentence in each pair. Complete the second sentence so that it has a similar meaning. Use between two and five words, including the word in bold.

1 It's better now than it used to be.
   It was _____ than it is now. **PAST**

2 There are fewer jobs available these days.
   There _____ jobs available. **USED**

3 I was really surprised by how good it was.
   I honestly didn't _____ anything special, but it was amazing. **THINK**

4 They said they don't expect to find any survivors.
   They said there's _____ finding any survivors. **CHANCE**

5 Very few museums are free to get into these days.
   _____ an entrance fee these days. **CHARGE**

6 Inflation was 5% at the start of the year and now it's almost 18%.
   Inflation _____ the start of the year. **DRAMATICALLY**

4 ▶ Listen and write the six sentences you hear.

VOCABULARY

5 Match the two parts of the collocations.

1	learn	a	quite a young crowd
2	attract	b	their latest album
3	keep	c	three months' notice
4	put	d	an extension
5	promote	e	halfway through
6	give	f	my feet up
7	build	g	an eye on my bag
8	leave	h	my lesson

6 Decide if these words and phrases are connected to houses, the arts or areas.

balcony	cosy	green spaces	in a state
neighbourhood	newly built	outskirts	plot
scenery	sculpture	portrait	well connected

7 Complete the sentences with the correct form of the words in bold.

1 We went to see this really funny new stand-up _____ last night. **comedy**

2 There's a new _____ of my favourite Shakespeare play on at the National Theatre. **produce**

3 It was good. It was a _____ play set in the 1930s. **history**

4 It's an amazing play. The acting's wonderful and the _____ is very clever. **light**

5 I'd like to study _____ at art college if I can. **photograph**

6 It's a nice place. It's much more _____ than her old flat. **space**

7 It's not a cheap place to live, but it is quite _____ . **centre**

8 To be honest, I thought the special effects were a bit of a _____ . **disappoint**

8 Complete the text with one word in each gap. The first letters are given.

My partner and I take [1]t _____ to choose things to go to and last week, I was the one to choose. We went to see this new [2]an _____ film. It was much better than I thought it would be, actually. It was surprisingly [3]m _____ – I even cried a bit at the end! The [4]so _____ was amazing too. It's lucky we booked in [5]a _____ because it was totally [6]s _____ o _____ . The building the cinema is in used to be a factory, but they [7]co _____ it a few years ago – and it was absolutely [8]pa _____ that night. It's very [9]ce _____ too, so it was easy to get home from, even if you live out in the middle of [10]n _____ like we do.

11

The natural world

IN THIS UNIT, YOU:

- share stories about encounters with animals
- tell each other about different challenges, ambitions and achievements
- discuss how the profits from natural resources might best be used

SPEAKING

1 Work in groups. Discuss the questions.

1 Look at the photo. Why do you think these animals might be in danger?

2 What animals or natural areas are under threat in your country? Is anything done to protect them?

3 Are there many charities supporting animals in your country? Do you think they do a good job? Why? / Why not?

4 Would you volunteer to help animals or support an animal charity?

2 Work in pairs. Discuss the questions.

1 Are pets popular where you live? What kind are most popular?

2 Are there many abandoned pets where you live? How are they treated?

3 Would you ever take an abandoned animal as a pet? Why? / Why not?

Releasing olive ridley turtles on the beach in Baja California Sur, Mexico.

So what happened?

SPEAKING

1 Work in groups. Look at the photos in File 12 on page 198 and discuss these questions.

1 Which of these animals do you like? Why?

2 Are you scared of any of these animals? Why?

3 Would any of them make good pets?

VOCABULARY Identifying animals

2 Work in pairs. Check you understand the words in bold. Then think of two animals the speaker may have seen or heard for each sentence.

1 Oh, look! What's that thing **crawling** along the floor? Can you catch it?

2 What was that? Did you see it? It just disappeared into that **hole** in the ground.

3 What's that lying on that **branch** in the tree?

4 It jumped out and **raced** across the road. We were lucky not to hit it.

5 What's that up there above the cliff? It's got huge **wings**.

6 You could see it just below **the surface of the water** and it looked like it was **chasing** something.

7 Look! Two backs above the surface of the water! You can see them there **in the distance**.

8 Can you hear that? There's something moving around **in the bushes**. Look – the branches are moving.

9 You can hear their **calls** at night. They make an awful noise.

10 I disturbed their **nest** by mistake and had to **run away** fast before they attacked me.

11 We found it **abandoned** in our street. It was such a cute little thing. We had to keep it.

3 🅿 ▶ Listen to words from Exercise 2 said on their own and then in a phrase. Practise saying them. Which words / phrases do you find hard to say? Practise saying them again.

4 Work in pairs. Tell your partner about six animals you've seen in the wild or in your town / city. Use language from Exercise 2.

When I went to Spain last year, I saw some eagles with big wings flying high above our campsite.

The other day, I saw a rat crawling along the railway tracks.

LISTENING

5 ▶ Listen to three stories about animals. Answer the questions.

1 What animal(s) is each story about?

2 Where were the speakers at the time? What were they doing?

3 How did each speaker feel?

6 ▶ Work in pairs. Decide in which story you heard the sentences (a–i). Explain how you think each sentence is connected to the story. Then listen again and check your ideas.

a I really thought they were going to eat me.

b I managed to catch it with a box.

c They were all making this awful noise.

d It's so cute!

e It must have escaped from somewhere.

f She crawled through a little hole.

g Honestly, I hope I never see another crocodile in my life!

h We were forced to call the fire service in the end.

i Everyone ran away.

Humpback whales at Inside Passage, Southeast Alaska, US.

GRAMMAR

Managed to, be able to and *be forced to*

We can use *managed to* + verb or *was / were able to* + verb to talk about an ability to do a specific action in the past.

They **managed to stop** them by shouting and waving these sticks at them, so I **was able to escape**.

He was here for ages, but he still **didn't manage to** solve the problem.

We **weren't able to help** them, unfortunately.

We can use *was / were forced to* + verb to show that something was the only possible action in a particular situation.

We **were forced to** call the fire service in the end.

7 Complete the sentences with one word or two words in each gap.

1   I heard the wolves calling, but we _____ actually manage to see any.

2   We took the animal to the vet's, but sadly they _____ able to save it.

3   We were _____ to take a longer route because the river had flooded, but luckily we still _____ to get there on time.

4   We _____ to get quite high up the mountain, but before we got to the top, there was a storm and we _____ forced to turn back.

5   I wasn't _____ to reach it because it was too high up, but my friend Sensio _____ to.

8 Work in pairs. Choose two of these situations. Write two sentences for each situation using *managed to*, *be able to* or *be forced to* that explain what happened and how the situation was resolved.

1   Your cat got stuck in a tree.

2   You were driving in the countryside and some sheep ran out in front of you.

3   You fell and hurt yourself when walking in the mountains.

4   Your bag was stolen just before you travelled home from holiday.

5   You locked yourself out of your second-floor flat.

G See Grammar reference 11A.

DEVELOPING CONVERSATIONS

Helping people tell stories

Good listeners ask questions when people tell stories to show interest and encourage the speaker to share more details with them.

A: *I really thought they were going to eat me.*

B: **Really?** That sounds terrifying! **So what happened?**

A: *Well, luckily, the guides managed to stop the lizards.*

An urban fox in London, UK.

9 Complete the conversations with these questions.

> Seriously?   So what happened in the end?   What?
> What was that?   What was that doing there?

1   A: You'll never guess what happened last night.

    B: Go on. [1] _____

    A: Well, I was walking home when I suddenly saw a horse standing there in the street!

2   A: I saw something really strange while we were away.

    B: Oh yeah? [2] _____

    A: We saw this whale stuck on the beach.

    B: [3] _____ Still alive?

    A: Yeah, it was actually quite upsetting! We phoned the police to see if they could organize help.

3   A: I was just about to put my shoes on when I found a scorpion hiding in one of the shoes!

    B: Really? [4] _____

    A: I don't know. I guess it was just looking for somewhere to sleep.

4   A: Then, after we failed to catch it the first time, it ran away up a tree and we spent hours trying to persuade it to come down.

    B: Oh no! [5] _____

    A: Well, eventually we gave up, but an hour later it walked into the kitchen, looking for its dinner!

10 ▶ Listen and check your answers. Then work in pairs and practise reading the conversations.

CONVERSATION PRACTICE

11 Choose one of the story ideas below. Spend a few minutes making notes on it, then work with a partner. Tell each other your stories, starting with *Did I tell you what happened … ?* Use the language in Exercise 9 to help your partner.

- a story about a pet you have / had
- a story about a time you saw a wild animal
- a story based on the ideas in Exercise 9
- a story based on one of the photos in this lesson

Challenges and achievements

IN THIS LESSON, YOU:
• tell each other about different challenges
• discuss your relationship with nature and places you've been to
• practise reading the story of a mountain climber and making personal responses

SPEAKING

1 Work in groups. Discuss the questions.

1 Do you spend much time in nature? Where do you go?

2 Have you been to any of these places? If so, When? Where? What was it like? If not, which would you like to visit? Why?

- a desert
- rainforest
- a glacier
- a mountain peak
- a long way out on the sea / ocean

3 Do you know any stories of people doing the following challenges? Were they successful? Why? / Why not?

- sailing round the world
- reaching the North Pole
- crossing a desert
- jumping from a great height

READING

2 Work in pairs. Read the first three paragraphs of the article about climbing Chomolungma on page 111. Then discuss the questions.

1 What kind of skills and equipment do you think you need to reach the peak?

2 What kinds of things might go wrong?

3 What things do you think were different 80 years ago?

3 Read the rest of the article. Decide what similarities (if any) Maurice Wilson had with modern amateur climbers.

4 Work in pairs. Are these statements true (T), false (F) or not given (NG)? Then read again and check your answers.

1 The Chomolungma climbing season is in the summer.

2 Not everyone pays as much as $160,000 to get to the top of Chomolungma.

3 Wilson had a physical disability.

4 He flew to the East Rongbuk Glacier.

5 People who had organized expeditions to climb Chomolungma supported Wilson.

6 Wilson was the first person to go beyond 6,500 metres.

7 He had some support to get beyond Camp 2.

8 The Sherpas didn't go further up the mountain because they thought Wilson would be fine.

9 Wilson didn't reach the top of Chomolungma.

5 M Work in groups. Discuss the questions.

1 What do you think of Wilson's story?

2 What do you think drove him?

3 What do you think generally about climbing Chomolungma?

4 Have you heard of any similar stories or issues in the news?

6 ▶ Work in pairs. Listen to someone talking about the article you read. How does she answer the questions in Exercise 5? Do you agree with the speaker? Why? / Why not?

VOCABULARY Challenges and achievements

7 Complete the sentences with these pairs of words and phrases.

ambition / achieving my goal   barriers / disabled
challenge / get through the pain   set / missed its target
dreamed / my dream's come true
drowning / overcame my fear
took several attempts / determination

1 A year ago I did the Marathon des Sables _____ , a 254 km race through the Sahara Desert. It was very tough, but I managed to _____ and finish.

2 Until last year, I'd never been in the sea because I was so scared of _____ , but last year I had some swimming lessons and I finally _____ .

3 I always _____ of becoming a marine biologist and now _____ because I've got a job protecting sea life in the Pacific Ocean.

4 The government _____ a goal of planting six million new trees last year and it only just _____ .

5 My biggest ever challenge was giving up smoking. It _____ and a lot of strength and _____ , but I finally managed to do it. My son is very proud of me!

6 My _____ is to become a millionaire before I'm 40 and I'm well on the way to _____ .

7 I'm blind, so I think getting my degree and a good job has been a big achievement as you have to overcome many _____ when you're _____ .

8 Work in pairs. Decide which idea in Exercise 7 is the greatest achievement and which is the easiest.

SPEAKING

9 Work in groups. Choose two sets of questions to discuss.

1 Have you heard of any other very tough races or challenges related to mountains? Why do you think people want to take on these challenges?

2 What challenges does the planet face? Do you know any goals that the government has set to deal with them? Are they hitting those targets or missing them?

3 What examples can you think of successful people who have overcome a barrier? How easy it for everyone to achieve their dreams and ambitions where you live?

4 What are your three biggest achievements so far? Why? What happened?

Dangerous Amateurs

Amateurs on Chomolungma may be in the news, but it's an old story, as the strange case of Maurice Wilson illustrates.

Maurice Wilson

Looking at the photo – the clear blue sky and the queues of people – you might think this is a group of walkers on a summer's day, climbing a popular local peak. But this is Chomolungma (also known as Mount Everest) – almost 9,000 metres high, with temperatures of -26 degrees and winds blowing at 60 km/h on a 'normal' day in the climbing season. What's more, at this height, the lack of oxygen can cause confusion, slow your movements and make it almost impossible to keep warm. It's so dangerous they call this place the 'death zone'.

The photo shows the increasing problem of amateurs on this mountain – people without the necessary skills who don't fully understand the risks involved. They just have the ambition to reach 'the top of the world' and are rich enough to pay up to $160,000 for everything, including experienced climbers and local Sherpa people to carry equipment and guide them. Apart from adding to the environmental damage caused by climbers, these amateurs simply can't cope when things go wrong, and that puts *everyone's* lives in danger.

Amateurs climbing Chomolungma is not a new thing. In the 1930s, a man called Maurice Wilson attempted to climb the mountain. His plan was to fly from the UK and land on the East Rongbuk glacier at the foot of the mountain, and from there go to the top. There were only two problems – he didn't know how to fly a plane and he'd never climbed before.

In fact, these weren't the only barriers to achieving his goal. He'd been shot during the First World War and couldn't fully use his left arm. Previous organizers of Everest expeditions thought he was a fool and tried to block his

efforts. It's incredible, then, that after just two months of flying lessons, he managed to fly solo all the way to India in a tiny second-hand plane – a huge achievement for the time. The 4,500-mile journey had taken 17 days, but his final destination was still 300 miles away. He was forced to walk there, with the support of three local Sherpa people.

When the group arrived in Rongbuk, they stayed at the monastery there, but Wilson was impatient to climb and soon set off up the glacier on his own with a 20-kilo rucksack. He frequently got lost among the towers of ice and it took him three days to reach Camp 2, established by a previous expedition. There was climbing equipment there, but he ignored it and continued up the mountain. At 6,500 metres a storm hit and he was forced to sit in his tent for two days and nights. When the storm eased, he struggled back to Rongbuk – starving, experiencing problems with his sight and in great pain. But he was determined to try again.

He rested for 18 days before his second attempt. This time, he took two of the Sherpas to carry supplies up the mountain and guide him through the glacier. They managed to go higher, to Camp 3, before strong winds and snow stopped them going any further. After the weather cleared, Wilson climbed again on his own, reaching around 7,000 metres before returning to Camp 3. He was by this time exhausted – the many days spent so high up were giving him headaches. The Sherpas desperately tried to persuade him to give up, but Wilson insisted on a final attempt. The last words in his diary are still optimistic: 'Off again, gorgeous day.' He never returned. His body was found a year later. He was wearing grey trousers and a purple jumper – almost as if ready for a walk in the park on a cold London afternoon.

Climbers queue near the summit of Chomolungma, Nepal.

Natural resources

VOCABULARY Natural resources

1 Work in pairs. Don't use a dictionary. Discuss what you think the words in bold mean or decide how to translate them into your first language.

1 The US has the second greatest level of **natural resources** in the world – mainly coal, wood and gas.

2 China is the biggest **producer** of rare metals, which are used in a lot of green technology.

3 Saudi Arabia **exports** most of its oil to other countries, while it **imports** about 80% of its food.

4 Most countries have **renewable** resources like wind, sunshine and water. Uruguay now gets 98% of its electricity from renewables.

5 Morocco is doing a lot to **exploit** the long hours of hot sunshine it gets. It's building a series of **solar farms** that aim to provide clean energy in the future.

6 South Africa has the deepest **mine** in the world. Miners work almost four kilometres below the surface of the earth to **extract** the gold which is found there.

7 In the UK, there have been protests against mining coal and oil, because burning them is a cause of **global warming**.

2 Work in pairs. Discuss the questions.

1 What do you think are the most valuable natural resources now? Why?

2 Do you think any natural resources shouldn't be exploited? Why? Are there any that should be exploited more? How?

3 Do you know what your country's biggest exports and imports are?

4 Are there any mines in your country? Where? Have you ever visited one?

LISTENING

3 ▶ Work in pairs. You're going to hear the introduction to a short talk on the 'resource curse'. Discuss what you think this is. Then listen and check your ideas.

4 FS ▶ Listen to six extracts from the talk and write down the words / phrases that introduce an explanation or example.

5 ▶ Read the notes (1–8). Then listen to the rest of the talk and complete them with one to three words in each gap.

According to various academics, having large amounts of natural resources may be a barrier to investment for these reasons:

Conflict

1 Locals can be forced to _____ .

2 Regions try to _____ and armies may be sent to defend access to the resource.

Corruption

3 'Presents' are given to politicians for access to the resource or to avoid rules that _____ .

4 Politicians pay officials _____ .

Value of resource

5 Countries with a resource may need help because they _____ .

6 Bigger profits are made by _____ , which is done abroad.

Price changes

7 A high price for resource = _____ high, which makes selling products difficult.

8 Variations in price make it difficult _____ and develop other industries.

6 Work in pairs. Discuss the questions.

1 Do you think the notes cover the argument of the talk clearly? Why? / Why not? Is there anything you would add or change?

2 In what way does each of the four factors of the 'resource curse' create a barrier to developing a country?

3 Does the resource curse make sense to you? Why? / Why not?

7 ▶ Listen to the last part of the talk about a country that has a natural resource. Does the example support the resource curse theory?

8 Work in groups. Discuss the questions.

1 Can you think of examples where a country has suffered from the negative aspects of having natural resources?

2 What lessons can we learn from the example of Norway? Can you think of other countries that have managed to avoid or deal with issues related to managing natural resources?

GRAMMAR

Passives

We use a passive when we want to make the object of a verb the subject of the sentence.

a *Energy companies <u>discovered</u> **oil** off the coast.* (*oil* = object of the active verb)

b ***Oil** <u>was discovered</u> off the coast.* (*oil* = subject of the passive verb)

Passive forms use the appropriate form of *be* + the past participle of the verb.

c *Bigger profits **are** generally **made** by foreign companies producing products.*

d *Profits **have** always **been saved** in a public fund.*

e *Control of the resource **can** also **be won** with money.*

9 Look at the examples in the Grammar box. Answer these questions.

1 Do we know who or what 'does' each action in the examples? If yes, how do you know?

2 Why are different forms of *be* used in examples b–e?

3 Where do adverbs like *also* or *generally* go in a passive form?

10 Complete the sentences with the correct passive form of the verbs in brackets.

1 Most of their gas and oil _____ from abroad. (import)

2 The city grew a lot after gold _____ near there. (discover)

3 Wind farms _____ all over the country at the moment. (construct)

4 Solar energy is cheap here because it _____ by the government. (partly pay for)

5 Locals don't want the mining to take place because they believe their houses _____ . (damage)

6 The country has a lot of natural resources that _____ , but the public think the environment should _____ instead. (still exploit, protect)

7 A lot of money _____ from natural resources there, but it _____ well. (make, not invest)

11 Work in pairs. Use the passive to talk about and explain the following.

1 changes in how energy is produced

2 a new city / city that has grown a lot

3 what aspects of society have been improved

4 how the environment is doing in your country

G See Grammar reference 11C. »

SPEAKING TASK

12 Imagine a new natural resource was suddenly discovered in your country. What should the profits be spent on? Read the ideas below and then think of one more. Rank the ideas from 1 (= most important) to 7 (= least important).

a building more airports and motorways

b providing free university-level education for everyone

c building factories that can process the raw material

d giving $10,000 to every family

e removing barriers for people to get jobs

f improving healthcare

g increasing the wages of people enforcing laws (police, tax inspectors, judges, etc.)

13 **M** Work in groups. Compare your lists then try to agree on the best two ways to spend the money.

■ MY OUTCOMES ■

Work in pairs. Discuss the questions.

1 Which reading or listening texts were the most interesting?

2 What useful language have you learned to talk about the natural world?

3 What did you find hard to learn or use in this unit?

4 What do you most need to revise from this unit? How will you do that?

Production in the Gachsaran oil field, Iran.

12

People I know

IN THIS UNIT, YOU:

- have conversations about people you know and find similarities
- discuss the role of grandparents
- discuss findings of studies on friendship and age

SPEAKING

1 Work in pairs. Discuss the questions.

1 Look at the photo. What do you think the relationship is between the different people?

2 What are the advantages and disadvantages of living with your extended family?

3 Who are the oldest and youngest people in your family?

2 Talk to other students. Find out who:

1 lives with more than one generation of their family.

2 has the most brothers and sisters.

3 has the most nephews and nieces.

4 has the oldest relative.

5 has family members living in another country.

3 Work with your partner again and compare what you found out. What was the most interesting thing you learned?

Three generations of the Moraes family meet for Saturday lunch in Belo Horizonte, Brazil.

Family and friends

IN THIS LESSON, YOU:
• have conversations about people you know and find similarities
• practise describing and explaining character
• practise listening to five people talk about a shared friend

VOCABULARY Talking about character

1 Complete the sentences with these words.

been there	charming	direct	make fun of
make the most of	mature	panicking	sensitive
side		sorts out	stubborn	takes work seriously

1 She's very reliable – she's always _____ for me if I've been struggling.

2 He used to _____ me when I was growing up. Brothers can be quite cruel.

3 He's very smart, but he's a bit lazy and doesn't have the ambition to _____ his intelligence.

4 She's always very calm and relaxed in a crisis when everyone else is _____ .

5 He's very _____ . I mean, he gets upset very easily and he takes things quite personally.

6 In normal life, she's very relaxed and takes things easy, but if you ever play a game with her, you'll really see her competitive _____ come out.

7 He can be very kind and _____ . I just wish he was like that more often!

8 I know she can be very _____ , but I prefer people to be honest and not hide their true feelings.

9 I know her colleagues can find her a bit difficult because she really _____ , but she has a fun side when she's relaxing with friends.

10 She's the one who always _____ any arguments. She's good at calming people down and doesn't take sides.

11 A lot of kids wouldn't have the confidence to speak in public, but he's very _____ for his age.

12 It's good to be determined and sort things out yourself, but in this case, she's just being _____ in refusing help. She doesn't want to admit she's wrong.

2 P ▶ Listen to the words from Exercise 1 and practise saying them on their own and in a phrase. Which words / phrases do you find hard to say? Practise saying them again.

3 Work in pairs. Discuss the questions (1–8).

1 How do you cope in a crisis? In what ways can you be there for someone in a crisis?

2 Is it always bad / cruel to make fun of someone?

3 In what ways are being sensitive or stubborn negative characteristics? And in what ways are they positive?

4 What types of behaviour might be considered mature for a six-year-old? What about a teenager?

5 Do you always prefer people to be direct or are there times when it's better to be less direct?

6 How might someone show their fun / serious side? What might they be like normally?

7 How would you describe someone who is good at sorting out arguments?

8 Why might someone *not* make the most of a talent?

4 Work in groups. Use language from Exercise 1 to talk about:

1 yourself.

2 a person who is quite different to you.

3 a person who you're not sure if you like.

LISTENING

5 ▶ Listen to a man called Lewis talking to his friend, Jessica.

1 Which people does Jessica talk about?

2 How does she get on with them? Why?

6 ▶ Listen again. Choose the correct option (a–c) to answer the questions. Then compare your ideas with a partner.

1 Why does Lewis start asking about Noel?

   a He found out they share the same birthday.

   b Jessica had been speaking to Noel on the phone.

   c They're waiting for Noel to arrive.

2 In what way is Lewis's mum similar to Noel?

   a They share the same birthday.

   b They don't listen to what people say.

   c They like chatting.

3 Why does Lewis think Noel is clever?

   a because Jessica is smart too

   b because a university offered him a free place to study

   c because he always did well at school

4 What does Jessica think of Greg's art project?

   a He won't find anywhere to show it or anyone to buy it.

   b It shows his sensitive side.

   c It's too similar to his previous artwork.

5 Why does Jessica get a bit annoyed at the end of the conversation?

   a because she thinks Lewis is criticizing her

   b because she doesn't think Noel is ambitious enough

   c because people in the art world are cruel

7 With your partner, discuss the questions.

1 As a child, which is best: being the oldest, the youngest or in the middle?

2 Do you know any brothers or sisters who are very different to each other? In what way?

3 Do you know anyone who's won a scholarship? What to do and where?

4 How would you describe Jessica's character based on the conversation? Do you think she's too tough on Greg?

DEVELOPING CONVERSATIONS

That's like ...

When people tell us about the character or habits of someone, we often compare the person to someone similar that we know. To introduce our comments, we can use *That's like ...* .

A: *Once he starts talking, he doesn't stop!*

B: *Oh, **that's (just / a bit) like** my mum. She can talk for hours.*

8 Match the sentences (1–6) with the comments (a–f).

1 He gets in a panic, even when small things go wrong.

2 He's only three and whenever he sees me, he runs up and gives me a big hug. It's so sweet.

3 Honestly, it's impossible to change his mind once he's decided on something.

4 She just lets her son do whatever he wants. She really spoils him.

5 She's really shy. She's not very good with people.

6 She works really hard and is very determined and ambitious.

a That's like my cousin. He finds it quite hard to make new friends.

b That's like my father-in-law. He's so stubborn.

c That's like my step-sister. She's only 23, but she's already running her own company.

d That's a bit like a friend of mine. He never says 'no' either – and his kid's really naughty.

e That's just like my sister. She's an anxious person too.

f Ah! That's like my niece. They're so cute at that age.

9 Work in pairs. Take turns to read out a sentence (1–6) from Exercise 8. Your partner replies with an example that's true for them.

A: *He gets in a panic, even when small things go wrong.*

B: *That's just like my brother Dan. He's quite an anxious person too.*

10 Work with a new partner. Talk about the sentences in Exercise 1. Say if they are like anyone you know.

CONVERSATION PRACTICE

11 Think of three people you know that you want to talk about. Decide how to answer the questions below for each person.

1 How old are they?

2 What are they like? Do you get on well?

3 Are you close? Do you see them a lot?

4 What do they do?

5 Where do they live? Is it near you?

12 Work in groups. Talk about the people and show photos if you have any. Ask each other the questions in Exercise 11 and any others you can think of. Add comparisons with people you know when you can. Use *That's like ...* .

The older generation

IN THIS LESSON, YOU:
- discuss the role of grandparents
- read and analyse an article about becoming a grandparent
- share memories of your grandparents, childhood and family

READING

1 **Work in pairs. Discuss the questions.**

1 What are the typical images of a grandmother and grandfather where you're from?

2 Do you think these images are positive or negative? Why?

2 **Read the article about becoming a grandparent on page 119. Find out why Jean is struggling.**

3 **Work in pairs. Discuss:**

1 to what extent you understand Jean's feelings.

2 to what extent Jean's views might be shared by a man.

4 **Work in pairs. Look at the facts and say which views in the article they support.**

a Global life expectancy has risen from 51 to 72 since 1960.

b Studies in the US, Britain and Japan found kids with grandparent carers tended to be overweight.

c 60% of grandmothers in Belgium regularly look after grandkids. Mexican grandmothers provide day care for 40% of all Mexican kids under six.

d On average, people in the UK become grandparents for the first time before the age of 63. In Nigeria this age is 55 and in Japan it's 70.

e Of the five million grandparents providing regular care for their grandchildren in the UK, 50% said it kept them physically and mentally active.

f In the UK, the over-55s take 30% more trips and spend 52% more on trips than the under-35s.

g A study in the US found that 57% of grandparents caring for their grandchildren found it difficult to control them and nearly 20% thought physical punishment was OK.

h Nearly 1.5 million people work beyond 65 in the UK.

5 **Each group of phrases (1–9) has the same word missing (~). Find the missing words in the article.**

1 the cost of ~ / provide ~ / ~ facilities

2 take on a big ~ / have family ~s / a financial ~

3 put me in a difficult ~ / reach a ~ where / our ~ in society

4 ~ to help out / ~ to eat / ~ the offer

5 be ~ to give up opportunities / be ~ to try / be un~ to help

6 have ~ memories / be ~ of him / grow ~ of the place

7 ~ them for the situation / ~ the problem on them / be ~d

8 ~ to strict rules / ~ to a diet / ~ to the plan

9 ~ a break / ~ our thanks / ~ more respect

6 **Write four true sentences using the phrases from Exercise 5. Then work in groups and share your ideas.**

The cost of childcare is partly paid for by the government.

I'd like to buy a house, but it's a big financial commitment.

GRAMMAR

Talking about memories

To talk about our memories, we can use *remember* + *-ing*.

*I only **remember having** a fantastic time.*

To give details about our memories, we can use the past simple, *used to* + verb and *would* + verb.

a *They **retired** to a seaside town.*

b *My gran **was** old and she **had** white hair.*

c *We **used to visit** once or twice a year.*

d *My granddad **would make** model cars with us; my gran **cooked** us all our favourite food.*

7 **Match these meanings (1–3) with the examples (a–d) in the Grammar box. Notice the forms used in each case.**

1 It shows a habit or regular event in the past.

2 It shows a past state, such as *having*, *liking* and *being*.

3 It shows a single event in the past.

8 **Complete the texts with one word in each gap.**

1 My brother used to [1]_____ really naughty when he [2]_____ younger. He [3]_____ write on the walls and he [4]_____ never do what my parents told him. I [5]_____ him getting into trouble at school at school quite a lot.

2 I always [6]_____ camping with my family when I [7]_____ a kid. I [8]_____ to love it. We usually [9]_____ in a campsite next to this beautiful lake. We'd [10]_____ swimming every day and sunbathe and play in the woods nearby. One year, we went to Canada and [11]_____ a week there. I remember [12]_____ a great time there too.

9 **Work in pairs. Tell your partner about:**

1 your memories of a grandparent.

2 your memories of summer holidays.

3 the lunch break when you were at primary school.

G **See Grammar reference 12B.** »»

SPEAKING

10 **M** **Work in groups. Compare what you read in the article to the situation in your country. Talk about:**

1 the age of grandparents.

2 the role of grandparents.

3 childcare – the cost and who does it.

4 whether any of these things were different in the past.

5 whether your own experience is typical of your country.

Struggling to fit into the role of GRANNY

Jean is finding it hard to adapt to life as a grandparent – and claims she's not alone.

1 I am a grandma. I've been trying hard to get used to that idea ever since my daughter gave birth last year. Obviously, I'm happy for my daughter and think my grandchild Olivia, is gorgeous, but *Granny*? The name just doesn't seem right, especially when I compare myself to the grandparents I knew. Mine were old! They retired to a seaside town with lots of other old people. My grandfather actually used to smoke a pipe! My gran had white hair and wrinkles and would walk with a stick. That's not me! I'm 54. I do yoga. I work. I have big nights out and take unusual holidays in faraway countries. How can I be a granny?

2 I can't be alone in having these mixed feelings. Throughout the world, the percentage of grandparents in the population is growing as we all live longer and people often become grandparents when they are still young and fit like me. As a result, we're being asked to play a more active role in looking after grandkids, especially in countries where the cost of childcare is rising and there's little government support. Babysitting from time to time is one thing; taking care of little ones for up to 30 hours a week is a much bigger commitment – and one many grandparents don't really want to take on. But then saying no puts us in a difficult position – especially grandmas. Women like me fought hard for the freedom to get out of the home and have a career and our daughters rightly want the same opportunities, but if we refuse to help out with childcare, it can seem like we are creating barriers instead. Some grandparents provide financial support, but I've only just reached a position where I can afford leisure and travel for myself and I'm not willing to give up those opportunities.

3 I'd also worry about taking on the role of a major childcare provider now in terms of how that will affect my relationship with Olivia. I have fond memories of my grandparents because seeing them was special. We used to visit them once or twice a year and I only remember having a fantastic time. My granddad would make model cars with us; my gran cooked us all our favourite food. They would take us to the circus and buy us ice cream and sweets. I'd want to be that nice grandma and enjoy that relationship of unconditional love. However, being a daily carer is different. If you don't have any discipline, you'll produce horrible spoilt kids who refuse to eat their greens or scream when they don't get their way.

4 Not that anyone should blame grandparents for this situation. If they punish their grandkids, it can lead to conflict with parents who have a different approach at home. And grandparents might not want stick to strict rules because it's hard – and they've already done all that with their own kids. They deserve a break from it.

5 Still, research also tells me that if I can overcome my concerns, a longer and more regular relationship with my granddaughter might actually be good for me. Maybe I've thought too much about what I might lose and not enough about what I could gain. Apart from giving hugs and kisses, it seems grandkids actually can teach an old dog new tricks. And by keeping us up to date with changes in the world, they help us stay young – even as we get more wrinkles.

How do you know him?

IN THIS LESSON, YOU:
- discuss findings of studies on friendship and age
- tell each other how you met friends and changing relationships
- practise listening to different speakers talking about a shared friend
- talk about regrets with regard to relationships and life

VOCABULARY Friendships

1 **Work in pairs. Tell your partner about five people that you got to know in different ways.**

2 **Complete the story about a friendship with these verb phrases.**

been seeing	ended up	fallen out
followed	got talking	had nothing to do with
have a lot in common	hit it off	meet up
remain friends	split up	took offence

I first got to know Jing online. I ¹ _____ her as she did similar work to me and I would comment on her posts. Then she did the same and we sort of became friends. However, one day we got into one of those strange online arguments. I posted something which she thought was wrong; I ² _____ at her criticism; we both said things we shouldn't have. It was completely ridiculous, but we ³ _____ unfriending each other and we ⁴_____ each other after that and I forgot about her.

Then, a few years later, I was at a conference. Before the last session, I ⁵ _____ to this woman who was sitting next to me, and it was quite strange because we just ⁶ _____ straightaway and we quickly agreed to go for something to eat after the session finished. At some point during the meal, she mentioned her socials and I suddenly realized that this was the same person I'd ⁷ _____ with online. The argument we'd had was immediately forgotten and we couldn't believe the coincidence! We'd regularly ⁸ _____ after that and became close friends, because we really ⁹ _____ .

She was there for me when I ¹⁰ _____ with my ex, and she actually introduced me to my new partner, who I've ¹¹ _____ for almost six months now. I'm sure Jing and I are going to ¹² _____ long into the future and won't fall out again.

3 **Work in groups. Discuss the questions.**

1 Do you think you can be more than 'sort of friends' with someone you only got to know online? Have you ever ended up unfriending someone on social media? Why?

2 How did you get to know your best friend? How important is it for you to regularly meet up? Have you ever fallen out? What happened?

3 Do you ever get talking to strangers when travelling / on holiday? Have you ever hit it off with someone very quickly? Who? Why?

4 Do you know anyone who has split up with their partner recently? How are they doing? Would you ever introduce someone or organize a blind date for a single friend? Why? / Why not?

LISTENING

4 ▶ **Listen to five people talking about how they know a Belgian man called Nicolas. Match the speakers (1–5) with the sentences (a–g). There are two extra sentences.**

a They regret not dating Nicolas sooner.

b They shared a bad experience with Nicolas.

c They fell out with Nicolas.

d They hit it off immediately with Nicolas.

e They were flatmates with Nicolas.

f They studied abroad with Nicolas.

g They met Nicolas through a friend.

5 FS ▶ *Had* and *would* are often reduced to /d/ in fast speech and may completely disappear. Listen to ten extracts and decide if you hear *had*, *would* or neither.

6 ▶ Listen to the speakers again. Are these statements true (T) or false (F)?

1 Nicolas once spent a summer working as a waiter.

2 He complained to his boss about the way he was being treated.

3 Sandra remembers him being someone who liked going out and enjoying himself.

4 Sandra is glad they're no longer seeing each other as a couple.

5 Nicolas and Shane are very different to each other.

6 Two years ago, Shane visited Nicolas from New Zealand.

7 Brigitte thinks Nicolas has a very different character to her.

8 Brigitte made the first move in their relationship.

9 Franck tried to apologize to Jef.

10 Franck regrets not making more of an effort with Jef.

7 Work in pairs. Choose three set of questions to discuss.

1 What do you learn about Nicolas? Does he sound like anyone you know? Would he be the kind of person you would like? Why? / Why not?

2 Why do you think Sandra and Brigitte have such different views of Nicolas? Do you think you show different sides of your personality in different situations? Give examples.

3 Do you think you've changed in the last year? The last five years? The last ten years?

4 How different are your friendships between now and five or ten years ago? What has changed? Why?

GRAMMAR

Expressing regret using *wish*

To express regret about things that didn't happen, but that we wanted to happen, we use *wish* + past perfect with *had*.

*I sometimes **wish** we**'d stayed** together.*

To express regret about things that did happen, but that we didn't want to happen, we use *wish* + past perfect with *hadn't*.

*I **wish** we **hadn't split up**.*

8 Complete the sentences with the past perfect form of the verb in brackets. You may need to use a negative.

1 I wish I _____ . (know)

2 I wish she _____ him before he died. (meet)

3 Honestly, I wish I _____ anything. (say)

4 I wish I _____ harder at school. (try)

5 I wish they _____ me earlier. (tell)

6 I really wish we _____ house when we did. (move)

7 I sometimes wish they _____ me a different name. (give)

8 I wish I _____ to the meeting at all. (go)

9 Work in pairs. Think of possible things that were said before / after these sentences.

I asked her out on a date, but then she told me she was married. I wish I'd known before I asked her!

10 Write three sentences about things you wish you had / hadn't done in the past. Then work in groups and talk about your regrets.

G See Grammar reference 12C.

SPEAKING TASK

11 M Work in groups. Read the findings suggested by various studies on friendship and age. Then discuss the questions.

Friends are a greater source of happiness than a partner or children and those who value friendships more tend to be healthier and happier.

People think having three to five close friends is enough to feel happy and satisfied, but many want those relationships to be closer and more meaningful than they are.

You can get extra benefits from being friends with people from a different class, sex and age group.

Women who have a larger social network of friends who they meet up with regularly feel younger.

Ageism (having negative attitudes and creating barriers based on your age) is a big problem for both young people and old.

Loneliness is a huge problem which is bad for your health and affects all ages.

People are happiest at the age of 36.

As we get older, the ability to make and maintain friendships becomes harder and women find it more difficult than men.

1 Do any of the findings surprise you? Why might you doubt those findings? What do you think might explain each one?

2 Which of the findings is most true for you? Explain why based on your own friendships and context.

3 What issues do these findings raise? How might you address them on a personal level? How might society / policy help?

■ MY OUTCOMES ■

Work in pairs. Discuss the questions.

1 What speaking or writing activities did you find enjoyable in this unit?

2 In what new ways can you now talk about people in your life?

3 What problems with vocabulary did you have?

4 What will you do outside the classroom to revise language?

WRITING 6
Writing a short story

IN THIS LESSON, YOU:
- write a short story based on an opening or closing line
- discuss ideas for different stories
- respond to a short story from a personal point of view
- practise ways to create more impact in stories

SPEAKING

1 Work in pairs. You're going to read a short story that starts with the line: *It was dangerous, but I knew I had to do it.* Do the following.

1 Based on this first line, think of four possible things that the writer was about to do.

2 Think of ways in which each of these four stories might then develop.

WRITING

2 These four sentences are from the story. Check you understand the words in bold. Then, in your pairs, discuss the order you expect to read the sentences in. Explain your ideas.

a I could feel the wind **rushing** past me as I fell.

b I **floated** slowly down.

c I moved my feet closer to the **edge** and looked down.

d The **parachute** opened.

3 Read the story and complete it with the correct form (past simple, past continuous or past perfect simple) of the verbs in brackets. Then work in pairs to compare your ideas.

It was dangerous, but I knew I had to do it. People
¹_____ (laugh) when I'd said my ambition was
to do a parachute jump. They think I'm a quiet, sensitive
person who takes life very seriously. They couldn't believe
I'd do something so crazy! Well, here I was in a plane and I
was about to show my wild side!

Just as I ²_____ (move) towards the open door,
the clouds cleared and I saw the ground below. It was very,
very far down! I began to panic. What ³_____
(I do) up here? I was just about to tell the instructor I
⁴_____ (change) my mind, when she screamed in
my ear, 'Go! Go! Go!' – and I automatically jumped.

The wind rushed past me, and the panic and fear
disappeared. For a moment, I ⁵_____ (really fly).
Then I felt the sudden pull as the parachute opened.
I floated slowly down, enjoying the incredible views, and
⁶_____ (land) safely in a field.

I'd done it! I'd overcome my fears and achieved my
ambition – and I instantly wanted to do it again!

4 Work in pairs. Discuss the questions.

1 What do you learn about the character in the story? How does she feel? Can you relate to her experience? Why? / Why not?

2 Do you know anyone who has done a parachute jump?

3 Would you like to do one? Why? / Why not?

4 What other dangerous activities do people enjoy doing?

5 Would you do any of these activities? Have done any of them already?

USEFUL LANGUAGE

(*Just*) *about to* and *just as*

Was / Were (just) about to + verb is used to talk about something you intend to do in the next moment. We often then say something else happened to stop us – linked by *when* (*suddenly*).

I **was about to show** my wild side!

I **was just about to tell** the instructor I'd changed my mind, **when** she screamed, 'Go! Go! Go!'

Just as is used to emphasize that two actions happened at exactly the same time. It's more common to use the past continuous after *just as*, but the past simple is also possible.

Just as I was moving towards the open door, the clouds cleared.

Just as I turned on the computer, I heard a bang and the lights went out.

5 Rewrite each pair of sentences as one sentence. Link your ideas using the words in brackets.

1 We were planning to leave. Then they finally found us a table. (just about to)

We were just about to leave when they finally found us a table.

2 We reached the peak. The clouds lifted and the magnificent view opened up before us. (just as)

3 We'd decided to give up and go home. At that moment, we finally saw the eagle fly from its nest. (just about to)

4 We arrived back at the hostel, all completely wet. At that moment, the sun came out. (just as)

5 I was going to ask him out. But before I did, he got a message saying he needed to go home urgently. (just about to)

6 We were walking towards our car. A police car drove up and stopped right in front of us. (just as)

6 Work in pairs. Complete these sentences with your own ideas.

1 I was just about to hit the ball, _____ .

2 Just as we were leaving the restaurant, _____ .

3 I was just about to give up, _____ .

4 _____ , I realized I didn't have my passport

5 _____ , my parents walked in.

Descriptive adverbs and adverbs

We can make stories more interesting by using descriptive adverbs to show how you did something.

I **automatically** jumped.

I **instantly** wanted to do it again.

We sometimes use descriptive verbs to show how you did something. They may replace a simpler verb + adverb.

They **screamed**, 'Go! Go! Go!' (= They said this loudly.)

The wind **rushed** past. (= The wind went past very quickly.).

7 **Complete the text with these adverbs.**

angrily	completely	in a calm manner
instantly	into the air	politely
quickly	tightly	warmly

As we walked through the busy square, I held my grandad's hand ¹_____ . At one point, a young man stopped us and ²_____ asked us to show him where they were on a map. Just as my grandad was looking at the map, a young woman grabbed my bag and ³_____ walked away ⁴_____ , trying not to attract attention. I was so shocked I didn't say anything for a moment and my grandad was still talking to the young boy. Then I shouted ⁵_____ at her to stop. A man in a red jacket ⁶_____ turned round and rushed after the woman. But before she was caught, she threw my bag ⁷_____ and ran off. The man in the jacket brought the bag back and my grandad shook his hand ⁸_____ . The young man with the map had ⁹_____ disappeared.

8 **Replace the words in *italics* with the correct form of these verbs.**

crawl	grab	scream	slam	stare
rush	whisper			

1 I *moved on my hands and knees* along the edge of the cliff.

2 I *looked hard* at my friend. I couldn't believe what she was saying.

3 Just as I was sitting down at the table, a monkey suddenly appeared, *took* my food *quickly* from my plate and ran off.

4 The plane was moving wildly in the storm. Everyone was *shouting in a scared way*.

5 I tried to *say quietly* the answer to my friend, but the teacher heard me.

6 The poor animal was obviously in pain, so we picked it up and *went quickly* to the vet.

7 My son turned round angrily, went out of the room and *closed* the door *loudly*.

PRACTICE

9 **Work in pairs. Choose one of the options from the tasks below and agree on what happens in the rest of the story.**

a Write a story that starts with one of the following lines:
- I looked out and I couldn't believe my eyes.
- It was dangerous, but I knew I had to do it.

b Write a story that ends with one of the following lines:
- … and that was the most amazing experience of my life.
- … and that was one of the worst days of my life.

10 **Each of you should write your version of the story. Write 150–200 words.**

11 **With your partner, compare your stories. Decide:**
- which sounds more exciting / interesting and why.
- how you could improve each other's stories.

VIDEO Out and about

1 Work in pairs. Discuss the questions.

1 Who are the oldest and youngest people in your family?

2 What are they like?

Understanding accents

Some accents may add a /h/ sound to words beginning with a vowel sound, so *ate* /eɪt/ may sound more like *hate* /heɪt/.

2 ▣ Watch six people answer the same questions. How much can you remember about what they said? Then work in pairs. Which person has the most similar family to you? What did they say?

3 ▣ Watch again. Match one sentence with each speaker. There are two extra sentences.

a They are themselves an uncle.

b Their grandfather is no longer alive.

c Their grandmother is in her 80s.

d Their relative has lived so long because of their lifestyle.

e Their oldest relative is a retired businessman.

f They are very close to their father.

g Their father used to be in the military.

h Their oldest relative is 100.

4 Discuss the questions with your partner.

1 Would you like to live well into your 90s? Why? / Why not? How can someone achieve that?

2 Do you want to retire in your 50s? Why? / Why not? When would you like to retire? What would you do?

3 Are you very close to your parents? In what ways are you similar / different?

4 If someone is well-behaved as a young child, what do / don't they do? What about teenagers? How well-behaved were you at these ages?

5 Do you know anyone who has a baby? How are they all doing?

VIDEO Developing conversations

5 ▣ You're going to watch two people talking about animals. Watch and take notes.

6 ▣ Work in pairs. Compare what you understood. Watch again if you need to.

7 FS ▣ Watch again. Complete the sentences with three to five words in each gap.

1 I'd just come back from Alaska, right. _____ friends.

2 It was so, so scary, because _____ to do.

3 It must have been – _____ full-size bear – five, six foot tall.

4 You see them on the TV _____ gauge how big they are.

5 ... the bear most likely will run after you. _____ froze!

6 Then we ran – we ran _____ back to our car.

7 Wow! _____ that went through your head?

8 The first thing I thought: 'Oh _____ will. Um, never mind!'

CONVERSATION PRACTICE

8 Work in pairs. You're going to practise a conversation.

1 Choose a Conversation practice from either Lesson 11A or Lesson 12A.

2 Look at the language in that lesson.

3 Check the meaning of anything you've forgotten with your partner.

4 Have the conversation. Try to improve on the last time you did it.

Grammar and Vocabulary

GRAMMAR

1 Complete the text with one word in each gap.

I [1]_____ up in the countryside and me and my little brother [2]_____ to love looking for animals. We [3]_____ go into the forest and the fields to play and find berries and other food for the family to eat. One day, we were out and my brother [4]_____ bitten by a snake. His leg became big and sore from the bite and he wasn't [5]_____ to walk so I was [6]_____ to leave him in the forest while I ran to get help. I was scared that he might die and I kept wishing I'd [7]_____ better care of him. Luckily, I [8]_____ to find my dad and we got him to a hospital. The doctor [9]_____ us my brother would be fine as it probably wasn't a dangerous snake. Before that incident, I [10]_____ used to worry about the dangerous animals that were out there, but I was much more careful afterwards. It's actually unusual to [11]_____ bitten by animals. They tend to run away from humans, so you don't see them often. It's if they've [12]_____ disturbed suddenly or are starving that they might attack you.

2 Read the first sentence in each pair. Complete the second sentence so that it has a similar meaning. Use between two and five words, including the word in bold.

1 We've redecorated the flat since then.   **SINCE**
   The flat _____ then.

2 Pay the full fee before you arrive.   **SHOULD**
   The full fee _____ in advance.

3 They usually collect the rubbish every Wednesday.
   NORMALLY
   The rubbish _____ every Wednesday.

4 It was so cold we couldn't stay outside.   **FORCED**
   It was so cold we _____ back inside.

5 It's a shame I didn't practise more when I was younger.   **WISH**
   I _____ more when I was younger.

3 Choose the correct option to complete the sentences (1–7).

1 My throat was so sore I wasn't *able / forced* to speak.

2 I wish I *wouldn't have / hadn't* mentioned it now.

3 I looked, but I *didn't manage / managed not* to find it.

4 I *applied / used to apply* for about 50 jobs, and in the end I managed to find one.

5 I very clearly remember *to tell / telling* you about it.

6 My dad *used to / would* have a very competitive side. He certainly didn't always let me win!

7 I *went / used to go* to Texas for a month with my parents when I was 11.

4 ▶ Listen and write the six sentences you hear.

VOCABULARY

5 Match the two parts of the collocations.

1	get through	a	the most of it / a noise
2	set	b	oil from the sea / a tooth
3	make	c	a goal / tough targets
4	build	d	the pain / her exam
5	overcome	e	respect / thanks
6	sort out	f	natural resources / workers
7	extract	g	a solar farm / a mine
8	deserve	h	problems / your life
9	exploit	i	barriers / his fear

6 Decide if these words and phrases are connected to character, animals' homes or ways of moving.

branch	bush	charming	chase	crawl
hole	mature	nest	panic	race
run away	rush	sensitive	side	

7 Complete the sentences with the correct form of the words in bold.

1 We need to deal with _____ warming.   **globe**

2 The country is a huge oil and gas _____ .   **produce**

3 All our electricity comes from _____ energy.   **renew**

4 We heard the wolf calls in the _____ .   **distant**

5 He has this real _____ to win.   **determined**

6 Buying a house is a big _____ .   **commit**

8 Complete the text with one word in each gap. The first letters are given.

We met at school. On the first day, we sat together at lunch and immediately [1]h_____ it o_____ . We had a lot in [2]c_____ as we both had big [3]a_____ to get important jobs and we took school very [4]s_____ . I remember that in one class, he told everyone that he [5]dr_____ of becoming a lawyer, which was not the kind of [6]g_____ most of our classmates had. They made [7]f_____ of him about that, but he [8]s_____ to his dream and eventually he made it [9]c_____ true. It's funny how things happen. I always thought we'd stay close and be [10]t_____ for each other no matter what. However, after we left school, he started [11]s_____ this girl I didn't like and our lives went in different directions. I tried to talk about it with him once, but he took [12]of_____ at what I said and we [13]f_____ o_____ for a long while because we're both quite [14]s_____ . Then a year ago, we both went to an old friend's wedding and I found out he'd [15]s_____ u_____ with his girlfriend. We started talking about all our [16]fo_____ memories. Now we [17]m_____ u_____ regularly and I think we will [18]r_____ friends.

13 Journeys

IN THIS UNIT, YOU:

- describe a terrible journey
- reflect on past events
- roleplay a conversation about a travel problem

SPEAKING

1 **Imagine you're the person in the photo. Think about these questions.**

   1 Who are you? What do you do?

   2 Where are you from? Where are you trying to get to?

   3 What's happened? Why?

   4 What are you going to do next?

2 **Work in pairs. Take turns to tell your stories. Your partner should sympathize if appropriate and ask extra questions.**

3 **Work with a new partner. Discuss the questions.**

   1 Do you usually take a lot of luggage on holiday or do you travel light? Why?

   2 Do you know anyone who has spent a few months (or more) travelling? Where did they go?

   3 What's the longest journey you've ever taken? How long did it take door-to-door?

A woman runs down the road near Big Almaty Lake, Kazakhstan.

How was your journey?

IN THIS LESSON, YOU:
- describe a terrible journey
- discuss what's good / bad about different ways of travelling
- practise listening to two conversations about bad journeys
- look at phrasal verbs for talking about journeys and travelling

LISTENING

1 Work in pairs. What is good and bad about driving and flying? Which do you prefer? Why?

2 With your partner, decide whether the words below are more likely to be connected to car or plane journeys. Explain your choices.

brake	the check-in desk	go round in circles
hit a big storm	pour down	security
take a wrong turning		take-off

3 ▶ Listen to two conversations about journeys. Answer the questions.

1 How did the people in each conversation travel?

2 What three problems did they have?

4 M ▶ Work in pairs. Can you remember which words in Exercise 2 were used in which conversation? Try to use the words to retell the relevant parts of the conversations. Then listen again to check your ideas.

5 Work in groups. Discuss the questions.

1 How long before a flight do you think it's best get to the airport? Why?

2 Have you ever missed a flight / a train / a coach? Why?

3 Has anything strange or scary ever happened to you while flying / driving?

4 Can you drive? What are your strong points and weak points as a driver?

5 Have you ever got completely lost while travelling? What happened?

Passengers wait to board a train at Shanghai railway Station, China.

DEVELOPING CONVERSATIONS

How come?

In conversations, we often use *How come …?* instead of *Why …?*

A: *I had a bit of a nightmare getting here.*

B: *Oh really?* **How come?**

Notice that after *how come* we use sentence word order rather than question word order.

Why was it so busy? → *How come* **it was so busy?**

Why didn't you take the train? → *How come* **you didn't take the train?**

6 Complete the sentences with *how come* or *why*.

1 So _____ it took you so long to get here?

2 _____ was the plane delayed?

3 So _____ you left the car at home?

4 _____ you know so much about trains?

5 _____ are you going to Vietnam, then? Is it a work trip?

6 _____ they've decided to move to Australia?

7 Work in pairs. Take turns to ask and answer the questions in Exercise 6.

VOCABULARY Phrasal verbs

V See Vocabulary reference 13A. »»

8 Replace the words in *italics* with these phrasal verbs.

calm down	drop off	get away	get in
hang around	pick up	pull over	set off
stop over	work out		

1 We only got the airport an hour before our flight because we didn't want to *sit, wait and do nothing much* for ages.

2 It was still dark when I *started my journey*.

3 I couldn't *find an answer to the problem of* where I was or where I was going!

4 I had to stop and park the car for a few minutes to *stop feeling so angry and upset*.

5 It's really kind of you to *come and collect* us *in your car* and take us to the hotel. Thank you.

6 What time does your flight *arrive*? Do you know?

7 We both work a lot, so it's always nice to just *go somewhere and have a holiday* for a few days.

8 I had to *drive to the side of the road and stop* because I needed to make a phone call.

9 We had to *change planes and stay for some time* in Frankfurt before flying home.

10 I'm going past your hotel on my way home, so if you want, I can *take* you *there in my car*.

9 P ▶ Listen to the phrasal verbs from Exercise 8 and practise saying them on their own and in a phrase. Which words / phrases do you find hard to say? Practise saying them again.

10 Complete the sentences (1–10) with the correct particles. Don't look back at Exercise 8.

1 We set _____ at five in the morning, so I'm exhausted now.

2 Mum, can you pick me _____ after the party? I think it finishes around midnight.

3 We had to hang _____ at the station for an hour because my wife couldn't pick us up till four.

4 It was a long journey. I left home at six in the morning and I didn't get _____ till ten at night.

5 My child got scared and started to panic. She wouldn't calm _____ .

6 Some days I just want to go off somewhere and get _____ from it all.

7 I was totally lost. I couldn't work _____ where I was.

8 We were early so we dropped _____ our luggage at the hotel and went out to explore the city.

9 The police pulled me _____ on my way home because one of my back lights wasn't working.

10 We fly from Amsterdam, stop _____ in Singapore and then get to Bali at around one in the morning.

11 Work in pairs. Answer the questions.

1 What's the opposite of setting off?

2 Can you think of three places you could pick someone up from / drop someone off at?

3 Can you think of three places where you might have to hang around? Why?

4 Can you think of three situations when you may need to tell someone to calm down?

5 Can you think of three reasons why you might need to pull over?

CONVERSATION PRACTICE

12 You're going to talk about a terrible journey. This can be a real journey you've taken or you can invent details. Make notes about what happened, why it was so bad and how to describe it.

13 Work in pairs. Take turns to tell your stories. Remember to react to what your partner tells you and ask follow-up questions.

Journey to a new life

IN THIS LESSON, YOU:
- reflect on past events
- discuss different aspects of immigration
- read an article about one refugee's remarkable journey
- talk about imagined past situations

READING

1 Work in pairs. Think of five different reasons why people might decide to leave their country. Then discuss these questions.

1 What different kinds of challenges might people face when leaving one country and moving to another?

2 Do you know anyone who has moved to another country? Which one? Why?

2 Read the first three paragraphs of the article about Dr Waheed Arian on page 131. Answer these questions.

1 Where is Waheed from and where did he travel to?

2 Why did he make these journeys?

3 What difficulties did he face?

4 Where did he end up?

5 What do you think happened to him next?

3 Work in pairs. Can you remember why these dates, numbers, places and things are mentioned in the article? Then read the first three paragraphs again to check your ideas.

1 more than a decade   5 Peshawar in Pakistan

2 1983   6 ten

3 the BBC World Service   7 1989

4 a week   8 15

4 Read the rest of the article. Are these statements true (T) or false (F)? Identify the parts of the article that support your answers.

1 When Waheed arrived in the UK, he worked a lot because he was saving money to study at Cambridge University.

2 When he became ill in the refugee camp, he saw the positive impact doctors can have.

3 His charity pays for volunteer doctors to go and work in areas where there are wars.

4 Very few refugees have good qualifications.

5 The experiences that refugees have had often mean they don't give up easily.

6 The writer is critical of the way immigration is often discussed.

5 Work in pairs. Look at the words and phrases in bold in the article. Decide what they mean from the context.

6 **M** Work in groups. Discuss the questions.

1 What other special skills might people from refugee backgrounds bring with them?

2 What impact might hearing stories like Waheed's have on the general public?

3 Can you think of any successful immigrants in your country? What difference have they made?

GRAMMAR

Third conditionals

We use third conditionals to talk about imagined situations in the past. They usually have two parts: an *if* clause referring to the situation and a second clause showing results or consequences.

*He probably **wouldn't have become** a doctor **if** he'**d stayed** in Afghanistan.*

***If** he **hadn't been** so determined, Waheed **would have given up**.*

7 Look at the examples in the Grammar box. Complete these rules.

1 In the *if* clause, we use the _____ form of the verb.

2 The *if* clause describes an imaginary situation in the _____ that it is impossible to change.

3 The result clause uses _____ / _____ *have* + past participle.

8 Match the first parts of the sentences (1–6) with the second parts (a–f).

1 If it hadn't been for the war,

2 The economic situation would have been much worse

3 If I hadn't had that teacher,

4 If we'd left a bit earlier,

5 The team would probably have won

6 I'd never have met my partner

a I probably would never have gone to university.

b if I hadn't gone to that party.

c if all the players had been fit.

d if the government hadn't helped the banks.

e we would have stayed in our own country.

f we wouldn't have missed the train.

9 Work in pairs. How many third conditional sentences can you make about Waheed and the article you read?

G See Grammar reference 13B. ≫

SPEAKING

10 Think of three important moments in your life. Write third conditional sentences to show how things would have been different if they had never happened.

11 Work in groups. Explain your sentences to each other in as much detail as you can.

After I graduated from university, I spent six months travelling around Latin America. One day I was on a bus in Chile and I got talking to the guy next to me – and he ended up becoming my husband. We never would have met if I hadn't decided to go travelling.

From Surviving Bombs to SAVING LIVES

Dr Waheed Arian attends a reception hosted by the UK Prime Minister.

To mark World Refugee Day, we look at how one man's journey has brought hope to thousands.

The road to become a doctor is a hard one and generally takes more than a decade. For Waheed Arian, though, the journey was far longer and involved dangers many of us can hardly imagine. Born in Kabul, Afghanistan in 1983, he grew up during the Soviet–Afghan **conflict**, with his family frequently having to move home because of the fighting. The war meant schools were often forced to close and Waheed's education was **disrupted**, though he picked up some English by listening to the BBC World Service.

His family, along with several others, decided to **seek** safety in Pakistan, and spent a week crossing the mountains by night to avoid military planes. At one point during the crossing, Waheed and his father narrowly escaped being killed in a rocket attack before eventually reaching a **refugee camp** in Peshawar.

Here, conditions were poor and the family of ten had to live in a single room without electricity or running water. Arian caught tuberculosis and malaria and suffered from malnutrition before being treated by a volunteer doctor at the camp. His family returned to Kabul after the conflict ended in 1989, but soon after that, the **civil war** began. In 1999, as the fighting was getting worse, his family decided that at 15, he was old enough to go to the UK, where they hoped he could stay with a family friend.

He arrived in the UK as a child refugee with $100 in his pocket and then worked several different jobs, sent money home to his family, and studied really hard. Around this time, he met someone who had just graduated from Cambridge University and was persuaded to visit the city. Whilst there, he saw students from a variety of different backgrounds and after attending an open day, he decided that he would apply. Despite his disrupted schooling, he managed to obtain the grades he needed to get in and study Medicine. Waheed explains that his interest in the subject started in the Peshawar camps. If he hadn't fallen ill, he would never have seen how doctors bring hope and **healing** to horrific situations.

After qualifying as a doctor, Waheed set up a charity called Arian TeleHeal which uses technology to allow medics in war zones and **low-resource** countries to talk to expert volunteers around the world. The organization has saved hundreds of lives and helped thousands more recover from illness and injury.

This is just one of countless stories of refugees who have made **significant contributions** to the countries that have taken them in. As well as becoming doctors and nurses, people from refugee backgrounds have become Olympic medal winners and pop stars, scientists and film stars, successful politicians and business people.

Clearly, welcoming refugees can bring real benefits to a country. As well as helping to fill short-term labour shortages, many people seeking refuge are very well-qualified, experienced and bring different skills that local people might not have. This can mean they are more creative and better at problem-solving too. Furthermore, people seeking a safe place to make a new life are often determined to succeed, and many start businesses that create **wealth**, employ local people and **boost** the economy. Such skill sets are often forgotten in political debates. It's time to recognize it's not just individuals that develop and grow thanks to immigration – it's nations as well.

It's my own fault

SPEAKING

1 Work in groups. Discuss the questions.

1 How do you usually react when things go wrong? Do you do any of the following?
- I often panic.
- I go very quiet.
- I'm very relaxed. I usually believe the situation will sort itself out.
- I organize people and focus on solutions.
- I blame myself.

2 Who's the best / worst person you know in a crisis?

3 Give an example of a time something went wrong in these contexts. What happened? How did you react?
- on holiday
- at work or school / university
- while making or repairing something

LISTENING

2 ▶ Listen to four conversations about things going wrong on holiday. What is the main problem in each case?

3 FS ▶ When the word *have* is used as an auxiliary verb, it's often unstressed in fast speech, and is sometimes hardly heard at all. Listen and write down the six phrases that you hear.

4 ▶ Listen to the conversations again. Match each conversation (1–4) with two sentences (a–j). There are two extra sentences.

a They didn't book in advance.

b The weather was lovely, but it caused problems.

c The weather didn't spoil their holiday

d There was a problem at check-in.

e They had a problem with the accommodation.

f There was a problem going through security.

g They didn't bring the right kind of clothes.

h They wish they hadn't started sleeping.

i They used the wrong cream and it caused skin problems.

j They think the rules are stupid.

5 Work in pairs. Discuss the questions.

1 Have you ever had really bad weather on holiday?

2 Have you ever had to complain about a hotel or place you stayed in? If yes, what about?

3 Do you like to spend time in the sun? Why? / Why not?

4 Do you ever travel on low-cost airlines? What do you have to pay extra for?

VOCABULARY Extreme adjectives

6 Complete the conversations (1–10) with these extreme adjectives.

enormous	freezing	furious	packed
ridiculous	soaked	spectacular	starving
terrifying	tiny		

1 A: How did you find the museum? It was absolutely _____ when we went!

B: It was busy, I guess, but it wasn't that crowded.

2 A: You must be annoyed they've lost your luggage.

B: Yeah. I'm absolutely _____ !

3 A: You had to make an emergency landing? Wow! That sounds really scary.

B: It was _____ , yeah, but at least we all got out safely.

4 A: You must be hungry after such a long journey.

B: I'm _____ . Have you got anything to eat?

5 A: How was the journey? Did you get wet in that storm?

B: Yeah. We got completely _____ !

6 A: What was the weather like there? Was it cold?

  B: It was _____ , yeah. It was minus twenty the day we landed!

7 A: Did you get a good view from the top?

  B: Yeah, it was _____ . You can see for miles and miles from up there.

8 A: So, what was the place you stayed in like? Was it big?

  B: Yeah, it was _____ ! I can't believe how much space we had.

9 A: Hiking in those mountains in the winter doesn't sound like a smart thing to do.

  B: I know, right. Looking back, it was clearly a _____ idea, but we did it – and survived!

10 A: The seats on those planes are small, aren't they?

  B: _____ , yeah. It was an uncomfortable flight.

7 You're going to tell a story. Choose one of these ideas. Spend a few minutes thinking about what happened and how to tell your story. Then share your stories in groups.

1 a place you stayed that was tiny / enormous / freezing

2 a time you got absolutely soaked

3 a terrifying experience you've had while travelling

4 something you did when you were younger that you now think was a ridiculous thing to do

5 a journey you made that involved some spectacular views

6 a time when you were absolutely furious

GRAMMAR

Should have

We use should(n't) have + past participle to talk about things that went wrong in the past.

a We **should have looked** around more.

b I **shouldn't have stayed** in the sun for so long.

8 Work in pairs. Look at the examples in the Grammar box. Answer these questions.

1 In example a, did they look at lots of places? Was that the right decision? Why? / Why not?

2 In example b, did the speaker stay in the sun for a long time? Was that a good idea? Why? / Why not?

9 Complete the sentences with *should / shouldn't have* and the past participle form of these verbs.

| book | choose | eat | learn |
| leave | pack | set off | |

1 I _____ with that travel company. There's clearly a reason why they have such a bad reputation.

2 I was really sick on my second day there. It's my own fault, though. I _____ so much street food.

3 I didn't realize how cold it was going to be. I _____ some warmer clothes.

4 I couldn't understand a word anyone said. I guess I _____ some basic phrases before travelling.

5 We very nearly missed our flight! We really _____ earlier.

6 We _____ the accommodation until the last minute. We _____ somewhere earlier.

10 Work in pairs. Imagine what actually happened in the situations below. Then use a third conditional to explain what would have been a better idea.

1 I knew we should have taken the plane instead of the ferry.

  We took the ferry, but it took ages and the sea was really bad as well. If we'd taken the plane, we would have got there a lot quicker.

2 I should have worn something lighter.

3 She shouldn't have tried to drive in that kind of weather.

4 You should have read the instructions more carefully.

5 I knew we should have booked the tickets in advance.

6 His parents shouldn't have left him on his own at home.

7 I shouldn't have left my bag hanging from the back of my seat.

G See Grammar reference 13C.

SPEAKING TASK

11 Work in pairs. Read the situations in File 13 on page 199. Which pair can write the most *should / shouldn't have* sentences about each situation?

12 M Work in pairs. You're going to roleplay a conversation. Choose one of the situations from Exercise 11. Read your roles and plan what you want to say.

Student A: You have the problem. Try to blame Student B. Use these phrases to help you.

If you ask me, it's your fault.

If you hadn't … , I / we wouldn't have …

You should / shouldn't have …

You're the one(s) who …

Student B: You need to try and resolve Student A's problem. Use these phrases to help you.

Don't blame me. You should / shouldn't have …

It's not my fault. If you'd / If you hadn't … , you wouldn't have …

No-one's really to blame.

It's just one of those things. It could have happened to anyone.

13 Roleplay the conversation. Then exchange roles and repeat.

■ MY OUTCOMES ■

Work in pairs. Discuss the questions.

1 What interesting information about the topics of the lessons did you learn?

2 What collocations have you learned?

3 Was this unit more or less difficult than earlier units? In what way?

4 What do you most need to revise from this unit? How will you do that?

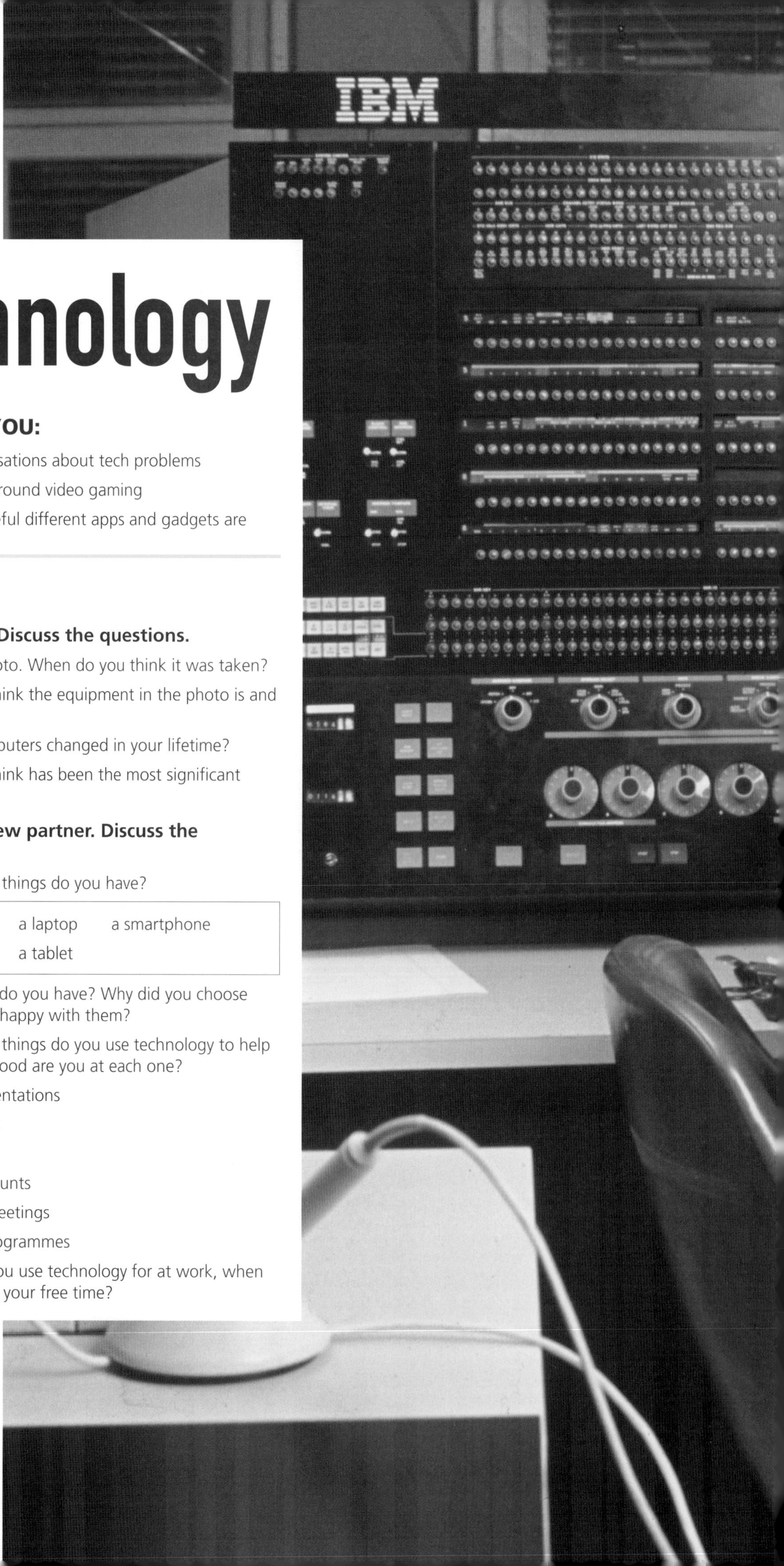

14

Technology

IN THIS UNIT, YOU:

- roleplay conversations about tech problems
- discuss issues around video gaming
- decide how useful different apps and gadgets are

SPEAKING

1 Work in pairs. Discuss the questions.

1 Look at the photo. When do you think it was taken?

2 What do you think the equipment in the photo is and what is it for?

3 How have computers changed in your lifetime?

4 What do you think has been the most significant change? Why?

2 Work with a new partner. Discuss the questions.

1 Which of these things do you have?

> a desktop   a laptop   a smartphone
>
> a smartwatch   a tablet

2 Which make(s) do you have? Why did you choose them? Are you happy with them?

3 Which of these things do you use technology to help you do? How good are you at each one?

- prepare presentations
- design things
- edit videos
- manage accounts
- hold video meetings
- code new programmes

4 What else do you use technology for at work, when studying and in your free time?

A man works on an IBM System Computer with 'virtual memory' technology.

My computer hates me

IN THIS LESSON, YOU:
- roleplay conversations about tech problems
- talk about computer problems
- practise listening to phone calls reporting IT issues
- practise phrases for sorting out problems

VOCABULARY Computer problems

1 Complete the sentences (1–10) with these words.

back up	blank	cable
the cloud	cursor	external hard drive
icon	plug	plug in
reset	scan	search for

1 I can click on the _____ and see the drop-down menu, but then, when I try to select one of the options, nothing happens!

2 The reason it's running so slowly is because the memory's almost full. You ought to move some of your files to a(n) _____ to free up some space.

3 It's weird. I _____ my laptop when I get to work, but later, I find it hasn't charged.

4 Try and _____ specific files by name and see if that works.

5 I tripped over a(n) _____ coming out of the back of the laptop and knocked the whole thing over.

6 You need to hold the _____ over the image and then the instructions should come up.

7 I might be wrong, but it sounds like the _____ on your power cable isn't properly connected.

8 My computer crashed and when I turned it back on again, the screen was completely _____ .

9 Make sure you _____ all the files. You don't want to lose them. Copy everything to _____ once you're done.

10 It doesn't sound good. If I were you, I'd _____ my password straightaway. You might want to run a security _____ as well, to be on the safe side.

2 🄿 ▶ **Listen to the words from Exercise 1 and practise saying them on their own and in a phrase. Which words / phrases do you find hard to say? Practise saying them again.**

3 Look at the sentences in Exercise 1 again. Which ones were said by someone who works on an IT help desk and which by someone calling with a problem? What advice would you give to the people calling?

4 Work in groups. Discuss the questions.

1 Can you think of three other things you can click on apart from icons?

2 Can you think of four things you plug in?

3 What kinds of things do you think people most often search for online?

4 What else apart from a computer might have a cable?

5 Why might you want to reset your password?

6 What kinds of things might a security scan find or prevent?

LISTENING

5 ▶ Listen to four phone calls to an IT help desk. For each call, answer these questions.

1 What's the problem?

2 What advice is given?

6 ▶ Work in pairs. Say which phone call (1–4) you think each sentence is from and why. Then listen again and check your ideas.

a You're not the worst offender.

b It's stupid of me, I know, but I always forget to copy them.

c Honestly, it's driving me mad!

d That's a disaster!

e It's the age we live in!

f One minute – let me just have one more look.

g OK. Well, try that and see what happens.

h I need these things in plain English, you see!

7 With your partner, discuss the questions.

1 Which of the four problems is the most serious? Why?

2 What do you think of the advice the IT help desk staff gave?

3 Have you ever had any similar problems? If so, when? What happened? Did you sort the problems out? How?

4 Do you know anyone who works in IT? Do they enjoy it?

5 Would you like to do that kind of work? Why? / Why not?

DEVELOPING CONVERSATIONS

Sorting out problems

There are some common phrases we use when trying to sort out problems.

A: *All my files have disappeared from the screen.*

B: ***Have you tried** turn**ing** it off and turn**ing** it on again?*

A: *Yes, I have and it **didn't do any good**.*

B: *OK. Have you tried searching for specific files by name?*

A: ***No, not yet**. Should I?*

B: *Yeah, **try that and see** if anything comes up.*

8 Put the two conversations (a–f) and (g–l) in the correct order.

Conversation 1

a OK. Well, it's probably just the wrong file type for your system, then. **Maybe you should** email the sender and ask them to resend it as a different file type.

b **Have you tried** download**ing** it to your desktop and seeing if you can open it from there?

c I hope that works. **Otherwise, I don't know what else to suggest.**

d Yeah, but I didn't have any success.

e I don't know why, but I can't open this file.

f **OK. I'll try that.**

Conversation 2

g **No, not yet. Do you think I should?**

h My boss wants us all to start using this new system, but I don't get how it works.

i **I've tried, but it didn't make any difference.** She just said we all have to switch over!

j **Yeah, try it. Otherwise, you're probably best** doing an actual course somewhere.

k **Have you tried** talk**ing** to her about it? **Maybe you should** tell her.

l Wow! **OK. Well, have you** looked online? There must be videos showing you how to use it somewhere.

9 Work in pairs. Take turns to say these problems and to give advice on them. Use the phrases in bold from the Developing conversations box and Exercise 8.

1 The printer isn't working.

2 I'm trying to download a file and it's taking forever!

3 I really want to get a new phone, but I can't afford one at the moment.

4 My boss wants me to run our social media campaign, but it's too much responsibility.

5 I worry about how much time my kids spend on their phones.

6 My boss has sent me a friend request on Facebook.

7 Something is wrong with the sound on my computer.

8 My keyboard isn't working properly. Some of the letters won't type when I press them.

CONVERSATION PRACTICE

10 Work in pairs. You're going to roleplay four phone conversations between someone who works on an IT help desk and someone with tech problems. Make a list of as many problems you could have with technology as you can.

11 Compare your list with another pair. Did they have any ideas you hadn't thought of?

12 Roleplay four conversations about your problems with your partner. Exchange roles after each conversation. Use as much language from this lesson as you can.

Games people play

IN THIS LESSON, YOU:
- discuss issues around video gaming
- read about jobs in the gaming industry
- practise understanding main ideas in a text
- locate specific information in a text

SPEAKING

1 Work in pairs. Discuss the questions.

1 How do you feel about video / online games?

2 Do you ever play them? If so, how often?

3 Do you know anyone who is very good at these kinds of games? Which ones?

4 What's the most popular game you know? How would you describe it to someone who doesn't know it?

READING

2 Read the first paragraph of an article about jobs in the gaming industry on page 139. Then work in pairs and discuss these questions.

1 How big do you think gaming is in your country? Do you know any locally produced games?

2 Do you have any stereotypes of what a typical gamer might be like?

3 How many different jobs within the gaming industry can you think of? Do you know anyone who works in the industry? Would you like to? Why? / Why not?

3 Read the rest of the article. With your partner, discuss:

1 which of the three jobs you would be best / worst at. Why?

2 what would be the best / worst things about them.

3 what else you would like to know about each job.

4 Read the article again. Decide which two points each person makes.

Lukman

a It's easy for gamers to make money.

b There are lots of similarities between e-sports and other sports.

c It's not easy to relax after a long day's training.

Kayla

d Being a game designer is a very creative job.

e The easiest way to get into game design is to study science.

f More and more women are becoming game designers.

Bryan

g A lot of people have the wrong idea about gamers.

h Skills that gamers develop can help in other areas of life.

i Bryan's next book is about how gaming spoils lives.

5 Work in pairs. Discuss the questions.

1 What qualities do you think Kayla's job and Bryan's job require?

2 What other kinds of things might drive parents mad?

3 What else can you come up with – apart from characters and storylines for games?

4 Can you think of three more things you can respond to?

5 What else might take over your life?

GRAMMAR

Articles

A and *an* are called indefinite articles. We use them:

a before nouns when they are one of several, when it's not important which one we mean, or when we mention something for the first time (e.g. **a** *friend of mine*).

b to say what people are (e.g. **a** *programmer*).

The is called the definite article. We use it:

c before nouns when we think it's clear which or things we mean (e.g. **the** *game I was telling you about*).

d when there's only one of something (e.g. **the** *moon*).

We don't use any articles:

e before uncountable nouns that we're talking about in a general way (e.g. *people*).

f before plural nouns to talk about things in general (e.g. *gamers*).

g after prepositions in some expressions with places (e.g. *in hospital*).

6 Work in pairs. Look at the Grammar box. Then match the rules (a–g) with the words and phrases in bold in the article (1–7).

7 Complete the sentences with *a*, *an*, *the* or *X* (= nothing).

1 I'm quite happy with _____ computer that I have.

2 _____ use of smartphones in _____ class should be forbidden.

3 No-one should ever download _____ illegal copies of _____ video games or software.

4 I think that _____ prize money you can win if you get into _____ pro-gaming is crazy.

5 Nowadays, _____ smartphone addiction is _____ extremely serious problem.

6 _____ video games can be _____ really good way of learning _____ foreign language.

8 Work in groups. Discuss how far you agree with each of the opinions in Exercise 7. Explain your ideas.

> **G** See Grammar reference 14B.

SPEAKING

9 Work in pairs. Discuss the questions.

1 How have video games changed over the years?

2 Do you know of any games that have made huge amounts of money? Have you ever played them?

3 What do you think should be done to help people with gaming addiction issues?

4 How is gaming used in education? In marketing? For recruitment purposes?

READING

GAME **CHANGER**

The computer and video games industry has experienced remarkable growth. Worth around $60 billion around a decade ago, interactive entertainment now generates well over $200 billion a year worldwide, a figure which is certain to rise in the coming years. With so much money floating around, it's no surprise that the industry is home to many different occupations and employs hundreds of thousands around the world. Today, we talk to three people working in very different parts of the field.

> "

Lukman

I've been a [1]**pro-gamer** for about three years now. You might think that getting paid to play video games is easy money, but e-sports require serious discipline and hard work – just like any other sport. I started just playing for fun when I was [2]**at school**, but I was spotted by a talent scout and offered the chance to join a team – Hunters Unlimited. We're a five-person squad and, like any team, we have a coach and a team captain and we train together a lot. Being part of a team means I get emotional as well as financial support. Next month, we're playing in [3]**the final** of [4]**a multiplayer battle game**. The prize money is $5 million dollars, and I think we're in with a chance. I sometimes play twelve or more hours a day, and it can be hard to switch off afterwards, but I love the feeling of power and control you get from really mastering a game.

Kayla

As a game designer, [5]**technology** has always been a huge part of my life. My mum often says that when I was little, I used to drive her mad by asking endless questions like 'How do planes stay in the air?' and 'How does electricity work?' and that kind of thing. I've never really lost that curiosity about how things work. Having said that, I'm not actually from a science background. I originally studied English Literature, but I was also really into gaming too and in the end, gaming won. All good game designers are big gamers too and I love the [6]**story-telling side** of my job. A lot of what I do is world building: I come up with characters and story lines, I plan everything you see on the screen and then it's just testing, re-working, talking to users, and improving the UX – the user experience. Here in the UK, the number of female designers is growing, so if you're a girl gamer and want to know more about getting into the field, get in touch!

Bryan

As a researcher with a special interest in technology, I spend a lot of time talking to gamers and I have to say, I think they're a misunderstood bunch. Many people expect gamers to be people who lack social skills and like to be alone, and we do see plenty of people with [7]**addiction issues**, where gaming has basically taken over their lives. However, gaming actually attracts all kinds of different people – and there's a strong community element to it too. Gamers don't just compete with strangers online; they make friends and build relationships as well. A lot of games involve people working together, and there's plenty of research that suggests gamers often become more creative, more confident and, yes, more social. Gamers also develop problem-solving skills, get better at making at decisions and learn how to respond to challenges. Lots of organizations now use multi-player games as a way of encouraging young people to join. In fact, that's what my next book will be about.

14C

There's an app for that

IN THIS LESSON, YOU:
- decide how useful different apps and gadgets are
- describe what different apps and gadgets do
- practise listening to a podcast about apps
- discuss how you feel about particular apps

Locals use the Mara EleApp to collect elephant data in the Serengeti-Mara region, Tanzania.

SPEAKING

1 Work in groups. Discuss the questions.

1 Do you know anyone who always buys the latest gadgets, technology or software? Give examples of what they've bought or use.

2 Do you know what a *technophobe* is? Do you know any?

3 Have you bought any new gadgets or downloaded any apps or software recently? What? Why did you get them?

VOCABULARY Apps and gadgets

2 Complete each pair of sentences (1–8) with one of these words.

allows	automatically	database	identifies
keeps	measures	runs	selects

1 a The app _____ pretty much any song you play it.

b It _____ all the different kinds of birds that you might see in the wild.

2 a The whole house _____ on solar power.

b He's got this new bike that _____ on a small battery.

3 a There's a new version out and it just _____ getting better and better.

b The app _____ working in the background, even when it's not open.

4 a It _____ you to record, edit and share videos.

b It _____ you to organize meetings, invite people and send reminders.

5 a The heater switches on _____ at whatever time you tell it to.

b It's amazing. The light just turns on _____ when you open the door.

6 a We used this software to help us build our own _____ of customers.

b It's quite exciting, because users are adding to the _____ all the time.

7 a It _____ how long each student takes to do each exercise.

b It _____ how many steps you take every day.

8 a It _____ different music for you depending on what you're doing.

B It _____ the latest news stories from a range of different sources.

3 Think of three gadgets, apps or pieces of software that you have. Then work in pairs and tell your partner as much as you can about them using language from Exercise 2.

140

LISTENING

4 ▶ **Listen to a podcast about new apps. Answer these questions.**

1 What three apps are reviewed?

2 Do they get positive or negative reviews? Why?

5 FS ▶ **In fast speech, the words *you* and *your* can sound similar. Work in pairs. Listen to eight extracts. Which contain *you* and which contain *your*?**

6 ▶ **Are the statements true (T) or false (F)? Listen to the podcast again and check.**

1 The host chooses the apps to review.

2 *what3words* can help you find places that don't have normal addresses.

3 *what3words* might be useful when you're meeting friends.

4 The host had seen the *Pl@ntNet* app before.

5 The *Pl@ntNet* app immediately tells you which plant you've photographed.

6 As more people use *Pl@ntNet*, it gets better.

7 The host thinks the *Real Razor* app is quite funny.

8 You can send money to the host if you want.

7 Work in pairs. Discuss the questions.

1 Do you know anyone who might use these apps?

2 Can you think of any other times that the *what3words* app might be useful?

3 Do you ever read / watch reviews of tech?

4 Do you ever listen to podcasts? What about?

GRAMMAR

Infinitive with *to* or *-ing* form

We often use verbs in the infinitive with *to* form or in the *-ing* form. The choice of form is sometimes decided by rules, and sometimes by patterns that you just need to learn.

a   Today I'm **looking** at three more apps.

b   **Having** a way of letting people know how to find you could save your life.

c   You can also use the app **to meet** friends.

d   You'll know how much I enjoy **gardening**.

e   It's **embarrassing** that I've not come across this before.

f   On **entering** a photo, you get a range of suggestions.

g   If you want **to keep** a note of your thoughts, you just click and record.

8 Look at the examples in the Grammar box. Match the examples (a–g) with these rules. One rule matches with two examples.

1 When we want to use a verb as the subject of a sentence, we use an *-ing* form.

2 When a verb follows a preposition, we use an *-ing* form.

3 We can use some *-ing* forms as adjectives.

4 We use *-ing* forms to make continuous forms.

5 We use an infinitive with *to* when we want to explain the reason or purpose for doing something.

6 When two verbs are used together, the second verb can take either the *-ing* form or the infinitive with *to*.

9 Complete the sentences with the correct form of the verbs in brackets.

1 I need a new computer. This one keeps _____ (crash).

2 I'm worried that students will use AI chatbots _____ all their homework for them. (do)

3 _____ your own films is much easier with this new software as it's so user-friendly. (make)

4 I saved a lot of money after _____ this gadget that measures how much electricity I'm using. (buy)

5 She decided _____ all her social media accounts. (delete)

6 I thought it was going to be great, but it was actually quite _____ . (disappoint)

7 We're probably all guilty of _____ our phones more than we should. (use)

8 I took the laptop back to the shop and luckily, they agreed _____ it. (exchange)

9 I've been _____ online for a few years now – and I have to say, I love it. (work)

10 I've started _____ the heating _____ energy. (turn down, save)

10 Complete the sentences to make them true for you. Use an infinitive with *to* or an *-ing* form. Then work in pairs and compare your ideas.

1 They should invent a machine …

2 … is OK for older people, but not for younger people.

3 I'm hoping … sometime in the future.

4 I keep …

5 I think … is better for you than …

6 I generally spend most of my weekends …

G   See Grammar reference 14C.   »»

SPEAKING TASK

11 Work in groups. Read the list of gadgets and apps. Decide how you think they work, why people might need them and how useful each one is.

- a waterless egg boiler
- a T-shirt that measures your heart rate and other data
- an app that works out how long food or drink will take to reach a specific temperature in the fridge or oven
- a pen that allows you to draw in 3D
- a pillow with built-in speakers
- a smart alarm-clock app that measures your sleep patterns and decides on the best time to wake you up
- a machine to exercise dogs

12 M **In your group, decide which of the gadgets and apps you think is most useful and which is the least useful. Say why. Explain your choices to the class.**

■ MY OUTCOMES ■

Work in pairs. Discuss the questions.

1 What was the best thing you learned in this unit?

2 What useful phrases have you learned to talk about technology?

3 What did you find challenging in this unit?

4 What will you do outside class to improve your English?

Writing an opinion essay

IN THIS LESSON, YOU:
- write an opinion essay
- discuss the pros and cons of car use
- read an essay that puts forward a particular opinion
- look at ways of describing trends, results and conclusions

Dustin Shuler's sculpture *Spindle*, Berwyn, Illinois, US.

SPEAKING

1 Work in pairs. Discuss the questions.

1 Do you / the people in your family have a car? If so, what kind?

2 Do you have a favourite kind of car?

3 What's the traffic like where you live?

4 Do you use a car much? Why? / Why not?

5 Look at the picture. What message do you think the artist was making with this car sculpture? Do you think the artist agrees or disagrees with the use of cars?

WRITING

2 Work in pairs. Look at the essay task. Think of three reasons why people might agree with the statement and three reasons why they might disagree. Discuss how far you personally agree with each reason you thought of.

'Cars are no longer the best means of transport.' How far do you agree with this statement?

3 Read the essay. Does the writer think the same as you?

'Cars are no longer the best means of transport.' How far do you agree with this statement?

The number of cars on our roads has increased a lot over the last twenty years. Traffic is getting worse and worse every year; it damages people's health and the environment, and we are also slowly running out of oil. Is it time to ask if cars are still the best way to travel? [1]_____ , I do not believe they are.

There are several reasons why cars remain so widely used. [2]_____ , they allow one to get directly from A to B. [3]_____ , people feel comfortable in their cars and [4]_____ , the car industry is a large employer and has influence with the government.

[5]_____ , in the long term we [6]_____ need to find alternatives to the car. [7]_____ , we will end up unable to move round our cities, as our streets become full of traffic. Road deaths will increase and there will be terrible environmental damage. It is time to limit car use and to encourage greater use of public transport and bicycles.

[8]_____ , while car users may want to continue using their vehicles, other options must be explored more fully.

4 Complete the essay with these words and phrases.

Firstly	However	In conclusion	obviously
Otherwise	Personally	Secondly	thirdly

5 Read the list of advice for writing essays. Find examples in the essay of where the writer follows each piece of advice.

> ### DOS AND DON'TS FOR OPINION-LED ESSAYS
>
> 1 Show you know why the question is being asked by giving examples of current trends or problems connected to it.
>
> 2 Make your own opinion clear in your introduction.
>
> 3 Allow space for points of view you disagree with and explain why you disagree with them.
>
> 4 Use paragraphs.
>
> 5 Avoid using *you*. Use impersonal forms like *people* or *one*.
>
> 6 Do not use contractions like *it'll* or *that'd*. Use full forms instead.
>
> 7 Have a clear conclusion where you repeat your main argument, but do not make new points or add new information.

USEFUL LANGUAGE

Describing trends with double comparatives

To describe trends, we often use a double comparative.

*Traffic is getting **worse and worse** every year.*

*Cycling is becoming **more and more popular**.*

***More and more people** have moved out of the city.*

***Fewer and fewer people** drive to work as a result of the new clean air zone.*

6 Complete the introduction sentences (1–6) by making double comparatives with these words.

bad	cheap	expensive	few
less	long	more	old

1 As property becomes _____ , it becomes ever harder for young people to buy.

2 Many parents are now seeing their children are living at home _____ , with the average home-leaving age now well over 30.

3 Public transport has improved dramatically over the last few years. Despite this, _____ people are driving into the city centre to work every day.

4 Crime is getting _____ at the moment. The government recently increased the amount of money available to the police, but this has not made much difference.

5 We are constantly demanding _____ food. As financial pressures grow, the risk of diseases resulting from poor conditions is growing every year, and animals are given _____ space to live in.

6 _____ people are having children these days. The birth rate is dropping quite dramatically, and the average age to become a mother is getting _____ .

7 Write similar introduction sentences to those in Exercise 6 for these two essay titles.

1 'Technology is making us less sociable.' Discuss.

2 'We should stop travelling by plane as it's bad for the environment.' Do you agree?

Introducing results and conclusions

To introduce results or conclusions, we often use linkers like *as a result*, *therefore* and *consequently*. They all basically mean 'because what has just been said is true' and they often begin a sentence and are followed by a comma.

*Traffic is getting worse and worse every year and we are slowly running out of oil. **As a result** / **Therefore** / **Consequently,** it is worth asking if cars are still the best way to travel.*

8 Match the sentences (1–5) with the results / conclusions (a–e).

1 Many people nowadays are too busy to meet potential partners by socializing.

2 Many refugees arrive with an amazing range of skills.

3 Over the last few years, the company has decided to do a lot more e-marketing.

4 More and more people are suffering from depression.

5 The school had the best results in the country last year.

a As a result, sales have grown dramatically.

b As a result, it is important to learn from its success.

c Consequently, dating apps are growing in popularity.

d Therefore, the countries that welcome them benefit from their presence.

e Consequently, research into the factors affecting happiness has become more and more important.

9 Work in pairs. Think of one more possible sentence that could follow sentences 1–5 in Exercise 8. Start each one with *As a result, Consequently* or *Therefore*.

PRACTICE

10 Work in pairs. Choose either the title below or one of the titles in Exercise 7. Discuss possible reasons why people might agree or disagree with the main statement in the title you choose. Then discuss your own opinions.

'Social media often has a negative impact on personal relationships.' How far do you agree with this statement?

11 Plan the content of each of your paragraphs. Use the model essay in Exercise 3 to help you.

12 Write your essay. Write 150–200 words. Use as much language from this lesson as you can.

13 [M] Work in pairs. Swap your emails. Can you see any ways your partner's essay could be improved? Discuss these questions.

1 Have they followed the advice given in Exercise 5?

2 Have they used double comparatives to describe trends?

3 Have they used phrases to introduce results / conclusions?

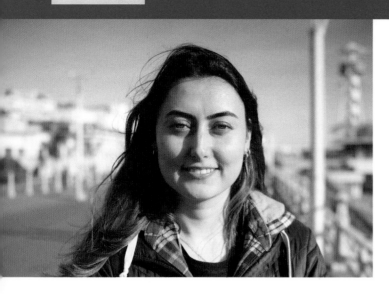

VIDEO Out and about

1 Work in pairs. Discuss the questions.

1 Do you ever play video games?

2 Do you have a favourite?

Understanding accents

Some accents use an /ɒ/ sound instead of an /əʊ/ sound, so *soak* /səʊk/ may sound more like *sock* /sɒk/.

2 � **Watch four people answer the same questions. How much can you remember about what they said? Then work in pairs. Did anyone have similar experiences to you?**

3 ▪ **Watch again. Match one or two sentences with each speaker. There are three extra sentences.**

a They've given up playing video games.

b Their friends prefer a different game.

c They would rather do something more worthwhile.

d They found a game exciting.

e They play a game with a partner to complete levels.

f They like competitive team games.

g They got a prize for winning a game.

h They lost the last game they played.

i They think people take games too seriously.

4 Discuss the questions with your partner.

1 What's good or bad about being competitive? How competitive are you?

2 Do you like team games? Why? / Why not?

3 What skills might video games help you develop?

4 Do you know any games, books or films which have won awards recently? What for?

5 What things have you given up as you've got older?

VIDEO Developing conversations

5 ▪ **You're going to watch two people talking about bad journeys. Watch and take notes.**

6 ▪ **Work in pairs. Compare what you understood. Watch again if you need to.**

7 FS ▪ **Watch again. Complete the sentences with three to five words in each gap.**

1 Well, first of all _____ I was 18 years old.

2 I have it all arranged. _____ our friends there.

3 I just didn't know. _____ only one airport.

4 Luckily, _____ the carry-on bag.

5 We had to go eight hours to meet our friends. _____ dinner.

6 Yeah, _____ find the humour.

7 I never planned a holiday ever again. _____ , my friend.

8 And I _____ this island was miles away.

9 They had to _____ to get me off.

CONVERSATION PRACTICE

8 Work in pairs. You're going to practise a conversation.

1 Choose a Conversation practice from either Lesson 13A or Lesson 14A.

2 Look at the language in that lesson.

3 Check the meaning of anything you've forgotten with your partner.

4 Have the conversation. Try to improve on the last time you did it.

Grammar and Vocabulary

GRAMMAR

1 **Complete the text with one word in each gap.**

I'm ¹_____ computer programmer and I love my job.
²_____ in IT means I can dress how I want, be as
creative as I want ³_____ be and work ⁴_____
hours I feel like working. Sometimes, though, it causes
problems. Last month, for example, a friend asked me
⁵_____ help her design a website for her company.
Looking back on it, I realize that I ⁶_____ have said no.
Honestly, if I ⁷_____ known how much work it'd be, I
would never ⁸_____ agreed to help. I spent night after
night ⁹_____ to sort out problems with ¹⁰_____
design – and all for nothing, because I didn't get paid for it!

2 **Read the first sentence in each pair. Complete the second sentence so that it has a similar meaning. Use between two and five words, including the word in bold.**

1 I blame myself for eating too much. **NOT**
   It's my own fault. I _____ so much!

2 I only forgot to do it because I was exhausted! **SO**
   If I _____ tired, I'd have remembered to do it.

3 If you text while you're driving, of course you're going to have an accident. **HAVE**
   It's not really surprising he had an accident. I mean, he _____ texted while he was driving.

4 I wanted to visit a friend there, so I stopped over for a few days on my way home from Sydney. **TO**
   I stopped over there for a few days on way home from Sydney _____ of mine.

5 It's really hard to find affordable accommodation in the centre of town. **PROBLEM**
   We're faced with _____ somewhere that's both cheap and central!

3 **Choose the correct option to complete the sentences.**

1 I *would / wouldn't* have probably been OK if the flight *had / hadn't* been so long.

2 Thank you so much. I *could / couldn't* have done it if you *had / hadn't* helped me.

3 It's my fault. I *should / shouldn't* probably have updated the software more often.

4 We shouldn't *stop / have stopped* for lunch. If we *did / had / hadn't*, we wouldn't *miss / have missed* the flight.

5 It's quite easy to play. Basically, you gather resources *for / for to / to* build your own little town.

6 He was caught *to try / trying / try* to take his pet dog on the plane.

7 *Work / To work / Working* as a computer programmer is far more exciting than many people realize.

8 *Life / The life* for students at *university / a university / the university* now is hard.

4 ▶ **Listen and write the six sentences you hear.**

VOCABULARY

5 **Match the two parts of the collocations.**

1	get in	a	how many steps you take
2	reset	b	for the file by name
3	search	c	for a few days
4	run	d	at around six in the morning
5	hold	e	on the icon there
6	measure	f	your password
7	get away	g	the cursor over the image
8	click	h	a security scan

6 **Decide if these words and phrases are connected to journeys or technology.**

back up	the cloud	a database	drop off
pull over	run on solar power	set off	stop over

7 **Complete the sentences with these words.**

enormous	furious	packed	ridiculous
soaked	starving	terrifying	tiny

1 Shall I get us something to eat? You must be _____ after such a long journey.

2 They cancelled the flight a day before our holiday. Honestly, I was _____ !

3 We very nearly had an accident on the motorway. It was _____ .

4 They spent an _____ amount of money on their new computer system.

5 I need to get changed. My clothes are absolutely _____ .

6 The room was _____ . There's no way two people could stay in there.

7 It was summer and the beach was _____ with tourists.

8 The cheapest room I've seen is $500 a night, which is just _____ !

8 **Complete the text with one word in each gap. The first letters are given.**

A friend of mine had promised to ¹p_____ me
u_____ from the station. When I arrived, she wasn't
there, though. I wanted to call her, but when I looked at
my phone, the screen was ²b_____ and I couldn't
find anywhere to ³p_____ it i_____ and charge
it, so I just had to ⁴h_____ a_____ and wait.
After an hour or so, I decided to walk. I'd been to her place
before, so I thought I'd be able to ⁵id_____ some of
the buildings along the way and ⁶w_____ o_____
where I needed to go. I was wrong! I ⁷k_____ getting
lost and was starting to panic, when I suddenly realized I
was in her street. I couldn't believe it! After giving myself a
minute or two to ⁸c_____ d_____, I knocked on
her door.

15
Injuries and illness

IN THIS UNIT, YOU:

- roleplay patient–doctor conversations in a hospital
- discuss health warnings and your response to them
- tell and retell stories about accidents

SPEAKING

1 Work in groups. Discuss the questions.

1 Look at the photo. What do you think it shows?

2 Do you think it shows a positive or a negative view of health and medicine? Why?

3 What kinds of things do you think the pills might be for?

4 What kinds of medication can you buy in a chemist's without a prescription?

5 How are these things usually treated?

| an allergy | a broken bone | a cut |
| depression | flu | heart disease |

A 73-year-old man counts out
one week's worth of pills.

What seems to be the problem?

IN THIS LESSON, YOU:
- roleplay patient-doctor conversations
- practise listening to patient-doctor conversations in a hospital
- identify and use different forms of adverbs
- practise using short questions with *any*

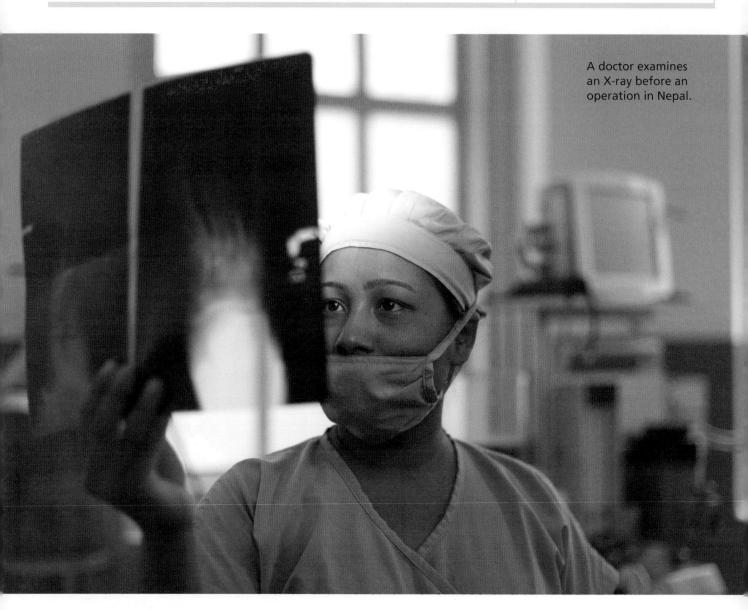

A doctor examines an X-ray before an operation in Nepal.

VOCABULARY Symptoms and treatments

1 Match the comments (1–4 and 5–8) with the replies (a–d and e–h).

1 I've hurt my **ankle**. I can hardly walk on it.

2 I've developed a **rash** on my hand. It's quite sore.

3 I've had a nasty **cough** for weeks.

4 I've had a high temperature and I **threw up** a couple of times.

a It's a chest infection. It should get better with **antibiotics**.

b I'm afraid there's **a virus** going round. Just rest and drink lots of water.

c It's probably just **sprained**, but we'll do **an X-ray** to check.

d It could be **a reaction** to an insect bite or an allergy.

5 Unfortunately, it's quite a nasty break.

6 You have a throat **infection**, but I think it's a virus, so there's no need for antibiotics.

7 Are you taking any **medication**?

8 You've got very high **blood pressure**.

e Well, I have been under a lot of stress recently.

f Oh no! Will it need **surgery**?

g Only some cream I have for my skin **condition**.

h Right. Is there anything that'll make swallowing less painful?

2 Work in pairs. Identify the collocations with the words in bold in Exercise 1. Can you think of one more collocation for each word?

I've broken my ankle.

3 **P** **▶** Listen to words and phrases from Exercise 1 said on their own and then in their collocations. Practise saying them. Which words / collocations do you find hard to say? Practise saying them again.

4 Work in a group. Take turns to say things which are true about your health or the health of people you know. Use the words in bold in Exercise 1.

LISTENING

5 **▶** Work in pairs. Look at the questions asked in two conversations in a hospital. What do you think is wrong with the patients? Listen and check your ideas.

Conversation 1

1 Can you put any weight on it at all?
2 How did you do it?
3 How long will I have to wait for the X-ray?
4 Are you taking any medication?
5 Have you ever had any bad reactions to any painkillers?

Conversation 2

6 What seems to be the problem?
7 How long have you been like this?
8 Any problems going to the toilet?
9 Has he been able to drink anything?
10 Does it hurt? And here?

6 **▶** Listen again. Note down the answers to the questions in Exercise 5.

GRAMMAR

Adverbs

We use adverbs to add information to verbs. They can show:

- the way we do something.
  *I'm going to press **hard**.*
- how frequently / much we do something.
  *He's **hardly** slept.*
- when we do something.
  *We've been a bit short of staff **lately**.*
  *He **first** said he felt sick **yesterday**.*
- our opinion or attitude about something we're saying.
  ***Hopefully**, it won't be more than half an hour.*

7 Look at the examples in the Grammar box. Answer these questions.

1 Do adverbs always end in *-ly*?
2 Could you put the adverbs in a different place in the examples? If so, where?

8 Make adverbs based on the words in brackets. Then decide where they should go in each sentence (1–10).

1 Have you had any of these symptoms? (previous)
2 Open your mouth and say 'ahhh'. (wide)
3 Can you just say it again, please? (slow)

4 It doesn't hurt. I can feel it. (hard)
5 You shouldn't go to bed. You need to get more rest. (late)
6 You shouldn't drive home. Shall I call a cab? (obvious)
7 It was my fault it happened. I was stupid. (incredible)
8 Leave pills where children can reach them. (never, easy)
9 It's nothing to worry about. It clears up with antibiotics. (basic, usual, quite quick)
10 I've been under a lot of stress because I've been working. (late, hard)

9 Work in pairs. Take turns to make new example sentences for the adverbs from Exercise 8.

*A: Have you studied English **previously**?*

*B: You left the door **wide** open.*

G See Grammar reference 15A. »»

DEVELOPING CONVERSATIONS

Short questions with *any*

We often shorten questions with *any*, especially when they follow other related questions.

*Has he had **any** problems going to the toilet?* →
***Any** problems going to the toilet?*

*Do you have **any** questions?* → ***Any** questions?*

10 Match the first parts of the questions (1–8) with the second parts (a–h).

1 Any news	a	what it is, doctor?
2 Any advice	b	apart from the cough?
3 Any pain	c	if I press here?
4 Any idea	d	you need to call?
5 Any symptoms	e	on how he's doing?
6 Any questions	f	for the weekend?
7 Anyone	g	on reducing blood pressure?
8 Any plans	h	about the surgery before I go?

11 Write your own endings for the first halves of the questions (1–8) in Exercise 10. Then work in pairs. Practise asking and answering the questions.

A: Any pain when you stand on it?

B: A little.

CONVERSATION PRACTICE

12 Work in pairs. You're going to roleplay a conversation between a patient and a doctor. First, decide together on a medical problem.

Student A: You're the patient. Think of details of your problem and plan what questions to ask the doctor.

Student B: You're the doctor. Decide what advice to give.

13 Roleplay the conversation. Then exchange roles and repeat.

Wise words?

IN THIS LESSON, YOU:
- discuss health warnings and your response to them
- read and respond to a blog post about parental health warnings
- understand the meaning of technical words from context
- develop the ability to recognise and understand suffixes

READING

1 Work in pairs. Look at the warnings (a–h). Then discuss:

1 why each of the warnings might be given.

2 what the consequence of not following them might be.

3 if they are aimed at a particular age group.

a Don't eat chocolate.

b Don't drink so much coffee.

c Don't eat a high-fat diet.

d Don't sit so close to the TV.

e Don't sit around all day.

f Don't go out with your hair wet.

g Don't bother the doctor with a cold.

h Don't put your thumb in your mouth.

2 Quickly read the post from a health blogger on page 151. Match the paragraphs (1–5) with the best warnings from Exercise 1 (a–h). There are three extra warnings.

3 Based on the blog post, match the statements (1–5) with these words. You can use the words more than once.

acne	cholesterol	myopia	superbugs

1 Genes play a role.

2 It's a recent issue.

3 It's important for good health.

4 People who sit a lot may get more.

5 Being outside can help.

4 Work in pairs. Discuss the questions. According to the writer:

1 what is / was the reason for each warning?

2 is each warning is based on scientific evidence or not?

5 With your partner, discuss these questions.

1 Have you ever received any of these warnings? What did you do?

2 Have you ever given such warnings? Who to? How did they react?

3 Did you learn anything new from or disagree with anything in the blog post? Explain your answers.

6 Work in groups. Discuss the questions.

1 Do you ever look online to check symptoms or find out about health issues? If you do, which sites do you use? If you don't, why not?

2 Have there been any news stories about health issues recently? What do you think about them?

VOCABULARY Word class and suffixes

V See Vocabulary reference 15B.

7 Choose the correct form of the words to complete the sentences.

1 Many people don't listen to *warn* / *warnings* about their health.

2 There is nothing we can do about *gene* / *genetic* conditions.

3 Ill health is *large* / *largely* due to poverty.

4 It's important to have *regular* / *regularly* check-ups with a doctor.

5 A *major* / *majority* factor in good health is getting enough sleep.

6 It's easy to make *adjust* / *adjustments* in your life to improve health.

7 A variety of diseases have *links* / *linked* to smoking.

8 We all show *addictive* / *addiction* behaviour at times.

9 Older people should do weights to *strength* / *strengthen* their muscles.

10 People suffering from *infection* / *infectious* diseases like colds and flu should always stay off work.

11 The biggest *contribute* / *contribution* to poor sleep is stress.

12 People aren't taught cookery at school and *consequence* / *consequently* they choose *unhealthy* / *unhealthily* options.

8 Work in pairs. What are the collocations with the words you chose? Can you think of a collocation for the other word form?

9 Work with a new partner. Discuss if you agree or disagree with each statement in Exercise 7. Why?

SPEAKING

10 M Work in groups. Discuss the questions (1–3) about these factors.

air travel	loneliness	mobile phones
red meat	sugar	video games

1 What warnings or advice have you heard about each factor?

2 How are these factors supposed to affect health, wellbeing or other areas of life?

3 How much attention do you pay to these warnings / advice and why?

11 In your group, discuss any other warnings / advice you know about health issues. Do you think they should be taken seriously? Why? / Why not?

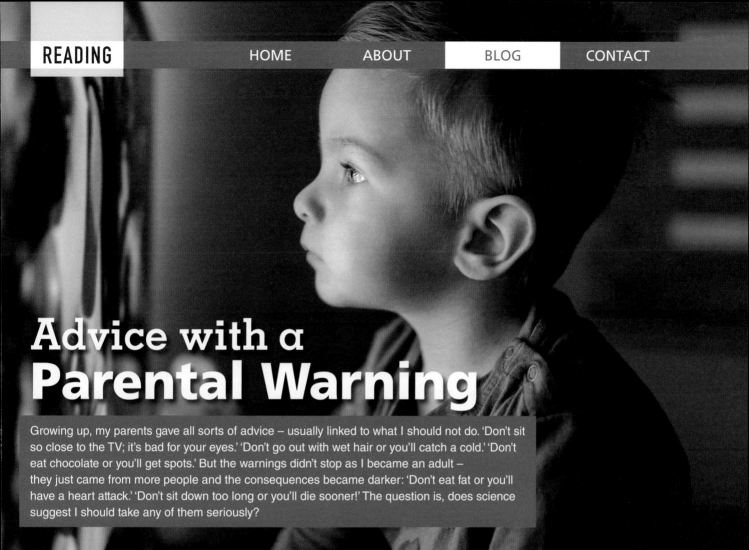

Advice with a
Parental Warning

Growing up, my parents gave all sorts of advice – usually linked to what I should not do. 'Don't sit so close to the TV; it's bad for your eyes.' 'Don't go out with wet hair or you'll catch a cold.' 'Don't eat chocolate or you'll get spots.' But the warnings didn't stop as I became an adult – they just came from more people and the consequences became darker: 'Don't eat fat or you'll have a heart attack.' 'Don't sit down too long or you'll die sooner!' The question is, does science suggest I should take any of them seriously?

1 _____

I'm sure having me stuck in front of the screen annoyed my parents and older brothers, but it seems the warning that I'd end up wearing glasses if I continued was wrong. Myopia – not being able to see objects far away clearly – is more likely caused by genetic factors rather than a TV screen or reading a book in bed under the blanket when you should be asleep. What we do know is that six-year-olds who spend at least one hour a day outside tend to have better eyesight.

2 _____

Apart from the effect on my eyesight, my dad also seemed more generally concerned about me lying around. 'Get up and do something. It'll do you good.' While I largely ignored him at the time, it seems I shouldn't ignore the advice any longer. Sitting for more than eight hours a day is apparently as bad as smoking and is linked to increases in blood pressure and bad cholesterol. Studies in the 1950s found bus drivers were twice as likely to have a heart attack compared to their colleagues who stood and sold tickets. So, yes, I do now follow the advice to get up and do something every hour.

3 _____

How many arguments did I have with my parents before I went out? 'You need to wrap up more.' 'Dry your hair properly.' What was that about? Colds are viruses! Walking around in a T-shirt or with wet hair in winter may look silly and make you feel cold, but you can only get one if you come into contact with someone

who has an infection. What's more, Dad would get annoyed when the doctor refused to give me a prescription when I got one, but again, if a cold is a virus, then antibiotics won't help. In fact, their over-use has contributed to creating new 'superbugs' which resist all previous antibiotics. So the best way to avoid colds is to wash your hands regularly when there's one going around, and unless it develops into a bacterial infection in the throat or chest, the cure is rest, lots of liquids and patience.

4 _____

As someone with acne, I was first told eating chocolate was bad for my skin because of the fat. I took the warning seriously and never touched it. However, acne isn't caused by fatty foods, though some studies do suggest sugary foods, like chocolate, can make it worse. Though I now tend to avoid all sweets and sugar, the truth is it's a condition which tends to run in families and is caused by the skin naturally producing too much oil.

5 _____

As I've got older, my mum's added butter, nuts and red meat to chocolate (the list seems endless!) as she worries about me having high levels of cholesterol and a heart attack. So, don't eat food high in fat, right? Not necessarily. Some people actually benefit from a high-fat diet and studies have found few reliable links between dietary fat and poor health. For example, cholesterol is essential for life and is produced naturally by the body. A few people have a condition which means cholesterol levels can rise, but most people's bodies adjust levels according to the amount of cholesterol they consume.

Accidents and injuries

IN THIS LESSON, YOU:
- tell and retell stories about accidents
- explain how accidents happen
- practise listening to a conversation about an accident
- report what different people said when telling a story

SPEAKING

1 **Look at these activities and places. Rank them from 1 (= most dangerous) to 8 (= least dangerous). Then work in pairs and compare your lists. Explain the dangers that might be involved.**

- cooking in the kitchen
- swimming in the sea
- going up a mountain
- sitting around all day
- doing gardening
- a workout in the gym
- jogging in the park
- cycling to work

VOCABULARY Accidents and injuries

2 **Complete the sentences with these words.**

banged	bleeding	bruised	fainted	fell off
ran into	recovery	rushed	slipped	stung
tripped	unconscious			

1 I trapped my finger in the door as it was closing and I _____ it really badly. It was black and blue for days.

2 I was jogging and I _____ over a rock and hurt my knee really badly.

3 I was out riding and the horse got scared by a loud noise and jumped. I _____ and broke my arm.

4 I was driving my car when a van pulled out in front of me. I _____ the side and hurt my neck.

5 It was really hot on the underground and I felt a bit strange, and then I just _____ and fell down.

6 It was freezing cold, and I was just walking down the street and I _____ on the ice.

7 This bee _____ me on the arm and I had a really bad reaction to it. It got quite big and was really sore.

8 I had quite a few injuries and it took me weeks to make a full _____ .

9 I _____ my head really hard when I fell over and apparently I was _____ for a while.

10 It was _____ really badly, so they _____ me to hospital before I lost too much blood.

3 **Work in groups. Discuss the questions.**

1 What are two other things you can trip over, apart from a rock?

2 What are two other things you can fall off, apart from a horse?

3 What are two other reasons why people sometimes faint?

4 What are two other things you can slip on, apart from ice?

5 What are two other things that can sting you, apart from a bee?

6 How can you stop bleeding?

7 What might happen if a car runs into another car?

8 Do you normally treat a bruise? If not, why not? If so, how?

LISTENING

4 **FS** ▶ **When people speak fast, you don't always hear sounds or whole words. You may hear different words joined together as one. Listen to seven extracts. Write down what you hear.**

5 ▶ **Listen to a conversation about an accident Dana's friend James had. Work in pairs. On a scale of 1–7, where 7 is life-threatening, decide how serious the accident was.**

6 ▶ **Listen again. Complete the sentences with no more than three words in each gap.**

1 Dana was in Austria on a _____ holiday.

2 The accident took place on _____ of a steep hill.

3 In the accident, James hit _____ and knee.

4 James was _____ to the hospital.

5 At the hospital he had _____ .

6 The doctors said he should take _____ or so to recover.

7 He couldn't cycle for a week, which _____ .

8 The man has a friend who slipped and fell while _____ .

7 **Work in pairs. Discuss the questions.**

1 Do you like cycling? What's the longest bike ride you've done? When? Where?

2 When was the last time someone was very kind to you? What did they do?

3 When was the last time you were very kind to someone else? What did you do?

4 Does Dana's story about James remind you of any other stories you've heard?

GRAMMAR

Reported speech

When we tell stories, we often report speech using *said / told me (that)* + clause. We report questions using *asked (me)* + clause.

a *The woman said she'd take James to the nearest hospital.*

b *She told me he was waiting to have an X-ray.*

c *He said he's going to have to buy a new bike now.*

d *He was asking us where he was and what had happened.*

e *We asked if we could buy her dinner or something.*

8 **Work in pairs. Look at the examples in the Grammar box. Answer the questions (1–5).**

1 Can you name the verb forms in bold?

2 What do you think the people actually said in each example?

3 When we report what people said, what often happens to tenses and words like *will* and *can*?

4 What's different about example c? Why is it different?

5 How is the word order in reported questions different to normal questions?

G See Grammar reference 15C.

9 Complete the sentences with the correct past form of the verbs in brackets.

1 The doctor told me I _____ a chest infection and _____ me some antibiotics. It cleared up after a week. (have, give)

2 The doctor said he _____ too much and he _____ to go on a diet, but he refused. (eat, need)

3 The doctors said she _____ some problems in the future, but that she _____ incredibly lucky to survive the crash. (have, be)

4 The doctor told me the injection _____ , but it _____ really painful! (not / hurt, be)

5 She told me they _____ several tests already, but they still didn't know what _____ the problem, so they had to do more. (do, cause)

6 They asked me how it _____ and whether or not it ever _____ me any pain. (happen, cause)

7 He asked if I _____ his phone conversation and if I _____ more or less what it meant. (hear, understand)

10 Work in pairs. Decide if the present form would also be possible in each sentence in Exercise 9.

11 With your partner, take turns to ask each other *So what did the doctor say?* Report something different each time.

A: *So what did the doctor say?*

B: *She said I'm quite unfit and I need to do more exercise. So what did the doctor say?*

A: *He asked how much red meat I ate and then told me I need to cut down.*

SPEAKING TASK

12 Think about an accident you've had or imagine you're the person in photos a–d below. Spend five minutes preparing your story. Think about the following.

1 The circumstances – When was it? Where were you? What were you doing?

2 The accident – What happened and how?

3 The immediate result – What injury did you have? Did anyone help you? Did you go to hospital? What was said?

4 The recovery – How? How long?

5 The 'lessons' – Did you learn anything from the accident? Did anyone say anything about it?

13 M Work in pairs. Do the task.

1 Work in groups. In pairs, tell each other your stories.

2 Change partners and tell each other the stories you just heard to your new partner.

3 Change to another new partner. Again, retell the story you just heard.

MY OUTCOMES

Work in pairs. Discuss the questions.

1 What did you enjoy doing the most in this unit?

2 In what new ways can you now talk about this topic?

3 What vocabulary problems did you have with the reading or listening texts?

4 What will you do outside the classroom to revise?

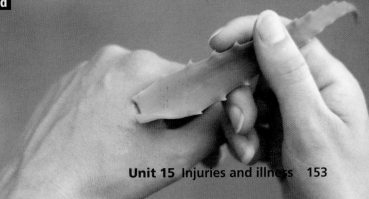

16 News and events

IN THIS UNIT, YOU:

- have conversations about different news stories
- discuss your views on fame, celebrities and culture
- create and do a quiz about people in history and the news

SPEAKING

1 **Look at the photo and imagine what the news story is. Think about the following.**

1 Who is the man being interviewed?

2 What did he do or what happened to him?

3 Where is he now?

4 What will happen next?

2 **Work in pairs. Tell each other your stories from Exercise 1.**

3 **Work in groups. Tell each other which of the types of news below you are most interested in and say where you get your news from. Who is most similar to you in the group?**

business and economics	celebrity news
crime and law	funny news stories
international news	national politics
reviews and entertainment	sport
technology	weather and the environment

A TV news team film an interview in Foggy Bottom, Washington D.C., US.

In the headlines

VOCABULARY News stories

1 Work in pairs. What area of news is each group of collocations (a–c) connected to? Explain your answers.

1 a **be elected** as leader / as president

  b **introduce** a policy to reduce crime / a law to protect children

  c **resign** as foreign minister / for breaking the rules

2 a **result in** job losses / a crisis

  b **expand** into new markets / their product range

  c **share prices** on Wall Street / have risen

3 a experience terrible floods / very high temperatures

  b result in a lot of damage / global warming

  c **negotiate** a new climate agreement / with other countries

4 a **lead to** a loss of confidence / winning the championship

  b **be suspended** for three matches / for missing training

  c **sign** a new contract / for Bayern Munich

5 a catch the robber / the person who did it

  b **investigate** the incident / a robbery

  c the **victim** of the robbery / is recovering in hospital

2 🅿 ▶ **Listen to the words from Exercise 1 and practise saying them on their own and in a phrase. Which words / phrases do you find hard to say? Practise saying them again.**

3 Work in groups. Give an example of recent news for each area in Exercise 1. Try to use at least one word from each group of words.

LISTENING

4 ▶ **Listen to five short conversations about possible news stories. Match the conversations (1–5) with the subjects (a–f). There is one extra subject.**

a a sportsperson   d a crime

b a politician   e a factory

c a celebrity   f a weather event

5 ▶ **Listen again and note down which of the words from Exercise 1 were used in each conversation. Then work in pairs and summarize each news story.**

GRAMMAR

Reporting verbs

We can use other verbs, apart from *say* and *tell*, to report speech: for example, *announce, claim, apologize* and *accuse*. These verbs are followed by different patterns.

say, announce, claim, state = verb + (*that*) + clause

He **claimed** <u>(that) the fan said something awful.</u>

apologize for, be accused of, insist on
= verb + preposition + (*not*) + -*ing*

He **apologized** <u>for causing</u> difficulties.

promise, refuse, offer, be warned
= verb + (*not*) + infinitive with *to*

He's **refused** <u>to apologize.</u>

A woman sells magazines in Peru.

6 Complete the sentences using the correct form of the phrase in brackets.

1 They have **promised** _____ (protect jobs).
2 He's just **announced** _____ (they split up).
3 She's **been accused** _____ (steal from her boss).
4 He **claims** _____ (he not know about it).
5 I can't believe she **refused** _____ (play the match).
6 Why did they **insist** _____ (sign him)?
7 I'm surprised they **offered** _____ (improve the deal).
8 They had **been warned** _____ (not employ her).

7 Work in pairs. Think of an example from the news where a person or organization:

1 was accused of something.
2 had to apologize for something.
3 announced something important.
4 refused to do something.
5 was warned.
6 offered to do something.

G See Grammar reference 16A.

DEVELOPING CONVERSATIONS

Introducing and commenting on news

Conversations about the news often have common features. You can start a conversation using this pattern or similar questions.

Did you see that thing about *the steel plant closing down?*

If you know a story, you can comment using *It's … , isn't it?*

Yeah, ***it's*** *shocking,* ***isn't it?***

Report details you heard or read about a story with *apparently*.

Apparently, *he took illegal payments …*

8 Complete the questions about news by putting the words in brackets into the correct order.

1 Have you seen that thing _____ (on / about / Threads / that / suspended / tennis player / being)?
2 Have you seen that thing _____ (on / of / the prime minister / YouTube / dance / trying / to) to hip-hop?
3 Did you see that thing _____ (TV / about / on / them / the shopping centre / expanding)?
4 Did you see that thing _____ (the news / on / about / the / near here / robbery) last night?
5 Did you see that thing _____ (arrested / the *Times* website / about / Shaynee Wilson / getting / on)?

9 Match the responses (a–e) with the questions (1–5) in Exercise 8.

a Yeah, it's good news, isn't it? Apparently, it's going to create loads of new jobs.
b Yeah, it's sad, isn't it? She's had so many problems in her life.
c Yeah, it's awful, isn't it? The victim was so young.
d Yeah, it's so funny, isn't it? Apparently, it was from before he went into politics, though.
e Yeah, what an idiot. Apparently, it's been shared a million times already.

10 Work in pairs. Take turns to say these sentences. Respond with an *It's … , isn't it?* comment.

1 Did you hear about Jay and Selma splitting up?
2 Did you hear about John getting fired?
3 Did you see that thing about the new trade deal they've negotiated?
4 Did you see that new law they're introducing to limit air travel?
5 Did you see that thing about that man paying $500,000 for a watch?
6 Did you hear that Jay and Selma are back together?

CONVERSATION PRACTICE

11 Think of two news stories you've read or heard about recently. Write one question for each story using the patterns in Exercise 8.

12 M Work in groups. Discuss the stories. Start your conversations with your questions from Exercise 11.

Gossip column

IN THIS LESSON, YOU:
- discuss your views on fame, celebrities and culture
- summarize the main ideas in a news article
- discuss your responses to a text and how you might report it to others
- identify useful language in a text to talk about celebrity

READING

1 Think of one celebrity you like and one you don't like. Then compare your ideas in groups and explain your choices.

2 Work in pairs. Read the first paragraph of the article about celebrity news on page 159. Then discuss these questions.

  1 Have you heard or read any celebrity stories like those mentioned? Who about? Where did you get the news?

  2 What would be your answers to the two questions at the end of the paragraph?

3 Read the rest of the article. Summarize the answers to each question in the introduction in one sentence.

4 Work in groups. Compare your summaries and decide which ones you like best. How far did the writer's answers to the questions match your own ideas?

5 Complete the sentences with three words from the article in each gap.

  1 Papers reporting on the rich and famous started in _____ .

  2 Scandal sheets didn't always have to be completely truthful because names were _____ .

  3 The way gossip was shared and discussed makes coffee-houses similar to _____ .

  4 A 19th-century newspaper and a 21st-century streaming service each boosted sales with stories about _____ .

  5 Over $2 million and _____ were needed to do an investigation into the secret finances of the wealthy.

  6 Stories in *Photoplay* like Lila Lee's love of hard work were written by _____ .

  7 The YMCA suggests celebrity news _____ about body image.

  8 Andrea McDonnell thinks celebrity gossip can enable discussions _____ without making friends feel uncomfortable.

6 **M** Work in pairs. Explain to each other:
- what you liked / disliked about the article and why.
- if there are any facts you'd like to remember and why.
- two or three different people you might mention the article to and what you'll tell them.
- four or five words or phrases from the article that you'd like to remember.

7 Find words in the article to complete each pair of examples.

  1 becoming ~ difficult / ~, celebrity cases are headlines on serious news programmes

  2 a ~ candidate / ~ elections

  3 ~ 'celebrity worship syndrome' / ~ 'scandal sheets'

  4 spread ~ / ~ about celebrities

  5 ~ the truth / ~ their emotional side

  6 cause a terrible ~ / avoid any mention of ~

  7 make ~ demands / have ~ expectations

  8 an ~ situation / an ~ subject with friends

8 Work in pairs. Think of one more example for each missing word from Exercise 7.

SPEAKING

9 Work in groups. Read the quotes about fame. What do you think they mean? How far do you agree with each quote? Explain why.

> *Fame means millions of people have the wrong idea of who you are.*
> Erica Jong

> *Wealth is like seawater; the more we drink, the thirstier we become; and the same is true of fame.*
> Arthur Schopenhauer

> *There is no celebrity quite so powerful as the local homegrown celebrity.*
> Tony Wilson

> *Fame is a constant effort.*
> Jules Renard

> *I wonder why the celebrities remodel themselves with plastic and then proclaim in ads to be ourselves!*
> Gayathri Jayakuma

> *Celebrity is … the punishment of talent.*
> Nicolas Chamfort

10 Work with another group. Which of the quotes do you think is the best? Why?

CELEBRITIES are OLD NEWS

Type *celebrity gossip* into a search engine and you'll find thousands of sites producing millions of stories about 'stars' announcing they're expecting a baby, splitting up with their partner, falling out with another 'celeb' or adopting some new diet. But it's not just gossip websites and magazines which run these stories. Increasingly, celebrity court cases, or reports from the red carpet at award ceremonies, are headlines on serious news programmes next to stories of presidential elections, factory closures and natural disasters. So why is this happening? And is all this celebrity news good for us?

In fact, the production of celebrity news is nothing new. In Britain, in the 18th century, so-called 'scandal sheets' reported the social life of wealthy families and royalty featuring stories such as a suspected affair, a poor fashion choice or the 'news' that the Prince Regent was no longer eating meat. Writers got their 'exclusives' by attending events, paying servants to tell all or simply making the stories up. There was no fact-checking, and the subjects of the stories were usually referred to indirectly (for example, as 'Lord B' or 'a daughter of a well-known gentleman'), which gave writers the freedom to focus more on entertainment than truth. The sheets were distributed in coffee houses – the social media platforms of that time – where the stories were hotly debated, and the gossip further developed and spread.

Gossip columns and stories about celebrities have been a feature of newspapers ever since, for the simple reason that they remain popular. In the 19th century, a special edition reporting a British prince's marriage tripled the sales of one newspaper, and 150 years later another British prince and his wife attracted millions of viewers to a streaming service for a series where they talked about their romance and family troubles.

But the current volume of celebrity news is not just because it sells, it's also because its cheap. 'Hard' news which involves major investigations or sending reporters to war zones is expensive. For example, one story into the secret finances of the rich and powerful cost $2 million to investigate – not counting the salaries of the 300 journalists involved. War reporting might cost $10,000 a day. In contrast, paying a journalist to keep an eye on social media feeds or attend an event is cheap, and sometimes a writer is not even required.

This is because celebrity news is often provided by a celebrity's publicist, something which has been done since at least the 1920s, when film studios wrote stories about their stars for fan magazines like *Photoplay*. One such article was about new star Lila Lee's love of hard work and featured a photo of Lila in perfect hair and make-up 'caught' washing her kitchen floor. Studios also provided articles with a star's advice on fashion or romance and enabled 'in-depth' interviews like Gloria Swanson's *The Confessions of a Modern Woman* which revealed the star's emotional side while avoiding any mention of scandal or even any real personal problems. In short, they presented celebrities as 'normal people', just better-dressed.

This manufactured view of celebrity is one reason why some feel that celebrity news might be bad for us – especially now it's available 24/7 on our smartphones. Some charities like the YMCA suggest it creates unrealistic expectations about body image and life in general. However, for researchers like Andrea McDonell, gossiping about celebrities can be positive. She argues such conversations not only allow people to dream, but also allow us to talk about serious subjects that might be awkward if they're directed at real friends. Put another way, by being fans of one celeb and criticizing others, we can define what we consider good or bad and make clear how we think people should generally behave.

I've never heard of them

IN THIS LESSON, YOU:
- create and do a quiz about people in history and the news
- talk about people you recognize and why they're famous
- practise listening to conversations about historic figures
- add information and ask questions with relative clauses

SPEAKING

1 Work in groups. Do you know who the people in the photos are?

VOCABULARY Important figures

2 Work in pairs. Don't use a dictionary. Discuss what you think the words in bold in the sentences mean. Can you translate them into your first language?

1 Christiane Nüsslein-Volhard is a German scientist who **was awarded** a Nobel prize for discovering the genes that control the development of animals.

2 Lee Byung-chul was the **founder** of South Korea's biggest company, Samsung. He started with a store making and exporting noodles.

3 Takako Doi was head of the Japanese **socialist party** at a time when few women got elected to parliament. She **inspired** other women to become politicians.

4 Argentinian writer Julio Cortázar's work has **influenced** many other writers and filmmakers. He**'s recognized as** one of the most important authors of the 20th century.

5 Serena Williams is a US **former** tennis player who completely **dominated** the sport at the start of the 21st century. She has won 23 singles titles and holds 25 Guiness World Records. Here she is competing at the 2017 Australia World Open.

6 Kemal Atatürk was the founder of modern Turkey, where he led **the struggle** for freedom and became the first president.

7 Hypatia was an ancient mathematician and philosopher whose life and murder made her **an icon for feminists**. Her story **was made into** the film *Agora*.

8 Beatriz Milhazes is a Brazilian artist whose **work combines** Latin and European styles. Her **pieces** are often very colourful, such as the sculpture *Marilola*, from the exhibition *Rio Azul*, which is made from metal, paper, plastic and wood.

3 Work in groups. Use as many of the phrases from Exercise 2 as you can to talk about other famous people, living or dead.

LISTENING

4 **FS** ▶ In fast speech, pronouns often join other words or almost disappear. Listen to eight phrases from the listening task. Which pronouns do you hear?

5 ▶ Listen to three conversations about historic figures. Answer the questions.

1 Why do the speakers start talking about historic figures in each conversation?

2 Which of the historic figures had you heard of before?

6 ▶ Listen again and complete the table with no more than two words and / or a number in each gap.

Name	Nationality	What were they?	When	Famous for
Garibaldi	Italian	1 _____	2 _____	Independence struggles in Italy, 3 _____ and Uruguay
Rosalind Franklin	–	4 _____	5 _____	Structure of 6 _____
Eddy Merckx	7 _____	8 _____	late 60s early 70s	Greatest ever 9 _____ record
Magritte	Belgian	10 _____	–	*Ceci n'est pas une pipe*

7 Work in pairs. Choose three sets of questions to discuss.

1 How important is it to learn about history? Who are seen as national heroes in your country?

2 What statues are there where you live? Who or what are they of? Do you like them? Why? / Why not?

3 Can you think of any historic figures that weren't recognized in their time? Why might some people's stories from history be hidden? Does it matter?

4 What awards, places etc. are named after someone? What's good or bad about naming things after people?

5 Do you know anyone who is a big fan of a historic figure? How do they show their interest?

GRAMMAR

Defining relative clauses

We use defining relative clauses to add information after nouns. Clauses can begin with a relative pronoun as the subject or object of the clause.

*Magritte was the guy **that** did pictures of office workers.*

*It's the station **where** they have the bike **that** he used.*

*He was a Spanish doctor **who** led a team **which** developed a vaccine.*

*She lived at a time **when** there were few women in politics.*

*She's a painter **whose** work combines Brazilian and European styles.*

*He's the reason **why** I got into cycling.*

We can usually leave out *who, which, why, when* or *that* before a subject + verb.

*Magritte was the painter **I was telling you about**.*

8 Look at the examples in the Grammar box. Complete these rules with the correct relative pronoun.

1 _____ and *who* refer to people.

2 *That* and _____ refer to things.

3 _____ and *which / that* refer to a time.

4 _____ refers to possessions.

5 _____ or *which / that* … *in / at / to* refer to places and positions.

6 _____ and *that* refer to a reason.

9 Choose the correct option to complete the sentences. Sometimes more than one option is possible.

1 He was a military leader from ancient history *who / that / which* conquered most of Asia.

2 It's a European Union scheme *that / who / which* provides grants to student teachers.

3 It's the gallery *which / – / where* they have Rembrandt's most famous paintings.

4 Reading her books is the reason *that / – / why* I wanted to become a writer myself.

5 He set up a charity *where / – / which* has helped thousands of poor children.

6 He's a composer *who / that / whose* most famous work is based on the sounds of the Amazon Rainforest.

7 At the time *that / who / when* he was writing, his ideas were seen as strange.

8 Do you know any cities *where / – / that* there are a lot of artists?

9 Who's the writer *whose / – / who* ideas have most influenced the world?

10 Work in pairs. Take turns to complete the questions with a relative clause. Your partner should answer.

1 What's the place _____ ?

2 Who is the person _____ ?

3 What do you think is the period of time _____ ?

4 What is the last thing _____ ?

5 Is there a reason why _____ ?

6 Who is the person whose _____ ?

G See Grammar reference 16C. »

SPEAKING TASK

11 Work in three or four teams. You're going to write a quiz about the news and history. In your team, write 6–8 questions.

Who was in the news recently for saying … ?
What's the name of the city where … ?

12 As a class, do the quiz. Do the following.

- Each team should take turns to read out their questions. Each question is worth one point.

- Give the other teams time to discuss their answers and write them down on a piece of paper.

- When every team has asked their questions, each team should take turns to give the correct answers. The team with the most points wins.

- Add up your final scores and find out who is the winner!

■ MY OUTCOMES ■

Work in pairs. Discuss the questions.

1 What have you enjoyed most overall about this course?

2 How much have you learned?

3 Was this unit more or less difficult than earlier units? In what way?

4 What language from this course do you need to revise and practise? How will you do that?

Writing a news story

SPEAKING

1 Work in pairs. Look at the local newspaper headlines. For each one, discuss what you imagine the rest of the story is about and say if you'd want to read it.

1 Car crash closes major road

2 Supermarket says sorry after Mother's Day flower problems

3 Teenager awarded prize for good citizenship

4 Swimming pool to be knocked down to build new one

5 Abandoned factory to be replaced by park

6 500 new homes to be built next year

7 Pensioner arrested after man hit with baseball bat on street

8 Reading volunteers meet mayor to discuss work

2 Work with a new partner. Discuss the questions.

1 Do you know much about what's happening where you live?

2 How do you find out this news?

3 Are the headlines in Exercise 1 things that might be reported where you live? What other kind of things might be reported?

WRITING

3 Read the news stories. Match them with the correct headlines in Exercise 1. How similar were your ideas to the actual stories?

Text A

Mayor Michelle Wang has announced that work will start next month to pull down an abandoned clothes factory in the north of the city to be replaced by a park and sports grounds. During the recent election, Wang promised to introduce a new green policy to improve the environment in the city and that one of her first acts as mayor would be to deal with the factory. The building has been empty for nearly ten years and is hated by local residents, who claim it is a centre for criminal activity. The Mayor said removing the factory would reduce crime and the park would create much-needed facilities in an area where there is little green space. The project will cost around $20 million and should be completed within two years.

Text B

Fifteen-year-old student Wan Bissako has won a Good Citizen Award for saving the life of a 73-year-old woman after she suffered a heart attack. The incident happened last year in the city centre while Wan was returning home from school. He noticed the woman, Lian Clovis, looked unwell as he passed her in the street and then turned to see her faint. Wan, who had previously taken first aid classes at school, instantly recognized Ms Clovis was having a heart attack and called an ambulance. He managed to keep the pensioner's heart beating while they were waiting and when paramedics arrived, they said Wan had saved the woman's life. Ms Clovis has since made a full recovery. The student hero was the youngest of the six people to win an award. Each winner received a medal and a £1,000 prize, which Wan said he would use to take his family out to dinner and to buy himself a new games console.

4 Work in pairs. Choose one set of questions to discuss.

1 Are there any abandoned buildings where you live? What were they? Do you know why they are abandoned?

2 Are there any awards for good citizens in your country? What kind of things do people win them for?

5 Work in pairs. Look at the news stories again and answer these questions.

1 How similar are the first lines of each story and the headline? What differences can you see?

2 What information is given after the first lines?

3 How many ways are the people in the stories referred to? What information do we learn about each person?

USEFUL LANGUAGE

Describing people in different ways

In news stories, we often refer to the same person in different ways. We do this so we can add information about the person, avoid too much repetition and make clear which person is being referred to.

Mayor Michelle Wang announced … Wang promised … The Mayor said …

Fifteen-year-old student Wan Bissako … Wan was returning … The schoolboy hero was the youngest …

6 Complete the first lines of the news stories (1–7) with these people. Then identify the other ways these people are referred to.

lead guitarist	motorist	MP
rider	schoolkids	senior citizen
soap star	suspect	victim

1 79-year-old Renata Casales finished her first ever marathon yesterday. The _____ from Concepción in Chile took just over seven and a half hours to compete the 49-kilometre course.

2 A new arts space was officially opened in Wood Green today by _____ , Misha Barry. The actor said it was an honour to be invited.

3 Sandra Fischer, _____ of the band NeinMine, has announced she is splitting from the group. The 35-year-old musician said she wanted a new challenge.

4 Three teenagers who had gone missing in the Pyrenees during a school trip have been found. The _____ , who attend Erasmus College, became separated from the group while they were walking.

5 _____ Baber Javid has criticized the government's education policy. The 63-year-old politician said more needed to be done to support young people.

6 A man was arrested yesterday for murder of restaurant owner, Razak bin Hassan. Police have not named the _____ . The brother of the _____ has asked for privacy.

7 A woman was badly injured yesterday when she was knocked off her motorbike by a car. The _____ , who was delivering pizzas, was taken to the General Hospital while police arrested the _____ for possible dangerous driving.

7 Write three similar news-story beginnings. Use the words from Exercise 6 along with other ways of referring to the same person / people.

Explaining time and order of events

We can use different kinds of words to show the time and order of events:

Conjunctions that join two clauses (*as, while, when, after, before*).

*He saved her life **after** she had suffered a heart attack.*

*He noticed the woman looked unwell **as** he passed her.*

Prepositions that join a clause to a noun / as a noun phrase (*during, after, before*).

***During** the election, she promised a new green policy.*

*The supermarket had to apologize **after** problems with deliveries.*

Adverbs that go with a verb phrase (*previously, instantly, immediately, suddenly*).

*Wan, who had **previously** taken first aid classes at school, **instantly** recognized Ms Clovis was having a heart attack.*

8 Choose the correct option to complete the sentences. Sometimes more than one option is possible.

1 Several arrests have been made *before / as / during* the current investigation.

2 The car was stolen from the garage *as / instantly / while* the owner was paying for the petrol.

3 The young man tried to grab his bag and the 50-year-old father of two *after / instantly / previously* screamed for help.

4 *During / After / While* the match, several people in the crowd came on to the pitch.

5 The 19-year-old singer *before / previously / while* worked in a shoe factory.

6 Historic remains were found *during / suddenly / when* the building was pulled down.

7 *After / When / While* the work is finished, the sports centre will provide jobs for 60 people in the area.

8 There is expected to be a lot of noise and traffic problems *during / while / as* the building work.

9 Add one or two sentences to each of the stories you wrote in Exercise 7. Use different ways to show the order of events.

PRACTICE

10 M Work in pairs or on your own. Do the following.

1 Find an interesting local news story in your first language.

2 Find two different sources about the story if you can and note down some details.

3 Based on your notes, write a headline in English and a story of 150–200 words.

11 Work in groups. Read each other's stories and write questions:

1 about any part of the story you don't understand.

2 about something you'd like to know more about.

3 about any language you're uncertain about.

12 In your groups, share your questions and discuss how your stories could be improved. Then rewrite them.

VIDEO Out and about

1 **Work in pairs. Discuss the questions.**

1 Would you like to be famous? Why? / Why not?

2 Who is the most famous person in your country at the moment / in the past?

Understanding accents

Some accents use an /uː/ sound instead of an /ʌ/ sound, so *but* /bʌt/ may sound more like *boot* /buːt/.

2 🎥 **Watch three people answer the same questions. How much can you remember about what they said? Then work in pairs. Do you know any of the famous people they mention?**

3 🎥 **Watch again. Match two sentences with each speaker. There are two extra sentences.**

a They think it's easier to get rich through fame than corporate life.

b They wouldn't like the attention from photographers.

c They don't like to talk about their life with strangers.

d They talk about some who makes comedy videos.

e They talk about someone promoting a film.

f They talk about someone who represented their country and way of life.

g They talk about an Olympic athlete.

h They talk about a political leader.

4 **Discuss the questions with your partner.**

1 Have you seen any interviews recently with famous people promoting a film, book, album, etc.? Were they any good? Why? / Why not?

2 What writers / artist / musicians represent your culture well? In what way?

3 Do you agree fame is an easy way to make money? Why? / Why not?

4 Do you follow any famous people on social media? If so, who and why? If not, why not?

VIDEO Developing conversations

5 🎥 **You're going to watch two people talking about an accident. Watch and take notes.**

6 🎥 **Work in pairs. Compare what you understood. Watch again if you need to.**

7 FS 🎥 **Watch again. Complete the sentences with three to five words in each gap.**

1 I was running with my kite, all happy and jolly, and then _____ I find myself on the ground.

2 It has swelled up quite a bit – _____ lie.

3 Yeah _____ … Have you been to the doctor's?

4 _____ sprained it, because I didn't hear anything break.

5 I know, _____ getting a medical opinion.

6 _____ medicine?

7 I can run you to the hospital – _____ an X-ray.

8 Don't worry … _____ to help you.

CONVERSATION PRACTICE

8 **Work in pairs. You're going to practise a conversation.**

1 Choose a Conversation practice from either Lesson 15A or Lesson 16A.

2 Look at the language in that lesson.

3 Check the meaning of anything you've forgotten with your partner.

4 Have the conversation. Try to improve on the last time you did it.

Grammar and Vocabulary

GRAMMAR

1 Complete the text with one word in each gap.

A few years ago, the company [1]_____
I was working for officially [2]_____ that they
[3]_____ starting this new scheme that
[4]_____ provide us all with excellent health
insurance. My employers [5]_____ to pay us all sick
pay and to cover most medical bills. All we had to do was
go for a quick check-up with the doctor. Sounds great,
right? Well, I went the [6]_____ week and got a bit
of a shock. The doctor [7]_____ asking me loads of
personal questions – you know, like [8]_____ I was
married, [9]_____ I didn't have any kids yet, and so
on. I couldn't believe it! The next thing I knew, the company
sent me an email apologizing [10]_____ bringing me
bad news, and saying I didn't qualify. Incredible! I briefly
considered complaining [11]_____ the experience to
someone, but a colleague warned me [12]_____ to.

2 Read the first sentence in each pair. Complete the
second sentence so that it has a similar meaning. Use
between two and five words, including the word in
bold.

1 I offered to pay, but he refused to listen!   **INSISTED**
   He _____, even though I offered myself.

2 During the exam, a teacher said two students were
   cheating.   **ACCUSED**
   Two students _____ during the exam.

3 I went to a studio. The Beatles recorded there.   **THE**
   I went to _____ The Beatles recorded.

4 Can you speak a bit more slowly?   **TOO**
   You're speaking a bit _____ for me.

5 He seemed sure it was going to be fine.   **WOULD**
   He kept saying _____ fine.

3 Choose the correct option to complete the sentences.
Sometimes more than one option is correct.

1 That's the hospital *that / which / where* I had my
   operation in a few years ago.

2 We met during the time *when / which / that* I was
   working in the Munich office.

3 He was a military leader *who / that / which* inspired great
   loyalty in his army.

4 He said he *was going to / is going to / would* do it
   sometime later in the year.

5 He *suggested / complained / refused* to consider my idea.

6 He kept asking what *had happened / was happening /
   was going to happen*.

7 She promised *she'd help / helping / to help* me.

4 ▶ Listen and write the six sentences you hear.

VOCABULARY

5 Match the two parts of the collocations.

1	resign	a	a law / a new system
2	introduce	b	rapidly / into the Asian market
3	expand	c	disaster / job losses
4	negotiate	d	your knee / easily
5	investigate	e	her to hospital / home
6	result in	f	as a minister / over the issue
7	rush	g	on a banana skin / on the ice
8	bruise	h	a murder / the incident
9	slip	i	a new deal / with us

6 Decide if these words and phrases are connected to
illness, accidents or the news.

bang	condition	elected	fall off
medication	rash	shares	sprain
suspect	suspended	throw up	trip
victim	virus	X-ray	

7 Complete the sentences with the correct form of the
words in bold.

1 She was knocked _____ when she banged her
   head.   **conscious**

2 There were job _____ in many companies.   **lose**

3 They've signed a new trade _____ .   **agree**

4 Things are becoming _____ difficult.   **increase**

5 Smartphones can be quite _____ .   **addict**

6 His illness is due to not eating _____ .   **health**

7 I had a nasty _____ to the sun cream I was using.
   react

8 They need to _____ people's rights!   **strength**

8 Complete the text with one word in each gap. The
first letters are given.

The Mexican artist Frida Kahlo only started painting
following a traffic accident, when a tram [1]r_____
i_____ the bus she was travelling in. It
[2]re_____ in terrible injuries and during her
[3]re_____ , she began to paint. Her work then was
[4]inf_____ by her husband, the artist Diego Rivera,
who [5]do_____ the Mexican art scene at
the time. However, she created her own style, which
[6]co_____ surrealist art and aspects of Mexican
culture, in many self-portraits. She was awarded a national
prize in 1946, but only was [7]re_____ as a truly
great artist internationally in the 1970s. Her popularity
has grown ever since. She became an [8]i_____ for
feminists for her strong independent attitudes and look,
and she has [9]ins_____ many people in her
[10]st_____ with pain and disability that she shows in
[11]pi_____ such as *Tree of Hope, Remain Strong*. Her
life was [12]m_____ i_____ a film in 2002 –
Frida starring Salma Hayek.

Grammar reference

1A AUXILIARY VERBS

There are three auxiliary verbs: *be, do* and *have*. They are used with different forms of a main verb to make questions, negatives and other structures.

Be

We use forms of the verb *be* (*am / is / are / was / were*) with the *-ing* form of the main verb to form the present continuous and the past continuous. Note that we add *not* or *-n't* to the auxiliary verb *am / is / are / was / were* to form the negative.

She **isn't feeling** very well. (*present continuous*)
What **are** you **studying**? (*present continuous*)
They **weren't living** in Porto at the time. (*past continuous*)
What **was** she **doing** in Kazakhstan? (*past continuous*)

We also use the verb *be* with the past participle to make passive forms of the verb.
What language **is** that **written** in? (*present simple passive*)
The film **was made** about ten years ago. (*past simple passive*)

Do

We use forms of the verb *do* (*do / does / did*) with the infinitive (without *to*) of the main verb to form negatives and questions in the present simple and past simple. Note that we add *not* or *-n't* to the auxiliary verb *do / does / did* to form the negative.

He **doesn't** really **like** this kind of music. (*present simple*)
We **don't live** near each other. (*present simple*)
Do you **like** Indian food? (*present simple*)
I **didn't go** anywhere last night. (*past simple*)
Did you **have** a good time last night? (*past simple*)

Have

We use forms of the verb *have* with the past participle form of the main verb to form the present perfect simple. Note that we add *not* or *-n't* to the auxiliary verb *have / has* to form the negative.

Have you ever **eaten** snake?
Has your brother **been** to Lisbon before?
I**'ve been** there a few times.
She **hasn't arrived** yet.

To form the present perfect continuous, we use *have / has + been*.
How long **have** you **been studying** English?
He **hasn't been working** there very long.

We also use *had* to form the past perfect.
I didn't see them. They **had** already **left** when I arrived.
We **hadn't met** before. Yesterday was the first time.

See Grammar reference 2B for more about the past perfect.

Exercise 1

Choose the correct option to complete the sentences.

1 I heard you were ill yesterday. *Is / Are / Does* you feeling better now?
2 *Do / Does* you and your sister get on OK?
3 Where *did / were* you born?
4 *Did / Have / Were* you visited many different countries?
5 *Have / Has / Is* your parents met your girlfriend yet?

6 Where *were / did / does* your parents first meet?
7 How long *are you been / has you been / have you been* waiting?
8 How long *is / have / has / does* he been married?
9 When *has / was / were* the book written?
10 The taxi *didn't / hasn't / wasn't* arrived yet.

Exercise 2

Make negative sentences by adding the correct auxiliary verb + *not / -n't*.

1 She working today, I'm afraid. I think she's sick.
2 Can we go somewhere else? I really like this place.
3 I don't see my sister very often. She live very near me.
4 I working at the moment. I need to find a job!
5 When I told them, they believe me. They said I was lying!
6 We going away during the holidays. We're just staying at home.
7 He studied for his exams at all. He's going to fail!
8 She went home because she feeling very well.
9 I feel bad because I done the homework for today.
10 He been studying French for very long, but he speaks it really well.

Exercise 3

Are these sentences true for you? Rewrite the sentences that aren't true as negative sentences.

1 I play the piano.
   I don't play the piano.
2 I live in a village.
3 I'm feeling tired.
4 I watched TV last night.
5 I like rock music.
6 I've been to the US.
7 It's raining at the moment.
8 It's been sunny all day.

There is further practice of auxiliary verbs in:
- Unit 1, when you look at the present simple and present continuous.
- Unit 2, when you look at the past simple, past continuous and past perfect.
- Unit 3, when you look at the present perfect simple and past simple.
- Unit 4, when you look at the present perfect continuous and past simple.
- Unit 9, when you look at the present perfect simple and present perfect continuous.
- Unit 11, when you look at passives.

1C PRESENT SIMPLE AND PRESENT CONTINUOUS

Present simple

We use the present simple to talk about both the present and the future. The main uses are to talk about:
- habits and regular repeated activities. Note that we can say 'how often' using adverbs such as *usually, often, sometimes, hardly ever* and *never*.
  I **train** on Saturdays.
  I **don't** usually **play** football on Wednesdays.
  Does he always **cycle** to work?

- facts and things that we see as permanent.

  I **live** in Bucharest.

  He **doesn't speak** any other languages.

  Does she **work** in the city centre?

- future events that are part of a timetable or a schedule.

  The bus **leaves** at 2:10.

  My classes **finish** at 5:30.

Present continuous

We use the present continuous to talk about both the present and the future. The main uses are to talk about:

- temporary, unfinished activities that are in progress at the time of speaking. Note that to emphasize that something is temporary, we often use expressions such as *at the moment, currently, this week* and *this month*.

  She**'s staying** with her brother this week.

  I**'m** not **working** at the moment.

  Is it **raining** again out there?

- things in the future that are already decided and planned or agreed / arranged with other people.

  I**'m going** out for dinner with a client on Friday.

  We**'re getting** married in the summer.

  They **aren't meeting** tomorrow.

DID YOU KNOW?

Verbs which express states (such as attitude, feelings or possession) are generally used in the simple form, even to describe unfinished or temporary states. These verbs include:

agree	believe	belong	depend	disagree
doubt	forget	hate	know	like
matter	mind	owe	own	prefer
realize	seem	suppose	taste	want

  Are you OK? You **seem** a bit sad.

  I **don't want** to talk about it at the moment.

  I'm tired. I **need** to go to bed.

Note that we can use some of these verbs in the continuous form. This is usually when we want to emphasize the feeling or situation is temporary.

  I**'m** really **liking** this risotto. It's delicious.

  Are you **wanting** anything more to eat?

Exercise 1

Choose the correct option to complete the sentences.

1 A: What are the hours like where you work?

   B: OK. *I'm usually just working / I usually just work* nine to five, but at the moment *I'm doing / I do* a lot of extra hours because we've got a deadline to meet. So, just for this month, *I'm starting / I start* at nine in the morning and *finishing / finish* at nine or ten at night.

2 A: Where do you work?

   B: Well, *I'm normally working / I normally work* in the centre of town, but next week *I'm working / I work* from home because *they decorate / they're decorating* our office.

3 A: What does your job involve?

   B: It's general office work, really. *I'm answering / I answer* the phone and *making / make* appointments for my boss, that kind of thing. But *we're holding / we hold* a conference in a couple of weeks, so at the moment *I'm sorting out / I sort out* lots of things for that as well.

4 A: When's the conference?

   B: Next month, over the weekend of the 26th. *It's going on / It goes on* until the 29th, I think. *Are you going? / Do you go?*

Exercise 2

Which six sentences are incorrect? Correct them.

1 Can you phone back later? I have dinner at the moment.

2 I'm sorry, but I disagree with you.

3 Is she seeing anyone at the moment?

4 I'm annoyed with him. He's still owing me money.

5 I don't need any help thanks. I just look.

6 I go to the shops. Do you want anything?

7 I'm not a tea drinker. I'm preferring coffee.

8 I love cycling. I'm belonging to a local cycling club.

Exercise 3

Complete the sentences to make them true for you.

1 I … at the moment.

2 I usually …

3 Next week, I …

4 I never …

5 I … at the weekend.

2 FEELINGS

2A   LINKING VERBS

Use

A linking verb is a verb that is followed by an adjective, a noun or a clause that tells us something about or describes the subject.

The hotel is **great**.

Jenny seems **tired**.

Their holiday sounds like it was **a disaster**.

The most common linking verb is *be*. Other common linking verbs are *look, seem, feel, sound, taste* and *smell*.

Form

We use different patterns when linking verbs are followed by an adjective, a clause or a noun.

Linking verb + adjective

We can use a linking verb + adjective without adding any other words. We can also use modifiers such as *very, a bit, slightly, really* and *too* before the adjective.

I **feel fine**.

This cake **tastes strange**.

He **looked** a bit **upset**.

Linking verb + noun

When we use a linking verb followed by a noun, we use linking verb + *like* + noun. The meaning is *the same as* or *similar to*. We can also use modifiers such as *a bit, quite*, etc. before *like*. We can use *nothing* to say there is no similarity.

The journey **sounds like** a nightmare!

It **tastes** a bit **like** chicken.

He **looks** nothing **like** a model!

Linking verb + clause

When a linking verb is followed by a clause, we use linking verb + *as if* / *like* + clause.

You **look as if** you're in a good mood. How come?

You **sound like** you're feeling better.

Note that we can use *as though* with the same meaning as *as if*.

I feel guilty. I **feel as though** it's my fault.

Note that we can use *seem* and *sound* without *as if* / *as though* or *like*.

It seems ~~as though~~ she's a bit annoyed about something.

The party sounds ~~like~~ fun.

DID YOU KNOW?

As if, as though and *like* mean the same thing when used after a linking verb. However, we usually use *like* in more informal contexts, such as conversation. In exams and when writing, it therefore may be better to use *as if* and *as though*.

Exercise 1

Which five sentences are incorrect? Correct them.

1 Do you understand? You still look like a bit confused.
2 She said the flight would cost €50 and the hotel €30 a night, which sounds like a really good deal.
3 I had to tell him the bad news. I felt as if terrible afterwards.
4 Don't eat that. It tastes like really disgusting.
5 It's quite frustrating in class. It sometimes seems as I'm the only person who wants to study and learn.
6 She sounded like quite upset the last time I spoke to her.
7 I've only met him once, but I enjoyed talking to him. He seemed like a very interesting guy.

DID YOU KNOW?

Linking verbs are most commonly used in the simple form. We sometimes use a continuous form, but the meaning is usually the same. If in doubt, use the simple form.
You're looking well. = You look well.
I'm feeling a bit ill. = I feel a bit ill.

Exercise 2

Complete the sentences with one or two words in each gap. Three sentences don't need words added.

1 I'm feeling a bit _____ tired.
2 This tofu tastes _____ fish.
3 She sounds a bit _____ nervous.
4 You look _____ you're worried about something.
5 They look _____ they are lost.
6 Their holiday sounds _____ a disaster.
7 It sounds _____ you had a great time last night.
8 The new neighbours seem _____ very nice.
9 It looks _____ we're going to be about an hour late.
10 I look nothing _____ my parents.

2B TELLING STORIES

When we tell a story, we often use a combination of the past simple, past continuous and past perfect forms.

Past simple

We use the past simple to tell the main events of the story, usually in the order they occurred. It is the most common form we use when telling stories.

*I **heard** a noise and **turned** round to look. I **didn't see** the hole in the ground in front of me and so I **tripped** and **fell**. I **hurt** my knee quite badly.*

We usually add *-ed* to form a past simple verb. Remember that some past forms are irregular, such as *spoke, fell* and *met*. To make a negative, we use *didn't* + verb.
*We arriv**ed** at 6:30.*
*I **spoke** to a few people.*
*They **didn't wait** for us.*

Past continuous

We often use the past continuous to give background information about the situation or about events taking place at or around the time of a story. We also use it while we're telling the story to give background to some of the main events.

*Something similar happened to me when I **was living** in Dubai. One day, I was at work ...*

We often use the past continuous to show that a background activity or situation was interrupted or stopped by another action.

*I **was walking** through the park when suddenly it started to rain. We quickly turned around and ran home.*

We use *was(n't) / were(n't)* + *-ing* to make the past continuous form of the verb.
*He **was** wait**ing** for us at the station.*
*We **were** walk**ing** on the beach.*
*They **weren't** work**ing**.*

Past perfect simple

We use the past perfect simple to show that something happened before something else in the past. When we're telling a story, we use it to talk about something that happened either before the beginning of the story or before an event in the story. We often use the past perfect simple with words like *already, previously* or *before*. Note that we usually use the past simple for the more recent action or situation.

*I suddenly remembered I **hadn't turned off** the cooker, so I ran home, but by the time I got there, the kitchen **had already caught** fire.*

*We**'d previously met** a few times, but this was the first time we spoke to each other.*

We use *had(n't)* + past participle to form the past perfect simple.
*She**'d spoken** to him a few times already.*
*I **hadn't seen** the film before.*

Exercise 1

Match the beginnings of the sentences (1–8) with the endings (a–h).

1 He didn't come out last night because
2 He didn't post the letter, even though
3 I was really surprised he failed the exam because
4 I think he got upset because
5 By the time we got there Nina had already left, so
6 When we got there the show was just starting, so
7 We first met while
8 I met my girlfriend at around eight and then

a he'd studied a lot.
b we went to a friend's for dinner.
c we didn't really miss much.
d I'd reminded him at least three times.
e we were laughing at him.
f he was doing some exam revision.
g we were travelling in South America.
h I didn't manage to speak to her.

Exercise 2

Complete the story with the correct form of the verbs in brackets.

I remember a mistake I made when I [1]_____ (teach) English in Argentina. I [2]_____ (learn) a bit of Spanish before in the UK, but I wasn't very accurate or fluent. Anyway, I was in class one day trying to get the students to talk, but they [3]_____ (not say) anything, so I said in Spanish, 'Don't be embarrassed! We all make mistakes. Just try.' The students [4]_____ (look) surprised and said '*Embarazada*?' 'Yes,' I said, 'I know how you feel because I'm a Spanish student and I'm embarrassed too sometimes.' I later found out I [5]_____ (not use) the right word – *embarazada* actually means pregnant! After that, being 'embarrassed' [6]_____ (become) a joke in class and I never [7]_____ (make) that mistake again! Funnily enough, the students actually [8]_____ (start) talking a bit more in English in class as a result. And I [9]_____ (decide) it was a good idea to learn a bit more Spanish too!

Exercise 3

Complete the story extracts with your own ideas.

1 The other day, I was _____ in the park when I _____ and old friend who I hadn't _____ for a long time. It _____ really good to see him and we _____ for ages.

2 At the weekend, my friends _____ to the cinema, but I didn't _____ because I had already _____ the film. Instead, I _____ at home and _____ TV.

3 Last month, I was _____ to work, when another car _____ into me. Luckily, no-one _____ hurt and there _____ only a little damage to the cars. That _____ the first time I had ever _____ an accident.

---

3 TIME OFF

3B FUTURE PLANS

Definite plans, intentions and arrangements

We generally use the present continuous to talk about things that are arranged, agreed or finalized.

We're staying in a five-star hotel.
I'm seeing my grandparents on Sunday.

We generally use *be going to + verb* to talk about things that are planned or intended, but not arranged, agreed or finalized.

She's going to stay in this evening.
We're not going to have a holiday this year.
I'm going to see my grandparents soon.

However, sometimes the difference between using the present continuous and *be going to* isn't clear, so we can use either form with no real difference in meaning.

I'm seeing my cousins at the weekend. / I'm going to see my cousins at the weekend.

He's watching the rugby this evening. / He's going to watch the rugby this evening.

DID YOU KNOW?

Instead of saying *be going to go*, we often just say *be going*. This is easier to say and avoids repeating the verb *go*.

I'm going ~~to go~~ to the shops. Are you going ~~to go~~ away?

Less certain plans

When we haven't completely decided on a plan or we want to show uncertainty, we can use *will, might* or *be thinking of*.

- *will + probably / possibly + verb*, or *probably / possibly won't + verb*

  I'm not absolutely sure, but I'll probably go out later.
  We'll possibly go out later, but it probably won't be for long.

- *might / may (not) + verb*

  We might not go on holiday this year.
  I may have to work right through the summer.

- *be thinking of + -ing form*

  I'm thinking of going to China. I have a friend there who's invited me to visit.
  When are you thinking of going?

Questions about plans

We generally use the present continuous or *be going to* to ask about plans.

What are you doing this afternoon?
Are you doing anything at the weekend?

Are you going away in the summer?
Where are you going to stay?

You can also ask:

Do you have any plans (for) *today / this afternoon / the summer?*

Do you have any plans to *look for a new job / get a new car / take a holiday?*

Exercise 1

Choose the correct option to complete the sentences. Sometimes both options are correct.

1 I can't wait for the holiday. *I'm visiting / I'm going to visit* my grandparents in Hong Kong.

2 My dad probably *won't come / isn't coming* with us. It depends how much work he has.

3 *We're meeting / We might meet* at 6:30. Don't be late or we'll miss the beginning of the film!

4 *We're thinking of going / We're going* to Cuba in April, but we haven't decided for sure.

5 *I might go / I'm thinking of going* travelling after I finish university. I'll see how much money I have.

6 A: What *are you doing / will you do* in the summer holidays?
   B: I haven't decided. *I'm going to / I might* just stay at home.

7 A: Do you have any plans *to / for* this evening?
   B: No, *I'm not doing / I'm not going to do* anything.

8 A: *Are you doing / Will you do* anything interesting at the weekend?
   B: Yeah, *I'm meeting / I'm going to meet* some friends. *We're thinking of going / We might go* to the beach.

Exercise 2

Complete the sentences with a future form of the verbs in brackets. Sometimes more than one answer is possible.

1 A: I _____ (meet) Marco and Letitia this evening. Do you want to join us?
   B: Thanks, but Ginny _____ (come) round for dinner. I _____ (not do) anything on Friday, though.

2 A: What _____ you _____ (do) tomorrow? Do you have any plans?
   B: I _____ (see) a client in the morning, but after that I'm free.

3 A: Do you fancy going out this evening?
   B: Thanks, but I _____ (probably stay) in this evening.

4 A: Have you got any plans for the summer?
   B: Well, we _____ (possibly go) to Greece again, but we haven't decided yet? What about you?
   A: We _____ (go) to Canada for two weeks in August.
   B: Nice. Whereabouts _____ (you go)?
   A: I've got relatives in Toronto, so we _____ (stay) with them. And we _____ (probably hire) a car at some point and have a bit of a road trip.

Exercise 3

Complete the sentences about next weekend to make them true for you.

1 I'll probably …
2 I'm going to …
3 I might …
4 I'm not going to …
5 I'm thinking of …
6 I'm _____ ing …

3C PRESENT PERFECT SIMPLE

Use

One common use of the present perfect simple is to talk about our experiences. We can use it to start a new conversation, often as a question to ask about someone's experience. We also use it to talk about experiences connected to a present discussion or topic. The experience has relevance now.

A: **Have** you **been** to Cologne?
B: Yes, I**'ve been** there a few times. I went there when I was living in Germany.

A: I'm going to London next month. **Have** you ever **been** there?
B: No, never. But I'd love to one day.

A: Why do you think you'll make a good English teacher?
B: Well, I**'ve done** some teaching before. I**'ve travelled** a lot, I**'ve been** to several countries in Europe and Asia and I**'ve also experienced** learning a language myself.

Note that when we use the present perfect simple in this way, we don't usually say when the experience happened.
~~I've done some teaching a few years ago.~~
~~I've been there last year.~~

Form

The present perfect simple is *have / has* + past participle.
I**'ve been** to Hiroshima.
He**'s been** there before.
Have you ever **visited** there?

To form the negative, we add *not* or *-n't*. We also often use *never* to mean *'not in my life'*.
I **haven't been** to Hiroshima.
She **hasn't travelled** much.
I**'ve never been** to Germany.

When we ask a question about someone's experiences, we sometimes use *ever* to emphasize 'at any time in your life'.
Have you **ever** been to Mexico?
Have you **ever** done a bungee jump?

Answering present perfect questions

When we answer present perfect questions, we often add details to help develop the conversation. Here are some common answers to the question *Have you (ever) …?*

Yeah (I have).	A couple of times.
	Last week, actually.
	I've been there a few times.
	I went there last year on holiday.
	I saw it a couple of years ago.
No (I haven't / never).	It's never really appealed to me.
	I've heard it's really good, though.
	But I'd love / like to one day.
	But I want to / I've always wanted to.
	But I'm (thinking of) going there next month, actually.
	What's it like?

We can add more details about an experience using the past simple. Here, we can use a time phrase to say when something happened.

Well, I've done some teaching before. I **taught** computer skills **a couple of years ago** to unemployed people back home.

I've travelled a lot. I've been to several countries in Europe and Asia. I actually **went** to Japan **a few months ago.** I **learned** some Japanese **before I went there**.

Common mistakes

We don't use the present perfect with a time phrase that says when the event happened.
I've been there ~~in 2022~~.
He's lost his passport ~~last week~~.
They've already had lunch ~~at 12:30~~.

Exercise 1

Complete the sentences with the present perfect simple or past simple form of the verbs in brackets.

1 One of the best places I ¹_____ (visit) is Hampi in India. It's a very historic place. About 700 years ago, it ²_____ (be) the capital of the Vijayanagara Empire, which later ³_____ (become) part of India.

2 It sounds strange, but I ⁴_____ (be) to Ireland three times, and I ⁵_____ (never go) outside Dublin, the capital. The last time I ⁶_____ (be) there, I ⁷_____ (plan) to visit more places, but in the end I just ⁸_____ (not have) time.

3 A: ⁹_____ (you / ever / be) to Malta?
   B: Yes, a few times. I ¹⁰_____ (go) there mainly for work, but it's a great place for a holiday.
   A: We're actually thinking of going to Gozo, the island next to Malta. ¹¹_____ (you / go) there?
   B: I have, but it ¹²_____ (be) quite a long time ago. That ¹³_____ (be) for a family holiday.
   A: What ¹⁴_____ (you / think) of it? ¹⁵_____ (you like) it?
   B: To be honest, I ¹⁶_____ (not / see) very much of it. We ¹⁷_____ (stay) mainly at the hotel.

Exercise 2

Which of B's answers are incorrect? Correct them.

1 A: Have you been to that new market yet?
   B: Yes, I have, actually. I've been shopping there yesterday – and guess what? I bumped into Rick while I've been there.

2 A: We went to see the musical *We Will Rock You* last night. Have you seen it?
   B: No, but I'd like to. I've heard it's really good.

3 A: We went to that Ethiopian restaurant round the corner. Have you eaten there yet?
   B: No. What it's like?

4 A: Have you ever done a parachute jump?
   B: No, never, but I always want to ever since I was a kid.

5 A: Have you been to that fish restaurant on the high street?
   B: Yeah! I went there loads of times. It's one of my favourites.

6 A: Have you ever been to Japan?
   B: Yes. I went there last year, actually.

Exercise 3

Complete the sentences to make them true for you.

1 I've been to … a few times. I first went there in …
2 I've never … , but I'd like to.
3 I've … only once. That was … ago.
4 I've always wanted to …
5 I haven't … since …
6 I've wanted to … since …

4A HABIT AND FREQUENCY

Present and past habits

To talk about present habits, we use the present simple and frequency adverbs (e.g. *sometimes, often, usually, hardly ever never*) and / or a frequency phrase (e.g. *every day, every couple of months, twice a week, once a month*).

I *sometimes go* cycling by the river. *It's lovely there.*
I *never watch* TV. *I just don't have time.*
I *usually go* the gym *twice a week*.
We *go there every couple of months*.

To talk about habits in the past, we use the past simple or *used to* + verb and frequency adverbs and phrases.
When I was a kid, we **always went** *to Blackpool.*
Until recently, I **went** *to the gym* **two or three times a week**.
I **hardly ever used to go** *swimming when I was younger.*

Position of frequency adverbs and phrases

Frequency adverbs normally go between the subject and the verb, but they go after the verb *be*.
In my old job, I **sometimes had** *to work late, but* **I hardly ever worked** *weekends.*
We usually go *skiing every year.*
He's **often** *late for work these days.*

Frequency phrases normally go at the end of the sentence or clause, although other positions are sometimes possible.
We usually go skiing **every year**. *I try to go* **two or three times**, *if possible.*
She goes running **almost every day**.

Asking about frequency

When we ask about frequency of habits, we use questions with *How often, ever* and *much / a lot*.
How often *do you go fishing?*
Do you **ever** *go swimming?*
Do you play tennis **a lot**?
Did you (use to) go climbing **much** *when you lived in Switzerland?*

Answering about frequency

To answer questions about frequency, we can use frequency adverbs and phrases as well as a range of other phrases. We often add details to our answers.

How often do you meet up?	**Usually every week,** *if we can.*
Do you ever go to the theatre?	*Maybe* **two or three times a year**. *But it's a bit expensive these days.*
Do you see each other much?	*We* **usually** *see each other* **once or twice a month**.
Do you eat out much?	**Hardly ever, these days**. *The last time was two months ago.*
Do you read much?	*Yeah,* **all the time**.
How often do you go to the cinema?	**Quite often / Quite a lot**. *Probably twice a month.*
Do you exercise much?	**Sometimes**. *It depends how I feel.*
How often do you go away for the weekend?	**Not that often**. *I don't have much spare time.*

We can also answer questions about frequency with *whenever* meaning 'every time'.

How often do you exercise?	**Whenever** *I can.*
	Whenever *I get the chance.*

We also often answer using phrases that compare one thing with another.

How often do you exercise?	*Not as much as I used to.*
	Not as often as before.
	Not as much as I'd like to.
	Not as much as I should.

Exercise 1

Correct the incorrect frequency phrases.

1 A: Do you ever go swimming?
　B: No, hardly never. I don't really like it.
2 A: How often do you go out?
　B: Not much often. I'm very busy with my studies.
3 A: Did you use to go and watch them play a lot?
　B: Yeah, basically once a two weeks.
4 A: Did your parents ever take you to art exhibitions?
　B: Yeah, sometimes. Probably twice or once a year.
5 A: Can we meet on Tuesday evening?
　B: I'm sorry, I can't. Always I go to my art class on Tuesdays.
6 A: So how often do you go walking?
　B: Whenever I will get the chance.
7 A: Do you go to the gym a lot?
　B: Not as much how I should.
8 A: Do you do much sport?
　B: Not as much as I used. I had a foot injury for a while which stopped me.

Exercise 2

Put the frequency adverb or phrase in the correct place in the sentence. Sometimes more than one position is possible.

1 When I was a kid, my parents let me stay out late. (never)
2 My brother goes swimming before I get up. (every morning)
3 Do you go running? (ever)
4 I see my parents. (usually, once or twice a week)
5 When I was at school, I studied hard and I did my homework. (always, always)
6 I go the gym, but I go more than that. It depends how I feel. (generally, twice a week, sometimes).
7 I used to read. But now it's just two or three books. I just have the time. (all the time, a year, never)
8 I don't see my best friend these days. We're both very busy. (as much as I'd like to, usually)

Exercise 3

Complete the sentences to make them true for you.

1 I usually … every week.
2 I … whenever I can.
3 These days, I hardly ever …
4 I … once or twice a week.
5 I used to … a lot, but not anymore.

4C PRESENT PERFECT CONTINUOUS AND PAST SIMPLE FOR DURATION

Present perfect continuous or present perfect simple?

To talk about duration when an activity or situation is still taking place or affects the present situation, we usually use the present perfect continuous (*have / has + (not) been + -ing*).
How long **have** *you* **been learning** *English?*
He **hasn't been working** *here for long.*
*Aren't you tired? You***'ve been driving** *all day.*

However, verbs that describe states (such as *know, have* and *belong*) are usually used in the present perfect simple (*have / has + (not) + past participle*) rather than the present perfect continuous.

*How long **have** you **known** each other?*

*They**'ve had** that car for years.*

***Have** you **belonged** to the club for a long time?*

We can also use the present perfect simple for situations that we see as being more permanent.

*She's **worked** here for over 30 years.*

*How long **have** they **lived** here?*

To talk about duration when an activity or situation is finished, we use the past simple.

*I **lived** in Brazil for ten years before I moved back to the US.*

*I **played** padel for years until I injured my knee.*

A: I used to be in an athletics team.

*B: How long **did** you **do** that for?*

A: About five years, I guess.

Since and for

- ***Since*** or ***ever since*** show when a current activity or situation started.

  since 2018 / April 10th / last Monday

  since his injury / the election / the start of the season

  ever since I was a kid / I got injured / we got married

- We usually use *since* phrases with perfect forms.

  *I**'ve been** really into martial arts **ever since I went to Thailand.***

- ***For*** shows the length / period of time something lasted.

  for five minutes / six months

  for ages / hours / weeks / years

  for a while / a long time / a week

- We can use *for* with both perfect and simple forms.

  *I**'ve been waiting** for 20 minutes.*

  *I **waited** for 20 minutes.*

DID YOU KNOW?

In spoken English, we sometimes miss out *for*.

A: How long have you been waiting?   *B: ~~For~~ Half an hour.*

I worked there ~~for~~ a long time before I got to know people.

Exercise 1

Choose the correct option to complete the sentences.

1 A: I have my yoga class tonight.

   B: Really? How long *have you been doing / did you do* that?

2 A: I think I spent too long in the gym yesterday. I'm really stiff this morning.

   B: How long *have you been / were you* there for?

3 A: My brother*'s been skiing / skied* ever since I can remember. He's really good.

   B: I'm jealous! *I've been going / I went* skiing for a week once and kept falling over!

4 A: Are you still going to karate classes?

   B: Yeah, but I have an injury at the moment, so I *haven't been going / didn't go* for the past few weeks.

5 A: How long *did you run / have you been running*?

   B: *Since / For* last year. I feel so much fitter.

6 A: Do you know anyone who'd like to play handball? We *haven't had / haven't been having* enough players *since / for* the end of last season.

   B: You said. *I've been trying / I've tried* to persuade my friend to play *since / for* ages, but she says she can't commit to playing every week.

Common mistakes

- *You speak German very well. How long ~~are you living~~ **have you been living** here?*

- *How long ~~do you know~~ **have you known** each other?*

Don't use the present simple or the present continuous to talk about the duration of an activity that started in the past but is still taking place or affecting the present situation – use the present perfect.

- *I waited for the plane ~~during~~ for two hours and they told us it was cancelled.*

Don't use *during* to show how long something continues – use *for*.

- *She's lived there ~~during~~ **for** three years.*

Exercise 2

Which sentences are incorrect? Correct them.

1 I've been doing these exercises during three years. I usually do them for an hour a day.

2 I've been studying Korean for six years now, but can still only have very basic conversations.

3 My grandparents have been married since fifty years and apparently they've never argued once.

4 I banged my head this morning and I've been having a headache since then.

5 I lived in Cali for ten years. We left last year and moved to Bogotá.

6 He's working here since he left school. It's the only job he's ever had.

Exercise 3

Complete the answers to the questions to make them true for you.

1 How long have you been learning English? For …

2 How long have you been living in your current home? Since …

3 How long did you go to primary school for? For …

4 How long have you had your current phone? Since …

Exercise 4

Complete the sentences to make them true for you.

1 I've … since I was a child.

2 I've … for a few months.

3 I didn't … for years.

4 I haven't … for long.

5 WORKING LIFE

5A *MUST / CAN'T* COMMENTS AND REPLIES

Making *must / can't* comments

We often use *must* or *can't* + verb when we comment on other people's experiences, situations or feelings. We use them to show we're making an assumption or guessing about things.

- We generally use *must* when we think something is the case.

  A: I'm a travel writer.

  *B: Really? That **must be** a great job.*

  (= we think the job is great)

  A: I've been working here for ten years now.

  *B: Wow. You **must enjoy** it, then.*

  (= we think the person enjoys working there)

- We use *can't* when we think something is not the case.

  A: Is that Bruno over there?

  *B: It **can't be** him. He's in Brazil at the moment.*

  (= we don't think it's Bruno)

  A: At the moment, I'm working full-time as well as looking after the kids.

  *B: That **can't be** easy. (= we don't think it's easy)*

  A: I spend about four hours getting to and from work each day.

  *B: That **can't be** much fun. (= we don't think it's fun)*

Responding to *must / can't* comments

When we reply to *must / can't* comments, we usually use a present (or past) tense to show facts or our own true feelings / experiences. We may use a form of the auxiliary verb *be* to avoid repeating an adjective, or a form of the auxiliary verb *do* to avoid repeating a verb.

A: *It must be difficult.*
B: *It **is** (difficult) sometimes. / It **was** to begin with, but I'm used to it now. / No, not really. / Actually, it **isn't** (difficult).*

A: *You must enjoy it.*
B: *Yeah, I **do** (enjoy it). / I **do** (enjoy it) most of the time. / I **did**, but I'm a bit bored with it these days. / Not really.*

A: *That can't be easy.*
B: *No, it **isn't** (easy). / Oh, it**'s** OK. / Actually, it **is** (easy).*

A: *You can't enjoy it that much.*
B: *No, I **don't** (enjoy it very much). / Well, I **do** sometimes (enjoy it). / Actually, I **do** (enjoy it).*

Exercise 1

Complete the conversations with one word in each gap. Contractions count as one word.

1 A: We're so busy right now. I've worked 70 hours this week.
  B: Wow. You _____ be exhausted.
  A: I _____, but it's going to be the same next week too.
2 A: Between emergencies, we often have nothing to do.
  B: You _____ get quite bored.
  A: Yeah, we sometimes _____ , but I read a lot and we also play cards.
3 A: My partner is away a lot with work at the moment.
  B: That _____ be easy when you have three young kids.
  A: _____ , it's fine. My family help me quite a lot.
4 A: The chemicals we use have a very strong smell.
  B: That _____ be horrible.
  A: _____ really. I mean, it _____ to begin with, but you quickly get used to it.
5 A: We're having meeting after meeting at work these days.
  B: That _____ be fun.
  A: It's _____ ! I'm having to do much longer hours.

DID YOU KNOW?

We can also follow *must / can't* with *be* + *-ing* to form a present continuous meaning.

A: *They're going to give me a bonus.*
B: *You **must be doing** well.*
A: *Yes, I am.*

Exercise 2

Rewrite B's responses with *must / can't* to show that you're making an assumption.

1 A: He works a 60-hour week and drives for three hours to and from work.
  B: ~~That's not fun.~~ *That can't be fun.*
2 A: I haven't eaten since breakfast.
  B: You're hungry.
3 A: She didn't get the job.
  B: She's disappointed. I know she really wanted it.
4 A: I really don't get on with my new colleague.
  B: That's not easy.
5 A: Dani's just bought a fancy new sports car.
  B: She's earning good money in her new job.
6 A: Valentin got that promotion.
  B: He's so pleased. He totally deserves it.

7 A: Sam left work early today.
  B: He isn't feeling well. He didn't look so good earlier.

5C TALKING ABOUT RULES

Must / Mustn't

We can use *must(n't)* + verb to talk about rules and other obligations. *Must(n't)* is often used when the speaker makes the rule.
*You **must arrive** to class on time. I don't allow anyone in if they are late.*
*You **mustn't use** these computers for personal use.*

We can also use *must* to ask questions about rules and obligations, though we usually use *have to* in questions.
***Must** we **wait** here? Or can we sit over there?*

Have to

We can use *have to* + verb as an alternative to *must*. We also often use *have to* to ask about rules.
*We **have to be** there by six at the latest.*
*We **don't have to wear** a uniform at work.*
***Do** I **have to attend** all the staff meetings?*
We can also use *have got to* + verb in more informal contexts, especially in speaking.
*We**'ve got to be** there at 6:30.*

Be supposed to

We use *be supposed to* + verb to say what is the correct thing to do according to a rule or other obligation. We often use *be supposed to* when a rule has been broken or is not followed.
*I**'m supposed to be** available to cover if anyone is off sick.*
*Hey, don't leave your dirty cup in the sink! You**'re supposed to wash** them yourself.*
*We**'re not supposed to be** in here. It's just for senior staff.*

Can't, be not allowed to, be not supposed to

We use *can't* or *be not allowed to* + verb as an alternative to *mustn't* when it isn't possible to do something.
*We **can't work** from home in my company.*
*Sorry, but you**'re not allowed to bring** dogs in here.*

We often use *be not supposed to* + verb when a rule has been broken or not followed.
*You**'re not supposed to use** this entrance into the building, but it's more convenient.*

Can, be allowed to

We also use *can* and *be allowed to* + verb to show there is no rule or to say that it's OK to do something.
*I **can** work at home one day a week.*
*They**'re allowed to start** work late if they also finish later.*

We use *can* or *be allowed to* + verb to ask about rules.
***Can** I **use** any of the computers in the building?*
***Are** you **allowed to work** from home?*

Exercise 1

Choose the correct option to complete the sentences.

1 Sorry, *you're not allowed to / you have to* smoke in here. Can you go outside please?
2 *Is Julia allowed to / Is Julia supposed to* wear jeans at work? I'd be surprised if she can.
3 *We're supposed to / We can* carry our ID with us at all times, but nobody ever asks for it!
4 *Do you have to / Can you* ask your manager if you want to leave the office?

5 *We're allowed to / We aren't supposed to* go on the roof of the building, but it's a nice place to have a break!

6 *You can't / You're not supposed to* eat or drink in the classroom, so please take your coffee cup with you.

7 *We have to / We're allowed to* belong to a trade union, but not many people are members.

8 *I can't / I have to* start really early some days, but at least *I have to / I'm allowed to* go home early.

DID YOU KNOW?

In more formal contexts, we sometimes use *is (not) permitted* to talk about rules.

*Parking **is permitted** between 8 p.m. and 6 a.m.*

*Taking photographs **is not permitted** inside the building.*

Exercise 2

Read the first sentence in each pair. Complete the second sentence so that it has a similar meaning. Use between two and five words, including the word in bold.

1 You shouldn't really leave before five, but there's nothing left to do now. **SUPPOSED**

I know you _____ before five, but there's nothing left to do now.

2 We're not allowed to give out the personal details of clients. **PERMITTED**

Giving out the personal details of clients _____ .

3 You mustn't make any noise while the exam is taking place. **HAVE**

We _____ really quiet while the exam is taking place.

4 The balcony is the only place where you are allowed to have a break. **CAN**

You _____ on the balcony.

5 You can't send personal emails from the company computers. **ALLOWED**

You _____ the computers for personal emails. It's a company rule.

6 Don't tell anyone I'm here. I told everyone else I'm working from home. **SUPPOSED**

_____ working from home, so don't tell anyone I'm here.

Exercise 3

Think about your place of work or study. Complete the sentences to make them true for you. Write about a different rule for each sentence.

1 You have to …

2 You're supposed to …

3 You're not allowed to …

4 You can't …

5 … is not permitted.

6 BUYING AND SELLING

6A COMPARISONS

Comparative adjectives

We form most comparative adjectives by adding *-er* or using *more*.

A: *This one is **cheaper**.*

B: *Yes, but this one is **easier** to use and the camera is **more powerful**.*

- For **one-syllable** adjectives, we add *-er*. Note that for adjectives and adverbs ending in *e*, we just add *-r* and for adjectives ending vowel-consonant, we double the final letter:

  cheap – cheap**er**   small – small**er**   old – old**er**
  late – lat**er**   big – bi**gg**er

- For **two-syllable** adjectives ending in *-y*, we change the *-y* to *-ier*.

  easy – eas**ier**   busy – bus**ier**   happy – happ**ier**

- For adjectives and adverbs with **two or more syllables**, we generally use *more*.

  expensive – **more** expensive
  powerful – **more** powerful
  interesting – **more** interesting

- Remember that some comparative forms are irregular.

  bad – worse
  far – further / farther
  good – better

DID YOU KNOW?

Some adjectives can be formed with either *-er* or *more*. For example, we can say *friendlier* or *more friendly* and *simpler* or *more simple*. This is common with two-syllable adjectives ending in *-y, -le, -ow* and *-er*.

Than

When we directly compare two things, we use *than*.

*I'm with Blue. They're **cheaper than** the other companies.*

*These jeans fit **better than** the other ones.*

Big and small differences

To say there's a big difference, we can add *much, so much, way, far, a lot* or *quite a lot* before the comparative adjective.

*The signal is **a lot better** over here.*

*The new model is **much more expensive** than the last one.*

To say there's a small difference, we can add *a bit, slightly* or *a little bit*.

*This one is **slightly bigger**, but it's also **a bit heavier**.*

Negative comparisons

To make negative comparisons, we can use *not (nearly / quite) as … as*.

*It looks nice, but it's **not as fast as** the other tablet.*

*Their selection **isn't as varied as** it used to be in the past.*

Note that *as … as* means two things are equal or the same.

*My phone is **as good as** yours.*

We can also use *less* to make negative comparisons.

*Their selection is **less varied than** it used to be.*

Twice / three times, etc.

We sometimes make comparisons using *twice, three times*, etc.

- *twice / three times / half + as + adjective (+ as)*

  *It's not cheap. It's about **twice as expensive as** this phone.*

  *It's a lot cheaper than the other one we looked at, but it's only **half as powerful**.*

- *twice / three times / half + the + noun (+ of)*

  *Their new place is **three times the size of** their old flat.*

  *It is a bit better, but it's more than **twice the price**.*

Exercise 1

Complete the sentences with the correct form of the adjectives in brackets. Add any other words that are needed.

1 This phone looks much __*nicer*__ , but the problem is, the battery doesn't last __*as long*__ . (nice, long)

2 These speakers are quite a lot _____ so the sound quality on them is far _____ . (big, good)

3 This one is way _____ , but it's probably worth it. It's not _____ the other phones, so it's much _____ to carry. (expensive, heavy, easy)

4 I know these boots aren't _____ the other ones, but they're a lot _____ and they look so much _____ , don't you think? (cheap, comfortable, cool)

5 When it comes to clothes, the brand name is a lot less _____ how an item fits and feels. (important)

6 If the screen is a bit _____ , then usually it's slightly _____ to navigate and it's not _____ to see all the icons and everything. (large, easy, difficult)

Exercise 2

Find the words and phrases in Exercise 1 that show the size of the difference.

1 *This phone looks <u>much</u> nicer, but the problem is, the battery doesn't last as long.*

Exercise 3

Complete the second sentence with an adjective and any other words you need so that it has a similar meaning to the first sentence.

1 The screen on this one is twice the size of the one you have at the moment.
 The screen on this one is twice <u>as big as</u> the one you have at the moment.
2 My old phone was almost double the weight of this new one.
 My old phone was almost twice _____ this new one.
3 The new shopping centre is three times the size of the old one.
 The new shopping centre is three times _____ the old one.
4 The wi-fi here is terrible. It's half the speed of my home wi-fi.
 The wi-fi here is terrible. My home wi-fi is twice _____ .
5 The business has really grown since last year. We have three times the work.
 The business has really grown since last year. We're three times _____ .
6 My old deal was twice the cost of my current one.
 My old deal was twice _____ as my current one.

Exercise 4

Choose the best options to make the sentences true for you.

1 I'm *less / slightly more / much more* interested in technology than I was five years ago.
2 Texting someone is *not as quick as / far quicker than / a bit quicker than* calling someone.
3 Using mobiles while driving is *a lot more dangerous than / a bit more dangerous than / as dangerous as / not as dangerous as* eating and drinking while you're driving.
4 For me, battery life is *a lot more important than / a tiny bit more important than / not as important as* a phone brand.
5 Now that so many people have smartphones, quality of life is *way better / quite a lot better / slightly better / a bit worse / much worse* than it was in the past.

6C NOUN PHRASES

Compound nouns (noun + noun)

Compound nouns are formed by adding two nouns together. The first noun acts like an adjective and describes or defines the main noun.

a silk scarf   several fridge magnets   a dining table
a shopping centre   two pizza restaurants

Remember, the first noun is never plural.

a couple of silks scarves
several fridges magnets

Noun phrases

We often add information before and after a noun or a compound noun to give more detail about it. This group of words is called a noun phrase.

We do this by adding one or more adjectives in front of the noun and / or adding a phrase beginning with a preposition (known as a 'prepositional phrase') after the noun.

*I met a friend. – I met an **old** friend **from university**.*

*I bought a painting. – I bought a **really unusual** painting **of New York**.*
*We stayed in an apartment. – We stayed in a **lovely big** apartment **with its own swimming pool**.*
*I got a fridge magnet. – I got a **cool** fridge magnet **of the Eiffel Tower**.*

Adjective order

We usually only use one or two adjectives before a noun. However, when we use more, there are some rules about the order of the adjectives.

• An opinion adjective (*horrible, lovely, cool, unusual,* etc.) usually goes before a fact (*old, yellow, silver, big,* etc).
 *a **horrible yellow** jacket*
 *a **lovely big** bunch of flowers*

 NOT a yellow horrible jacket
 a big lovely bunch of flowers

• If we use more than one fact adjective, they generally go in this order:
 size – age – colour – place / origin – nationality – material
 *an **enormous 1990s** mobile phone*
 *an **old red Italian** sports car*

 NOT a 1990s enormous mobile / phone a red Italian old sports car
 Note that this order can be flexible and not all adjectives fit into these categories.

Prepositional phrases

We can add information after nouns using phrases beginning with a preposition.

• We use *with* to show a feature of the main noun.
 *a tie **with** a picture on it*
 *a shirt **with** horrible buttons*
• We use *of* to explain the specific thing you see on the main noun or what it contains.
 *a photo **of** Niagara Falls*
 *a model **of** the Eiffel Tower*
 *a bottle **of** water*
• We use *from* to show the origin of the main noun or where you met a person.
 *some cheese **from** Norway*
 *a friend **from** school*
 *a song **from** the 1960s*
• We use *for + -ing* to show the purpose of the main noun.
 *a pan **for** cooking paella*
 *a machine **for making** coffee*

Exercise 1

Choose the correct option to complete the sentences.

1 I wanted to buy this *beautiful Turkish / Turkish beautiful rug*, but I couldn't afford it.
2 They brought us some fancy chocolates *from / of* their town.
3 I bought a huge pan *for / of* cooking this rice dish they make called *plov*. It was a nightmare to bring home on the plane!
4 The café is next to that *grey big old / big old grey* building *of / with* the red door over there.
5 The town has a *fantastic new / new fantastic* shopping centre. It attracts people from miles around.
6 We watched *an old wonderful / a wonderful old* film last night *from / of* the 1930s.
7 They sell a lot of *horrible plastic cheap / horrible cheap plastic* toys in the market in the main square.
8 He was wearing a *big black / black big* t-shirt *with / of* a picture *with / of* a cat on it.

Exercise 2

Which six sentences are incorrect? Correct them.

1 I bought some red really nice leather boots.
2 My son works in that French new restaurant on the High Street.
3 I had an amazing vegetarian meal the other day.
4 My daughter bought me an Italian beautiful silk tie for my birthday.
5 I bought this thing for cut apples into slices. It's really useful.
6 You should buy some cheese of this area to take home with you.
7 My friend bought me this pink awful comedy tie with a cartoon of Superman on it.
8 It was a horrible cold rainy day, so we spent most of it in the shopping centre.

7 EATING

7B GENERALIZATIONS AND *TEND TO*

Adverbs

We can use adverbs like *usually, generally, normally* or *hardly ever* to make generalizations. They usually go before a verb, but after the verb *be*.

I **normally** stay at home during the week.
I **hardly ever** eat meat these days.
The food is **usually** pretty good here.

Note that in negative sentences, the adverb can go before or after the negative auxiliary verb.

People **generally don't** have dinner before 8 o'clock.
I **don't normally** eat lunch. **I'm usually** too busy.
This dish **isn't usually** so spicy.

Adverbial phrases

We can also use adverbial phrases. They usually go at the beginning of the sentence or clause, but can go at the end.

In general, people here don't eat much foreign food.
On the whole, people meet in a café rather than at home.
Generally speaking, I eat after seven at night.
As a rule, we didn't eat much meat when I was a kid.
I have a pretty good diet, **in general**.

Tend to

We can also use *tend to* + verb to make generalizations.

Do you **tend to eat** many vegetables?
We generally didn't go out much at night. We **tended to eat** in the hotel.
Since I saw that documentary about factory farming, I've **tended to avoid** eating chicken.

The negative form is *tend not to*. However, *don't tend to* is also possible.

I **tend not to eat** after seven at night.
We **tended not to go** to restaurants much when I was a child.
I **don't tend to eat** after seven at night.

DID YOU KNOW?

It's possible to combine these ways of expressing something is generally true.

As a rule, we **tend to eat** in front of the TV most evenings.
Generally speaking, I **usually** order a takeaway twice a week.

Exercise 1

Complete the sentences with one word in each gap. Sometimes more than one answer is possible.

1 I don't like cooking, so I _____ to eat out a lot.
2 _____ general, the food here is really good.

3 I don't _____ eat shellfish, but this is really nice.
4 He has a terrible diet. I mean, he hardly _____ eats vegetables or fruit.
5 As a _____ , I eat as healthily as I can, so I _____ ever eat fried foods.
6 I tend _____ to do much exercise. I should do more.
7 On the _____ , food from my country is fairly unhealthy, but I still love it.
8 _____ a rule, people here _____ complain if the service is bad. It's just that I personally tend _____ to. I'd just never go there again.

Exercise 2

Complete the sentences to make them true for you.

1 I tend to eat a lot of _____ .
2 I generally _____ once or twice a week.
3 I tend not to eat _____ .
4 I hardly ever drink _____ .

7C FIRST CONDITIONALS

Use

We use the first conditional to talk about a possible present or future situation and the result or consequence of this situation. This is often to give advice, make an offer or promise, make a prediction or to explain a plan.

Form

The *if* clause

The *if* clause refers to a possible present or future situation. We use a present form in the *if* clause.

If customers **enjoy** the meal, they'll come back again.
If you **don't have** a good business plan, you might not be successful.
If it **rains**, we won't have the barbecue today.
Get something to eat **if** you**'re feeling** hungry.

Note that we don't use *will / won't* in the *if* clause.
~~If it will rain, we'll have the barbeque another day.~~

The result clause

The result clause refers to the consequence of an action. We can use different forms in the result clause.

- To give advice, we use an imperative form.
  If you're feeling hungry, **get** something to eat.
- To make an offer or promise, we use *will* + verb.
  If you do the shopping, I**'ll cook** dinner.
- To make a prediction or to talk about general possibility, we use *will* or *might* + verb.
  If customers enjoy the meal, they**'ll come back** again.
  If you don't have a good business plan, you **won't be** successful.
- To talk about a possible plan, we use *might* + verb.
  We **might open** a second café next year.
- To talk about a definite plan, we use be *going to* + verb.
  We**'re going to open** a second café next year.

Questions

We form a question with *will* + subject + verb.
If we haven't got any milk, **will you get** some?
What **will you do** if all the shops are closed?

DID YOU KNOW?

We can put the *if* clause first or second in the sentence. When we put it first, we use a comma after it. When we start with the result clause, we don't use a comma.
If I this restaurant is full**,** we'll go to a different one.
We'll go to a different restaurant if this one is full.

Exercise 1

Complete the sentences with the correct form of the verb in brackets.

1 If you _____ (want) something to eat, just _____ (help) yourself. There's plenty of food.
2 I _____ (help) you cook if you _____ (like).
3 If you _____ (be) thirsty, _____ (get) yourself a drink. There's some juice in the fridge.
4 If you _____ (pass) your exams, we _____ (have) a party to celebrate.
5 I've waited long enough. If they _____ (not serve) me soon, I _____ (leave).
6 If you _____ (fancy) eating out tonight, I _____ (book) us a table at that new vegan place.
7 I'm not sure, but I _____ (not join) you for dinner, you _____ (not mind). I'll let you know.
8 If there _____ (not be) any milk, I _____ (have) my coffee black. Either way is fine.

Exercise 2

Which sentences are incorrect? Correct them.

1 If you'll eat less junk food, you'll feel a lot better in general.
2 If there isn't a red onion, will use a regular one instead.
3 If we've got the ingredients, I might make a risotto tonight.
4 What you will do if there's no vegetarian food on the menu?
5 They're going to expand the restaurant if they will get a loan from the bank.
6 It'll help climate change if we'll all eat less meat.
7 If you want a lift to the restaurant, I pick you up at about 7:30, OK?
8 If you have any special dietary requirements, let us know when you make your booking.

8 EDUCATION

8A FUTURE TIME CLAUSES

To specify the time at which a future action will happen, we often use a clause starting with a time expression:

after   as soon as   before   once the moment
until   when   while

Present forms, future meaning

Even though we're referring to a future situation or action, we use a present tense after these time expressions. This can be the present simple or the present perfect. The present perfect emphasizes that the action / situation is completed before the other event.

I'll tell him the news **when** he **gets** home.
I'll tell him to call you **the moment** he **comes** through the door.
We'll cook dinner **as soon as** the kids **have got back** from school.

We can also begin sentences with the time clauses.
The moment he **comes** through the door, I'll tell him to call you.
Once I**'ve finished** this bit, I'll come and help you.

Remember that we don't use a future form such as *will* or *be going to* after time expressions.
The moment I ~~will~~ arrive, I'll call you.
We'll cook dinner as soon as the kids ~~are going to~~ get back from school.

DID YOU KNOW?

We can use *just before* and *right after*. The meaning is similar to *immediately*.
I'll let you know **just before** we arrive.
I'll call you **right after** the class finishes.

Exercise 1

Choose the correct option to complete the sentences.

1 I'll phone you *the moment* the class *will finish / finishes*.
2 *I give / I'll give* you the book as soon as I've finished with it.
3 After I *will finish / finish* my Master's, I'm going to do a PhD.
4 I'll phone you *when* I *get / will get* home.
5 Call me just before you *will get / get* to the station.
6 *Once* my final exams *are / will be* over, I'm going to have a long holiday.
7 I'm going to study English before I *will start / start* university.
8 I'll say goodbye before I *leave / will leave* on Friday.

Exercise 2

Rewrite each pair of sentences as one sentence.

1 I'm going to leave school next month. Then I might go away for a few weeks.
After *I leave school*, I *might go away for a few weeks*.
2 The course finishes soon. Then I'll have to start paying back all my debts.
Once _____ , I _____ .
3 You're going to move to Germany soon. Are you going to look for a job there?
Are _____ when _____ ?
4 I have my final exams soon. I'm not going to go out.
I _____ until _____ .
5 I'm in a lecture at the moment. It finishes at three. Then I'll call you back.
I _____ right after _____ .
6 He's going to graduate next year. He said he's immediately going to burn all his notes!
He said he _____ the moment _____ !
7 I'm waiting to hear from my boss. I promise I'll call you right after she calls me, OK?
I _____ you as soon as I _____ .
8 I graduate next spring, but I think I'll start looking for a job before then.
I _____ a job before I _____ in the spring.

Exercise 3

Complete the sentences to make them true for you.

1 I'm going to …. after …
2 I think I'll … when …
3 As soon as … , I …

8C SECOND CONDITIONALS

Use

We use the second conditional to talk about an imagined situation in the present or future and its imagined result or consequence. We can also use it to talk about things we feel are possible in the future, but unlikely. A second conditional has two parts: the *if* clause and the result clause.

Note that this contrasts with a first conditional, which talks about things which are possible or likely in the future. See Grammar reference 7C for more about first conditionals.

Form

The *if* clause

The *if* clause refers to an imagined or unlikely situation, action or event in the present or future. We use a past form (past simple or past continuous) in the *if* clause.
If I **had** more time, I'd study a lot more.
(= I don't have enough time)
She'd do much better **if** she **worked** harder.
(= she doesn't work hard)

If it **wasn't raining**, I'd go to get some fresh air.
(= it's raining at the moment)

We don't use *would / wouldn't* in the *if* clause.
~~If I would have more time, I'd study a lot more.~~

DID YOU KNOW?

We can use both *if I / he / she / it* **was** ... and *if I / he / she / it* **were** ... .
If I **was / were** *more interested in science, I'm sure I'd enjoy the classes more.*
I think she'd be happier if she **was / were** *in a different school.*
To give advice, we can use **If I were you**, *I'd* ... . You may sometimes hear *If I was you*, ... but this is generally considered to be incorrect.

The result clause

The result clause refers to the imagined result or consequence. We use *would / wouldn't* + verb in the result clause.
*If I had more time, I***'d study** *harder.*
*She***'d do** *much better if she worked more.*
*If it wasn't raining, I***'d go** *to get some fresh air.*
I **wouldn't do** *that if I were you.*
We can use the result clause without the *if* clause in a separate sentence when the *if* clause is understood or when the situation is obvious.
A: *If I could, I'd go and live in the UK for a while.*
B: *Yeah, you***'d** *certainly* **improve** *your English a lot quicker.*
A: *And I***'d be able to see** *my British friends more often.*

Note the contrast in structure between a second conditional structure (*If* + past form + *would*) with a first conditional (*If* + present form + *will*).

Might and *would probably*

We can use *might* or *would probably* + verb in the result clause to show that we're less certain about the result.
If the courses weren't so expensive, I **might do** *another one.*
*She***'d probably do** *much better if she worked harder.*

Questions

We form questions with *would* + subject + verb.
What **would** *you* **study** *if you could study anything at all?*
Would *you* **take** *the job if they offered it to you?*

DID YOU KNOW?

We can put the *if* clause first or second in the sentence. When we put it first, we use a comma after it. When we start with the result clause, we don't use a comma.
*If I didn't have the exam tomorrow***,** *I'd go out tonight.*
I'd go out tonight if I didn't have the exam tomorrow.

Exercise 1

Complete the sentences with the correct form of the verb in brackets.

1 I'd love to go out tonight, but I have to write an essay. If the deadline *wasn't* (not be) tomorrow, *I'd come* (come) for sure.
2 Danny failed all his exams? Oh no! I don't know what I _____ (do) if that _____ (happen) to me.
3 I _____ (be) *very* happy to help you with your essay if I _____ (not be) so busy.
4 I need a bit of fresh air. If it _____ (not rain) at the moment, I _____ (go) for a walk.
5 A: If you _____ (know) that a classmate had cheated in an exam, what _____ (you do)? _____ (you tell) the teacher?
    B: Yes, if I _____ (be) you, I think I _____ (probably tell) the teacher. I think it'd be the right thing to do.

Exercise 2

Which six sentences are incorrect? Correct them.

1 I'd ask to change classes if I were you. I think you might enjoy a different one more.
2 If I can go back in time, I'd do engineering at university.
3 I think I'd enjoy my yoga classes more if we would have a different teacher.
4 He might do a bit better if he worked a bit harder.
5 If I could learn any language, I probably choose Spanish.
6 I'd be very surprised if I'll pass the exam.
7 I know you're busy right now, but I wouldn't ask you if I wouldn't really need your help.
8 If I'm you, I'd do what your professor tells you. I'm sure she's trying to be helpful.

Exercise 3

Complete the sentences with your own ideas.

1 If I had more free time, ...
2 If I could visit any city, ...
3 If I were more adventurous, ...
4 If I could study any subject, ...

9 HOUSES

9B PRESENT PERFECT SIMPLE AND PRESENT PERFECT CONTINUOUS

Present perfect simple

We can use the present perfect simple (*have / has* + (*not*) + past participle) to talk about trends that continue from the past until now. We often use an adverb to say how quickly the change happened, or by how much. We use a time phrase to show the period of time.
Spending **has increased** *since last year.*
Visitor numbers **have dropped** *slightly in the last year.*
Unemployment **has increased** *significantly since the last election.*
The population **hasn't grown** *much over recent years.*
Have *prices* **changed** *much recently?*

Present perfect continuous

We can use the present perfect continuous (*have / has* + (*not*) + *been* + *-ing*) in a similar way to the present perfect simple to talk about trends that continue from the past until now.
Sometimes, there is little or no difference between the two forms. However, we use the present perfect continuous to emphasize the duration of an activity or the fact that it is regularly repeated.
The situation **has been** *gradually* **improving** *over recent months.*
Unemployment **has been rising** *steadily over the last year.*
*They***'ve been building** *a lot of new houses round here.*
I **haven't been spending** *much recently.*
How long **has** *she* **been working** *here?*

Present perfect simple or continuous?

- We use the present perfect simple to express a quick change, or when we say exactly how much something has changed.
  Prices ~~have been suddenly dropping~~ **have** *suddenly* **dropped**.
  Inflation ~~has been falling~~ **has fallen** *from 3% to 2.25%.*
- We also use the present perfect simple for something that is already finished.
  They ~~have been building~~ **have built** *a new estate by the river.*
  (= the building project is finished)

Verbs, adverbs and time phrases

Verbs we can use to talk about trends include:

decrease	drop	fall	go down
go up	increase	rise	

Adverbs that we often use to talk about trends include:

a bit	by (15%)	dramatically	gradually	a lot
sharply	slightly	slowly	steadily	suddenly

Time phrases that we often use to talk about trends include:

over / for the past few months / ten years
over / for the last few months / years
for ten years / six months
in recent months / years
since 2022 / last year / January / the last election
recently / lately / in recent years

Exercise 1

Choose the correct option to complete the sentences. Sometimes both options are possible.

1 Inflation *has been gradually falling / has gradually fallen* over the last two years.
2 The population *has grown / has been growing* dramatically in recent years.
3 The government *has introduced / has been introducing* a new law to prevent people buying property and leaving it empty.
4 More and more young adults *have been leaving / have left* the country because of the economic problems.
5 Unemployment *has increased / has been increasing* by 6% since the crash.
6 Things *have improved / have been improving* slowly over the last few years.
7 *We've moved / We've been moving* house three times in the last five years.
8 I've been under a bit of stress, because *I've changed / I've been changing* my job a couple of times recently.

Exercise 2

Complete the sentences with one word in each gap. Sometimes more than one answer is possible.

1 The crime rate has _____ falling steadily over the last 20 years.
2 Unemployment has risen sharply _____ the start of the economic crisis.
3 The global birth rate has been falling _____ for the last 50 years, by a few percent each year.
4 In the last decade, the population has grown _____ 25% to reach 100 million people.
5 Oil prices have _____ dramatically in the _____ six months. It was $125 a barrel at the beginning of the year and now it's $80.
6 House prices _____ more or less stayed the same _____ the last two years.

Exercise 3

Complete the sentences with your own ideas about where you live. Use a time phrase and an adverb in at least two of the sentences.

1 … have / has been increasing …
2 … have / has gone up …
3 … have / has gone down …
4 … have / has been falling …

9C COMPARING NOW AND THE PAST

Comparisons with nouns

We can make comparisons between now and the past using the following patterns.

There are many more cars on the road *than before*.
There are far fewer independent shops *than there were a few years ago*.
There isn't nearly as much pollution *as there used to be*.
There's much less crime *than when I was a kid*.
There's much more litter on the streets *than there was*.
There isn't as much to do in this town *as when I lived here*.

Note the following:

- We use *fewer* or *not as many* with plural countable nouns (e.g. *cars, schools, people*). We use *less* or *not as much* with uncountable nouns (e.g. *pollution, investment, traffic*).
- We use *more* with both countable and uncountable nouns.
- We use *more / fewer / less … than* and *not as many / much … as*.
- We can use *many, much, far* and *nearly* to emphasize a difference.
- We can also use time phrases such as *than / as before, than / as in the past, than / as there used to be, than / as it used to do / be, than / as when I was at school, than / as a few years ago*, etc.

DID YOU KNOW?

We more commonly start a comparison with the present situation, but can also start with the past.
There **were** *fewer problems in the past than there* **are** *now.*
Twenty years ago, parents **spent** *more time with their children than they* **do** *now.*

Comparisons with adjectives

We can also compare the past and present using comparative adjectives and a time phrase.
The area is **more popular** *than* **it used to be**.
That part of town used to be **much nicer** *than* **it is** *now.*
I'm **not as fit as** *I was when* **I was** *at university.*

For more about comparative adjectives, see Grammar reference 6A.

Exercise 1

Add the missing word in each sentence in the correct place.

1 It's far international than it was ten years ago.
2 It wasn't nice as the last time we went there.
3 There aren't as people living here as when I was a kid.
4 There's less unemployment there used to be.
5 There are more restaurants than were before.
6 The area isn't as dirty as used to be.
7 There isn't as pollution since the laws were changed.
8 There didn't use to be as many shops here as there now.
9 It's much easier to get around than it used to.
10 It takes me much less time to get to work than it used do.

DID YOU KNOW?

We sometimes use an auxiliary verb as a second verb when we make comparisons. This might be different to the first verb or auxiliary verb.
It's not as interesting as it **was** *twenty years ago.*
It **didn't** *seem to rain as much as it* **does** *now!*
The area **has** *more cultural events than it* **did** *before.*

Exercise 2

Complete the sentences with these verbs.

can	did	do	is	was	were

1 It's not as difficult to get round the city as it _____ .
2 There are so many more cars on the street than there _____ a few years ago.

3 I used to work a lot harder than I _____ now.
4 We spend less money at the supermarket than we _____ in the past.
5 Before they changed the laws, we could work more hours per week than we _____ now.
6 It never used to be as international as it _____ now.

Exercise 3
Complete the sentences about where you live.
1 There are more … than …
2 There aren't as many … as …
3 There is far less … than …
4 It's not nearly as … as …

10 GOING OUT

10B QUANTIFIERS

We use quantifiers when we want to give information about the number or amount of something. The table shows some of the most common and useful quantifiers.

no not any	There are **no** cinemas nearby. There are**n't any** cinemas nearby.
hardly any almost no (very) few (very) little	**Few / Hardly any** locals can afford to go to the top restaurants. I heard it can be dangerous, but we saw **almost no / very little** trouble.
some a few a little not much not many	**Some** of us went home, but **some / a few** people went on to a club. I do**n't** drink **much**, but I may have **some / a little** wine at dinner. There were**n't many** people there. There is**n't much** nightlife here. There are **a few** places that are good.
a lot of (so) many (so) much	**A lot of / Many** people are living in poverty. Apparently, things are expensive because there's **a lot of / so much** corruption.
almost all almost every most	**Almost all / Most** clubs charge you to get in. Hardly any have free entry. **Almost every** place we went to had a TV with a fashion channel on.
all every	The DJ plays **all** kinds of music. **Every** time I go out, I spend **all** my money.

No and not any
We don't use *not* directly before a noun – we use *no* or *not any*.
I **have no / don't have any** idea where it is.
There **are no / aren't any** clubs round here.
NOT ~~There are not clubs round here~~.

Some
While *some* can have the same meaning as *a few / a little / not much / not many*, it often expresses a neutral (neither a small or large) quantity.
Some people like the new development, **some** people don't.
I was looking at **some** old photos the other day.

Few and many, little and much
We use *(a) few* and *many* with plural countable nouns, e.g. *people, cinemas, locals, cars*.
We use *(a) little* and *much* with uncountable nouns, e.g. *money, corruption, poverty, rain*.
There weren't **many** people at the park.

There hasn't been **much** rain recently.
There **a few** clothes shops in town.
We had **a little** snow this morning.

We use *so* with these quantifiers to link a cause and result.
We have **so much** daylight in summer that it's difficult to sleep.
There was no real atmosphere in the place because there were **so few** people.

Note that we use *a lot of* with both countable and uncountable nouns.
There are **a lot of** coffee shops in the town centre.
There's **a lot of** poverty round here.

DID YOU KNOW?
In spoken language, we often use *a lot* in positive sentences and *much* and *many* in negative sentences and questions.
There **were a lot of** people at the party.
There **weren't many** people at the party.
Were there **many** people at the party?

However, in formal or academic writing, *much* and *many* are often used in positive sentences.
The development **has many** environmentally friendly features.

A few and few, a little and little
A few and *a little* generally have a more positive meaning than *few* and *little*. *Few* and *little* (without *a*) often mean less than wanted, needed or expected. To add emphasis, we often use *very few* and *very little*.
I had **a little break** and took **a few days** off work.
After the redevelopment, **few old buildings** remain and the area has **very little character**.

All and every
We use *all* with singular and plural nouns. We often use *all* + a determiner such as *the, my, your* or *these* with plural nouns.
The party lasted **all** day and all night.
We saw **all the** sites while we were there.
I spent **all my** money.

We use *every* with singular nouns.
We visited **every museum** and gallery in the city!

Exercise 1
Complete the text with one word in each gap.
I live in a fairly small place, so there's not ¹_____ entertainment at night and not ²_____ places to go. There are a ³_____ discos, but only one is open late, which is a bit boring. So ⁴_____ weekends, I travel to the city where there are a ⁵_____ of clubs playing ⁶_____ kinds of music, such as salsa, reggaeton, rock and pop. Personally, I'm a big fan of electronic dance music and I know a ⁷_____ clubs there that play this. It's mainly local DJs, but we get ⁸_____ international DJs coming over and there's also a big festival ⁹_____ year. I'd like to move to the city because I spend so ¹⁰_____ time there, but there are ¹¹_____ jobs available in my area of work at the moment, so I'll have to see. I hope there'll be ¹²_____ job opportunities soon.

DID YOU KNOW?
When we use pronouns (*us, them*, etc.) or *the* after quantifiers, we add *of*. With *all*, we can use or not use *of*.
Some **of** us are going out this evening.
I haven't met all (**of**) the people on my course – just a few **of** them.
I work from home most **of** the time these days.
Many **of** the best restaurants are in this area.

Exercise 2

Read the first sentence in each pair. Complete the second sentence so that it has a similar meaning. Use between two and five words, including the word in bold.

1 I went to the cinema with a couple of friends last night. **FEW**
   A _____ went to the cinema last night.
2 We could hardly move because the place was so busy. **PEOPLE**
   There _____ there we could hardly move.
3 There won't be anything to eat at the party. **FOOD**
   There'll _____ at the party.
4 There's hardly any crime, so you can walk safely at night. **VERY**
   You can walk safely at night as there _____ crime.
5 A lot of restaurants in town have discounts for students. **MANY**
   If you're a student, you can get a discount at _____ town's restaurants.
6 Just about every restaurant serves vegetarian food. **ALMOST**
   You can get vegetarian food at _____ restaurants.
7 The town has almost no visitors these days. **FEW**
   Very _____ the town these days.
8 There aren't any spaces left in the car park. **NO**
   There _____ in the car park at the moment.

Exercise 3

Are these sentences true about where you live? Rewrite the sentences to make them true for you.

1 There aren't many good clothes shops.
   There are some good clothes shops, but there aren't many good restaurants.
2 There are a lot of coffee shops these days.
3 There are a few clubs.
4 There are no museums or galleries.
5 Almost all the shops are closed on Sundays.
6 Most of the time, I enjoy living here.

10C FUTURE IN THE PAST

Plans and intentions

We can use the structure *was / were going to* + verb to talk about things that were planned or intended, but didn't happen. We also use *wasn't / weren't going to* + verb for something that wasn't planned or intended, but did happen. To explain why the thing did or didn't happen, we often add a clause starting with *but*.

*I **was** just **going to go** out for a walk when it started raining.*
*Some friends **were going to come** for dinner, **but** they rang to say they couldn't make it.*
A: Did you go out last night?
*B: Yeah, I **wasn't going to do** anything, **but** some friends invited me out for dinner.*

Predictions, promises and offers

We often use *would(n't)* + verb to talk about predictions, promises and offers in the past. This is often when things were not as we expected, or they didn't happen. We often report speech or thoughts with *would(n't)* and the past tense of verbs such as such as *said, promised, thought, hoped*, etc.
*The play was much better than I **thought** it **would be**.*
*I **hoped** we**'d get** there earlier, but the traffic was terrible.*
*I **didn't think** the restaurant **would be** anything special, but it was amazing.*
*I **said** I**'d go** with her. (= but I didn't)*
*He promised he **wouldn't be** late. (= but he was / is late)*

Exercise 1

Complete the conversations with one word in each gap.

1 A: So, did you go and see that film last night?
   B: No, I was going _____ , but I had an essay to write and it took longer than I thought it _____ , so by the time I'd finished, it _____ too late.
2 A: What did you do at the weekend?
   B: Nothing much. We _____ going to go to the beach, but the weather was so awful, we just stayed at home.
   A: I know. It was terrible, wasn't it? It was so annoying, because the forecast said it _____ be sunny!
3 A: So, how was your summer? Did you go away anywhere?
   B: Bad question, I'm afraid! My brother and I _____ going to visit our uncle in Spain. He'd promised he _____ pay for the flights, but in the end he couldn't afford it, so we just had to _____ at home instead.
4 A: How was the new restaurant?
   B: Not as good as I thought it _____ be. I thought it'd _____ a bit fancier, but the food was pretty plain. I was going _____ suggest going there for Greta's birthday, but I don't think I will now.

Exercise 2

Read the first sentence in each pair. Complete the second sentence so that it has a similar meaning. Use between two and five words, including the word in bold.

1 A friend rang and said he had tickets for the Sepultura concert, which is why I didn't stay in. **OUT**
   I wasn't _____ , but a friend gave me a ticket for the Sepultura concert.
2 I expected him to be rubbish, but he was actually quite good. **THOUGHT**
   His performance was much better _____ be.
3 It's so sunny! The forecast was for rain. **IT**
   They said _____ , but it's turned out really sunny.
4 My dad promised to help me later. **SAID**
   My dad _____ me later.
5 The government has broken their promise not to raise taxes. **INCREASE**
   The government said _____ , but they have.
6 I feel a bit guilty about not going to the party because I promised to be there. **DEFINITELY**
   I told her _____ at the party, so I feel guilty I didn't go.

Exercise 3

Complete the sentences with your own ideas.

1 I was going to _____ , but I didn't because _____ .
2 I thought _____ would be much better than it was.
3 I hoped I'd _____ , but _____ .
4 I was going to _____ , but _____ .

11 THE NATURAL WORLD

11A *MANAGED TO*, *BE ABLE TO* AND *BE FORCED TO*

Managed to

We use *managed to* + verb to show an ability to do something specific that was difficult and / or required a lot of effort in the past. We use *didn't manage to* when we didn't have the ability to do something. The question form is *Did you / he / they manage to … ?*
*The fire service took ages to get the cat out of the tree, but they **managed to do** it in the end.*
*I screamed and screamed and eventually **managed to attract** someone's attention.*

*The birds were moving very quickly and I **didn't manage to get** a photo of them.*
***Did** you **manage to leave** on time?*

DID YOU KNOW?

We often use *managed to* when talking about stupid mistakes.
*I somehow **managed to lose** my passport.*
*We **managed to get lost** everywhere we went.*

Be able to

We use *was(n't) / were(n't) able to* + verb in a similar way to *managed to*.
*I screamed and screamed and eventually I **was able to attract** someone's attention.*
*We **were** finally **able to find** a tour company that visited the nature reserve.*
*The birds were moving very quickly and I **wasn't able to get** a photo of them.*
***Were** you **able to get** an appointment with the vet in the end?*

Eventually, finally, in the end

Note how we often use *managed to* and *be able to* with words and phrases such as *eventually, finally* and *in the end*. This helps to emphasize the time and the effort needed.

Be forced to

We use *was / were forced to* + verb to show that something was the only possible action in a particular situation. We do not usually use *forced to* in the negative.
*We **were forced to wait** under the trees until the rain stopped.*
*I **was forced to take** a different route as the road was closed.*
We can also use the active form *forced* + object + verb.
*The rain **forced us to wait** under a tree.*

Exercise 1

Complete the sentences using the words in brackets.

1 I was cycling along and this dog suddenly chased after me, but I _____ (able, cycle) fast enough to escape.
2 We went on a whale watching trip, but we _____ (not manage, see) anything because the weather was terrible.
3 The road was totally blocked after the snowfall, so we _____ (force, turn) back.
4 We arrived at the campsite late at night and we had to use the torches on our phones. It wasn't easy, but finally we _____ (manage, put) the tent up.
5 It got so dark we _____ (not able, see) anything. I'm amazed we _____ (able, get) back down the mountain.
6 There were cockroaches in the house and I _____ (not able, get) rid of them. So, in the end we _____ (force, call) a specialist to deal with the problem.
7 The car broke down in the middle of nowhere. But luckily, I _____ (manage, get) it to start and we _____ (able, get) home.
8 We _____ (not manage, make) it all the way to the top of the mountain. The rain and wind _____ us _____ (force, go) back down.

DID YOU KNOW?

We can sometimes use *couldn't* as an alternative to *wasn't / weren't able to* or *didn't manage to*.
*The birds were moving very quickly and I **couldn't get** a photo of them.*
*We **couldn't find** a hotel that allowed pets in the rooms.*
*I chased the mouse for ages, but I just **couldn't catch** it.*

However, we can't use *could* as an alternative to the affirmative forms *was / were able to* or *managed to* when we are talking about ability to do something difficult in a specific situation in the past.

*I screamed and screamed and eventually I ~~could~~ **managed to attract** someone's attention.*
*The animals ~~could~~ **were able to escape** through the fence.*

Exercise 2

In which sentences in Exercise 1 can we use *couldn't*?

Exercise 3

Read the first sentence in each pair. Complete the second sentence so that it has a similar meaning. Use between two and five words, including the word in bold.

1 The light wasn't good, but I finally managed to take some good photos. **ABLE**
   I was eventually _____ some good photos, despite the bad light.
2 We weren't able to get tickets for the balloon trip, which was a real shame. **MANAGE**
   Unfortunately, we _____ any tickets for the balloon trip.
3 We had no option but to turn back. The weather was awful. **FORCED**
   Because the weather was awful, _____ back.
4 Finally, after three attempts, they succeeded in getting to the top of the mountain. **MANAGED**
   They finally _____ to the top of the mountain after three attempts.
5 Unfortunately, I didn't manage to work out what the problem was. **COULDN'T**
   I _____ what was wrong, I'm afraid.
6 I didn't manage to find a suitable campsite in the area. **ABLE**
   I tried, but I _____ a nearby campsite that was any good.

Exercise 4

Complete the sentences with your own ideas.

1 It took a long time, but I eventually managed …
2 After several attempts, I was finally able …
3 I tried and tried, but I just couldn't …

11C PASSIVES

Use

We use passives when we don't know who does an action, we don't want to say who does an action (because the person is unimportant or obvious), or an action occurs naturally.
*Oil **has been discovered** in the north.*
*Most of the coal **is exported**.*
*Taxes **are not being spent** wisely.*
*The first solar panel **was invented** in the 1880s.*
*The volcano **was formed** a million years ago.*

To say who or what does an action, we use *by*.
*The first solar panel was invented in the 1880s **by** Charles Fritts.*
*Taxes are not being spent wisely **by** the current government.*

Form

Compare these active and passive sentences.
Active: *Sailors **discovered the island** in 1750.*
Passive: ***The island was discovered** in 1750.*
To form the passive:

* we make the object of a verb in an active sentence (e.g. *the island*) the subject of the passive sentence.
* we use a form of the verb *be* + past participle (e.g. *was discovered*).

Passives can be used in different forms:
* Present simple
   *Most wheat **is exported**.*
   *The mines **aren't inspected** very often.*
   *How many people **are employed** in the fishing industry?*

- Present continuous

  *More gas than ever **is being exported** from the country.*

  *The equipment **isn't being looked after**.*

  *How **are** the prices **being controlled**?*

- Past simple

  *The factory **was opened** over 50 years ago.*

  *The stolen equipment **wasn't found**.*

  *How many homes **were destroyed** in the storm?*

- Past continuous

  *About 80% of the oil **was being sold**, the rest **was being kept**.*

  *The diamonds **weren't being mined** legally.*

  *How much **was being exported**?*

- Present perfect simple

  *Oil **has been discovered** in the north of the country.*

  *The area **hasn't been visited** for many years.*

  *How much of the profits **have been invested** in healthcare?*

Modal verbs

We form modal passives using modal verb + *be* + past participle.

*The resources **can** now **be extracted** more easily.*

*Most natural resources **will be used up** in the next 50 years.*

*The company **won't be sold** just yet.*

***Should** more **be done** to help developing countries?*

Frequency adverbs

Most frequency adverbs (*also, generally, often, always*, etc.) go between *be* and the past participle or between the two auxiliary verbs if there are two in passive structures.

*The park is **often** used for festivals and concerts.*

*The public is not **usually** consulted on these matters.*

*This land has **always** been used for farming.*

*Gas will **also** be extracted during the process.*

Exercise 1

Choose the correct options to complete the text.

I recently [1]*attended / was attended* a conference on how profits from the sale of natural resources can best [2]*use / be used* for human development. It's an important question, because oil and gas have recently [3]*discovered / been discovered* in my country. In many countries, natural resources [4]*managed / are managed* badly. Interestingly, I learned that in countries with lots of natural resources, people often [5]*don't tax / aren't taxed* very much. This means they usually [6]*aren't expected / don't expect* a high level of public services – because they pay less they have less reason to worry about how the money [7]*uses / is used*. This gives governments more freedom to decide how to spend money that has [8]*made / been made* from natural resources. It also means that people have less control over how the national budget is [9]*spends / spent*.

Exercise 2

Read the first sentence in each pair. Complete the second sentence so that it has a similar meaning. Use between two and five words, including the word in bold.

1 They discovered oil there back in the 1970s. **WAS**

  _____ back in the 1970s.

2 The government controls petrol prices, which is why they are so low. **BY**

  Petrol is so cheap there because _____ the government.

3 They generally test the equipment every week. **USUALLY**

  The equipment _____ once a week.

4 The government could do more to stop corruption if it wanted to. **DONE**

  More _____ stop corruption if the government wanted to.

5 They are building a new motorway which will destroy the area. **BUILT**

  The area will be destroyed by a new motorway which _____ .

6 They should do more to prevent people cutting down trees illegally. **DONE**

  More _____ to prevent trees being cut down illegally.

7 You can get to the island by boat or by the new bridge. **REACHED**

  The _____ by boat or by driving over the new bridge.

8 Because there will be more visitors, they will extend the opening hours. **EXTENDED**

  Because of the increased number of visitors, the opening _____ .

12 PEOPLE I KNOW

12B TALKING ABOUT MEMORIES

Remember + -ing

We can use *remember + ing* to talk about memories. We can also use *remember + someone / something + -ing*.

*I **remember meeting** them for the first time.*

*I **don't remember** Karina **buying** all those gifts for her friends.*

***Do** you **remember going** to that museum in the city centre?*

We can also use *remember + noun* and *remember + wh-* clause.

*I **remember the party**, but I **don't remember who was there**.*

Past simple, used to and would

We can use the past simple, *used to* + verb and *would* + verb to talk about memories.

- We use the past simple to talk about past habits and past states. We tend to use the past simple if we say when the situation existed.

  *I **played** computer games all the time in my early teens.*

  *I **didn't live** in Scotland until I was ten.*

  ***Were** you in any sports teams at school?*

- We use **used to** to talk about past habits and states. *Used to* emphasizes that the situation no longer exists.

  *I **used to spend** hours playing computer games.*

  *I didn't **use to like** rock music.*

  ***Did** you **use to eat** meat?*

  Note that the pronunciation of *used to* is the same with or without the *-d*. When forming the negative with *never*, we keep the final *-d*.

  *My grandparents **didn't use to visit** us very often.*

  *I **never used to read** much. But I read a lot these days.*

- We use **would** to emphasize that events were regularly repeated in the past. Note that *would* is often contracted to *'d*, especially in speaking.

  *I**'d spend** hours playing computer games.*

  *We**'d visit** my grandparents every weekend.*

  We don't use *would* to talk about past states.

  ~~I would have really long hair.~~

  Note that we rarely use *would* in the negative form or question form to talk about past habits.

We often combine all three of these forms when we are describing memories.

*We **used to live** next door to my cousins, so we**'d spend** a lot of time together. We **didn't have** a garden, so we**'d play** together most days in the street in front of our block of flats. There **was** a park nearby and we **used to play** there, as well.*

Single events

Remember that for single events, we use the past simple, not *used to* or *would*.

*When he **died**, my mother **moved** to a town by the seaside.*

*They **got** married and **had** their first child a year later.*

Exercise 1

Complete the conversations with *remember* and the correct form of these verbs.

buy	fall	get	go	jump	stay

1 A: Do you _____ to school for the very first time?

   B: I do, actually. It was raining and I _____ completely wet from head to toe on the way there.

2 A: I don't _____ in this hotel. Are you sure it was this one?

   B: Yes, I'm sure. I _____ you _____ into the swimming pool over and over again and splashing water everywhere.

3 A: Ah, I _____ my very first bike in this shop. Do you remember it?

   B: I do. It was that red and gold one, wasn't it? And I _____ you _____ off it all the time.

Exercise 2

Choose the correct options to complete the conversation. Sometimes both options are correct.

A: Arnedo is a lovely place, isn't it? How do you know it?

B: Well, my parents ¹used to have / would have a house near there. We ²would go / went there every summer for a month.

A: Really? Whereabouts?

B: The house ³was / would be just outside the town.

A: Lovely. Did you ⁴use to go / go walking round there?

B: Not really. In fact, we ⁵would never do / never used to do much while we were there. We ⁶would go / went swimming in the river, we ⁷went / used to go for bike rides, but to be honest, none of us were into walking.

A: Oh, OK. So how come your parents ⁸used to sell / sold the house?

B: Well, when we ⁹would get / got older, we ¹⁰would always complain / always used to complain so much about going that they ¹¹would decide / decided to sell it.

Exercise 3

Complete the sentences to make them true for your childhood.

1 I used to _____ all the time.

2 I'd often _____ .

3 I remember _____ for the first time.

12C EXPRESSING REGRET USING *WISH*

We use *wish* + past perfect simple to express regret about things in the past.

- To express regret about something that <u>didn't</u> happen, we use the affirmative form of the past perfect (*had* + past participle). Note that *had* is often contracted to *'d*.

   *I **wish** I**'d been** a bit stricter with my children.*

   (= I wasn't strict enough)

   *I **wish** I**'d worked** a bit harder at school.*

   *She **wishes** she**'d gone** there when she had the chance.*

   *I **wish** we**'d left** a bit earlier.*

- To express regret about something that <u>did</u> happen, we use the negative form of the past perfect (*hadn't* + past participle).

   *I **wish** I **hadn't eaten** so much.* (= I ate too much)

   *He **wishes** he **hadn't got** so angry with them.*

   *I **wish** we **hadn't met** in the first place.*

DID YOU KNOW?

We can use *really* + *wish* to emphasize our regrets. We can also use *never* instead of *not* as a stronger way of expressing regret about something that happened.

*I **really wish** I'd spoken to her earlier.*

*He **really wishes** he hadn't bought it.*

*I wish we'd **never** moved house.*

Exercise 1

Choose the correct option to complete the sentences.

1 I often wish *I'd / I hadn't* travelled more when I had the chance. It's impossible with the children.

2 I wish *I'd / I hadn't* gone. It was such a waste of time.

3 All the flights are really expensive. I wish we *had / hadn't* left it till the last minute to book them.

4 She really wishes she *had / hadn't* said something at the time. But it's too late now.

5 I wish I *had / hadn't* ignored him. He was right.

6 You've been so helpful. I wish *I'd / I hadn't* spoken to you earlier.

7 I shouted at her and now I wish I *had / hadn't* got so angry.

8 I sometimes wish I *had / hadn't* been stricter with my children. They would have thanked me for it.

9 I wish *we had / we'd never* met. Life would be so much easier now if we hadn't.

10 I'm so fed up at work. I really wish *I'd / I hadn't* applied for that other job when I had the chance.

Exercise 2

Complete the second sentence so that it has a similar meaning to the first sentence.

1 I really regret saying all those things.

   I really wish *I hadn't said all those things*.

2 I really regret not asking her.

   I wish _____ .

3 It's a shame you didn't tell me.

   I wish _____ .

4 I regret being so hard on my children.

   I wish _____ .

5 It's a shame I lost touch with them.

   I really wish _____ .

6 It's a shame I didn't move when I had the chance.

   I wish _____ .

Exercise 3

Complete the sentences to make them true for you.

1 I wish I'd _____ .

2 I wish I hadn't _____ .

3 I really wish _____ .

13 JOURNEYS

13B THIRD CONDITIONALS

Use

We use the third conditional to talk about an imagined situation in the past and its imagined past result or consequence. A third conditional has two parts: the *if*-clause and the result clause.

Note that this contrasts with the first or second conditional, which talk about things in the present or future.

Form

The *if* clause

The *if* clause refers to an imagined past situation, action or event. We use the past perfect in the *if* clause. In more informal writing and speaking, we can use the contracted form (*'d*).

*If I'd **stayed** in Afghanistan, none of this* would have happened. (= I didn't stay in Afghanistan)
*If he **hadn't fallen** ill, he would never have seen how doctors bring hope.* (= he did fall ill)

We can use the past perfect continuous in the *if* clause to express an action in progress.
*If he'd **been driving** more slowly, he wouldn't have crashed.*

The result clause
The result clause refers to the imagined result or consequence in the past. We use *would have* + past participle in the result clause. In more informal writing and speaking, we often use the contracted form (*'ve*).
*If I'd stayed in Afghanistan, none of this **would have happened**.* (= it did happen)
*I **wouldn't have gone** if I'd known how bad it would be.* (= I did go)
*If he hadn't fallen ill, he **would never have seen** how doctors bring hope.* (= he did see)

Note that we use *wouldn't have* or *would never have* for negative structures.

Common mistakes
*If I ~~would have~~ **had** had more time, I would have stayed longer.*
Remember that we do not use *would have* in the *if* clause.

DID YOU KNOW?
We can put the *if* clause first or second in the sentence. When we put it first, we use a comma after it. When we start with the result clause, we don't use a comma.
*If we hadn't met**,** my life would have been very different.*
My life would have been very different if we hadn't met.

Exercise 1
Complete the sentences with the correct form of the verbs in brackets.

1 I *would have called* you last night if I *'d had* your number. (call, had)
2 I _____ if I _____ she was going to be here. (not come, know)
3 If you _____ your bag in such a stupid place, I _____ over it. (not leave, not trip)
4 We _____ lost if the battery on my phone _____ . (not get, not die)
5 There's no way I _____ my own business if I _____ in my own country. It just _____ possible. (set up, stay, not be)
6 If there _____ so much traffic on the way to the airport or if we _____ earlier, I _____ my flight (not be, set off, miss)

Exercise 2
Which five sentences are incorrect? Correct them.

1 If we would have set off an hour earlier, we would have missed the rush hour.
2 If you'd asked me earlier, I would come yesterday.
3 The accident would have been worse if she hadn't been wearing a seatbelt.
4 I don't know what I would have did if I hadn't come here. It changed my life.
5 If it hadn't been for that long journey, we would never have got to know each other.
6 If I'd seen you at the party, I would say hello.
7 We wouldn't have got lost if we'd been given better directions.
8 We would never met if I hadn't been working that day.

13C *SHOULD HAVE*

We use *should(n't) have* + past participle to express a better alternative to something that actually happened in the past. In more informal writing and speaking, we often use the contracted form (*'ve*). We use *should have* to talk about what we didn't do and *shouldn't have* to talk about what we did do.
*My mobile's dead. I **should have charged** it before I left.* (= I didn't charge it)
*I overslept. I **should have set** my alarm clock.* (= I didn't set my alarm clock)
*I **shouldn't have eaten** so much earlier. I feel dreadful.* (= I ate too much)
Note that we can also use *never* to make a negative.
*I **should never have said** anything!*

DID YOU KNOW?
We often use *so* or *such* after *shouldn't have* to say that something was too much or too many.
*He shouldn't have been driving **so** fast.*
*I shouldn't have eaten **such** a big meal.*

Continuous form
We can use *should(n't) have* + been + *-ing* to express an action in progress over a period of time.
*You **should have been listening**. Then you'd know what to do.*
*You **should have been working**, not looking at Instagram.*

Exercise 1
Complete the sentences using *should have* / *shouldn't have* and the past participle of the verbs in brackets.

1 It's crazy! They *shouldn't have let* so many people into the building. (let)
2 Look at the traffic! I knew we _____ the train. (take)
3 We _____ somewhere else to eat. That place was terrible. (go)
4 It's my own fault I didn't finish everything. I _____ to do so much. (try)
5 You _____ me you were having difficulties. I could've helped you. (tell)
6 It was my mistake. I'm sorry I _____ so stupid. It won't happen again. (be)

Exercise 2
Complete the second sentence using *should(n't) have* so that it has a similar meaning to the first sentence.

1 We didn't set off early enough.
  We _____ earlier.
2 I wish I hadn't left it till the last minute.
  I really _____ so late.
3 It's a shame you didn't come to the party. It was great.
  You _____ party. You would have enjoyed it.
4 They didn't tell us about the change until it was too late.
  They really _____ about the change sooner.
5 I'm not surprised you don't understand. You weren't paying attention.
  It's your own fault you don't understand. You _____ attention.
6 If he'd been skiing a bit slower, he wouldn't have lost control. It's his own fault he fell. He _____ fast.

Exercise 3
Think about some things that you recently did and didn't do and that you should have done differently. Complete the sentences.

1 I should have …
2 I shouldn't have …
3 I shouldn't have … so …

14 TECHNOLOGY

14B ARTICLES

Indefinite article: *a / an*

We use *a / an* is when something we are referring to is one of several. This is usually because the exact thing is not important or because we don't know what exactly it is. We also use *a / an* when we mention something for the first time.

*I've got **a new computer**.* (= this is the first time the computer is mentioned and the exact computer is not important)

*The feeling of driving **a fast car** is incredibly exciting.* (= it doesn't matter which fast car; all fast cars are exciting to drive)

*Internet speeds and connectivity are still **a real issue** here.* (= there are other issues too; this is one among many)

Another common use of *a / an* is to say what someone is, such as what their job is.

*I'm **a software engineer**.*   *I'm **a programmer**.*   *He's **a student**.*
*You're **a genius**!*

Common mistakes

Remember that we do not use *a / an* with uncountable nouns. We use *a / an* only with singular countable nouns.

I need ~~an~~ some information.

It's important to do ~~a~~ careful research.

DID YOU KNOW?

We use *a* before a word that begins with a consonant sound and *an* before a word that begins with a vowel sound. Note that for some words that begin with the vowels *e* and *u*, the sound at the beginning of the word is actually the consonant sound /j/.

a euro	*a gadget*	*a phone*	*a university*
an apple	*an engine*	*an image*	*an umbrella*

Definite article: *the*

We use *the* when it is clear which thing we are referring to. This is sometimes because it is understood from the context or situation and sometimes because there is only one of something.

*Did you watch **the film** I told you about?* (= both people know the exact film because they spoke about it)

*I imagine the best thing about your job is **the flexible hours**.* (= both people know that the job has flexible hours)

*Did you read all **the comments** below **the photo**?* (= both people know that there's a photo and there are comments below it)

*Shall I turn off **the computer**?* (= there is only one computer in the situation)

*When was **the internet** invented?* (= there is only one internet)

We can use *the* with singular, plural and uncountable nouns.

the computer   *the computers*   *the information*

No article

We don't use an article before plural and uncountable nouns to talk about things in a general sense.

***Technology** is developing faster than ever.*

*I love watching **films**, especially **romcoms**.*

*I became obsessed with **roleplay games**.*

*It's taking money away from **designers** and **programmers**.*

We also don't use an article in some expressions of place that use preposition + noun. There is no fixed rule, but it is usually when we are talking more generally about the place.

*I started gaming seriously when I was **at university**.*

*I almost completely stopped going **to class**.*

*We're not allowed to use our phones **in class**.*

*We met **at school** about 15 years ago.*

*I sometimes work **from home**.*

*Do you have a study or office **at home**?*

*Can you wear jeans **at work**?*

*I walk **to** and **from work** most days.*

Exercise 1

Choose the correct option to complete the sentences.

1 *The technology / Technology / A technology* has completely changed the way people work.

2 *The technology / Technology / A technology* inside the camera is really clever.

3 My brother is *games designer / a games designer / the games designer*.

4 I've always been interested in *the computers / a computer / computers*. That's why I studied software engineering *at university / at a university / at the university*.

5 *Today, developing the green technology / a green technology / green technology* is *number one / the number one / a number one* priority for many companies.

6 I'll call you back later. I'm still *at work / at the work / at a work*. But I'll be *at the home / at a home / at home* all day tomorrow if you want to call me then.

7 *A thing / Thing / The thing* I love about gaming is that it brings *people / a people / the people* together.

8 It was *a very popular game / very popular game / the very popular game* when I was *a kid / the kid / kid*.

Exercise 2

Complete the text with *a*, *the* or *X* (= no article).

It is impossible to say that ¹_____ single person is responsible for ²_____ invention of the internet. The internet was the work of dozens of ³_____ scientists, programmers and engineers from across ⁴_____ globe. Each of them developed ⁵_____ new features and technologies that eventually combined to become ⁶_____ online world that we know today.

Exercise 3

Which six sentences are incorrect? Correct them. Some sentences have more than one mistake.

1 Not many of the people I know play the computer games these days.

2 I've had a smartphone since I was twelve or thirteen.

3 I can't call you this afternoon because I'll be in the class.

4 Copper is important metal used in the computer manufacturing.

5 I love online gaming. It's the great way to connect with people all over world.

6 My sister works for big computer company in Bangalore.

7 I love watching films, especially with a few friends.

8 I've loved the gadgets since I was child.

14C INFINITIVE WITH *TO* OR *-ING* FORM

-ing forms as subject or object

When a verb is a subject or object, we use an *-ing* form.

***Playing video games** is one of my favourite pastimes.*

***Gardening** always helps me to relax.*

*We didn't do **programming** in our IT classes at school.*

-ing forms after prepositions

When a verb follows a preposition, we use an *-ing* form.

*What's wrong **with using** your own voice?*

*We were all involved **in organizing** the event.*

*I'm really looking forward **to going** to the tech fair in Barcelona.*

-ing forms as adjectives

We can use some *-ing* forms as adjectives.

*It was so **embarrassing**.*

*It's a very **exciting** development.*

-ing forms in continuous tenses

We also use an -ing form to make continuous tenses.

She's watching TV at the moment. (present continuous)

I was talking to Erica the other day. (past continuous)

You've been playing that game for three hours! (present perfect continuous)

Infinitive with *to* for purpose

We use an infinitive with *to* to explain the purpose or reason for doing something.

Do you use facial recognition to unlock your phone?

I need to go to the bank to sort out a problem.

I'm going into town to get some printer ink.

Verb + infinitive with *to* or + -ing form

When two verbs are used next to each other, the second verb can take the infinitive with *to* or the -ing form. The choice of form depends on the first verb. There are no rules for this, you have to learn the patterns.

- Verbs usually followed by the infinitive with *to* include:

(can/can't) afford	agree	arrange	ask
decide	deserve	expect	fail
help	hope	intend	learn (how)
manage	need	offer	plan
promise	refuse	threaten	wait
want	would	like	

I promised to help Ali with his homework.

I can't afford to get a new phone at the moment.

Do you want to come to the cinema with us?

- Verbs usually followed by the -ing form include:

avoid	can't stand	consider	deny
enjoy	fancy	feel like	finish
imagine	involve	keep (on)	like (don't)
mind	miss	practise	recommend
risk spend (time)	stop	suggest	

I feel like watching a film this evening.

He used to spend hours playing online games.

Do you miss living by the sea?

We sometimes use verb + object + infinitive with *to*. Note that some verbs (e.g. *ask, expect, help, need, want*) can be used with or without an object, whereas some verbs (e.g. *advise, allow, encourage, persuade, remind*) must have an object.

Gardening always helps me to relax.

He's always asking us to help him.

It's an app that allows you to speak in a foreign language.

They finally persuaded me to go with them.

Exercise 1

Complete the sentences with the correct form of the verbs in brackets.

1 The company finally agreed _____ me a refund for the faulty gadget. (give)

2 I was involved in _____ the website at work. (develop)

3 They should invent a robot _____ your pets while you're away. (look after)

4 _____ computer games can be very educational. (play)

5 The app allows you _____ if any of your friends are nearby. (find out)

6 I can't stand people _____ their smartphones while I'm _____ to them. (look at, talk)

7 I was thinking of _____ engineering, but I decided _____ business studies instead. (study, do)

8 You should get a cover for your phone _____ it from _____ damaged. (prevent, get)

9 _____ up with all the latest online trends is _____. (keep, exhaust)

10 I was involved in _____ a series of webinars last month, helping _____ speakers for the event. (organize, find)

Exercise 2

Choose the correct option to complete the sentences.

1 My job involves *travelling / to travel* a lot.

2 Do you fancy *going / to go* out somewhere this evening?

3 Sorry, I've arranged *meeting / to meet* a friend.

4 I'd rather stay in. I don't feel like *going out / to go out*.

5 He played well. He didn't deserve *losing / to lose*.

6 I asked her *emailing / to email* me a response, but I'm still wating *hearing / to hear* from her.

7 I avoid *talking / to talk* to him as much as I can. But he keeps *trying / to try* to start conversations with me all the time.

8 I recommend *to set / setting* your computer to save automatically or you risk *losing / to lose* your work.

Exercise 3

Match the beginnings of the sentences (1–6) with the endings (a–f).

1 I can't afford

2 I'm not interested in

3 I spend too much time

4 I really need

5 I'm looking forward to

6 I'm learning English

a sitting in front of the computer.

b to eat better and do more exercise.

c to get a new phone at the moment.

d getting away for a few days next week.

e keeping up with the latest gadgets.

f to help me get a better job.

Exercise 4

Complete the sentence beginnings (1–6) in Exercise 3 with your own ideas.

1 I can't afford *to go on holiday at the moment.*

15 INJURIES AND ILLNESS

15A ADVERBS

Use

We use adverbs in a number of ways. The main uses include:

- to say how or the way we do something. These are sometimes called adverbs of manner.

  She read the notes carefully.

  I fell badly and I hit the ground hard.

- to say when we do something. These are sometimes called adverbs of time.

  I saw the doctor yesterday.

  He hasn't been feeling well recently.

- to say how frequently we do something. These are sometimes called adverbs of frequency.

  I never eat meat these days.

  She usually does some exercise twice a week.

- to say how much or to express the degree of something. These are sometimes called adverbs of degree.

  They hardly spoke at the meeting.

  I really tried to do my best.

- to give our opinion or show our attitude about something. These are sometimes called adverbs of attitude.

  Hopefully, it's nothing serious.

  Obviously, she was happy with the outcome.

  Personally, I don't agree.

DID YOU KNOW?

Adverbs that say how much or express the degree of something (e.g. *incredibly, really, absolutely*) can modify adjectives.

I was **incredibly** tired.

She made a **really** quick recovery.

Form

Adverbs have a range of different forms. However, it is useful to know that:

- a lot of adverbs are formed by adding *-ly* to an adjective. Adverbs ending with *-ly* often show how we do something (*wait **patiently**, look **carefully**, walk **slowly***), express the degree of something (e.g. **hardly** *understand*, **really** *serious*, **incredibly** *painful*) or show frequency (e.g. **occasionally** *visit*, **usually** *eat*, **rarely** *go*).

- some adverbs (e.g. *early, fast, hard, late*) have the same form as the adjective.

  He can run **fast**. He's a **fast** runner.

  We started **early**. We had an **early** start.

  She's working **hard**. She's a **hard** worker.

- some adjectives have two adverb forms (e.g. *hard / hardly, late / lately*) The two forms have different meanings.

  They **work hard**. (= they work a lot)

  He **hardly sleeps**. (= he doesn't sleep very much)

  I **get up late** most weekends. (= I get up at a late time)

  I've been feeling ill **lately**. (= I've been feeling ill recently)

Position

- Adverbs that show our opinion or attitude about what we're saying usually go at the start of a sentence (or clause). They are often followed by a comma.

  Hopefully, it won't be more than half an hour.

  Fortunately, the hospital didn't charge us for the treatment.

  There was a lot of traffic, but **luckily**, we arrived on time.

- Adverbs that show frequency or express the degree of something usually go before the main verb.

  He **often** cycles to work.

  I've **never** been here before.

  I **really** enjoyed it.

  However, note that they go after the verb *be*.

  They are **usually** on time.

  My ankle was **badly** sprained.

- Adverbs showing how we do something generally go after the verb.

  I listened **carefully** to what he was saying.

  She works **very hard**.

  They arrived **late**, as usual!

  Note that if the verb has an object, the adverb usually goes after the verb + object.

  They read the notes **quickly**.

- Adverbs showing when things happen often go at the end of a sentence (or clause).

  I haven't been sleeping well **lately**.

  I went to see a specialist **a few days ago**.

  I have an appointment **tomorrow afternoon**.

Exercise 1

Choose the correct option to complete the sentences.

1 They arrived *late / lately* and missed the beginning of the film.

2 I *usually eat / eat usually* meat only once or twice a week.

3 It was a big needle, but I *hard / hardly* felt it in my arm.

4 They *early set off / set off early* to avoid the traffic.

5 I was *incredibly lucky / lucky incredibly* that I wasn't injured.

6 Sara has *tomorrow a test / a test tomorrow*.

7 *Late / Lately*, I've been working really *hard / hardly*.

8 Luckily, I *never have had / have never had* an operation or spent a night in hospital.

Exercise 2

Put the adverb(s) in the correct place in the sentence. Sometimes more than one position is possible.

1 I need to give you an injection, but you'll feel it. (hardly)

2 He's never had a day off work because of illness in 40 years. (amazingly)

3 I have been very tired. Maybe I'm getting a virus. (lately)

4 I was walking, but I still slipped on the ice. (carefully)

5 She is very fit and healthy, but she's had a few days off work. (usually, recently)

6 She came out of hospital. I think she's making a good recovery. (last week, really)

7 I broke my arm and I had to have an operation. (badly, unfortunately)

8 I fell over and was lucky I didn't hurt myself. (really, seriously)

9 I have to get up, but I don't mind. (sometimes, early, usually)

10 They can do the operation. You'll only be in the hospital for a few hours. (very quickly these days, apparently)

15C REPORTED SPEECH

Said and *told*

When we report things, we generally use *said* and *told*. Note that *told* must have an object (e.g. *me, her, us, them*).

She **said** she was going to be a bit late.

He **told me** he was feeling much better.

NOT ~~She said me she was going to be a bit late~~.

Note that we can omit *that* with no difference in meaning.

He said / told me **that** he was fine.

He said / told me he was fine.

Tense change

When we report things, especially when something is finished, not relevant or untrue now, we generally move one tense back from the direct speech. The changes we make are:

- Present simple → Past simple
- Present continuous → Past continuous
- Present perfect simple → Past perfect simple
- Past simple → Past perfect simple
- *be going to* → *was going to*
- *will* → *would*
- *can* → *could*
- *must / have to* → *had to*

'We**'ve given** him an X-ray and luckily nothing **is** broken.'
(present perfect simple, present simple)

They rang and told me they**'d given** James an X-ray and that there **was** nothing broken.
(past perfect simple, past simple)

'He **needs** to stay here a bit longer, I'm afraid. He**'s waiting** to have a few more tests.'
(present simple, present continuous)

They said he **needed** to stay there a bit longer, though, as he **was waiting** to have a few more tests.
(past simple, past continuous)

'I**'ll** take him to the nearest hospital.' (will)

She said she**'d take** James to the nearest hospital. (would)

No tense change

Sometimes, we do not change the tense in reported speech. This is usually when we want to show or emphasize that what we are reporting is still true.

*'I **live** in Madrid now.'*
*She told us she **lives** in Madrid now.*

*'Sam**'s going to** have to go to hospital.'*
*He said Sam**'s going to** have to go to hospital.*

*'We**'re working** tomorrow, so I'm afraid we can't come.'*
*They said they can't come tomorrow because they**'re working**.*

Reporting questions

When we report questions, the word order is different from direct questions. There is no inversion of the subject and verb, and we do not use *do, does* or *did*. We can use *asked* with or without an object, e.g. *She asked …* or *She asked me …* .
*'When **did you start** feeling ill?'*
*She asked me when **I'd started** feeling ill.*

*'Where **am I**?'*
*He kept asking where **he was**.*
NOT ~~He kept asking where was he.~~

When we report *yes / no* questions, we use *if* or *whether*.
'Have we met before?'
*He asked me **whether we'd met** before.*

'Can I have a look at it?'
*She asked **if she could have** a look at it.*

Note that reported questions follow the same rules of tense change as reported statements.

DID YOU KNOW?

Time and place words and pronouns often change when we report things people said.
*'I saw him **yesterday**.'*
*She said **she**'d seen him **the day before** / **the previous day**.*

*'**We** can arrange an appointment for you **tomorrow**.'*
***They** said I could see a doctor **the next day** / **the following day**.*

*'Is there a hospital near **here**?'*
***He** asked if there was a hospital near **there**.*

Exercise 1

Complete the sentences with the reported speech.

1 'I'm feeling much better, thanks.'
   I saw her yesterday and she said she _____ .
2 'I've worked here for over ten years.'
   She told me she _____ .
3 'You need to eat a more balanced diet.'
   The doctor told me _____ .
4 'You'll probably be in hospital for a few days.'
   She said _____ , but I was back home after just two.
5 'It doesn't hurt. I'm fine.'
   He said _____ and that he _____ .

Exercise 2

Complete the sentences below with the correct form of these verbs. You will need to add modal verbs in two sentences. Sometimes more than one answer is possible.

be	cancel	have	qualify	suffer	take

1 A: I feel guilty because we didn't help.
   B: You shouldn't. We did offer, but he said he _____ fine.
2 A: I saw James in the gym last night.
   B: Really? I thought he said he _____ his membership.

3 A: He's looking really well, isn't he?
   B: I know. It's amazing! The doctors told him it _____ years to recover.
4 A: He's got his final exams next month.
   B: That's strange. I thought he said he _____ as a doctor already.
5 A: She's having an operation to sort out the problem.
   B: I thought she said she _____ it done already.
6 A: He's suffering from stress.
   B: Really? He told me he _____ from a heart condition.

Exercise 3

Report the doctor's questions. Sometimes more than one answer is possible.

1 'Has anything like this happened before?'
   She asked me _____ .
2 'Does it hurt if I press here?'
   She asked _____ if she pressed on my arm.
3 'How do you think it happened?'
   She asked me _____ .
4 'Are you free to come in again next week?'
   She asked _____ .
5 'How did you manage to do that?'
   He asked me _____ it.
6 'Have you lost weight since the last time I saw you?'
   He asked _____ since the last time _____ .
7 'Do you ever have problems sleeping?'
   He asked me _____ .
8 'Do you have any other questions you want to ask me?'
   He asked _____ .

16 NEWS AND EVENTS

16A REPORTING VERBS

We use a range of verbs to report what someone says. Different reporting verbs are followed by different patterns.

Verb + (*that*) clause
*She's just **announced** (that) they're splitting up.*
*The new management **claim** (that) it's too expensive to run.*
Verbs like this include:

admit	announce	claim	deny	explain
mention	promise	reply	say	state

Verb + object + (*that*) clause
*He **told** me (that) he's getting divorced.*
*They **informed** us (that) that there would be a delay.*
Verbs like this include:

inform	promise	remind	tell	warn

Verb + infinitive with *to*
*They **promised** to expand last year.*
*No-one **offered** to help.*
*He's **refused** to play in any friendly matches.*
Verbs like this include:

agree	ask	demand	promise	refuse	threaten

Verb + object + infinitive with *to*
*I **warned** him not to do it.*
*They've **persuaded** her to stay.*
Verbs like this include:

advise	encourage	invite	persuade	order
remind	tell		warn	

Verb + preposition + -ing

He just **apologized** <u>for causing</u> the government difficulties.
She **insisted** <u>on travelling</u> by train and not flying.
Verbs like this include:

admit to   apologize for   complain about   insist on

Verb + object + preposition + -ing

She **accused** <u>him of lying</u>.
They **thanked** <u>me for helping</u> them.
Verbs like this include:

accuse … of   congratulate … for / on   thank … for
warn … against

DID YOU KNOW?

Verbs that are followed by an -ing form can also usually be followed by a noun.
They apologized for **all the problems** we'd had.
I complained about **the service** at the hotel.
I thanked them for **all of their help**.

Verbs with more than one pattern

Note that some verbs have more than one pattern.
He **promised that** he'd not be late. (verb + (that) clause)
He **promised me that** he wouldn't be late.
(verb + object + (that) clause)

The company has **warned staff that there may** be some cuts.
(verb + (that) clause)
The police have **warned people not to approach** the prisoner.
(verb + object + infinitive with to)

The government **insisted its policy would work** eventually.
(verb + (that) clause)
He **insisted on paying** for everything.
(verb + preposition + -ing)

Exercise 1

Choose the correct option to complete the sentences.

1 The company finally agreed *to increase / that they increase* the workers' wages.
2 She was accused *to cheat / of cheating* to win the match.
3 The police are advising the public *not to travel / not travelling* because of the bad weather.
4 The company has stated *not to know / it didn't know* about the problem until very recently.
5 She threatened *to tell / telling* the newspaper about the stolen money.
6 Before the election, the government promised *to lower / lowering* taxes.
7 I'm not surprised you're ill. I did warn you *not to eat / not eating* the food at that place!
8 The police questioned him about the murder, but he refused *to say / saying* anything.

Exercise 2

Read the first sentence in each pair. Complete the second sentence so that it has a similar meaning. Use between two and five words, including the word in bold.

1 He said he was sorry he was late. **APOLOGIZED**
   He _____ late.
2 His exact words were, 'If you tell anyone about this, you're fired!' **THREATENED**
   He _____ if I told anyone about it.
3 She said there was no way she was signing the contract. **REFUSED**
   She _____ the contract.
4 She kept telling me I should apply for the job. **ENCOURAGED**
   She _____ the job.

5 They said I shouldn't walk on my own at night. **WARNED**
   They _____ at night on my own.
6 He told me he would definitely pay me tomorrow. **PROMISED**
   He _____ pay me tomorrow.

Exercise 3

Which four sentences contain a mistake? Correct them.

1 They announced us that some roads would be closed in the city centre.
2 The airline informed that the flight was delayed by two hours.
3 He denied that he was involved in the bank robbery.
4 We demanded to speaking to the manager about the bad service.
5 The government apologized for causing so much confusion about the new law.
6 They accused the minister to lie about where the money came from.

16C DEFINING RELATIVE CLAUSES

We use a defining relative clause to add information to a noun. The relative clause comes immediately after the noun and begins with a relative pronoun (*that, who, which, whose*) or a relative adverb (*where, when, why*).

- To add information about a person, we use *who* or *that*.
  Roentgen was the scientist **who discovered radiation**.
  She's the woman **that spoke to me earlier**.
- To add information about a thing, we use *which* or *that*.
  It's a government scheme **which helps unemployed people**.
  She wrote a book **that was a huge bestseller**.
- To add information about possession, we use *whose*.
  That's the couple **whose child went missing last year**.
  He made a film **whose main character becomes the US President by accident**.
- To add information about a reason we use *why* or *that*.
  Increasing online sales was part of the decision **why we closed the shop**.
  He was ill and **that's the reason he cancelled the concert**.
  The reason **that he had to leave** was that his visa had run out.
- To add information about a time, we use *when* or *that*.
  I remember the day **when the Queen died** very clearly.
  At the time **that he was writing**, there was a war going on.
- To add information about a place, we use *where*.
  That's the office **where Sami works**.
  What's the name of that place **where you went for your birthday**?

DID YOU KNOW?

We can use *which / that … in / at / to* as an alternative to *where*.
This is the church **that** we got married **in**. (= this is the church where we got married)

The picture shows the building **which** the gang was hiding **in**.

We can also use the more formal alternative *in / at which*.
The picture shows the building **in which the gang was hiding**.

Leaving out the pronoun

We can leave out *that, who* or *which* when the word following it is a subject (*I, he, you, Monica* etc). This is common in spoken English.
This is the book ~~that~~ Monica was telling us about.
Luci is my colleague ~~who~~ you met the other day at the conference.
The reason ~~that~~ he had to leave was that his visa had run out.

Common mistakes

Note that a relative pronoun / adverb replaces the noun / pronoun it refers to.

She wrote a book that ~~it~~ was a huge best-seller.
The people I was speaking to ~~them~~ are colleagues.
The scientist who ~~she~~ made the discovery won a Nobel prize.

Exercise 1

Match the beginnings of the sentences (1–6) with the pairs of relative clauses (a–f).

1 Did you apply for that job
2 He's the writer
3 What's the name of that company
4 We met that woman
5 We went to that café
6 Did you read about that guy

a which you recommended. It was really good!
  where all the stars go, but we didn't see anyone famous!
b which went bankrupt last week?
  that Maria works for?
c whose novel was banned.
  who won the Nobel prize a couple of years ago.
d that you were telling me about?
  which was advertised in the paper yesterday?
e who works with you. I've forgotten her name!
  that we spoke to at the conference last month.
f who they arrested for that big robbery?
  that was awarded the Nobel peace prize?

Exercise 2

In which sentences in Exercise 1 can we leave out the relative pronoun?

1 *Did you apply for that job ~~that~~ you were telling me about?*

Exercise 3

Complete the review with the correct relative pronouns / adverbs. Sometimes more than one answer is possible.

Lorenzo's Oil is a film [1]_____ tells the true story of a couple [2]_____ child, called Lorenzo, develops medical problems at the age of seven. The first doctors [3]_____ see him have no idea what's causing the problem, but he's eventually diagnosed with a rare and incurable disease called ALD. The parents ask about hospitals [4]_____ they're doing research on this disease, but they're told that ALD is so rare that no-one will provide the money [5]_____ is needed to research it. The couple, who have no medical training, then start to study medical literature to find something [6]_____ will help their son. They hear about a special oil [7]_____ they believe can help their son and they eventually find a scientist [8]_____ is prepared to produce the oil for them. It works, and their son's condition starts to improve. Lorenzo's oil is then also given to other people [9]_____ are suffering from ALD.

Irregular verbs

Infinitive	Past simple	Past participle
be	was / were	been
beat	beat	beaten
become	became	become
begin	began	begun
bite	bit	bitten
blow	blew	blown
break	broke	broken
bring	brought	brought
build	built	built
burn	burned / burnt	burned / burnt
buy	bought	bought
catch	caught	caught
choose	chose	chosen
come	came	come
cost	cost	cost
cut	cut	cut
deal	dealt	dealt
do	did	done
draw	drew	drawn
dream	dreamed / dreamt	dreamed / dreamt
drink	drank	drunk
drive	drove	driven
eat	ate	eaten
fall	fell	fallen
feed	fed	fed
feel	felt	felt
fight	fought	fought
find	found	found
fit	fit / fitted	fit / fitted
fly	flew	flown
forget	forgot	forgotten
get	got	got
give	gave	given
go	went	gone
grow	grew	grown
have	had	had
hear	heard	heard
hide	hid	hidden
hit	hit	hit
hold	held	held
hurt	hurt	hurt
keep	kept	kept
know	knew	known
lead	led	led
learn	learned / learnt	learned / learnt
leave	left	left
lend	lent	lent

Infinitive	Past simple	Past participle
let	let	let
lie	lay	lain
light	lit	lit
lose	lost	lost
make	made	made
mean	meant	meant
meet	met	met
pay	paid	paid
prove	proved	proven
put	put	put
read	read	read
ride	rode	ridden
ring	rang	rung
rise	rose	risen
run	ran	run
say	said	said
see	saw	seen
sell	sold	sold
send	sent	sent
set	set	set
shake	shook	shaken
shine	shone	shone
shoot	shot	shot
show	showed	shown
shut	shut	shut
sing	sang	sung
sink	sank	sunk
sit	sat	sat
sleep	slept	slept
smell	smelled / smelt	smelled / smelt
speak	spoke	spoken
spend	spent	spent
spill	spilled / spilt	spilled / spilt
stand	stood	stood
steal	stole	stolen
stick	stuck	stuck
swim	swam	swum
take	took	taken
teach	taught	taught
tell	told	told
think	thought	thought
throw	threw	thrown
understand	understood	understood
wake	woke	woken
wear	wore	worn
win	won	won
write	wrote	written

Vocabulary reference

2 FEELINGS

2C   ADJECTIVES ENDING WITH *-ED* AND *-ING*

A small group of common adjectives can end in both *-ed* and *-ing*. The *-ed* form describes people's feelings. The *-ing* form describes the thing(s) that cause the feelings.

*I felt much more **relaxed**.* (= because the new way of doing things is more relaxing)

*An **embarrassing** silence followed.* (= and I felt embarrassed)

5 WORKING LIFE

5B   PHRASES WITH *BE* AND *GET*

Lots of adjectives can be used with both *be* and *get*. We often use *be* to describe states and *get* to focus on a change in state (where *get* means *become*).

*I'm much **better**, thanks. / Is he **getting better**?*

*We've **been married** for a year now. / I **got married** last year.*

We can use *be* and *get* in a similar way with other phrases.

be / get in trouble

be / get into (= interested in)

be / get sick of (= bored of)

be / get in touch with (= in contact with)

be / get used to (= something is / becomes familiar or normal to you)

8 EDUCATION

8B   FORMING NOUNS

One way to build your vocabulary is to learn the verb and the noun forms of words, e.g. *achieve – achievement*. Common noun endings (suffixes) are *-ment, -tion, -ation, -ance, -ence* and *-ist*. Many nouns, such as *worry*, are used as verbs without adding a suffix. A few verb-to-noun changes are more unusual, e.g. *compare – comparison*, *know – knowledge*. Some also involve changing one letter, e.g. *affect – effect*, *practise – practice*.

In all cases, make sure you learn the pronunciation of the different forms to help you use them correctly. Sometimes when a verb has the same form as the noun, the stress changes.

*pro*test *against the policy*   *go on a* pro*test*

It's also important to learn collocations for the different forms.

differ widely   *a big difference*

analyse the results carefully   *a careful analysis of the results*

10 GOING OUT

10B IDIOMS

An idiom is a fixed group of words that mean something different to the meaning of the individual words. You can sometimes work out the meaning of an idiom from the words and the context. If you look up the idiom in a dictionary, it's usually listed as a whole phrase, but sometimes you might find it under the entry for the noun.

*I tend to go for walks out **in the middle of nowhere**.*

13 JOURNEYS

13A PHRASAL VERBS

A phrasal verb is a verb (*put, throw, take*, etc.) plus a particle (*up, off, out, down*, etc.) Often the meaning is not obviously connected to either the verb or the particle. For example, when a plane *takes off*, it's not taking anything – it goes up into the sky!

When you translate phrasal verbs, you may use just one word in your language for some, while others may be translated into a phrase.

Phrasal verbs appear in all kinds of text – formal and informal, written and spoken – but are generally more common in informal language. It's best to learn them as you would any other verb: for example, in groups connected to a topic or as they appear in a text. Notice collocations and other phrases connected to each phrasal verb.

15 INJURIES AND ILLNESS

15B WORD CLASS AND SUFFIXES

Many words in English have the same verb and noun form (we add the suffix *-s* for plurals or *-ed* for past forms, passives, etc).

diet   head   link   sprain

Other forms in a word family may have different suffixes to show their word class. Removing the suffix and paying attention to the base form can help you guess the meaning of words:

*give a **warn**ing*   *a natural **occur**rence*

__modern__ize the health service   *an in**cura**ble condition*

Learning to recognize common suffixes for different word classes can help you build your vocabulary.

Adjective:	-able	-al	-ed	-ful	-ing
	-(i)ous	-ive	-less	-(t)ic	-y
Noun:	-ance	-ence	-er	-ing	-ist
	-ity	-ment	-ness	-or	-(t)ion
Verb:	-en	-ise	-ize		
Adverb:	-ly				

Information files

8B EXERCISE 10, SPEAKING

Student A

Hattie gives an average 'effect-size' score which allows comparison of the relative strength of each influence. Anything with a negative score has a negative effect. 0 has no effect. 0.4 is the average positive effect.

Teachers' subject knowledge

Teachers obviously need to know the subject they teach, but the level of qualifications that teachers have in their subject doesn't appear to have very much impact compared to other influences. This may be because in many classes the level of knowledge the students are learning is quite low, for example primary-school maths. What's more important is the teacher's ability to be clear, to show students how new knowledge connects to old, and to give feedback on how to improve.

Vocabulary programmes

Trying to increase the amount of vocabulary students know seems to work well, especially when you provide examples of how words are used as well as definitions. It's an example of challenging students and helps with several subjects by improving reading skills, which is maybe why it had an effect size of 0.62.

Self-reported grades

When you ask students to grade themselves or to predict their grades in exams (sometimes called 'self-reported grades'), they are often very accurate. Hattie suggests this is because they have learned what level they are by what teachers say or how they are grouped in class. He says self-reported grades are such a powerfully positive strategy because teachers understand their students' expectations better, and can then challenge them and show them how to do much better.

3C EXERCISE 13, SPEAKING TASK

Cruise: One- or two-week cruises, all-inclusive. Cruise ship includes luxury accommodation and a wide range of meal options. On board there's a spa, pool, golf, gym, evening entertainment, casino, disco. The trip includes a minimum of three days in port, with day-tours. Available cruises: Caribbean, Mediterranean, Alaska

Cultural encounters: One- or two-week tours where you get to hear a variety of perspectives on the country's history and culture through guides from different communities, visits to historic sites and educational talks. The tours include hotel accommodation and some meals. Available countries: Ireland, Israel and Palestine, US, Colombia, Egypt, Croatia

Home swap: Swap your home with a person or family from another country from our online community. Register on the site and then find a match with someone who'd like to have a holiday where you live. You can choose to visit each other's places at the same time of year or arrange visits at different times. Available countries: US, UK, Germany, Israel, Brazil, UAE, Kenya, Japan, Thailand, Italy

FILE 3   UNIT 1

1A EXERCISE 13, CONVERSATION PRACTICE

FILE 4 UNIT 3

3B EXERCISE 4, READING

Sette Giugno

Sette Giugno, or 7th June, is a public holiday in memory of a tragic day in our history and the people who fought for our independence. In 1919, there were a lot of protests against the British government, who controlled Malta at that time. On 7th June several people were shot and two years later we became independent. Of course, Maltese people learn about this event at school, and on the day there are some official ceremonies, which are televised, such as the president laying flowers at the Sette Giugno monument. However, to be honest, it's not something most people pay a lot of attention to these days. We just think of it as a day off work to enjoy. It's the start of summer, the sea is warming up, so it's typical to get together with friends and family at the beach. This year the festival falls on a Friday, so I'm thinking of taking an extra day off work on Monday to take full advantage of the long weekend. I might take the boat to Sicily or maybe a take a flight to somewhere a bit further away, like Madrid or Berlin.

Marcellino, Malta

Inti Raymi

Inti Raymi is a celebration of Inca culture. During Inca times, it was a religious event to give thanks to the sun god, Inti, and took place on the shortest day of the year, when the sun is furthest away. In the 16th century it was banned in Peru, but in 1944 a historian and a writer got together to create a new version of the ancient ceremony. It has become more and more popular over the years and it's now a public holiday for the people of Cusco. It's held every year on 24th June and it attracts a lot of tourists from all over the world. There are three performances during the day in different places in the city. Two are free, but the tickets for the main one in the ruins of an Inca temple costs around $200. It's a pretty spectacular event, with hundreds of performers. A friend took part in it once and we watched it on TV. I don't normally watch or attend the actual performances during the day, but there's always lots of partying and dancing at night, which I love, so I'll probably go out with my friends as usual. It's a shame I have to work the next day, but I can survive a day without sleep occasionally!

Gabriela, Peru

FILE 5 UNIT 3

3C EXERCISE 13, SPEAKING TASK

Volunteering: Volunteer in projects throughout the world for one to twelve weeks. Fee includes airport pickup, project training, host family accommodation and meals. Projects include animal care, youth programmes, farm/construction work in rural areas and teaching assistant roles. Available countries: Portugal, Costa Rica, Jordan, Madagascar, New Zealand, Morocco

Staycation: A week of group tours and visits within your region. No need to spend excessive amounts on travel and accommodation – our expert guides will show you the history, wildlife and culture of the area you live in that perhaps you've never seen before. Includes all travel, including transfers from your home and two overnight stays, plus lunches in some of the top restaurants your region has to offer. Available wherever you are!

Adventure, activity: One-week stays in spectacular mountain scenery. Activities include hiking, mountain-biking, skiing, climbing, white-water rafting, bungee jumping and zip lines. Prices include three-star accommodation or hostel, breakfast and lunch, all activities, equipment hire and instructors. Available countries: Chile, Switzerland, US, Italy, Romania, India, Vietnam, South Korea

FILE 6 UNIT 6

6A EXERCISE 12, CONVERSATION PRACTICE

Student A

You're a customer. Decide:

- how much you currently pay for your phone.
- how long the battery lasts.
- how much storage you have – and if you're happy with that.

Then decide what questions you want to ask about the new phone:

- camera?
- battery life?
- screen size?
- how easy is it to use?
- how much you have to pay upfront?

FILE 7 UNIT 8

8B EXERCISE 10, SPEAKING

Student B

Hattie gives an average 'effect-size' score which allows comparison of the relative strength of each influence. Anything with a negative score has a negative effect. 0 has no effect. 0.4 is the average positive effect.

Reducing class sizes

The overall score Hattie's analysis produces for reducing class sizes is quite small. Hattie suggests that one reason for this may be that teachers don't change the way they teach when class size is reduced. However, some studies suggest the effect size might have is nearer the average for smaller classes in secondary schools or with kids who are under-performing.

Deliberate practice

'Deliberate practice' is practising with the aim of improving – rather than just repeating similar tasks and checking the answers. For deliberate practice, students need information on assessment and feedback on how to improve. This is because students will often be more motivated when it is clear how they can get a higher grade. If the teacher then shows the next steps needed to improve, this is more encouraging than just saying 'well done' or 'you need to study more'.

Charter schools

Several countries have schools (e.g. charter schools in the US) which are more independent from government: they can choose what to teach, which teachers to employ, etc. They get some money from the government and some from private sources, so students do not have to pay. They do make a difference, but just a tiny one.

FILE 8 UNIT 6

6A EXERCISE 12, CONVERSATION PRACTICE

Student B

You're a salesperson in a mobile phone shop. Think about the phone you want to sell. Decide the details of the phone:

- camera?
- battery life?
- screen size?
- how much storage it has?

- how easy it is to use?
- how much it will cost upfront?
- what sort of monthly deal you can offer?

Think about how you'll sell the phone. What makes it better than other phones?

- battery life?
- the price?
- special features?
- something else?

FILE 9   UNIT 6

6B EXERCISE 7, READING

Add up your score:

a answers = 1

b answers = 3

c answers = 5

12–25

You really can't stand shopping and spending money on clothes just isn't your priority. Being fashionable doesn't interest you and you tend to wear fairly plain clothes most of the time. You're more concerned with things like protecting the environment. You buy second-hand items: they're cheaper and don't harm the planet as much.

26–38

You don't mind shopping, but you're quite careful with your money and you often keep an eye out for bargains. You want to look good, but you also want clothes to last, so the latest fashions don't interest you so much. There's more to life than shopping.

39–50

You're quite fashion-conscious and love shopping. It's one of your main leisure activities and often cheers you up. You probably have a particular obsession – shoes, shirts, suits, coats – and you generally make sure you get the items you really want. Sometimes you buy things without thinking and then later realize it was a bad idea.

51–60

Shopping and fashion are clearly your two main interests. You can't go shopping without buying something – even if you don't need it. You follow all the latest fashions and have drawers and wardrobes full of clothes you hardly ever wear.

FILE 10   UNIT 8

8A EXERCISE 12, CONVERSATION PRACTICE

Role card 1

You're studying a course in Java (explain this is a coding language for software / computer programs).

It's a sixteen-week intensive course. Explain what stage you're at.

Decide how the course is assessed.

You're positive about the course, your tutors and classmates. Think of reasons why.

The course will help you find a job.

Role card 2

You're studying a degree in Business Management. Decide which year you're in.

One of your current modules is Tax and Accounting.

You're struggling. Think of reasons why.

The tutors aren't very good. Think of reasons why.

You want to get work in finance or an accountancy firm.

Role card 3

You're doing a first-aid course. Decide why.

You do it at weekends. Decide how long it lasts.

You're enjoying it. Explain why.

Explain something you've learned already. In the next session you're learning CPR (what to do when someone stops breathing).

Decide how the course is assessed and what qualification you'll get.

FILE 11   UNIT 8

8C EXERCISE 11, SPEAKING TASK

a **We should ban exams in schools.**

For

- Reduce stress
- Internet makes exams unnecessary

Against

- Companies need to know standard people have
- Fairest judge of level

b **We should provide a healthy free school meal to every child every day.**

For

- Good food helps concentration
- Reduce obesity

Against

- Too expensive
- Should spend money on educational equipment

c **We should get a yearly amount of money to pay for education throughout our lives.**

For

- Fair
- Encourage life-long learning

Against

- Some important courses more expensive
- People more likely to give up

d **No-one should be able to get a degree if they haven't got an Intermediate level of English.**

For

- English essential in the modern world
- Science is a global subject using English

Against

- Students might not have access to quality teaching
- English unnecessary for a lot of jobs

e **Teachers should be paid according to the exam results of their students.**

For

- Reward good teachers
- Performance pay is normal in industry

Against

- Make teachers focus more on passing exams
- Unfair on teachers working with lower-level students

11A EXERCISE 1, SPEAKING

13C EXERCISE 11. SPEAKING TASK

Situation 1

You checked in for a flight and went to have something to eat. When you went to the departure lounge, there was an enormous queue to transfer to the terminal and extra security. When you walked up to the boarding gate, the airline said it was closed and they would charge you for a new ticket.

Situation 2

You went on a weekend break with a friend. When you got to the flat they'd booked online, you found out you were sharing a room, which you weren't happy about. Your friend said they didn't check, but just went for the cheapest option. Also, there was no wi-fi in the flat – a fact which wasn't mentioned in the advert online. On your first night, there was a huge noisy party upstairs. When you got home, you realized you'd left something in the flat. The owner offered to send it to you, but wanted to charge you three times what you think it should cost for postage.

Situation 3

You reserved a seat on a train to attend an important meeting. The first train arrived five minutes late, so you missed the connection. The next train was packed and you had to stand for two hours. You arrived at the meeting tired, late and absolutely furious. Unsurprisingly, the meeting didn't go well. Now you want compensation from the train operator.

Situation 4

You and a friend hired a car to go to a wedding. Your friend entered the destination in their phone, but used the wrong address so you set off in the wrong direction. Then you left the motorway to avoid a traffic jam and got completely lost. When you got back on the motorway, you started driving fast because you were worried you were going to be late. You got caught speeding and now you have to pay a fine. You think your friend should pay it.

8B EXERCISE 10. SPEAKING

Student C

Hattie gives an average 'effect-size' score which allows comparison of the relative strength of each influence. Anything with a negative score has a negative effect. 0 has no effect. 0.4 is the average positive effect.

Spaced practice v mass practice

Mass practice is when students have a long training period to cover one area of a subject. In many schools, students are given several lessons on the same area, often followed by a test. Lessons then move on to a new area. However, evidence from Hattie's research suggests that students remember much more if an area of learning is covered in shorter lessons over a longer period of time and is mixed with other areas. This is called 'spaced practice'.

Doing homework

Students everywhere might be happy to hear that homework isn't anywhere near as effective as people think. However, it depends on the age of the student and what kind of homework is given. In primary school, it has almost no effect at all. In secondary school, the effect is around the average, especially if it is a simple, short practice of what has been learned (see *Spaced practice v mass practice*). For this reason, Hattie still recommends giving it.

Summer holidays

There are complaints that long summer holidays impact badly on student achievement, and unfortunately, if you are a student or teacher, it is true! It seems that students do forget what they have learned over the long break. However, the negative effect is tiny, so there are many other issues that are of more concern.

Audio scripts

UNIT 1

Lesson 1A, Exercises 4 & 5

Conversation 1

H = Harry; O = Olivia

H: Hi, nice to meet you. I'm Harry.

O: Hey. Olivia. How's it going?

H: Yeah, I'm OK, thanks. I'm a bit nervous though, to be honest.

O: Yeah? Why?

H: I don't know. You know … first class, new people.

O: Yeah, I remember that feeling. Don't worry. You'll be fine. It'll be fun.

H: So, have you studied here before?

O: Yeah, I was here last term.

H: Oh, really? OK. And did you enjoy it?

O: Yeah, it was amazing. Our teacher Ángel was brilliant. Really great. So patient and helpful, you know. So, what about you? How long have you been learning Spanish?

H: For about three years now, I guess, but just on my own online. There's so much stuff available these days.

O: Yeah. So, have you learned much?

H: Well, my listening's improved and I've learned quite a lot of vocabulary, but I really need to practise my speaking more, you know. That's why I'm here. What about you? Why are you learning?

O: Well, I'd like to be a translator and Spanish is an official EU language and UN language, so … you know.

H: Wow! OK.

Conversation 2

N = Noah; G = Giuliana

N: So, what did you make of that session?

G: Oh, um. Well, it was … um … different, wasn't it?

N: I'm glad I'm not the only person that didn't really enjoy it.

G: So, what's your name, then? Where are you based?

N: Oh, I'm Noah.

G: Giuliana. Hi.

N: Hey. And I'm originally from Canada, from Halifax, but I'm working in Santiago now.

G: Oh really? Nice. How long have you been there?

N: A couple of years now. Do you know it? Have you been there?

G: Yeah, loads of times. I'm from Mendoza, just the other side of the mountains. We can drive there in five or six hours. Great city.

N: I like it, yes.

G: What are you doing there? Are you working?

N: Yeah. I'm a researcher – attached to the university there. I'm doing work on climate change.

G: Wow, interesting. And are you presenting at the conference?

N: Yeah. I was on yesterday, actually. What about you?

G: No, goodness! The whole idea really scares me. I don't think I could do it. I'm happy just attending and going to the talks.

Lesson 1C, Exercises 2 & 5

1: My business partner is Māori and so I've tried to learn Te Reo Māori a few times over the years – without much success. I've picked up a few words here and there, of course – things like 'kia ora', meaning 'hello', and so on – but it's only these last few months that I've really had time to improve. I'm taking classes twice a week and I'm not there yet, but I'm getting more fluent. I can feel it. The language is an important part of the culture and identity of New Zealand and though most people in my class are Māori themselves, interest in the language is really growing. You'll often hear it in advertising and in music on the radio now, for example.

2: A: That was great. I really enjoyed that.

B: Me too. I think Marie is maybe the best French teacher I've ever had.

A: Hey, listen. I was wondering. Do you want to maybe meet sometime and practise a little bit?

B: Um. Well … maybe, I guess. It depends.

A: How about tomorrow?

B: Oh, I can't I'm afraid. I'm working all day tomorrow. I don't finish until nine.

A: So, how about Saturday? Are you working then as well?

B: Um … I'm not, no, but I'm meeting someone, I'm afraid. Sorry.

A: Oh, OK. Well, let me know if you ever have a bit of free time, anyway.

3: I'm Brazilian, so I speak Portuguese, but I actually speak German at home. People are surprised when they find that out, especially because my parents are from Russia and Turkey! They first met when they were both working on a cruise ship. He worked in the engine room and she was a cleaner. There was a kind of party every week and they met there. My Mum said Dad was a really good dancer, which I find hard to believe. Anyway, neither spoke the other's language, but my mum had worked in Germany and Dad knew German from school, so that's how they communicated. They chose to settle in Rio because the cruises usually stopped here and they often had short holidays here. It also stopped them arguing about whose country to live in.

4: It's not easy – that's for sure. The thing I find the hardest is remembering all the new vocabulary. What I usually do is record myself saying new words and phrases in my own language first and then in English. I listen and stop after I hear the words in French, then try to say them in English and then play the recording and check. So for instance, I might hear 'un fort accent', and stop the recording, try to remember the translation, and then say 'a strong accent'. Like that. And I'm getting better. I understand more when I read and listen and the recordings help me see my progress too.

UNIT 2

Lesson 2A, Exercises 4 & 5

Conversation 1

R = Ryan; C = Clara

R: Hey, Clara!

C: What is it, Ryan?

R: Have you seen Karim this week?

C: Yeah, I saw him yesterday. Why?

R: Is he OK? I haven't spoken to him for a while, but the last time I saw him he seemed a bit down.

C: Hmm, I know. I think it's his mum. Apparently, she's quite ill and he's very worried about her.

R: Oh no! That sounds like a nightmare. What's wrong with her? Is it very serious?

C: I think it must be. He was quite upset when I spoke to him and he didn't want to say much.

R: Oh dear. That's awful. I feel a bit guilty now that I haven't rung him – I had a feeling something was wrong.

C: Why?

R: Well, I met him outside the university with Chris. Chris and I were chatting, but Karim didn't say much. In fact, he hardly said anything at all.

C: Really?

R: And Karim normally loves to talk.

C: I know. Well, he probably isn't in the mood to talk to anyone at the moment.

R: Oh dear. Well, if you see him, tell him I'm thinking of him.

C: Of course I will, yeah.

Conversation 2

B = Belinda; A = Alisha

B: Hello, Alisha! How's it going?

A: Great, actually, Belinda. I've just finished all my exams!

B: That must be a relief. How did they go?

A: Quite well, I think. I was really pleased with how I did.

B: That's great.

A: Are you alright? You look as if you need cheering up.

B: Yeah, sorry. I'm just a bit fed up with my accommodation situation.

A: Oh dear. What's the problem?

B: Oh, I've just found out I can't continue to stay where I am at the moment.

A: Oh no! What a pain!

B: Yeah, I know. So basically, I need to find another place and, to be honest, I just don't need the stress.

A: I can imagine. Can I do anything to help?

B: No, it's OK. I'm sure it'll sort itself out, but thanks.

A: Well, at least let me buy you a drink.

B: OK. That'd be nice.

A: What would you like?

B: A cappuccino would be good.

A: Anything else? A bit of cake? Go on, It'll cheer you up.

B: Well, I have to say that chocolate cake looks nice.

A: I think I'll join you – to celebrate finishing my exams.

Lesson 2C, Exercises 3 & 5

1: When I started doing talks at conferences, I used to get incredibly nervous. Even though I'd spent hours writing and preparing a speech, I was often sick in the toilets before the session, and sometimes forgot what I was going to say during it, which made things worse. Eventually, I started to question why I was doing this. When I teach normally, I have a plan, but I don't write everything down and I don't worry if I forget something. Once I started thinking of talks and workshops more like a normal class, I felt much more relaxed.

2: I went in feeling confident and it started OK. They asked me a bit about myself and why I wanted to join the police. It all seemed like it was going well – until they asked me to describe a situation where I'd had to resolve an argument. Looking back on it, I now see that it's an obvious question for them to ask, but I just wasn't ready for it. I just sat there umming and ahhing. Then they asked if I could give an example of a time when I'd been under pressure and how I'd dealt with it. Again, nothing. Just an embarrassing silence followed by my nervous laughter. Obviously, I didn't get a place on the course, which was a shame.

3: I was going to work and this car passed very close by me and almost knocked me off my bike. I shouted out something – partly because I was scared – and the car stopped. The driver then got out and started screaming at me, saying I'd almost caused an accident and that I shouldn't be allowed on the road. Then just at that moment, a police car stopped behind us. Luckily, the officer had seen what had happened and got out and managed to calm things down. We kind of apologized to each other and then carried on with our journeys.

4: Some people are already anxious when they come to see me. I mean, let's face it, most people don't actually enjoy the experience. We have a few different techniques to distract patients and help them relax while I'm working on their teeth. One is playing gentle music in the examination room and I also have a screen with calming images on it. Another thing that seems to work is asking patients to take some deep breaths before I start and then asking them to focus on moving their toes while I work.

UNIT 3

Lesson 3A, Exercises 7 & 8

C = Claire; R = Receptionist

C: Hello, there. I wonder if you can help me. I'm thinking of going sightseeing today. Can you recommend anywhere good to go?

R: Well, it depends on what you like. There are lots of places to choose from. What kinds of things are you interested in?

C: I don't know. Um, something cultural?

R: Oh, right. OK. Well, quite close to here is St Mary's Church. It's Kraków's most famous church and very beautifully decorated. You can walk there in five or ten minutes.

C: OK. I'm not really a big fan of looking around old religious buildings, to be honest.

R: That's OK, I understand. What about Oskar Schindler's factory? That's very popular.

C: Actually, I've actually already booked to go there later in the week.

R: Well, in that case, you could try Kazimierz, the old Jewish Quarter, where Steven Spielberg filmed some of Schindler's List. It's actually quite a lively area now. There are lots of good bars and restaurants round there.

C: Oh, so that might be nice for this evening, then.

R: Yes, maybe. Let me know if you want more information about places to eat or drink there. Erm, then if you'd prefer something a bit different, how about a guided tour of Nowa Huta? It was a model town built in communist times. You can see what life was like in those days and there's quite an interesting museum too.

C: Oh, that sounds interesting. How much is that?

R: About 40 euros. I can call and book a place for you if you want.

C: What times does that leave?

R: Every two hours from outside the hotel and the tours last around 90 minutes. They leave at 10, 12, 2 and 4 o'clock.

C: OK, that's great. Can you book me onto the 2 o'clock tour? Then I can do some shopping in the main square in town beforehand.

R: Sure.

Lesson 3A, Exercise 10

Conversation 1

A: I'm thinking of doing some shopping today. Can you recommend anywhere?

B: Well, you could try Oxford Street. There are lots of big department stores there.

A: To be honest, I'm not really a big fan of department stores.

B: Oh, OK. Well, in that case, how about Portobello Road? It's a big street market. You can find lots of bargains there.

A: Oh, that sounds great. I love that kind of thing. Is it easy to get to?

B: Yes, very. I'll show you on the map.

Conversation 2

C: I'm thinking of doing some sightseeing today. Can you recommend anywhere?

D: Well, you could try the local museum. That's quite close to here. They've got lots of interesting things in there.

C: Right. I'm not really into museums, to be honest.

D: That's OK. In that case, how about going to the Roman ruins down by the lake? There are also some nice cafés and you can swim there.

C: Oh, that sounds better. Are they expensive to get into?

D: No, it's quite cheap. It should only be about 10 dollars.

Lesson 3C, Exercise 3

H = Holly; L = Lois

H: Welcome to a new episode of *The Road Less Travelled*, with me, Holly Bakewell. For those new to the show, I'm a blogger with an interest in everything about travel and in this show, I interview people I've met on my journeys in the real world and on social media, who are all doing something a bit different. With me today is Lois Schultz.

L: Hi! Thanks for inviting me.

H: And thank you! Now Lois is, I think, what some might call a dark tourist.

L: Well, some might, but I don't.

H: No – as we'll discuss – but before we'll get there, let me ask the question we always start the show with, which is … have you visited anywhere interesting recently?

Lesson 3C, Exercises 5 & 6

H: … have you visited anywhere interesting recently?

L: Yeah, a few weeks ago I went to a place you probably know – Glasgow, in Scotland.

H: You know what? I've never been there!

L: No way! Oh, you should.

H: I know, I know … I'd definitely like to – the nightlife is supposed to be amazing.

L: It certainly is. We had a great night in a karaoke bar – super friendly people, super good time.

H: That's what I've heard, but that's not the only reason you chose to go there.

L: No … so … I also wanted to visit the cemetery there.

H: Because this is a thing you do, right?

L: I mean not only that, but it's something that helps decide my travel destination.

H: So tell us about that. I mean, why cemeteries? What do you do there? How did you get into it? Don't you find it sad?

L: Oh right – yeah, so many questions! Well to begin at the beginning, maybe the first time I went to one was when I was a teenager. I went to Paris with my family and because my Dad's a big fan of The Doors, we had to go to the Père Lachaise cemetery, where the lead singer Jim Morrison is buried. So, I was feeling pretty fed up about going anyway, but also I hate The Doors. But then, when we got there, we had this guide and she was great – actually quite funny – and she told us about all kinds of people there and the stories about the place and it was just … really, really interesting.

H: Yeah, I think a good guided tour can make such a difference.

L: For sure. Then, when I started travelling on my own, you know, I couldn't always afford museums and big attractions and so when I went to different places, I'd go and see the main cemetery.

H: Because they're usually free to enter, right?

L: Yeah, but also they … they have this history and they're often beautiful. Like the one in Glasgow – it's set in these really beautiful surroundings and has some amazing works of art.

H: Yeah. You have some fantastic photos of it on your social media.

L: Thanks!

H: I notice you never feature in them, though. Are you camera-shy?

L: Not at all. I have lots of photos of me in other places, but cemeteries aren't somewhere to take smiling selfies. It's not respectful.

H: I understand. They're sad places, right? Which is why I talked about dark tourism. But you don't agree.

L: No, no, because, I think dark tourism is more about focusing on tragic events – battles, murders, natural disasters – and events which are often still quite recent. But the thing I like about cemeteries – and it's why I visit them – is all the interesting historic figures, poets, politicians, scientists you can find out about. I see cemeteries as a kind of celebration of past lives. I mean, some cemeteries actually promote that idea, like the Merry – or Happy – Cemetery in Romania.

H: Yes! What an amazing place.

L: Have you been there?

H: No, but I saw it on a travel programme here. And, as you say, it looks very … bright and happy.

L: It is. It's great.

H: So where next? More cemeteries?

L: Probably, but actually what I want to do now is explore my local region more – it's amazing how little you know about what's near you.

H: Absolutely.

L: And I can't really afford to travel far now, so if I go abroad, I'll probably do something like WWOOFing.

H: WWOOFing?

L: Yeah, it's basically volunteering on small organic farms, in return for accommodation and the opportunity to learn about farming …

UNIT 4

Lesson 4A, Exercises 4 & 5

Conversation 1

A: So, what did you do last night Brenda?

B: I had a rehearsal for this play I'm going to be in.

A: You're going to be in a play! I didn't know you're an actor.

B: I mean, it's not professional or anything. I'm in a drama group at university. We put on all kinds of shows during the year.

A: Wow, great. So what's the play? Do you have a big part?

B: No. It's this play called *101 Break-ups*, there are lots of people in it and there's no main character.

A: Sounds fun. So how often do you rehearse?

B: Well, we usually meet once a week, but now we're getting nearer the performance we have rehearsals three or four times a week.

A: Cool. Well, let me know when it's on and I'll come and see it.

Conversation 2

C: Did you have a good weekend, Domi?

D: Yeah, it was great. I went sailing with some friends. We hired a boat and went to an island off the coast.

C: Sounds amazing – it was so hot last weekend!

D: I know. It was boiling. It was actually nice to have the sea breeze.

C: So were you actually doing the sailing?

D: Yeah. I grew up in Brittany, on the coast of France, and my dad used to take me out and taught me how to sail.

C: Wow, lucky you. So how often do you go now?

D: I mean, whenever I can, but it's been a while because of work – and it's pretty expensive to hire a boat here too.

C: I can imagine.

D: Have you ever tried it?

C: No, never, but I'd love to. It looks amazing.

D: It is. It's great. I'll let you know next time we go.

C: Sure! That'd be brilliant.

Conversation 3

E: Are you OK, Finn? You look a bit tired.

F: I know. I didn't go to bed until two thirty.

E: Really? Why?

F: Oh, I invited some friends round for something to eat and to play chess.

E: Oh really? Do you do that a lot?

F: Yeah, a fair bit. Maybe once every couple of months.

E: Nice. So are you any good?

F: Not bad. When I play my friends, we play speed chess and I usually win.

E: Nice! So do you ever play standard games?

F: Yeah, I play online sometimes, but not as much as I'd like to. I want to improve, but I don't have enough time to play.

Lesson 4C, Exercises 3 & 4

I = Ian; R = Rika

I: What happened there, Rika? Did you just sign that guy's book?

R: You saw that?

I: Yeah! It was like you were famous or something.

R: That's because, er … I don't know. I guess I am, kind of – if you're a judo fan.

I: What?

R: Well, in my other life, away from selling books, I do judo and last week I was in a competition on TV. That guy recognized me from there.

I: Seriously? That's amazing!

R: Oh, it's no big deal. I didn't win it or anything. I lost in the semi-finals.

I: You got to the semi-finals! I can't believe it! I mean, no offence, but you don't look big enough to fight.

R: Well, you fight according to your weight in judo, so size doesn't matter. Although being big isn't always an advantage. It's more about balance. Someone can be big and strong, but if they're off-balance, you can easily throw them. I bet I could throw you over!

I: Hey, I believe you! So how long have you been doing it, then?

R: Ever since I was a kid. At school, the big kids often used to bully me because I was so small and I got into fights, so my dad suggested I did a martial art to defend myself and that was it, really.

I: Well, you've kept very quiet about it. I mean, how long have I known you now? Six years?

R: Yeah, well, I don't really feel like it's connected to what I do at work and, I don't know, I think it's strange for me to just tell colleagues I'm a judo champion for no reason.

I: I guess. So, how often do you have to train?

R: Well, I usually practise all the techniques for at least an hour a day once I get home in the evening, and then two or three times a week I go to the dojo, which is like a martial arts gym, to practise with others.

I: Wow! And this competition the other week … what was it exactly? Was it a big thing?

R: Um, yeah … it was the women's national finals!

I: No! And you got to the semi-finals!

R: Yeah! I've actually won it before, so I'm a bit annoyed I didn't win it this time, but I had quite a bad back injury last year, which stopped me doing any training or fighting.

I: Really? How long did you stop for?

R: Well, I didn't do anything for a couple of months and I only started full training a few weeks before the finals.

I: OK. Well, it sounds as if you did well to get to the semi-finals then.

R: I guess. And the girl who beat me went on to win the whole thing, so … still, I hate losing!

I: Amazing. You learn something new every day!

UNIT 5

Lesson 5A, Exercises 4 & 5

Conversation 1

I = Ivan; A = Amanda

I: So what do you do, Amanda?

A: I work for a mobile phone company.

I: Oh yeah? Doing what?

A: I work in the design department. I'm involved in designing what you see on the screen of the phone.

I: Oh right. How long have you been working there?

A: It must be seven years now. No, wait … maybe it's eight. I was 25 when I joined, so yeah, eight years. Wow! Time goes so fast!

I: You must enjoy it.

A: Yeah, I do, generally. It's quite varied because they're constantly changing the phones and designs, and it's quite a creative job, which is nice. But, you know, it's like any job. It gets a bit dull sometimes – and the hours can be quite long.

I: Yeah? How long?

A: Well, it depends how busy we are, but sometimes I do 50 hours a week.

I: Really? Oh! That can't be easy.

A: It's actually OK. I mean, it is a bit stressful sometimes, but to be honest, I think I work better under pressure.

Conversation 2

M = Marie; C = Carlo

M: So what do you do, Carlo?

C: I work for the government, actually.

M: Oh right, OK. Doing what?

C: I'm an engineer. I'm involved in designing and building new roads and bridges and that kind of thing.

M: OK. That must be interesting. Do you enjoy it?

C: Yeah, very much. It's good to feel you're doing something useful, you know. And the money's good, plus we get a bonus every year, so ….

D: Oh, that's great.

C: And my job's nice and secure too, which is unusual at the moment with the economy not doing so well.

M: I hear you. How long have you been doing that, then?

C: Since I graduated from university, so about ten years now. Anyway, what about you? What do you do, Marie?

Conversation 3

D = Deborah; E = Ella

D: So where are you based these days, Ella?

E: Well, my apartment is in Munich, but I seem to be travelling pretty much all the time at the moment, so it's hard to say, to be honest.

D: I'm sure it's fun, but it can't be easy.

E: No, but my partner's great. They stay home with our daughter – so I don't have to worry about that – and I do love my work. The company made me manager for the whole of Europe and the Middle East last year, so …

D: Wow, congratulations! That must be quite demanding, though, no?

E: Yeah, it is. It's a lot of responsibility, but I have a great team. We all work really well together.

D: Well, that's good. And how's business?

E: Great, actually. We're having a very good year – in a very competitive market.

Lesson 5C, Exercises 3 & 5

Conversation 1

A = Almir; L = Laura; D = Davina

A: I don't get it. You're not allowed to turn your video off? That's just strange.

L: I know, right. I mean, when we have team meetings online, we're generally obliged to keep our cameras off and to turn the sound off too.

D: Well, lucky you. They just told us that they think it'll help create a better atmosphere and that if we can all see each other when we're talking, we can read body language and see facial expressions and stuff – and that's supposed to reduce misunderstandings.

A: OK. Fair enough, I guess. How big is your team?

D: There's only six of us, so it does kind of feel more like face-to-face when we can all see each other.

A: Yeah. Maybe.

L: We sometimes have over fifty in our meetings, so …

D: To be honest, I'm just grateful we're still allowed to work from home.

L: Yeah? You don't miss going into the office at all?

D: Not even slightly, no.

Conversation 2

F = Francesca; U = Ulrika

F: Are you thinking of buying that?

U: Yeah, what do you think?

F: It's alright, I guess, but it's not very you. I mean, I don't usually see you wearing such dark colours.

U: No, I know, but I've got this new job working in a law firm.

F: Oh really? Congratulations, that's great news! What are you going to be doing there?

U: It's just office work, really – secretarial stuff – but they have a very strict dress code. You have to wear blue, black, grey or white. That's it. No other colours allowed. Guys can't have beards; oh, and no tattoos – they're totally banned; we have to wear heels … it makes us look 'professional' they say.

F: You're joking! Is that even legal?

U: Apparently. They sent one of my colleagues home the other day just for wearing flat shoes.

F: Wow! That's just mad.

J: Yep. But I was looking for a job for ages, so I'm not going to complain! I'm just going to keep my head down and obey the rules.

F: Fair enough.

Conversation 3

A = Adam, B = Bill

A: Bill, sorry to interrupt, but can I have a quick word?

B: Yes, of course. What's up?

A: Listen, I'd like to take the day off on Friday. My son's performing in a school concert.

B: Friday? I'm afraid that's impossible.

A: Are you sure?

B: Sorry, Adam. It wouldn't be a problem normally, but we've got a bit of a crisis this week. Vicky's off sick and we really have to complete this order by Saturday.

A: Can't someone else help? My son will be so disappointed if I don't watch him play. And I do have some holiday left for this year.

B: I'm sure. But if we're late with this order, we might lose the whole contract.

A: I see.

B: You're supposed to arrange time off with me a month in advance, you know.

A: I know, I know. It's just I've asked you at short notice before and it hasn't been a problem.

B: Well, as I say, normally it isn't.

A: Well, I guess that's all. I don't know what I'll tell my son.

B: I'm sorry. You'll be really helping me and the company.

UNIT 6

Lesson 6A, Exercises 5 & 8

S = Sales assistant; C = Customer

S: Hello there, can I help you?

C: Yeah, hi. I'm thinking of switching phone companies.

S: Alright. Well, you've come to the right place! Who are you with at the moment?

C: Blue. But I'm looking to see if there are any better deals around.

S: I'm sure we can find you something. What phone do you have at the moment?

C: This one, but they've offered to upgrade it to the S620.

S: OK, that's a nice phone. It certainly looks very stylish. How much are you paying every month?

C: I think it's 50 pounds and they said that that would stay the same. I get unlimited calls and messages for that and 15 gigs of data.

S: OK. Well, we could offer you a better model for the same price. For example, this one – the N570.

C: OK. What's the difference? They look pretty similar to me.

S: Well, with this one, the N570, you get a much better user experience. It's a bit easier to use and, as you can see, the screen folds out so it's about twice the size of your current phone's.

C: Wow! That's nice.

S: I know. It's impressive, isn't it? It's got a great battery life as well. It lasts for up to 25 hours, whereas the battery in the other phone isn't as good. It usually needs charging after 15 or 16 hours, so this one lasts a lot longer.

C: Oh, OK.

S: And then the camera is much better too. This one is 48 megapixels, whereas the one on the S620 is just 20 – meaning this one's more than twice as powerful.

C: Right. And how many photos can the N570 store?

S: It obviously depends on what else you have on your phone, but it can easily hold at least ten thousand – that's double the amount of storage that the S620 has. And, of course, you can always just store all your images in the cloud if you'd prefer.

C: OK. And what about sound quality?

S: Well, the N570 has a fairly large speaker built in on the back here. See? It's about twice as big as the speaker on the S620, so no worries there.

C: OK. Well, I must admit, it is a nice phone. I'm tempted. And how much would I need to pay upfront for the phone itself?

S: Just 89 pounds.

C: 89 pounds! That's quite a lot more than Blue are currently asking.

S: Well, I'm not sure we can go any lower for that phone. What price have they told you?

C: 65 pounds.

S: OK. Well, let me check with my manager, but I think we probably could match that – and still give you the better phone.

Lesson 6C, Exercises 5 & 7

1: I don't like typical souvenirs like those little model Big Bens or tourist T-shirts or whatever. They're a waste of money. Far better to have something you can consume. My neighbour's Italian and he gave us this delicious fruitcake. Apparently, it's very typical. Oh, what do you call it … um … comes in a box … oh, *panettone* – that's it! Anyway, yeah, we also went to Spain recently and I bought a few bottles of this drink called *mosto*, which is a kind of grape juice. Lovely, it is. We finished the drink in about two days, but I kept the bottle, as it's actually perfect for keeping oil in.

2: My wife's an English teacher and she gets all kinds of presents from her students. I guess it's nice of them to think of her – and I know this makes me sound awful – but I just don't want them all over the house! One student once gave her a present for me – a bright red silk tie with pictures of scary masks printed on it! Another time we got this plastic model of the Eiffel Tower with a light in it. I mean, it's fine if you like that kind of thing, but I'm a designer! They're not to my taste and I really don't need them. My wife refuses to throw them away, though, so we've agreed to keep them in a box under the stairs.

3: One of my friends spent last summer travelling round Europe by train and she brought me back an apron from Lithuania, I think it was, to wear while I'm cooking. It's the best souvenir I've ever had. It's made from this beautiful material and it has a lovely stripy pattern which she said is typical from there. She's clever, because she knows I love cooking and she's also seen what happens when I cook. Maybe I'll look a bit less messy now!

4: I visited the Czech Republic last year with my family and we went to Prague. While we were there, my daughter bought a glass paperweight with an image of the Charles Bridge inside as a souvenir. She was really happy with it. Then on the way home, the airline lost our luggage. The paperweight was in her bag so she was really upset … but then they found the bags and when they arrived the paperweight was there and it was all fine. Big relief! Then, though, as she was putting it on her shelf, she somehow dropped it! It was awful! She cried for ages.

UNIT 7

Lesson 7A, Exercises 5 & 6

A = Aurora; C = Claes

A: They don't have the menu in English, so shall I talk you through it?

C: Sure.

A: Anything I need to know? Any allergies?

C: Yeah, I'm allergic to shellfish.

A: Oh, right – so nothing with *marisco* then. *Marisco* is seafood.

C: OK.

A: So, for starters, the *papa rellena* is a potato ball, filled with beef, raisins and olives, and then deep-fried so it's crispy on the outside.

C: Mmm, that sounds tasty – though isn't it quite heavy?

A: Not really – I mean, the portions are quite small here. Then the *anticuchos* are a kind of Peruvian kebab, made from sliced cow heart grilled on a stick.

C: Right. I've never had heart.

A: No? But you're not vegetarian, right?

C: No, not at all. I suppose we've just never eaten those parts in my family.

A: Really? It's so good. Not tough and chewy – just nice and juicy.

C: What about the *cevishi*…?

A: *Ceviche*! That's Peru's national dish. It's a cold fish dish. Are you OK with fish?

C: Yeah, usually. What else is in it?

A: It's basically cooked in lime or lemon juice, maybe special vinegar and spices.

C: OK. What do you mean by cooked? You said it's cold …

A: Yeah, the raw fish is left in the lemon or vinegar for a while and the acid in the juice does the same as heat, so it's like cooked … but it's cold.

C: Hmm, I'm not sure about that. I think I'll go for the heart. What are you having?

A: *Ceviche*. You can have a bite if you want.

C: Thanks. What about the main course?

A: Well, the *bistec apanado*, that's steak.

C: OK. I'm not sure I want beef if I'm having heart.

A: Right, so not the *lomo saltado* either. Do you like duck?

C: Sure.

A: You could have the *arroz con pato*. It's a bit like a Spanish paella, but much tastier of course!

C: Well, you would say that! And the *seco de* …

A: *Seco de cabrito*. That's goat meat cooked in a thick sauce – and served with beans on the side.

C: OK. I've never had goat either! What's it like?

A: Oh, I guess it's a bit like lamb, but with a slightly stronger flavour. I love it. That's what I'm going to have.

C: I think I'll join you – it sounds delicious. Do we need to choose the desserts now?

A: No, see how you feel. But if you have room, you must try the *mazamorra* – it's made from fruit and purple corn. It's my favourite.

Lesson 7C, Exercise 2

P = Presenter; A = Antonia MIller

P: Almost certainly, if you're listening to this show, you're a real foodie, someone who loves to find new tastes and dishes, make the perfect coffee or create something delicious from what's left in the fridge. And without doubt there will also be a lot of you that have at least thought about turning that passion for food into something you could make a living from. Over the next few episodes, we're looking at the variety of opportunities for food businesses and giving some advice. This week, we start with restaurants, and joining me is Antonia Miller, who is in an investor in over 30 food businesses. Antonia, welcome.

A: Good to be here.

Lesson 7C, Exercises 4 & 5

P: Now Antonia, I've heard that 90 per cent of all new restaurants fail within a year, so maybe your advice should be don't try!

A: Well, yes, it is risky, but here in the US, the figure's actually more like 25 to 30 per cent and then maybe the same again over the next two years.

P: That still sounds pretty high.

A: Sure. But all businesses struggle to begin with and food services actually tend to do better than others. And there are huge opportunities. Some estimates suggest food services will be worth over five trillion dollars by 2029.

P: Wow, OK. I notice you refer to 'food services' there.

A: Yes, because 'restaurants' doesn't really cover everywhere serving food, like coffee shops, fast food places, takeaways, food trucks and so on.

P: Sure.

A: And I think that is the first advice I'd give. You don't have to invest in the perfect restaurant. With restaurants, people often spend their budget before the first customer has eaten anything. But what will you do if you don't get as many customers as you hoped? How will you pay for extra publicity? What if your chef is sick? How will you pay for a replacement?

P: So be prepared for unexpected costs, and if you don't have much money, start small?

A: That's right. These days, you don't even have to rent a shop or buy equipment to do takeaways. There are big kitchens set up in industrial parks where you can hire space to cook and have a website for orders.

P: And if you do that, you cut costs too.

A: Exactly. And then, if that makes a profit, you might then think about investing in your own place.

P: And if you are setting up your own place, how important is location?

A: Well, you can find it difficult if you don't have easy access and you don't benefit from being near other restaurants, but a clear concept is more important – I mean that's true of online food businesses too.

P: What do you mean by that?

A: Well, what are you offering? Is it a particular kind of meal? Breakfast is a growing market. Is there a health angle? Is it cheap and cheerful – basic ingredients and big portions? Who are your customers? Are they families, couples, groups of students? Again, people sometimes try to set up a business because they're into cooking, but they don't go beyond that. 'Nice food' is not a concept.

P: But you do need that quality and passion, don't you?

A: I mean, if you don't sell tasty food, you will fail – of course you will – but you need to ask yourself why customers should choose you in the first place. You have to offer something clear and different. And you certainly need passion to maintain a business because it's hard work with unsocial hours. But you need head as well as heart – you need people that are good with money, not just good in the kitchen. It is doable. Lots and lots of food businesses succeed.

P: What about you? Do you have any plans for any new investments?

A: Absolutely. I'm actually working on something called *Genuine*. It's using the idea of the industrial kitchen I mentioned earlier. We'll have a single website where people can order food from different cultures. And in the kitchen, there'll be chefs from those communities cooking their own cuisine. And if they're successful online, we might help them set up their own physical businesses.

P: Interesting. So when will we see that?

A: Well, if everything goes to plan, we're going to launch our first kitchen in around four months' time, serving *Genuine Moroccan* and *Genuine Vietnamese*.

UNIT 8

Lesson 8A, Exercises 4 & 5

D = Daniel, P = Paulina

P: Wow. It's busy today.

D: I know – it's crazy. I was supposed to take a break an hour ago.

P: Yeah, I'm going back after I've had this coffee.

D: OK. Are you going to the thing for Holly's birthday later?

P: No, I can't. I have a class.

D: Oh yeah? What are you studying?

P: It's a counselling course for speech therapists.

D: Oh, right. What does that involve?

P: Well, you learn basic counselling skills. You know, how to listen and guide people through problems, but it's focused on the kinds of psychological problems people have when they have a difficulty with speaking.

D: And how come you're doing that?

P: Well, I did speech therapy at college and, you know, that's still what I want to do.

D: Oh right.

P: So, it'll be good for my CV.

D: Yeah, I'm sure. So, how's it going? Are you enjoying it?

P: Yeah, it's good. It's very practical. I mean, we have some lectures and seminars which are about theory, but most of the time we just practise with each other and a tutor observes us and gives feedback.

D: So, what about the tutors? What are they like?

P: Great. They're all very experienced and knowledgeable, but they present things in a very clear way, you know, they're, like, on our level. They're really good, actually.

D: It sounds it. And what are the other students like? Do you get on with them OK?

P: Yeah, mostly.

D: Mostly?

P: Well, there are one or two guys that aren't as supportive as everyone else. Like when we do the feedback after the practice sessions, they can be a bit more critical than the others, which is a bit annoying.

D: I can imagine. You want encouragement, not criticism!

P: Exactly.

D: So how long does the course last? When do you finish?

P: I think there are 11 weeks left. It's a six-month course – an evening a week.

D: Do you have any coursework on top of that? I mean, is it assessed?

P: Not exactly. You just get a certificate for completing the course.

D: And to get that?

P: You have to attend 80 per cent of the classes and do an assignment, which is basically a kind of diary of our counselling sessions. Nothing too demanding.

D: OK. So you don't have to do much reading?

P: There's a bit connected to the seminars and you could do more, but I don't have time on top of my workload here.

D: I bet. So what are you going to do when it ends?

P: Well, I might actually do another course once I've finished this one.

D: Wow! You're keen!

P: Maybe, but as soon as I find a proper job, I'll probably stop doing any studying.

D: Sure.

P: I'd better get back.

D: OK.

Lesson 8C, Exercises 4 & 5

Conversation 1

A: How come there are so many kids around today?

B: Where have you been? The teachers are on strike. It's been all over the news.

A: Ah, I never watch the news …

B: Oh. Well, if you did, you'd know all the schools are closed this week because teachers are demanding a pay rise.

A: Fair enough – they deserve the money. I can't imagine being a teacher myself.

B: Really? I always thought you'd make a great teacher.

A: Me? Why do you say that?

B: I don't know. You're pretty good at explaining things; you like kids …

A: Ah, it depends on the kids. I mean, I like yours, but I'm not sure I'd be able to teach 30 of them, especially if they were causing trouble.

B: I'm sure you'd be OK.

A: Nah, I think I'd end up screaming at them. Honestly, I admire anyone who does that job – the pressure they're under – but I'll stick to my desk job, thank you very much!

Conversation 2

C: So what are you going to do at uni?

D: Medicine … if I meet the entry requirements – they're so tough!

C: Ah, you'll be alright. You've been getting straight As, haven't you?

D: Yeah, but … we'll see. I don't want to bring bad luck. What about you? You could do medicine, couldn't you?

C: Me! You're joking, aren't you? I'd never get the grades.

D: You could – if you wanted to.

C: Ahh, maybe, but I'm not interested anyway.

D: Really? I thought you liked biology and stuff like that.

C: Yeah, I love it, but my mum's a doctor, so I see what it's like. I don't think I'd enjoy it. I'd rather teach science or something like that.

D: Really? Your mum isn't disappointed that you don't want to do the same as her?

C: Well, if she is, she doesn't show it and she hasn't pushed me to study anything in particular.

Speaker 3

In recent years, it has become accepted here, and in many other countries, that university students should pay for their education – either by borrowing the money or by paying extra in tax. The argument is that students will earn more from having a degree, so they should contribute more. I disagree. We shouldn't measure the value of a degree in terms of money. We all need graduates – we need doctors, teachers, engineers and all the other jobs that help benefit society. And society also needs people with good learning skills and critical minds to deal with our changing world. If university education was free, more people would be able to gain those skills and help create a better world.

Conversation 4

E: So, how's Angela doing?

F: Oh, she's OK, although she does complain a fair bit. It seems several teachers struggle with discipline, and they spend a lot of time just getting the kids' attention and making sure they're focused on what they need to do. I don't think she's learning as much as she could.

E: What a shame. She's such a bright kid. Maybe she'd do better if she was somewhere else. Camp Hill has a very good reputation, and the facilities are excellent.

F: I don't know. She'd probably get pushed a bit more there, but I think moving might do more harm than good. She'd have to make new friends and she's in the basketball team now, which she really loves.

UNIT 9

Lesson 9A, Exercises 4 & 5

A = Andy; G = Gitte

A: Did I tell you I went round to see Jon and Sara the other day?

G: No, you didn't. How are they? I haven't seen them for ages.

A: Oh, they're fine. They said to say 'hello' to you. You know they've moved recently, don't you?

G: Oh really? No, I didn't, actually. The last time I heard from them they were still renting that place near the centre.

A: Oh, OK. Well, yeah, they've moved, umm … I think it was last month. To be honest, they seem much happier now.

G: Oh, that's good. So what's their new place like? Is it nice?

A: Yeah, it is. It's OK. It's quite a lot bigger than their old place. The front room is huge – it's about twice the size of this room – and the whole place is pretty spacious.

G: That must be nice for them now the kids are growing up.

A: I know. They said the old place was getting a bit small for them all. They wanted separate rooms for the kids. They didn't want them sharing forever! That's the main reason they moved out.

G: So, what kind of place is it? I mean, is it a house or an apartment?

A: Oh, it's an apartment. It's on the third floor of an old block. It's not in a great state and they'll need to do quite a bit of work on it, but they have actually bought this place, so they can do what they want to it.

G: Lucky them! And all those weekends spent painting and decorating to look forward to!

A: I know! I don't envy them! It's got real potential, though. It's got a great kitchen – it's a similar size to yours, maybe a bit bigger – and it's got these lovely old wooden floors everywhere. And huge windows, so it's nice and bright. Then there's a little balcony where you can sit and eat in the summer, and a shared garden out the back where the kids can play and everything.

G: Oh, it sounds lovely. I must go round and see them sometime soon.

A: Yeah, I'm sure they'd like that. The only problem is, though, it's not as central as their old place was. It's quite a lot further out, so it takes quite a long time to get there.

G: Oh, OK.

Lesson 9C, Exercises 4 & 7

Conversation 1

A: Hi, I'm here about the room.

B: Hi, nice to meet you. I'm Karina. And you must be Chloe, right?

A: Um … no. I'm Paula. I called earlier.

B: Oh, right. The 3.15 pm. Sorry. Chloe's the 3.45 pm. No … the 4.15 pm.

A: OK. So it's popular, then?

B: Well, we've had about fifteen people view it already and have six or seven more today.

A: Wow, OK.

B: So if you come through, you've got the bathroom on the left there, which all five of us share. Obviously, it gets quite busy in the morning.

A: I bet, yeah.

B: And this would be your room here.

A: This?

B: Yes. What do you think? It's nice and cosy.

A: That's one word for it, yeah. It's quite a lot smaller than I was expecting. I mean, I've seen bigger cupboards!

B: Well, that is reflected in the rent. You won't find anything else round here at this price.

Conversation 2

C: Remind me again where you're living?

D: Northgate.

C: That's it, yeah. How long have you been there now?

D: It must be about ten years, I guess.

C: Has it changed much in that time?

D: A bit, I guess, yeah. I'd say it's more popular than it used to be.

C: Yeah. It's quite fashionable now, isn't it?

D: It is, yeah. I'm glad we bought when we did. It was so much cheaper in the past. I don't think we could afford it here now.

C: I think that's the same everywhere. I mean, I'm renting and even where I am, it's not as cheap as it used to be.

D: Yeah, right. On the plus side, though, there's much less crime than there used to be and there are a lot more cafés and restaurants than there were when we first moved here, which is nice.

Conversation 3

E: How's the flat-hunting going? Have you had any luck?

F: We have, actually, yeah. We found a little place in Woodlands and we're moving in next week.

E: Oh wow, that's great. Congratulations! Do you need any help with the move?

F: No, we'll be fine, thanks. Grace's parents are going to drive us, so …

E: Oh, cool. I used to live out near there, actually. Back in the day. It was always a bit of a pain to get to, though, being on the outskirts – before they extended the train line.

F: Yeah? It's much better connected than it used to be. It's only about half an hour into the centre of town now.

E: Right, yeah. And I guess the highways are much better than they were as well. So how much are you paying?

F: Two thousand eight hundred a month. For two bedrooms. So if you ever feel like coming to revisit the old neighbourhood, you're always welcome.

Conversation 4

G: Hello?

H: Oh, hello there. I'm just phoning about your advert online for the room.

G: Oh, yes – OK.

H: Is it still available?

G: It is, yeah.

H: Good, good.

G: As you probably read, you'd be living with my wife and I. We're both retired now and our kids have all left home, so there are fewer people around than before and we've got plenty of room. So if you're OK with all that …

H: It sounds ideal. I like a bit of peace and quiet. So, can I just check that you've got wi-fi there? I work online a lot so it's quite important for me.

G: Yes, of course. We upgraded to high speed a year or so ago, so no problems there.

H: Ah, amazing. So when would it be possible for me to come and have a look at the room?

G: Well, we're free almost all the time. When works best for you?

UNIT 10

Lesson 10A, Exercise 5

L = Lyla; Z = Zahra

L: Hey Zahra. Do you fancy going out later?

Z: Yeah, maybe. What's on?

L: Well, do you like modern art?

Z: Yeah, sometimes, I guess. If I'm in the right mood. Why?

L: Well, there's this exhibition on in town that I'd really go to. It's only on for another week or so and I've been wanting to see it for ages.

Z: Oh right, OK. What kind of stuff is it?

L: So, the main thing is this series of sculptures by a Brazilian artist called Jac Leirner.

Z: OK.

L: All made from things she found on different flights – like plastic knives and forks and magazines and stuff.

Z: OK. That sounds … interesting.

L: And I think there are some other video pieces there as well.

Z: OK, cool. Let's give it a try. When do you want to go?

L: Well, the gallery's open late today. I think till 9 o'clock.

Z: Oh. I need to be up quite early tomorrow, so I'm not sure I can manage an evening thing.

L: That's OK. How about sort of mid-afternoon, then?

Z: Yeah, that'd work better for me. Where's it on?

L: This new place called Art Attack. Do you know it?

Lesson 10A, Exercise 6

Z: I think so. Isn't it that place near the river?

L: Nope. That's Hip Hub.

Z: Oh right. Well in that case, no, I'm not sure.

L: Art Attack's in the centre – on Crown Street.

Z: OK. I don't know it, then.

L: You know Oxford Road, yeah? That's the main street that goes past the railway station.

Z: Yeah, yeah.

L: Well, if you have your back to the station, you turn right down Oxford Road. You walk about 200 metres and you go past a post office.

Z: OK.

L: And the next street after that is Crown Street. The gallery's along there, about halfway down on the left.

Z: Oh yeah, I think I know the place now. There's a big clothes shop right opposite, isn't there?

L: Yeah, that's the one.

Z: OK. So what time do you want to meet?

L: Don't know. How about I just meet you outside at, say, four?

Z: Earlier is better for me, to be honest, so could we maybe make it three?

L: Yeah, OK. I doubt it'll be that busy anyway. Maybe whoever gets there first should get the tickets, OK?

Z: Yeah, sure, but I don't think we need to worry. I don't think that people will be queueing up for it.

L: Hey, you never know!

Lesson 10C, Exercises 3 & 5

Conversation 1

A: So, how was it?

B: Oh, it was brilliant – much better than I thought it'd be.

A: Really? I'd heard it wasn't that good.

B: Well, me too, but I actually really enjoyed it.

A: So, what's so good about it?

B: Oh, the plot, the acting – everything. It's just really funny and it's quite exciting too. I don't know. Maybe it's because I didn't think it'd be anything special.

A: I know what you mean. You see loads of films these days – especially Hollywood stuff – that are promoted so much in advance, and everyone on social media is saying you have to go and see this or that. Then you go and it just ends up being a bit of a disappointment. It's nice to go to something that's as good as everyone says it is.

Conversation 2

C: Did you have a good night out? How was the concert?

D: Oh, we didn't go in the end.

C: Really? What a shame.

D: I know! Hans was going to pick me up at seven, but as it happened, he had to finish some work at the office and by the time we got there, there was a massive queue for tickets. So we decided we weren't going to get in and we went to a club instead.

C: Oh right. So what club did you go to?

D: Radio City.

C: Well, that's supposed to be really good. It's quite trendy, isn't it?

D: That's what they say, but I hated it!

C: Really? What was so bad about it?

D: It was just awful – the people, the music, everything. It's one of the worst clubs I've ever been to.

C: Really?

D: OK, maybe I'm exaggerating a bit. I mean, it was OK to begin with, but then it got absolutely packed, so you couldn't really dance properly. And it was boiling hot, so you were sweating like crazy. And then they changed the music later to this heavy techno stuff, which I hate. And the drinks were a rip-off.

C: Oh dear. Maybe you just went on the wrong night.

Conversation 3

E: I'm so tired! I was out late last night.

F: Really? I thought you said you were going to have a quiet night in.

E: I know. I mean, I was going to stay in, but Clara phoned and while we were chatting, she mentioned she had a spare ticket for this play in town, and so I said I'd go with her.

F: Oh right. So what did you go and see? Anything good?

E: Yes, actually. It was called *A Man for All Seasons*.

F: Oh! I've been wanting to see that for ages! It's had some great reviews. How was it?

E: Brilliant! One of the best things I've seen in a long time.

F: That's what I'd heard.

E: Yeah. It's so moving. Honestly, I was in tears at the end. And the whole production – the lighting, the scenery, everything – it's just really well done.

F: I'll have to go.

E: Yeah, you should.

UNIT 11

Lesson 11A, Exercises 5 & 6

Conversation 1

A: That's a nice photo. Who's that?

B: Oh, it's a friend.

A: And is that your cat?

B: Yeah.

A: It's so cute!

B: I know. Mind you, she's lucky she's still alive!

A: Really? What happened?

B: Well, when she was a little kitten, she actually got stuck inside the wall of our house!

A: You're joking! How did that happen?

B: We're not absolutely sure, because we didn't see her disappear, but we think she crawled through a little hole in the floor in our bedroom and then she fell down the gap between the walls.

A: Oh no.

B: Anyway, we were watching TV and we could hear these little cries coming from somewhere, but we were going mad because we couldn't see her anywhere. And then we worked out she was actually inside the wall!

A: So how did you get her out?

B: We were forced to call the fire service in the end, and they basically broke a bit of the outside wall and they managed to get her out like that. Here, I think I still have a picture …

A: Oh, look at that! Oh that sad little face!

B: I know. I'm glad we found her.

Conversation 2

C: You'll never guess what happened last night.

D: Go on. What?

C: Well, I was working at home writing some reports when I suddenly noticed a group of crows looking quite excited. They were all making this awful noise, so I went outside to see what was happening.

D: And?

C: Well, the crows were chasing a little parrot up and down the street.

D: A parrot? What was it doing there?

C: I have no idea. I guess it must've escaped from somewhere. Anyway, it was obviously very scared and cold. I felt really sorry for it, so I chased the crows away. The parrot was then sitting on my neighbour's roof and I didn't want to leave it.

D: Yeah? So what happened in the end? Did you catch it?

C: Yeah, I put some fruit and seeds on the ground to persuade it to come down and then, when it did, I managed to catch it with a box. We took it to the vet to check it was OK and we're going to keep it as a pet now. It seems quite happy to stay with us!

D: Well, that's good. Actually, it reminds me of something I saw a few weeks ago. I was coming home from work on my bicycle …

Conversation 3

E: I really thought I was going to die. Honestly, I hope I never see another crocodile in my life!

F: I can imagine. That's awful! It actually reminds me of something that happened to me last year in Indonesia.

E: Oh yeah? What was that?

F: Well, I was there on holiday, and I'd decided to spend a few days walking through the jungle. On the second day, we were going along a path through the rainforest when suddenly these huge lizards came racing out of the bushes from all sides. They were enormous – maybe even bigger than me! Everyone ran away, leaving me with three of these monster lizards running towards me. I tried to scream, but just couldn't! I really thought they were going to eat me.

E: Really? That sounds terrifying! So what happened?

F: Well, luckily, the guides managed to stop them by shouting and waving these sticks at them, and I was able to escape.

Lesson 11A, Exercise 10

Conversation 1

A: You'll never guess what happened last night.

B: Go on. What?

A: Well, I was walking home when I suddenly saw a horse, standing there in the street!

Conversation 2

C: I saw something really strange while we were away.

D: Oh yeah? What was that?

C: We saw this whale stuck on the beach.

D: Seriously? Still alive?

C: Yeah! It was actually quite upsetting! We phoned the police to see if they could organize help.

Conversation 3

E: I was just about to put my shoes on when I found a scorpion hiding in one of the shoes!

F: Really? What was that doing there?

E: I don't know. I guess it was just looking for somewhere to sleep.

Conversation 4

G: Then, after we failed to catch it the first time, it ran away up a tree and we spent hours trying to persuade it to come down.

H: Oh no! So what happened in the end?

G: Well, eventually, we gave up. But an hour later it walked into the kitchen, looking for its dinner!

Lesson 11B, Exercise 6

Obviously, Wilson's story is a tragedy. He had no real idea of the power of nature and he died because of it. But I don't think he was stupid. Remember, he was shot in the First World War. Experiences like that can affect people in different ways and maybe those terrible memories are what drove him. Then think about his achievement. Just reaching the mountain was really amazing. All those difficulties he overcame – the flight to India, the walk, everything. And he showed skill in learning to fly, and amazing strength and determination to get up to the height he did – and he did so with very little support. That's so different to these people who pay to go up Chomolungma these days. They arrive in helicopters. They carry almost nothing and they're not just risking their own lives. If a rope broke, how many people would fall? If a guide got injured, these amateurs couldn't help. And with so many of them, serious climbers are often forced to wait in really dangerous conditions. And if that wasn't bad enough, they leave so much rubbish on the mountain – broken tents, ropes, empty oxygen bottles – things that stay there forever in the freezing cold.

Lesson 11C, Exercise 3

You've probably all seen films where people discover gold or oil, and they jump up and down celebrating their new wealth. Of course, oil brings riches, but academics have wondered if the discovery of natural resources is actually good for everyone. Surprisingly, they've found that economies whose main income came from, say, oil, tended to develop more slowly than countries with few natural resources. This discovery has been called 'the resource curse', because it seems that having a huge non-renewable natural resource might be a barrier to investment and development. Four main explanations are usually given for this: one, conflict; two, corruption; three, the higher value of manufactured products; and four, price changes. Let's look at them now.

Lesson 11C, Exercise 5

So, firstly, conflict. The argument is that because a natural resource can bring huge wealth, groups will use violence to win control of that resource. For example, local people may be forced to leave their homes so mining can start. That causes anger – especially if locals aren't paid to move. They might fight back and the region might try to gain independence from the rest of the country. But then, the central government, or even other countries, may send the army to defend access to the resource. And if a war's being fought, people invest in guns, not, say, education.

Secondly, control of the natural resource can be won with violence, but it can also be won with money. In other words, corruption. Companies give politicians huge 'presents' to be able to mine the resource or to avoid rules that protect the environment. Politicians may then try to hide this corruption by giving cash to powerful individuals and paying very high salaries to officials. They may also reduce everyone's taxes to keep the public happy. All this uses money that could be invested in schools, hospitals, factories, and so on, which would grow the economy faster.

The third point of the curse is the relative value of the resource compared to making products with it. The country with the natural resource may also lack technology to exploit it fully, so it needs foreign companies to help exploit it. While mining creates jobs and money, bigger profits are made by producing products from the resource – say, petrol from oil, or mobile phones from rare metals. These products tend to be manufactured abroad, so the country with the resource earns less money than the country with the factories.

You might think the country would therefore invest in manufacturing, but that brings us to the fourth aspect of the curse: price changes. When the price of the resource is high, the value of the country's currency is high. As a result, the country's exports are more expensive and so manufacturers sell fewer products abroad. But they also lose sales at home because imports are cheaper! So, it's understandable that fewer factories are built. On the other hand, if resource prices are very low, the country earns less and might have little money to invest in development. And on top of this, prices of the resource constantly rise and fall,

so along with the problems of conflict and corruption it's difficult to plan and develop other more profitable industries – which is why having the resource is a curse.

Lesson 11C, Exercise 7

But is the resource curse always true? In fact, there are resource-rich countries, such as Norway and Botswana, who some argue have managed to develop well. In fact, Norway was already a relatively wealthy country when oil was discovered off its coast around 50 years ago. However, since then it has continued to grow and pass its neighbours in income per person. But it's not just that Norway is wealthy, it's an equal society – in fact the most equal society in the world, according to the World Economic Forum. How has it managed to do it? Well, since the beginning, Norway took control of the industry and profits have been saved in a public fund. A small amount is used each year to pay for public projects and at the same time taxes remain fairly high, including a tax on wealth. This is possible because there is very high trust in the government. Data from the World Bank shows it is the fifth best country at controlling corruption. It has maintained and strengthened other industries so only 14 per cent of its income comes from oil and gas, and it owns one per cent of company shares in the world. So, while the discovery of oil may have been a curse for some countries, for Norway it really has been a cause for celebration – just like in the movies.

UNIT 12

Lesson 12A, Exercises 5 & 6

L = Lewis; J = Jessica

L: Where did you disappear to?

J: Yeah, sorry. I had to go and phone my brother, Noel. It's his birthday today.

L: Oh, OK. It's just that you were quite a long time.

J: I know. I was only going to be five minutes – just wish him 'Happy Birthday' – but once he starts talking, he doesn't stop!

L: Oh, that's like my mum. She can talk for hours. I sometimes think we could be on the phone and I could go off and have a coffee and then come back and she'd still be talking! She wouldn't have noticed I'd gone!

J: Right. That's a bit extreme … I'm not sure Noel is that bad.

L: OK, maybe not, but it is sometimes difficult to stop her once she's started on a topic. Anyway, it sounds like you and Noel get on well.

J: Yeah, really well. Unfortunately, I don't see him that much now because he's living in the US.

L: Really! What's he doing there? Is he working?

J: No, he won a scholarship to study Physics at MIT. They pay for his fees, accommodation, and maybe a grant for other stuff on top of that.

L: Wow! He must be clever.

J: He is. He's really smart – always top of his class. But, you know, he's not one of those super serious clever people. He's really charming and funny.

L: Sounds like a great guy. Do you have any other brothers or sisters? I don't think you've told me before.

J: Maybe not. Er, I've got a younger brother called Greg.

L: And what's he like? Do you get on well?

J: Yeah, I guess.

L: You don't sound too sure.

J: No. I mean, he's nice and everything. We're just … different.

L: Yeah? In what way?

J: I don't know. He's just so sensitive. I seem to upset him a lot, anyway.

L: Oh yeah?

J: Yeah, for example, he wants to be an artist, yeah?

L: Oh, right.

J: And the other week I saw him at my mum and dad's and he was talking about his big new art project – some kind of sculpture piece with video or something.

L: Right.

J: And I asked, 'So, where and when is this going to be on?', and he just got annoyed and went quiet.

L: Oh?

J: Basically, because it won't happen. He likes the idea of being creative, but he doesn't want to do the work. I've told him before: you need to be ambitious, push yourself more, or you'll never make any money.

L: Oh … right.

J: What?

L: No, you're right. It's tough being an artist. It's just that …

J: What?

L: Well … I guess you get plenty of criticism in the art world and he just wants his sister to be there for him rather than …

J: Oh, right. So you think it's my fault?

L: No! I'm just saying …

J: Whatever.

L: It's … hard … So, are we going for coffee?

J: I guess.

Lesson 12C, Exercises 4 & 6

Speaker 1 Caitlin

I met him while doing a summer job in England. We were both working in this café – he was in the kitchens and I was a server. Our boss was a bit of an idiot. She was really strict – she was always shouting at us and was just horrible. Anyway, we used to go out after work and we'd sit and complain about her. Nicolas would also make fun of her by copying the way she talked but saying ridiculous things. It helped us see the funny side of the situation.

Speaker 2 Sandra

We were dating for a while. I met him when we were studying in Rome on a student exchange programme. It was a great few months. He was always so much fun and so full of life. We tried to keep things going after he went back to Belgium, but it's difficult maintaining a long-distance relationship. We couldn't afford to visit each other very often and, in the end, we split up. We remained friends, which I suppose is important, but I sometimes wish we'd stayed together. Yeah, I wish we hadn't split up.

Speaker 3 Shane

I met him while I was backpacking. We were staying in a hostel and we had to share a room. We got talking and found we had a lot in common. We were joking and laughing straight away, and we ended up spending the next couple of weeks sightseeing together until I went back to New Zealand. We kept in touch via email and social media after that and two years ago I moved to the UK. Since then, I've been over to Belgium to see him a couple of times.

Speaker 4 Brigitte

I'd known Nicolas for a while before we got together. We were on the same course, but I didn't have much to do with him at first because we were often in different groups and we seemed so different. I think I'm quite sociable and outgoing and, as you probably know, he's a bit quiet and shy. It's not that we didn't get on at all. We'd see each other in class and in the library and we'd chat a bit. Over time, though, our chats got longer, and then, just before we left university, I asked him out on a date.

He looked a bit surprised, but he said OK and we've been seeing each other now for about two years. It's a shame it took so long for us to get together, really!

Speaker 5 Franck

Nicolas moved into a place where my friend Jef lived. I used to be round at the flat hanging out with Jef. We'd play video games and chat late into the night, and Nicolas would often join us, so I got to know him pretty well. At some point, though, I had an argument with Jef and we basically stopped talking to each other. We're both very stubborn and even though Nicolas tried to sort things out between us, neither of us were interested. I kind of wish I'd made more of an effort, but … there you go. Anyway, to cut a long story short, I haven't seen Jef for a couple of years now, but I stayed in touch with Nicolas and since he moved out, we meet up quite a bit.

UNIT 13

Lesson 13A, Exercises 3 & 4

Conversation 1

M = Maria; B = Belinda; A = Andre

M: Thanks for picking us up. It's really kind of you.

B: That's OK. It's no problem. So, how was your journey?

M: Oh, quite stressful, actually. It's a relief to finally be here.

B: No! What happened? You weren't delayed or anything, were you?

M: No, no, it wasn't that, thank goodness, but everything else that could go wrong did! To begin with, we almost missed the flight, because Andre didn't want to spend too long hanging around at the airport.

A: I've already said I'm sorry!

M: He said we'd be OK if we got there an hour and a half before take-off, but there was a huge queue at the check-in desk and then another one going through security, so in the end we only just caught the flight.

B: How come it was so busy? It's not really the holiday season.

A: Exactly. They were doing extra security checks for some reason.

B: Oh right.

M: Whatever! If we'd been there earlier …

A: OK, OK.

M: Anyway, the flight was dreadful too.

A: Awful. We hit a big storm coming over France and it all got a bit scary …

M: Honestly, at one point, I thought we were going to crash!

A: I was sweating!

B: That sounds terrifying.

M: It was! I don't want to go through that again, I can tell you!

A: Me neither.

B: I'm sure. What do you want to do now? Do you want to go and get something to eat, or do you want to check in at the hotel first?

Conversation 2

L = Lara; K = Kwab

L: Hi. There you are! I was starting to worry.

K: Yeah, sorry I'm so late. I had a bit of a nightmare getting here.

L: Oh really? How come?

K: Well, to begin with, it was still dark when I set off.

L: Really? What time did you leave?

K: Six. And then it immediately started to pour down, so the roads were really dangerous.

L: Oh, I hate driving in the rain – especially when it's dark.

K: So do I. That's probably why I took a wrong turning. I got completely lost and ended up going round in circles for ages. I couldn't work out where I was or where I was going! Then, when I finally got back onto the right road, I almost had an accident.

L: Seriously? What happened?

K: Oh, it wasn't anything bad. It was just this stupid guy in a big expensive car who drove straight across me. I had to brake to avoid hitting him. I wasn't hurt or anything, but I did have to stop and park the car for a few minutes to calm down.

L: Oh, you poor thing. That's awful.

Lesson 13C, Exercises 2 & 4

Conversation 1

A: What was the weather like in Peru? Was it hot?

B: No, it wasn't, actually. We arrived at night and it was freezing. Then during the day it was still chilly and cloudy.

A: Oh dear.

B: I wish I'd taken some warmer clothes. I only had T-shirts and one thin jacket.

A: Oh no!

B: It was stupid of me, really. I should have thought more carefully before setting off. I knew we'd be in the mountains and could have checked the forecast.

A: I guess, yeah. I don't know. Maybe it's just me, but I always assumed that most of South America would be hot, you know.

B: Well, me too, yeah! Silly, really! Anyway, we still had an amazing time!

Conversation 2

C: Hello?

D: Hello, Mum. It's me, Alan.

C: Oh, hello. I was worried. Did you arrive safely?

D: Yeah, sorry, we got here late – that's why I didn't phone.

C: Oh right. So, is everything OK? Are you both well?

D: Yeah, fine, except for the fact there didn't seem to be any heating in our hotel last night.

C: No heating? But it's the middle of winter!

D: I know. It was a really old building and the room was just freezing.

C: That's awful!

D: We were silly, though. We should have looked around more, but because we got here so late, we just chose the first cheap place we came across.

C: Oh, Alan!

D: Don't worry – we'll check the place out better next time.

C: I hope so.

Conversation 3

E: How was your trip to the coast? Nice and hot?

F: Yes, it was. It was boiling!

E: Lucky you! I bet that was nice.

F: It was, but I did get sunburnt on the first day.

E: Oh no!

F: It was really hot and I was sunbathing and just fell asleep. The next day, my skin went purple! It was horrible.

E: Oh you poor thing!

F: Oh, it was my own fault. I shouldn't have stayed in the sun for so long, especially with my skin. I should've at least put on some sun cream!

Conversation 4

G: Hello, sir, madam. Are all three of you flying together to Munich?

H: Yes, that's right.

G: In that case, I'll just need to weigh your bags.

H: Sure.

G: I'm afraid you have to pay an excess baggage charge of 100 euros on this bag.

H: What? But there are three of us! The baggage allowance is 23 kilos each.

G: I'm sorry, madam, but the rules are very clear: the maximum for any one bag is 23 kilos, and this one weighs 33. You can transfer some weight to your hand baggage if you like.

H: How can we fit 10 kilos in there? It's tiny!

G: Well, in that case, you need to pay extra.

H: That's ridiculous!

G: I'm sorry, but it really isn't my fault. The ticket conditions are very clear. I'm afraid you have to go back to the desk over there and pay the additional charge.

H: But the queue is enormous!

I: I told you we should have brought another suitcase.

H: I just thought it would be easier with two.

I: 100 euros! That's such a rip-off!

UNIT 14

Lesson 14A, Exercises 5 & 6

Conversation 1

A: Hello, help desk.

B: Yeah, hi there. I wonder if you can help me. I've just turned on my computer and found that the internet's not working.

A: What? No! All of it? That's a disaster!

B: What?

A: Oh, nothing. Just my little joke. Have you checked all the connections? Maybe something's not plugged in properly?

B: I think everything's OK, yes. One minute – let me just have one more look … yep, I've just checked all the plugs and everything again, but it hasn't made any difference.

A: Hmm. Well, in that case, there's probably an issue with the cable then. I'll come down and have a look in a bit, OK?

Conversation 2

C: Hello, IT.

D: Hi, I've got a bit of a problem. My computer crashed this morning and when I turned it back on, all the folders I keep my files in had disappeared from the screen.

C: OK. Well, you must have back-up copies somewhere, right? On an external hard drive or in the cloud?

D: I'm afraid not. It's stupid of me, I know, but I always forget to copy them.

C: Right. Well, in future, you might want to think about backing up more often. Have you tried rebooting at all?

D: Umm … what does that mean?

C: Turning it off and turning it on again.

D: Oh, OK. I need these things in plain English, you see! But yes, I have and it didn't do any good.

C: OK. Have you tried searching for specific files by name?

D: No, not yet. Should I?

C: Yeah, try that and see if anything comes up.

Conversation 3

A: Hello, help desk.

E: Hi there. I've got a bit of problem down in accounts. I'm trying to print some files and every time I go to select 'print' from the drop-down menu, my cursor just turns into that spinning wheel of death thing, you know, that circle that just goes round and round and round. I move it away with the mouse and it stops and goes back to normal. Honestly, it's driving me mad!

A: OK. That's a very specific problem. I'm not sure I've dealt with anything like that before. I think you may have got a virus. Have you run a security scan?

E: No, I haven't, but I could if you think it'll help.

A: OK. Well, try that and see what happens. It should find any unwanted software that's hiding away in there and it'll give you greater protection in future if you need it as well.

E: OK.

A: Otherwise, let me Google it and see what I can find.

Conversation 4

C: Hello, IT help desk.

F: Hi Bob. It's me, Martin again, I'm afraid.

C: Let me guess. Password problems?

F: Yes. Sorry. I'm just hopeless at remembering these things! What is it now? Three times this month?

C: At least. But don't worry. You're not the worst offender.

F: It's the age we live in! I've got more passwords than I have friends!

C: I'll reset it for you and email you a new one in a minute, OK?

F: Thanks.

C: Have you tried that app, by the way? I think it's called 'All My Passwords'.

F: No.

C: Well, try that. It might help. Otherwise, you might need to get some more memory installed.

Lesson 14C, Exercise 4 & 6

Hey there, what's up? Welcome to another episode of *What's App?* – my weekly show about what's going on in the world of apps. So today I'm looking at three more apps that you, my wonderful listeners out there, have suggested for me.

First up, we have something called what3words. Now, this is one of those things that's so clever it makes your brain hurt just thinking about it. In short, what it does is it gives everywhere in the world a unique, easy-to-say, three-word address that allows you to tell people exactly where you are – to the nearest nine square metres. That's like the size of the room I'm talking in now. So for example, if I wanted to tell people where I am, the app might give me something like 'chickens.heavy.package'. I then tell whoever I'm talking to those three words, they enter them into their app and hey presto – they can get directions to the exact spot I'm in. It's amazing. Imagine breaking down in the middle of nowhere or getting hurt while hiking in the mountains. In situations like this, having a way of letting people know how to find you could literally save your life. You can also use the app to meet friends in parks or at festivals, say, and I'm sure it has plenty of other applications too. Oh, and did I mention it's completely free?

Next up is a thing called Pl@ntNet, which quite a few of you seemed to think I'd find interesting, so thanks for that. Keep those recommendations coming. If you're a regular listener, you'll know how much I enjoy gardening, and so it's slightly embarrassing that I've not come across this one before. This app basically helps you identify plants simply by photographing them with your phone. It's got a huge database and on entering a photo, you get a range of suggestions that you can sort through. You can search by leaf, by flower, and even by region on Pl@ntNet and on top of all that, it's learning all the time. Every time someone adds a new entry, it helps the app identify things. In fact, a flower I entered that didn't have a match to begin with was then identified a few days later – because of new information someone in France had added.

Finally, we have a bit of a weird one called Real Razor. Which is a strange name, really, because it's clearly not a real razor, but to give credit where credit's due it does look like a razor – an electronic one – and as you can hear, it sounds like a razor too

… and it even knows when it's near your head. Run it up and down your face and it starts with the hair-cutting sound effects … but, of course, it doesn't actually cut off any hair. Because it's not a real razor. I'm guessing it's meant to be a joke, but I'm not sure what's funny about pretending to be shaving yourself with a phone. There you go. That's it from me for today. Remember, if you want to donate, please go to my …

UNIT 15

Lesson 15A, Exercises 5 & 6

Conversation 1

A: Hello, Mr Gomes?

B: Yes?

A: I'm sorry. Have you been waiting long?

B: About two hours.

A: I'm sorry, we're quite busy today. You've done something to your ankle?

B: Yes.

A: Hmm, it's quite big. Does this hurt?

B: Yeah, it's very painful.

A: Can you put any weight on it at all?

B: No, no. It hurts too much.

A: Hmm. And how did you do it?

B: I was just coming out of the hotel and I slipped on the stair and my ankle, it just …

A: You just fell over on it. Nasty. Well, I think we should do an X-ray. It might just be badly sprained, but it could be broken. You'll have to wait again, I'm afraid. We've been a bit short of staff lately. I'll ask the nurse to give you something for the pain.

B: Good. How long will I have to wait for the X-ray?

A: Hopefully, it won't be more than half an hour. Are you taking any medication?

B: Err … I take something for my dust allergy sometimes?

A: That's fine. Have you ever had any bad reactions to any medication – aspirin or anything?

B: No, never.

A: OK, fine. Well, I'll get the nurse to give you something and then take you down for the X-ray.

Conversation 2

A: Hello.

C: Hello.

D: Hello.

A: Take a seat. What seems to be the problem?

C: It's my son. He's been up all night throwing up. He's hardly slept, and he had a high temperature – 39 – and his heart was beating really fast.

A: And how long have you been like this?

C: Sorry, he doesn't speak much English. He first said he felt a bit sick yesterday afternoon and then he threw up about seven and he hasn't really stopped since.

A: Oh dear. Any problems going to the toilet?

C: Actually, no. None.

A: And has he been able to drink anything?

C: No, that's the problem. When he drinks water, he's sick again.

A: Right, well, let's have a look. Can you just take off your jumper and sit up here? Open your mouth and stick your tongue out. Lovely. And now take a deep breath. Again … breathe in … and out. Just lie down. I'm going to press quite hard. Does it hurt? And here?

D: Hmm. It's OK.

A: Maybe a bit uncomfortable – but no pain?

D: Yes … no pain.

A: OK, you can put your jumper back on. I think it's a nasty stomach infection – there seems to be one going round at the moment. We've had a few people in.

C: Will he need antibiotics?

A: It's a virus, so there's no need for antibiotics. I'll give him something to stop the vomiting and then he just needs to rest and take lots of fluids – water, tea, maybe some juice. OK? Any questions?

C: No, I don't think so. I'll explain to him.

Lesson 15C, Exercises 5 & 6

A = Alex; D = Dana

A: How was your holiday? You went mountain biking in Austria, didn't you?

D: That's right. It was great, except for James's accident.

A: Why? What happened?

D: Well, we'd been cycling in the mountains round Kaunertal, and we were going back to the hotel down this steep hill, so we were going really fast and James lost control of his bike on a corner and he went off the road. He just managed to avoid running into a wall and fell off. It was horrible.

A: It sounds it! Was he badly hurt?

D: Well, he was conscious when we got to him, but he was asking us where he was and what had happened.

A: That doesn't sound good.

D: Yeah, he certainly seemed a bit confused – and his helmet had come off so he must've banged his head.

A: Oh dear. Did he have any other injuries?

D: Yeah, he had a nasty cut on his knee which was bleeding really badly and he was obviously very bruised. He kept saying he'd be OK to cycle home, but he clearly wasn't in any condition to, and we were miles from anywhere and it was a really quiet road.

A: What a nightmare! Couldn't you call someone?

D: Well, we didn't really know who to call.

A: I guess. So what happened?

D: Well, we were waiting for about half an hour and eventually this car appeared and we waved at it to stop, and the woman driving said she'd give James a lift to the nearest hospital. So, we got him and his bike into the car, and she took my mobile number and said she'd call me once there was more news.

A: Wow! That was nice of her.

D: I know. She was so kind. Anyway, we then cycled back to our hotel and waited to hear from her.

A: And did she call?

D: Yeah, after a couple of hours, she rang and told me they'd given James an X-ray and everything was fine and any cuts and bruises should heal in two weeks or so.

A: Oh, poor guy! And what an amazing woman.

D: I know. We did ask her if we could buy her dinner or something to say thanks, but she just refused.

A: Ahh … People can be so good.

D: Yeah, I know. In the end, James spent the rest of the holiday hanging around in the hotel. He was desperate to go out with us, but the doctors told him not to cycle for a week. It spoiled his holiday, really.

A: I bet! It actually reminds me of this friend, Jess, who had to be carried down a mountain once.

D: No way!

A: Yeah, basically there was quite a tough section where she was climbing and she slipped and fell about 20 feet …

UNIT 16

Lesson 16A, Exercises 4 & 5

Conversation 1

A: Did you see that thing on the *Times* website about the steel plant closing down?

B: You're joking! Doesn't your friend Cathy work there?

A: Yeah. I haven't spoken to her yet.

B: So how come it's being shut down? Are they losing money?

A: Not at all! Apparently, they want to expand and the share price has gone up!

B: So why close it?

A: The usual. They want to cut costs and increase profits, so they're moving production somewhere cheaper.

B: That's terrible! So how many job losses will that result in?

Conversation 2

C: Did you see that thing on TV about that guy being robbed in town?

D: Yeah, shocking, isn't it? The victim's OK though, right?

C: Yeah – they said he's recovering in hospital. But how can someone do something like that in a crowded place in the middle of the day and just get away?

D: Really? No-one offered to help?

C: No, and apparently the police are investigating, but no-one has come forward. It's like no-one saw anything.

D: It is bad, but I guess people are scared to get involved in those kinds of incidents.

Conversation 3

E: Did you see that thing about it reaching 50 degrees in Morocco?

F: What? 50? That's crazy! How can people survive in that heat?

E: I know, I can't imagine it.

F: Apparently, those kinds of temperatures can result in all kinds of issues. I mean not just people getting ill or dying, but all kinds of stuff not working properly … I mean roads can melt in that heat!

E: Yeah, it's bad. I still don't think of heat in that way – causing damage – I only think about floods or hurricanes resulting in those kind of immediate issues.

F: Yeah, well, we'll have to get used to it – they say we could experience those kind of temperatures in Spain sometime.

E: Really?

F: Yeah, absolutely! It already often goes over 40 degrees in the south.

E: Wow, I didn't realize.

Conversation 4

G: Have you heard the news?

H: No, what?

G: The health minister has resigned.

H: Really? Why's that?

G: Haven't you been following the story? She's been accused of doing all kinds of things. Like apparently, she's been secretly working with one drug company to help them sign government contracts.

H: Right.

G: Not that she's admitted to doing anything. She just apologized for 'causing the government difficulties'.

H: Right. So what else has she been accused of?

Conversation 5

I: Did you see that video of the basketball player hitting a fan?

J: What? No.

I: Yeah, it was in the middle of the game, and he just went into the crowd and punched this guy – apparently, he claimed the fan said something and maybe threw a drink at him.

J: Wow. I mean, it's a difficult one. Obviously, you can never support violence, but these players must have to listen to so much horrible stuff, I can see why they might lose control.

I: Yeah. Apparently, he's refused to apologize and he's going to be suspended for the rest of the season.

J: Really? What about the fan – did they get banned too?

I: I don't know. He should do.

Lesson 16C, Exercises 5 & 6

Conversation 1

A: Who's the statue of?

B: That's Garibaldi.

A: Garibaldi?

B: You've never heard of him?

A: No, I don't think so. Who was he?

B: He was a military leader in the 19th century who helped create Italy as a modern country. He's like a national hero. He fought in South America as well. He was part of the independence struggles in Brazil and Uruguay. I think his first wife was even Brazilian.

A: When was this?

B: The late 1800s. I'm surprised you haven't heard of him.

A: Well, I'm not really interested in history.

Conversation 2

C: What do you do, then?

D: I'm actually studying to become a nurse.

C: Oh, right. Nice. Where do you do that, then?

D: Rosalind Franklin University.

C: OK, where's that?

D: It's just outside Chicago. It was originally, like, the Chicago Hospital-College of Medicine, and then I think something else, and then they renamed it in the early 2000s.

C: Oh, OK. Who's Rosalind Franklin then? I've never heard of her.

D: Oh, no? I mean I've seen a few things about her – films and documentaries – but basically, she was a scientist and she's like the mother of modern genetics, because she was a crucial figure in the discovery of the structure of DNA.

C: Really? Wow! I'm kind of surprised she's not better-known.

D: Yeah, well this is the thing. While she did a huge amount of work at the start of the 50s that led to the discovery, the final complete structure was declared by these two guys Crick and Watson. And they were the ones who were awarded the Nobel prize for it, while Franklin was kind of forgotten.

C: Right, so the university was recognizing her contribution to science.

D: Yeah. And maybe for the university it's a symbol of being inclusive. You know, like it's saying science and medicine is a career for everyone – no matter what gender, race or social class …

C: Interesting. I'd like to find out more about her.

Conversation 3

E: So, what are you going to do while you're in Brussels?

F: Work, mainly, but I'm hoping to go to the Eddy Merckx metro station while I'm there.

E: Really? Why do you want to go there?

F: It's where they have the bike that he used to set the hour record.

E: What? What are you talking about?

F: Eddy Merckx? He's like the greatest cyclist of all time – he completely dominated the sport in the late 1960s and early 70s! My dad was a huge fan and I guess that then inspired me to get into cycling myself.

E: Oh, right.

F: You've never heard of him?

E: Err … no. And you're not planning to go anywhere else, like the Magritte Museum?

F: Magritte?

E: The surrealist painter. He's Belgian too. He was the guy that did pictures of office workers raining down from the sky.

F: It doesn't sound familiar.

E: *Ceci n'est pas une pipe?*

F: Sorry, you've lost me.

E: You must know it! It's one of his paintings. It's a picture of a pipe and underneath it says, 'This is not a pipe' in French. You'd recognize it if you saw it. It's really famous.

F: Yeah, well, so is Eddy Merckx, but you didn't know him!

NATIONAL GEOGRAPHIC LEARNING

National Geographic Learning,
a Cengage Company

Outcomes Intermediate Student's Book,
3rd Edition
Hugh Dellar and Andrew Walkley

Publisher: Rachael Gibbon

Senior Development Editor: Laura Brant

Content Editors: Alison Sharpe and Nicole Elliott

Director of Global Marketing: Ian Martin

Senior Product Marketing Manager: Caitlin Thomas

Heads of Regional Marketing:

  Charlotte Ellis (Europe, Middle East and Africa)

  Justin Kaley (Asia and Greater China)

  Irina Pereyra (Latin America)

  Joy MacFarland (US and Canada)

Senior Production Manager: Daisy Sosa

Content Project Manager: Ruth Moore

Media Researcher: Jeff Millies

Operations Support: Hayley Chwazik-Gee

Senior Designer: Heather Marshall

Senior Media Producer: Monica Writz

Art Director (Video): Macy Lawrence

Inventory Manager: Julie Chambers

Manufacturing Planner: Eyvett Davis

Composition: MPS North America LLC

Audio Producer: Tom Dick & Debbie Productions Ltd

Contributing Writer: Jon Hird (Endmatter)

For permission to use material from this text or product,
submit all requests online at **cengage.com/permissions**
Further permissions questions can be emailed to
permissionrequest@cengage.com

Outcomes Intermediate Student's Book, 3e
ISBN: 978-0-357-91754-1

Outcomes Intermediate Student's Book with
the Spark platform, 3e
ISBN: 978-0-357-91753-4

National Geographic Learning
Cheriton House, North Way,
Andover, Hampshire, SP10 5BE
United Kingdom

Locate your local office at **international.cengage.com/region**

Visit National Geographic Learning online at **ELTNGL.com**
Visit our corporate website at **www.cengage.com**

Printed in Greece by Bakis SA
Print Number: 01 Print Year: 2023

MIX
Paper | Supporting
responsible forestry
FSC™ C169932

Credits

Illustration: All illustrations are owned by © Cengage Learning, Inc.

Photography:

Cover Fotografia Inc./E+/Getty Images

2 (tl1) The Washington Post/Getty Images, (tl2) © Life as Lived – Ami Vitale, (tl3) Ian Dagnall/Alamy Stock Photo, (cl1) Halfpoint/iStock/Getty Images, (cl2) Hugh Sitton/Stone/Getty Images, (cl3) Marc Bruxelle/Alamy Stock Photo, (bl1) MiRafoto/Alamy Stock Photo, (bl2) Brandstaetter Images/Hulton Archive/Getty Images; **4** (tl1) © Babak Tafreshi/National Geographic Image Collection, (tl2) © Greg Dale/National Geographic Image Collection, (tl3) Paul Souders/Stone/Getty Images, (cl1) © Life as Lived – John Stanmeyer, (cl2) Marina Pissarova/Alamy Stock Photo, (cl3) F8 Imaging/Hulton Archive/Getty Images, (bl1) © Joel Sartore/Digital Collection/National Geographic Image Collection, (bl2) Wiskerke/Alamy Stock Photo; **6–7** (spread) The Washington Post/Getty Images; **8** © Chris Frezza/Cengage, **11** © Richard Simcott; **12** © Amy Toensing/National Geographic Image Collection; **14–15** (spread) © Life as Lived – Ami Vitale; **16** (bl) © Jason Edwards/Digital Collection/National Geographic Image Collection, (bc) © Alex Treadway/Digital Collection/National Geographic Image Collection, (br) Jack Taylor/Getty Images News/Getty Images; **19** © Global Leadership Summit 2019; **20** (cl) EyeEm/Alamy Stock Photo, (cr) SDI Productions/E+/Getty Images, (bl) Boston Globe/Getty Images, (br) FG Trade/E+/Getty Images; **21** (cl) Morsa Images/DigitalVision/Getty Images, (bl) Javier Zayas Photography/Moment/Getty Images; **23** Jeff Gilbert/Alamy Stock Photo, **24** © Cengage; **26–27** (spread) Ian Dagnall/Alamy Stock Photo; **29** Zarnell/iStock/Getty Images; **31** (cl) Pacific Press/LightRocket/Getty Images, (br) AmbrosiniV/Shutterstock.com; **32** VW Pics/Universal Images Group/Getty Images; **34–35** (spread) Halfpoint/iStock/Getty Images; **36** Prisma by Dukas Presseagentur GmbH/Alamy Stock Photo; **39** Yinjia Pan/Moment/Getty Images; **41** © Xpacifica/National Geographic Image Collection; **43** (tl1) Caia Image/Collection Mix: Subjects/Getty Images, (tl2) Yelizaveta Tomashevska/Shutterstock.com, (tr1) Karelnoppe/Shutterstock.com, (tr2) DGLimages/Shutterstock.com, **44** © Cengage; **46–47** (spread) Hugh Sitton/Stone/Getty Images; **49** Zoonar GmbH/Alamy Stock Photo; **51** Justin Lewis/Stone/Getty Images; **52** (tr) © Mike Baldwin/CartoonStock, (cr) © Shannon Wheeler/CartoonStock, (br) © Jerry King/CartoonStock; **54–55** (spread) Marc Bruxelle/Alamy Stock Photo; **57** Andresr/E+/Getty Images; **59** (tl) Valery Rizzo/Alamy Stock Photo, (tr) Syda Productions/Shutterstock.com, (bl) Krakenimages.com/Shutterstock.com, (br) Alistair Berg/DigitalVision/Getty Images; **60** (bl1) Japanese Photograph/Moment/Getty Images, (bl2) Heather Leah Kennedy/Moment/Getty Images, (bc1) Mark Kerrison/In Pictures/Getty Images, (bc2) Roussel Images/Alamy Stock Photo, (br1) Tim Graham/Alamy Stock Photo, (br2) Annick Tartelin/Shutterstock.com; **62** Reuters/Alamy Stock Photo, **64** © Cengage; **66–67** (spread) MiRafoto/Alamy Stock Photo; **69** David Collingwood/Alamy Stock Photo; **71** VladyslaV Travel photo/Shutterstock.com; **72** Imke Lass/Redux; **74–75** (spread) Brandstaetter Images/Hulton Archive/Getty Images; **76–77** View Pictures/Universal Images Group/Getty Images; **79** © Kike Calvo/National Geographic Image Collection; **80–81** (spread) © John Stanmeyer/National Geographic Image Collection; **83** Barry Lewis/Corbis Historical/Getty Images, **84** © Cengage; **86–87** (spread) © Babak Tafreshi/National Geographic Image Collection; **88–89** (spread) Halfpoint Images/Moment/Getty Images; **91** VDB Photos/Shutterstock.com; **93** (bl) SeanPavonePhoto/iStock/Getty Images, (br) Iain Masterton/Alamy Stock Photo; **94–95** (spread) © Greg Dale/National Geographic Image Collection; **96** Anders Ryman/Alamy Stock Photo; **97** © Cengage Learning/National Geographic Image Collection; **99** (t) Weniliou/Shutterstock.com, (br) Tim Wright/Alamy Stock Photo; **100–101** (spread) © Ruben Salgado Escudero/National Geographic Image Collection; **102** Amedved/Thinkstock; **103** Bender Rodriguez/Alamy Stock Photo, **104** © Cengage; **106–107** (spread) Paul Souders/Stone/Getty Images; **108** Alaska Stock/Alamy Stock Photo; **109** Alex Witt/Alamy Stock Photo; **111** (tc) Keystone-France/Gamma-Keystone/Getty Image, Mint Images/Getty Images; **113** © Frank AND Helen Schreider/National Geographic Creative/National Geographic Image Collection; **114–115** (spread) © Life as Lived – John Stanmeyer; **117** Lechatnoir/E+/Getty Images; **119** Caia Image/Collection Mix: Subjects/Getty Images; **120** Flashpop/DigitalVision/Getty Images; **123** Mauricio Graiki/Shutterstock.com, **124** © Cengage; **126–127** (spread) Marina Pissarova/Alamy Stock Photo; **128** Jie Zhao/Corbis News/Getty Images; **131** John Stillwell/PA Images/Getty Images; **132** Henry Rose/Photodisc/Getty Images; **134–135** (spread) F8 Imaging/Hulton Archive/Getty Images; **136** Westend61/Getty Images; **139** Gorodenkoff/iStock/Getty Images; **140** © Joyce Poole and Petter Granli/National Geographic Image Collection; **142** Steve Skjold/Alamy Stock Photo, **144** © Cengage; **146–147** (spread) © Joel Sartore/Digital Collection/National Geographic Image Collection; **148** © Alex Treadway/Digital Collection/National Geographic Image Collection; **151** Dusan Petkovic/Alamy Stock Photo; **153** (bl1) Astrid860/iStock/Getty Images, (bl2) Tetra Images/Alamy Stock Photo, (br1) Fuse/Corbis/Getty Images, (br2) AnthonyRosenberg/E+/Getty Images; **154–155** (spread) Wiskerke/Alamy Stock Photo; **156–157** (spread) © Mike Theiss/Mike Digital Collection/National Geographic Creative/National Geographic Image Collection; **159** Transcendental Graphics/Archive Photos/Getty Images; **160** (tl1) Archive PL/Alamy Stock Photo, (tl2) Ulf Andersen/Getty Images Entertainment/Getty Images, (cl1) Bernd Weissbrod/picture alliance/Getty Images, (cl2) Xinhua/Alamy Stock Photo, (bl) Guy Bell/Alamy Stock Photo; **162** South_agency/E+/Getty Images, **164** © Cengage; **195** (tl) Shikhar Bhattarai/iStock/Thinkstock, (tc) JohnnyGreig/E+/Getty Images, (tr) SuperStock/Alamy Stock Photo, (cl) Wavebreak Media Ltd/Thinkstock, (c) NadoFotos/iStock/ThinkStock, (cr) Ingram Publishing/Alamy Stock Photo, (bl) Evgeny Sergeev/iStock/Thinkstock, (br) Fuse/Getty Images; **198** (tl) Eric Isselee/Shutterstock.com, (tc1) Molotok289/Shutterstock.com, (tc2) Lakov Filimonov/Shutterstock.com, (tr) (cl1) (cl2) (cr1) (cr2) (bc1) (bc2) Ingram Publishing/Alamy Stock Photo, (c1) Anat Chant/Shutterstock.com, (c2) Jules Frazier/Photodisc/Getty Images, (bl) Eric Isselee/Shutterstock.com, (bc3) Tagstock1/Shutterstock.com, (br) Photolinc/Shutterstock.com.

Acknowledgements

The Outcomes publishing team and authors would like to thank EC English for their collaboration on the new videos in this edition, and all of the students and staff at EC Dublin and EC Brighton who took part in the filming.

The team would also like to thank the following teachers who provided detailed and invaluable feedback on this course.

João Rodrigo Lima Agildo, Colégio São Luis, São Luis; Verliscia Alexander, EC Malta, St Julian's; Patrick Allman, EC Bristol, Bristol; Francesc Martí Aluja, EOI Lleida, Lleida; Jose Luis Piñeira Alvarez, EOI Tolosa, Tolosa; Marcel lí Armengou, EOI Terrassa, Terrassa; Desmond Arnold, EC Cambridge, Cambridge; Holly Bailey, EC Brighton, Brighton; Elisabet Prím Bauzá, EOI Manacor, Manacor; Daniel Beus, Fukuoka Communications Center, Fukuoka; Mónica Salgado Blesa, EOI Palma, Palma de Mallorca; Frederik Bolz, University of Bochum, Bochum; Malachy Caldicott; EC Oxford, Oxford; Elisa Roca Burns, EOI Palma, Palma de Mallorca; Eva Cantuerk, University of Bochum, Bochum; Ana Belén Gracia Castejón, EOI Palma, Palma de Mallorca; Ana María Serra Comas, EOI Palma, Palma de Mallorca; Michael Crowe, EC Dublin, Dublin; Rebekah Currer-Burgess, EC Bristol, Bristol; Luca de Santis, EC Dublin, Dublin; Hilary Donraadt, EC Dublin, Dublin; Julia Drzechovskaja, EC Dublin, Dublin; Jordan Duggie, EC Brighton, Brighton; Rachel Fenech, EC Malta, St Julian's; Armando Fernández, EOI Palma, Palma de Mallorca; Fabiana Fonseca, Associação Brasil América, Recife; Bruno Franco, Luzianna Lanna, Belo Horizonte; Natalia Fritsler, University of Bochum, Bochum; Lukas Galea, EC Malta, St. Julian's; Antonio Berbel Garcia, EOI Almeria, Almeria; Maria dels Angels Grimalt, EOI Palma, Palma de Mallorca; Honorata Grodzinska, Future, Gorzów; Abigail Hackney, IH Manchester, Manchester; Alicky Hess, EC Dublin, Dublin; Silvia Milian Hita, EOI Prat, El Prat de Llobregat; Richard Hill; EC Cape Town, Cape Town; Roxana Irimieia, BBE Languages, Bogota; Bronia Jacobs, EC Cape Town, Cape Town; Natalia Jakubczyk-Gajewska, Warsaw University of Life Sciences (SGGW), Warsaw; Georgine Kalil, Berlin; Jameelah Keane, EC Manchester, Manchester; Shelly Keen, EC Bristol, Bristol; Dariusz Ketla, Warsaw University of Life Sciences (SGGW), Warsaw; Gabriela Krajewska, University of Wrocław, Wrocław; Peter Kunzler, Gymnasium Kirchenfild, Bern; Juana Larena-Avellaneda, EOI Telde, Telde; Isabelle Le Gal-Maier, VHS Rottweil, Rottweil; Angela Lloyd, Polytech Brandenburg/Havel, Brandenburg an der Havel; Kenya Lopes, Luzianna Lanna, Belo Horizonte; Sandra López, EOI Palma, Palma de Mallorca; Lucía Marotta, EC Dublin, Dublin; Francesca Mesquida, EOI Manacor, Manacor; Nico Moramarco, EOI Santander, Santander; Sian Morrey, University of Sheffield, Sheffield; Vinicius Nobre, Toronto; Sue Nurse, University of Sheffield, Sheffield; Giuseppe Picone, Milan City Council, Milan; Maria Eugenia Perez Primicia, EOI Palma, Palma de Mallorca; Piotr Przywara, Warsaw University of Life Sciences (SGGW), Warsaw; Manlio Reina, EC Dublin, Dublin; Laura Rota i Roca, EOI Sabadell, Sabadell; Salvador Faura Sabe, EOI Sabadell, Sabadell; Justin Sales, Edinburgh College, Edinburgh; Paloma Seoane Sanchez, EOI Laredo, Laredo; Aïda Santamaria, EOI Palma, Palma de Mallorca; Sean Scurfield, EOI Santander, Santander; Pilar Riera Serra, EOI Palma, Palma de Mallorca;Tetiana Shyian, University of Bochum, Bochum; Vinicius Silva, Colégio Bandeirantes, São Paulo; Anna Soltyska, University of Bochum, Bochum; Glenn Standish, IH Torun, Torun; Andreas Tano, Makarios Christian School, Jakarta; Tran Thi Thu Giang, TEG international Education Centre, Hanoi; Sam Verdoodt, EC Malta, St Julian's; Aline Vianna, Colégio Humboldt, São Paulo; Rachael Worrall, IH Manchester, Manchester; Mehmet Yildiz, Bezmialem Vakif University, Istanbul

Authors' acknowledgements

Thanks to Alison Sharpe, Clare Shaw, Nicole Elliott, Rachael Gibbon and Laura Brant for their meticulous reading of our work and to all at National Geographic Learning for the continued support and enthusiasm.

Thanks also to all the students we've taught over the years for providing more inspiration and insight than they ever realised. And to the colleagues we've taught alongside for their friendship, thoughts and assistance.